The Promise of American Life

James Madison (signature)

THE JAMES MADISON LIBRARY IN AMERICAN POLITICS
Sean Wilentz, General Editor

Margot Canaday
Kevin M. Kruse
Julian E. Zelizer

The James Madison Library in American Politics of the Princeton University Press is devoted to reviving important American political writings of the recent and distant past. American politics has produced an abundance of important works—proclaiming ideas, describing candidates, explaining the inner workings of government, and analyzing political campaigns. This literature includes partisan and philosophical manifestos, pamphlets of practical political theory, muckraking exposés, autobiographies, on-the-scene reportage, and more. The James Madison Library issues fresh editions of both classic and now-neglected titles that helped shape the American political landscape. Up-to-date commentaries in each volume by leading scholars, journalists, and political figures make the books accessible to modern readers.

The Conscience of a Conservative by Barry M. Goldwater

The New Industrial State by John Kenneth Galbraith

Liberty and the News by Walter Lippmann

The Politics of Hope and the Bitter Heritage: American Liberalism in the 1960s by Arthur M. Schlesinger, Jr.

Richard Nixon: Speeches, Writing, Documents, edited by Rick Perlstein

The Promise of American Life

Herbert Croly

With a new foreword by **Franklin Foer**

PRINCETON UNIVERSITY PRESS
PRINCETON AND OXFORD

Copyright © 2014 by Princeton University Press
General Editor's introduction copyright © 2014 by Sean Wilentz
Published by Princeton University Press, 41 William Street, Princeton,
   New Jersey 08540
In the United Kingdom: Princeton University Press, 6 Oxford Street,
   Woodstock, Oxfordshire OX20 1TW

press.princeton.edu

First published 1909

First Princeton paperback edition, 2014

LIBRARY OF CONGRESS CATALOGING-IN-PUBLICATION DATA
Croly, Herbert David, 1869–1930.
     The promise of American life / Herbert Croly ; foreword by
        Franklin Foer.
        pages cm. — (The James Madison library in American politics)
        Originally published: New York : Macmillan, 1909.
        Includes index.
        Summary: "*The Promise of American Life* is part of the bedrock of
     American liberalism, a classic that had a spectacular immediate im-
     pact on national politics when it was first published in 1909 and that
     has been recognized ever since as a defining text of liberal reform.
     The book helped inspire Theodore Roosevelt's New Nationalism and
     Franklin D. Roosevelt's New Deal, put Herbert Croly on a path to
     become the founding editor of the *New Republic*, and prompted Wal-
     ter Lippmann to call him twentieth-century America's "first important
     political philosopher." The book is at once a history of America and
     its political ideals and an analysis of contemporary ills, from rampant
     economic inequality to unchecked corporate power. In response, Croly
     advocated combining the Hamiltonian and Jeffersonian traditions and
     creating a strong federal government to ensure that all Americans had a
     fair shot at individual success. The formula still defines American liber-
     alism, and *The Promise of American Life* continues to resonate today,
     offering a vital source of renewal for liberals and progressives. For this
     new edition, Franklin Foer has written a substantial foreword that puts
     the book in historical context and explains its continuing importance"
     — Provided by publisher.
        ISBN 978-0-691-16068-9 (pbk.)
        1. United States—Politics and government. 2. United States—Social
        conditions—1865–1918. I. Title.

HN64.C89 2014
     320.973—dc23   2013028106

British Library Cataloging-in-Publication Data is available

This book has been composed in Sabon, Didot, Helvetica Neue

Printed on acid-free paper ∞

Printed in the United States of America

10 9 8 7 6 5 4 3 2 1

Dedicated to the memory of the late David Goodman Croly

Contents

Preface

"Combining Hamiltonian ends with Jeffersonian means" is perhaps the most famous phrase summarizing the character of Progressive Era liberalism. Usually attributed to Herbert Croly, the co-founding editor of *The New Republic*, the phrase also captures the essence of Croly's highly influential book, *The Promise of American Life*.[1] That book's importance remains undiminished, despite its growing obscurity with the general public. Ever since *The Promise of American Life* appeared in 1909, Americans' perceptions of their political history have owed a great deal to Croly's thoughts on American liberalism—even if they have never heard of Croly or his book.

Writing at the close of the presidency of his hero, Theodore Roosevelt, Croly believed that an urgent, fundamental reform of American politics was at hand. Decades of industrial expansion and urban growth had rendered obsolete the competitive individualism that dominated the agrarian America of the nineteenth century. In order to advance, the nation would have to create and then master a new synthesis of its chief political traditions—a revitalized liberalism that merged Thomas Jefferson's inclusive view of justice and civic equality

[1] Croly certainly devoted large sections of his book to this theme, and to Jefferson and Hamilton. But as near as I can tell, the actual phrase first appeared nearly forty years later, and with reference not to Croly's thoughts but Theodore Roosevelt's New Nationalist program, in George A. Mowry, *Theodore Roosevelt and the Progressive Movement* (Madison: University of Wisconsin Press, 1947).

with the imperatives of order, economic expansion, and nationalism that Croly ascribed to Alexander Hamilton. The classical liberalism favored by old-line Jeffersonian democrats, Croly insisted, would only bring chaos to the new industrial America. Centralization, planning, and government by experts—what Croly called a "more highly socialized democracy"—had to supplant the Jeffersonians' "excessively individualized democracy," or the country would disintegrate.

These key observations of Croly's have led later writers to describe his book as a landmark in the intellectual history of American politics. Classical Jeffersonian liberals had posited that a powerful centralized federal government was bound to turn predatory and secure the interests of the powerful, wealthy, well-connected few at the expense of the many. Such had been a chief contention of the pioneering British political economists of the late eighteenth century, above all Adam Smith, in their arguments with monarchical mercantilism; and such were the ideas (and the fears) proclaimed by American liberals and democrats for decades after the American Revolution. By contrast, twentieth-century American liberalism, as enunciated by Theodore Roosevelt and later augmented by his cousin, Franklin D. Roosevelt, insisted that only a powerful federal government could promote the interests of the many (or, as some of them were more likely to put it, the nation) in the vastly changed circumstances of the new century.

In industrialized and corporate America, gigantic, irresponsible private interests, and not government authority, loomed as the greatest threat to national prosperity and social justice. Whereas government was once the indispensable power in creating overweening and artificial privilege, now government had to step in to restrain unbridled individualism, eliminate wasteful inefficiency, minimize abuses of corporate power, and maximize national wealth. Modern liberals would replace laissez-faire with coherent national regulation in order to promote social harmony and national greatness, all the while countervailing the voracious private interests of the few. *The Promise of American Life* has survived as the most thorough exposition of the philosophical as well as political reasoning behind this shift—or as close to such an exposition as would ever be published.

Important though it was and is, the book does have many manifest flaws. Although remembered largely for Croly's efforts to combine the Hamiltonian and Jeffersonian legacies, *The Promise of American Life*'s accounts of those legacies were badly skewed. Croly did not try to conceal his personal predilections: "On the whole," he wrote, "my own preferences are on the side of Hamilton rather than of Jefferson." But that was putting it mildly. Croly's distaste for Jefferson and Jeffersonian democracy was as systematic and palpable as it was ill-informed and at times willful. To claim, for example, as Croly did, that the Jeffersonians consented "to use the machinery of government only for a negative or destructive purpose" required ignoring, among much else, one of Jefferson's signal triumphs, the Louisiana Purchase.

Although Croly was aware that Hamilton's politics could never have governed the diverse and rambunctious American people, he turned to Jeffersonianism not out of admiration for Jefferson or his ideas, but by default, as a necessary democratic modification of the splendid Hamiltonian program.

This democratic corrective, nevertheless, was essential to Croly's appeal, as it helped to justify his book's strong insistence on social responsibility and care for the downtrodden in the new industrial era. And with its call for a bolstered nationalism and an enlarged sense of common purpose, *The Promise of American Life*

quickly became one of the rare commentaries on American political history and ideas to have an immediate political impact.

Theodore Roosevelt had recently departed from the
White House but by no means from politics when he
read the book in 1910. He may or may not have lifted
what would become his new catch phrase, "The New
Nationalism," from Croly. Indeed, the convergence may
well have been coincidental: Roosevelt certainly was
moving in the same direction as Croly was, albeit from
a different direction, long before the book's publication.
Still, apart from being greatly flattered by Croly's ef-
fusive praise of him and his presidency, Roosevelt could
read *The Promise of American Life* as a kind of explica-
tion and grand affirmation of his administrations' ac-
complishments and aspirations—what he had called,
in more piece-meal and pragmatic fashion, the Square
Deal. The book's Rooseveltian qualities certainly rec-
ommended it to the man who presented it to T.R., the
progressive jurist, Learned Hand, who singled out for
praise Croly's elaboration of the "neo-Hamilton" political ideas that Roosevelt, according to Hand, had made
real.[2]

Thereafter, a reinvigorated Roosevelt would carry
those ideas forward, reformulated under the Crolyesque
cognomen of the New Nationalism. In the momentous
1912 presidential campaign, as the candidate of the
"Bull Moose" Progressive Party, Roosevelt proclaimed
the use of "Government as an efficient agency for the
practical betterment of social and economic conditions
throughout this land"—a line he might as well have bor-

[2] Hand to Theodore Roosevelt, April 8, 1910, in Constance Jordan,
ed., *The Selected Correspondence of Learned Hand* (New York: Oxford
University Press, 2013), 15.

rowed from *Promise*.[3] Although defeated by the Democrat Woodrow Wilson, Roosevelt did finish a respectable second, besting the conservative Republican incumbent William Howard Taft and the Socialist Eugene V. Debs. In doing so, he advanced ideas and issues that would be contested for years to come and in some cases for a generation or more, ranging from social health and unemployment insurance to votes for women.

Croly, meanwhile, went on to help make another lasting contribution. Five years after the success of *The Promise of American Life*, with financial support from the heiress Dorothy Payne Whitney and her husband, Willard Straight, Croly joined with Walter Lippmann and Walter Weyl to launch an innovative journal of opinion, *The New Republic*. After its first issue appeared in November 1914, the magazine quickly established itself as a tribune of the new American liberalism, on a mission to push liberal politics as far as possible in the direction of active government in both domestic and world affairs. For an entire century, through editorial permutations that have kept shifting the magazine's positions across a broad spectrum of liberal thinking, *The New Republic* has remained at once a flagship and a battleground for American liberal thought.

It is thus altogether fitting that the James Madison Library edition of *The Promise of American Life* appears in the *The New Republic*'s centennial year, with an introduction by the magazine's current editor, Franklin Foer. A keen student of the Progressive era, Foer has thought hard about the ideas that helped initiate and then guide the magazine. He has also reflected on what is living and what is not in Croly's book. Most strik-

---

[3] "Address by Theodore Roosevelt before the Convention of the National Progressive Party in Chicago, July 1912," at http://www.ssa.gov/history/trspeech.html.

ingly, he takes the measure of Herbert Croly's strangeness as a man, thinker, and writer. Yet even when he enriches our understanding of Croly's peculiarities, Foer never loses sight of how Croly and his book helped to change the working assumptions of American political thought. Building in part on the Library's earlier republication of Walter Lippmann's *Liberty and the News*, this new edition of *The Promise of American Life* is also an important addition to the series. Together, Croly and Foer bring back to life a pivotal phase of the forever unfinished arguments over American democracy: what it has been, what it has become, and what its future ought to be.

Sean Wilentz

Foreword

When Theodore Roosevelt vacated the presidency in the spring of 1909, he also vacated the country. After nearly eight years in the White House, Roosevelt chose to restore himself with a bit of big game hunting. He journeyed across the savanna of British East Africa, then up the River Nile. His trip, financed by Andrew Carnegie, had an explicit purpose: collecting specimens for the Smithsonian Institution. But there was a salutary side effect to disappearing into the bush. It permitted him only periodic contact with news from home, allowing him to clear his mind of politics. Attention had to be paid to charging rhinoceroses and loafing elephants rather than the performance of his handpicked successor, William Howard Taft.

But even a hunting nut can fall victim to homesickness. Eleven months after he embarked, Roosevelt left the jungle with a museum's load of trophies—his expedition killed 11,400 animals—and began his meandering route home. With each stop on his return—Nairobi, Cairo, Naples, Vienna, Berlin, Stockholm, Paris, and London—he slowly caught up on events in Washington, DC. What he heard rattled and radicalized him. The portrait of Taft that his friends conveyed was dark. His protégé had trashed his legacy in his absence, pushing Roosevelt's reform-minded allies to the side and making common cause with the reactionaries in Congress.

Roosevelt had traveled to Africa with six-dozen books, yet had exhausted that supply. As he sifted through the bulging bags of unopened mail that greeted him, he found his friends insisting that he get his hands on a volume that had been published in his absence. The author was unknown and the book had landed with little notice, but the recommendations came from reliable sources, such as Henry Cabot Lodge and Learned Hand. Their enthusiasm was sufficiently robust that Roosevelt wrote to Macmillan of London to order a copy of Herbert David Croly's *The Promise of American Life*.

Without the missives vouching for the book, it is unlikely that Roosevelt would have ever touched it. Croly didn't write for the *Nation*, *Outlook*, or any of the muck-raking journals. He contributed to a small trade paper called the *Architectural Record*—a job he had scored thanks to family connections. That he had achieved this much was somewhat unexpected. He had started at Harvard, yet never managed to earn a degree. Debilitating stretches of undefined and prolonged illness plagued him—the type of malaise that mental health professionals would now precisely diagnose without shame.

When Roosevelt read *The Promise of American Life*, his pencil raced across the pages. On the book's flyleaf, he compiled his own index of Croly's ideas. He underlined vast chunks of the text. Returning to his home in Oyster Bay, Roosevelt wrote Croly a mash note. "I do not know when I have read a book which I felt profited me as much as your book on American life," he told him. "I shall use your ideas freely in speeches I intend to make."[1]

The outburst of reformism that greeted the onset of the twentieth century had exploded in all directions—a

---

[1] Quoted in Herbert Croly to Learned Hand, August 1, 1910, Learned Hand Papers, Law School Library, Harvard University.

push for the prohibition of alcohol and against the exploitation of child labor, for granting women's suffrage and against the new concentrations of wealth. Progressive agitators had cobbled together a slate of practical concerns for a series of disparate campaigns to achieve specific legislative goals. For all this frenzy of activity, though, there was little underlying theory and no well-defined set of ideas about the role of government guiding these campaigns; only an inchoate sense that the state could become a force for good.

Croly's big book took the emerging progressive faith in government and rigorously argued on its behalf. His thesis went like this: during the nineteenth century, the state was seen as the enemy of liberty. The ethos of the new nation celebrated self-interest, which made sense for a country of pioneers forced to fend for themselves on the frontier. But that age had passed. Large corporations now dominated the scene, especially the political one—and American life had grown far more complicated. Some of the reformers wanted to destroy these corporations, and return to an economy of small shopkeepers and artisan producers. Croly, however, thought it foolish to reverse the clock to a bygone time. The corporations had actually improved many facets of American life. What the new era required was a robust federal government capable of regulating these new corporations so they could be harnessed on behalf of the national interest.

In short, Croly had written the founding and defining text of American liberalism. Although he sympathized with labor unions, he had no patience for socialism, with its reification of the working class. And he had even less patience for unregulated, free market capitalism, which permitted unconscionable agglomerations of wealth. Yet the ideology he posited wasn't a mere splitting of the difference. He presented it as the ultimate expression of democracy, the only outlook that would fulfill the dreams of the Founding Fathers.

A year after reading Croly's book, Roosevelt delivered his famous fire-breathing speech at Osawatomie, Kansas, calling for a "New Nationalism" and announcing his own hard turn toward progressivism. On hearing Roosevelt's speech, pundits and reporters instantly credited Croly's book. Nationalism, after all, had played a central role in Croly's justification of government; other ideas in Roosevelt's speech seemed lifted directly from *The Promise of American Life*. To be sure, it was easy to overstate the extent to which Roosevelt had leaned on Croly's book for this speech. Roosevelt had been mulling many of its themes for years. But if the relationship between Roosevelt and Croly was partially a media concoction, it hardly mattered. Croly was suddenly launched as a national figure.

II

Croly's parents were prominent denizens of Gilded Age New York, and that city's first journalistic power couple. In their brownstone on Bank Street, they entertained the likes of Oscar Wilde and Louisa May Alcott. His father, David, had acquired such famous acquaintances from his perch as an editor at the *New York World*. The man made an instant impression. He wore a long, stringy mustache that drooped past his chin toward his shoulders. Although he couldn't write an unclouded sentence, he talked with fantastic ease. He dictated a regular column and a shelf of books, filled with his idiosyncratic theories of the world. If you enter his name into Google, you will find him remembered as a latter-day Nostradamus. David frequently wrote under the moniker "Sir Oracle"—a name he came to regard as far too glib for his futurism. In the 1880s, Sir Oracle presciently forecast a global conflagration instigated by Germany and envisioned travel in flying machines. (Of course, when you make so many guesses about the future, you will often later find yourself stranded on the wrong side of history. The United States never merged with Canada, as he imagined. Nor has humanity relocated inside massive temperature-regulated iron enclosures.)

Given the attitudes of the day, Jane Cunningham could have only married a man as enlightened and eccentric as David. She had rammed her way into the newsroom over the objections of her chauvinistic colleagues and created the first advice column. Her suggestions were published under the nom de plume Jenny June. The years after the Civil War had brought new conundrums for women. A modern industrial economy had created all sorts of wonderful conveniences, but also deprived women of the essential role they had once played in the household economy. Her column helped women navigate this change.

As a purveyor of advice, June could, on occasion, strike a strident pose. Husbands were among the targets of her thunderous judgments. She charged them with routinely reducing their spouses to a state of subservience and intellectual dormancy. Nor did she especially care for little boys. She deemed them unappreciative little pests. It is, she wrote, "galling to her who has suffered for him, who has protected his infancy, who has watched and fostered his growth, who has worked for him, lived for him, and woven into the web of his young life the best and brightest years of her own."[2] This sentiment perhaps explains Herbert's lifelong resentment toward his mother.

[2] Jane Cunningham Croly, *For Better or Worse: A Book for Some Men and All Women* (Boston: Lee and Shepard, 1875), 21.

It must have been difficult to be the son of David and Jane Croly. From a young age, Herbert was painfully shy—a condition that would inflict him for the rest of his life. Even as the editor of a prestigious magazine, he often disappeared into the room. T. S. Matthews, a colleague, recounted his awkward first interaction with Croly: "He just sat in his office. It seemed like an hour; it might have been five minutes: he didn't say a word and I didn't say a word." Another colleague, Francis Hackett, was a touch crueler, when he described how Croly would settle "like a stone crab in the middle of lively company."[3]

Croly's parents didn't just burden him with their personalities; they saddled him with their ideology. They had been devotees of the French philosopher August Comte. The attraction to Comte was understandable enough. His writings seemed to anticipate the intellectual movements of the twentieth century. Like Karl Marx, who carefully studied him, Comte saw history progressing toward utopia. He showed how ideas had proceeded in a linear fashion from the beginning of time—theology gave way to metaphysics, which gave way to the age of science. Over time, science itself had grown progressively more sophisticated. The history of ideas would soon culminate in the greatest of all sciences: the science of society.

Comte imagined that the science of society would be used to engineer a new order—a society that would be efficient and stable, neither socialist nor market based. Instead, he envisioned a government run by technocrats. Unlike the socialists, he didn't fear the concentration of wealth. Quite the opposite, he considered it inevitable

[3] Quoted in Charles Forcey, *The Crossroads of Liberalism: Croly, Weyl, Lippmann, and the Progressive Era, 1900–1925* (New York: Oxford University Press, 1961), 7.

and desirable. Such wealth accumulation was a necessary source of resources that would allow society to continually increase production. But the titans of wealth couldn't simply follow their own parochial interests; their economic importance demanded that they act out of altruism. Comte predicted that the spirit of the industrial age would shatter individualism and egotism. Machines and commerce would teach us the essential truth of mutual dependence; they would guide us toward altruism.

Then, in 1844, Comte fell in love with a young woman named Clotilde de Vaux. Her erstwhile husband had fled to the East Indies to escape arrest. Unfortunately, France did not permit divorce, leaving de Vaux miserably stranded. Compounding her calamitous state, she suffered from tuberculosis, keeping her bedridden for long stretches.

Although their relationship existed only on a platonic level—and only for a year—Comte worshipped her. When she died, he enshrined her in a new religion. In his state of mourning, he took positivism and turned into a full-born church, what he called the "Religion of Humanity," complete with rites and a catechism. Outposts of the Religion of Humanity sprouted up across the world, even in New York City. The Crolys were stalwarts of the New York church. Their son Herbert was one of the few children baptized into the sect; a priest held him in his hands and offered him to the Goddess of Humanity. For the rest of his days, David made it his mission to cultivate his son as disciple. "There never, indeed, was a time throughout my whole youth, when we were alone together, that he did not return to [Comte]," Herbert would later remember.[4]

[4] Herbert Croly, "In Memoriam, David Goodman Croly: Estimates of the Man," *Real Estate Record and Builder's Guide*, May 18, 1889.

That mission encountered an almost-insurmountable obstacle in the form of Harvard. Herbert had entered the college in 1886, when the institution was in the midst of reinventing itself as a modern university, no longer just a finishing school for Brahmin boys. The most stunning sign of the university's new seriousness was its philosophy department, where Croly took up his studies. In David's view, the department was a bed of temptation. There was the unkempt Josiah Royce, the great Hegelian philosopher, who spoke eloquently about the virtues of community and loyalty. The department also harbored the dangerous William James, who popularized the pragmatic school of American philosophy.

None of the Harvard philosophers were positivists. Their work, in fact, amounted to a devastating refutation of Comte. Where Comte had despised Christianity, Royce believed devoutly in it and anchored his philosophy in theology. (Croly began a lifelong interest in Christianity at Harvard.) Meanwhile, the pragmatists maintained that there was no such thing as truth—or certainly not anything like the iron laws of history that Comte claimed to have discovered. They held that the world could only be understood through a series of provisional observations, which required constant testing and revision.

The exposure of young Herbert to these teachers provided David with profound agita. Everyday, he wrote his son long letters—thirty or sometimes forty pages long—warning him to steer clear of these subversive thinkers, urging him to give Comte one more chance. "Life is too short to master the unfruitful thinkers like Hegel and the lesser lights," he contended. What made these letters so crushing was that they were written lovingly, and filled with obvious paternal affection and patience. "Do not indulge in feelings of morbid self-deprecation," the

elder Croly remarked in one of his many efforts to buck
up the sagging spirits of his son.[5]

Yet despite these pleas, Herbert often indulged in
these emotions. He felt terrible that he had disappointed
his father's hope that he would follow in his positivist footsteps. "Part of his life's work had failed," Croly
later lamented.[6] In these years of anxiety, he drifted. He
dropped out of school, then reenrolled and dropped
out again. His Harvard education remained forever incomplete, although his friend Learned Hand later cam-
paigned to get him a degree.

When he abandoned his quest to complete college,
Croly went to work for the *Architectural Record*. His
life acquired a certain genteel dignity. He had married into money and bought a house in Cornish, New
Hampshire—where he played tennis and bridge, and
befriended the other writers who summered there. It
should have made for a life of perfect contentment, except for the fact that his father had set a much higher
standard for him. "Take your place in the front rank of
modern thinkers," David urged.

III

The Promise of American Life has a quality of des-
peration; it was Herbert's last-ditch attempt to fulfill
the expectations that his father had laid out for him.
Herbert crammed a lifetime of reading into one sprawl-
ing argument. If Herbert had an important thought or
grand theory about, say, the French military or urban
life, he wasn't going to exclude it from his tome. The

[5] David G. Croly to Herbert Croly, January 9, 1888, Autograph File,
Houghton Library, Harvard University.
[6] Croly, "In Memoriam, David Goodman Croly."

book had started out as a side project—a hobby that Croly would indulge before heading into the office. But it began to swallow up his life, requiring him to take leaves of absence from his regular job. He constructed the book with overbearing attention, revising and then revising some more, using a method that helps explain the book's turgid prose.

Given all the anxiety that had inflicted Herbert, his book possessed a supreme self-confidence. He had no fear of arguing with prestigious targets, no apparent second thoughts about synthesizing the whole of American history into sweeping judgments. Some of his most savage passages were reserved for Thomas Jefferson. He denounced the "unscrupulous" Sage of Monticello, who he deemed "incapable either of uniting with his fine phrases a habit of candid and honorable private dealing or embodying those phrases in a set of efficient institutions."[7]

This hostility was hardly a lone act of courage. Jefferson bashing was on the rise in the early twentieth century. Roosevelt, Lodge, and other progressive Republicans were also working hard to revive Jefferson's nemesis, Alexander Hamilton. They saw a version of themselves in Hamilton: a proponent of a robust federal government who hardly threatened the underpinnings of American capitalism. If Jefferson was a naive idealist peddling the virtues of self-interest, Hamilton offered a hard-nosed debunking of this dangerous mythology. "He was not afraid to incur public unpopularity for pursuing what he believed to be a wise public policy," Croly observed.[8]

[7] Herbert Croly, *The Promise of American Life* (New York: Norwood Press, 1909), 20.
[8] Ibid., 31.

It is to Croly's credit, however, that he didn't join Roosevelt and Lodge in mythologizing Hamilton. Croly disdained Hamilton's elitist discomfort with democracy. "He was possessed by the English conception of a national state, based on the domination of special privileged orders and interests."[9] In short, Hamilton had placed far too much faith in the rich and educated classes—a bias that doomed his vision of activist government.

This reading of early American history isn't incidental to Croly's thesis. The argument of *The Promise of American Life* is frequently reduced to an aphorism: Hamiltonian means to achieve Jeffersonian ends. That is, Croly wanted to use a Hamiltonian conception of federal action to achieve the sort of individual autonomy and genuine democracy that Jefferson claimed to cherish.

It's a formulation that pretty neatly captures the spirit of American liberalism, too, with its faith in both affirmative government and civil liberties. And it shows how modern liberalism didn't abandon the precepts of classical liberalism but instead found new methods for defending them. The classical liberals—Locke, Montesquieu, and Jefferson—had exposed the horrors of an overbearing state; they pointed toward a market economy and new conception of liberty. What Croly showed is that the modern state wasn't the enemy of either capitalism or democracy but rather their necessary protector.

American life had changed since the founding of the United States, and the critical change was the birth of the corporation. There were some reformers like Louis Brandeis who cursed the new "bigness" of these omnipotent firms. Croly found this critique far too broad.

[9] Ibid., 29.

The modern corporation, he asserted, was capable of tremendous efficiencies. "The trusts have certainly succeeded in reducing the amount of waste which was necessitated by the earlier condition of unregulated competition," he wrote.[10]

But without a strong state looking over the shoulder of these new behemoths, the trusts would stifle the economy with their unfair tactics, thereby pocketing enormous profits and damaging competitors who abided the law. The corporations had exploited state governments to reap enormous political power, too—a condition that could only be remedied by shifting ever-increasing responsibilities to the far less corruptible structure of the federal government.

Croly's estimable biographer, David Levy, has found large traces of David in the book. The positivists were, after all, early fans of centralization; their heroes were the technocrats, very much like the ones Herbert had hoped would regulate the trusts. And it's true that *The Promise of American Life* contains many theories and passages that recall the copious writings of Croly's father. Nevertheless, the genius of the book is that it takes this positivist faith in social engineering and softens it. The book also betrays the strong influence of the Harvard professors who David distrusted. Herbert was not just personally modest; he shared pragmatism's belief in intellectual humility and experimentation. He instinctually hoped to extend the reaches of the federal government, but was willing to reverse himself if the evidence suggested the inefficiency of such an extension.

IV

Croly was a creature of the early twentieth century—and his thesis shares the values of his time. He believed

[10] Ibid., 81.

in the virtues of nationalism and even imperialism. The expansion of the state was justified on these grounds: a robust federal government would create a national community and something Croly called "the national spirit." This last idea sounds vaguely menacing—a phrase that certain European dictators would later exploit for horrific ends. Yet Croly meant nothing of the sort. In the parlance of contemporary American politics, Croly would be called a communitarian. He abhorred the selfishness of his society, and hoped that a sense of patriotism might replace it and that citizens would work altruistically on behalf of their compatriots in the name of bettering the nation. (This, too, echoes Comte and his rhapsodic visions of the brotherhood of man.)

There was more to his idea of nationalism than that, though. As an architecture writer, Croly had arrived at a dim view of American culture. He thought that it failed to appreciate genius. In part, he contended, this was a hangover from the pioneer days, when the country made a fetish out of the everyman. And in part, this was the fault of the market, which allowed clients to dictate to artists. But when Croly cast his eye over the buildings that Americans had constructed, he saw one giant pile of mediocrity. The same was true of our politics. Aside from one or two cases—Abraham Lincoln in particular—the profession had attracted few exceptional people.

He hoped that a revived sense of national purpose would reverse this culture of materialism and mediocrity. The European nationalist had invoked the homeland in order to achieve a sense of conformism. Croly wanted to cultivate a sense of nationalism in order to achieve a sense of radical nonconformity, to create a sense of ferment and higher purpose that would allow genius to truly express itself: "Any success in the achievement of national purpose will contribute positively to the liberation of the individual . . . by enveloping him in an invigorating rather than an enervative moral and intellectual atmosphere."[11]

Croly was hardly optimistic about the prospects of transforming the culture. He believed that it would require an elite that resisted the prevailing pressure of society; this vanguard would have to educate the nation, slowly improving the standards of society. And the book closes with a rousing call for the enlightened few to provide models for the rest of the country—to offer examples of heroism and saintliness.

The finale apparently had the desired effect. A couple called Willard and Dorothy Straight read *The Promise of American Life* together while on their honeymoon— not everyone's definition of a romantic time. She was the heiress to the Whitney fortune, arriving at her riches at an early age. Her wealth had allowed her to buck the expectations of her social station and donate with little self-consciousness to progressive causes. This wealth also meant that she had no compunction about marrying Straight, a self-made man who rose from a childhood as an orphan to spend much of his adult life as J. P. Morgan's representative in China. The couple was friendly with Roosevelt and wildly enthusiastic about his turn toward the New Nationalism.

Croly had struck a nerve with them. When they returned to their home on Long Island, the Straights invited him for lunch. They were patrons in search of an author, and he was an author in search of a new project befitting his new standing in the world. Over the course of their conversations, the Straights agreed to start a new weekly publication, edited by Croly, which would promote the ideas contained in his book. They initially called their magazine the *Republic*. When they discov-

[11] Ibid., 292.

ered that the name was already taken, they redubbed it the *New Republic*. The magazine would help re-create the meaning of liberalism in the American political vocabulary. Where it had only meant laissez-faire, the magazine identified the term with the affirmative use of government.

V

Once upon a time, *The Promise of American Life* was a book that liberals venerated. It's why Walter Lippmann called Croly "the first important political philosopher who appeared in America in the twentieth century."[12] There were New Dealers who spoke of the tome reverentially, which is fitting since they enshrined Croly's ideas as the policy of the land.

In the decades since the Great Depression, the book has plummeted from discussion. Conservatives are now largely the ones who invoke Croly's name, and only then to service a grotesque caricature of liberals' authoritarian tendencies. They point to a series of articles that Croly wrote in the mid-1920s expressing interest in Benito Mussolini's nascent regime. And it's true that Croly's emphasis on nationalism—and the special role that he assigned to enlightened elites—contained faint resonances with European fascism. But this flash of admiration for Mussolini should hardly matter. Croly wrote his articles about Italy in the earliest days of fascism; he recanted those views when Il Duce's authoritarianism, "his archaic imperialism," more clearly emerged.[13] Besides, those pieces appeared during one of Croly's periodic phases of dark introspection. World

[12] Walter Lippmann, "Notes for a Biography," *New Republic* (July 16, 1930): 243.

[13] Quoted in John P. Diggins, *Mussolini and Fascism: The View from America* (Princeton, NJ: Princeton University Press, 1972), 227–34.

War I and its reactionary aftermath had shaken his core faith in liberalism—and he spent the 1920s, his last decade, on a quest for new ideological and metaphysical certainties. This final decade saw him write obsessively about Christianity, and he even dabbled in the bizarre mystical teachings of Georges Gurdjieff. Few of Croly's writings from this period do much to bolster his reputation, but they don't really indict his earlier work either—except for those looking to smear him.

In some ways, though, it's fitting that conservatives now show greater interest in Croly than their liberal counterparts. The American Right cares more deeply about ideological history. It has its own clear creation myth that it tells—about how William F. Buckley helped shape a modern movement, and about how Ronald Reagan gave it a popular voice. Conservatives have a canon of thinkers—Russell Kirk, Whitaker Chambers, and Irving Kristol—who remain obligatory reading for young Republicans. They have books that are passed down from generation to generation. But then again, conservatives are the party of tradition.

American liberalism is made of different material. It is the ideology that denies its ideological tendencies as well as its intellectual origins. It likes to congratulate itself on its pragmatism along with how it amends its worldview in response to data and changing conditions. During the Bush era, it became especially fashionable for liberals to declare themselves members of the "reality-based community." Yet it's precisely this tendency that makes liberals prone to bouts of insecurity; it's the reason that liberals can't decide if they care to call themselves by that name or prefer to disguise themselves as progressives. Ever since the 1960s, liberals have found themselves on the defensive—and that condition has been exacerbated by the sense that they are improvising. Liberals have been ridiculed by those on both the Left and Right for weakness as well as equivocation.

The Promise of American Life is an eccentric book and hardly a beautiful work of literature. Yet it's also a wonderfully muscular work, an antidote to the neurosis suffered by Croly's heirs; it captures the patriotic spirit of liberalism, how government helps complete and perfect the nation. The faith in government that Croly articulates isn't just about social justice, and it doesn't pay any special attention to the poor or working class. It's about the "national interest"—a phrase that Croly repeats to the point of tedium. But it's worth the repetition, especially now, when it has faded so far from our politics.

Franklin Foer
MARCH 2013

The Promise of American Life

1.

What Is the Promise of American Life?

|

The average American is nothing if not patriotic. "The Americans are filled," says Mr. Emil Reich in his "Success among the Nations," "with such an implicit and absolute confidence in their Union and in their future success that any remark other than laudatory is inacceptable to the majority of them. We have had many opportunities of hearing public speakers in America cast doubts upon the very existence of God and of Providence, question the historic nature or veracity of the whole fabric of Christianity; but never has it been our fortune to catch the slightest whisper of doubt, the slightest want of faith, in the chief God of America—unlimited belief in the future of America." Mr. Reich's method of emphasis may not be very happy, but the substance of what he says is true. The faith of Americans in their own country is religious, if not in its intensity, at any rate in its almost absolute and universal authority. It pervades the air we breathe. As children we hear it asserted or implied in the conversation of our elders. Every new stage of our educational training provides some additional testimony on its behalf. Newspapers and novelists, orators and playwrights, even if they are little else, are at least loyal preachers of the Truth. The skeptic is not controverted; he is overlooked. It constitutes the kind of faith which is the implication, rather than the object, of thought, and consciously or unconsciously it enters largely into our personal lives as a formative influence. We may distrust and dislike much that is done in the name of our country by our fellow-countrymen; but our country itself, its democratic system, and its prosperous future are above suspicion.

Of course, Americans have no monopoly of patriotic enthusiasm and good faith. Englishmen return thanks to Providence for not being born anything but an Englishman, in churches and ale-houses as well as in comic operas. The Frenchman cherishes and proclaims the idea that France is the most civilized modern country and satisfies best the needs of a man of high social intelligence. The Russian, whose political and social estate does not seem enviable to his foreign contemporaries, secretes a vision of a mystically glorified Russia, which condemns to comparative insipidity the figures of the "Pax Britannica" and of "La Belle France" enlightening the world. Every nation, in proportion as its nationality is thoroughly alive, must be leavened by the ferment of some such faith. But there are significant differences between the faith of, say, an Englishman in the British Empire and that of an American in the Land of Democracy. The contents of an Englishman's national idea tends to be more exclusive. His patriotism is anchored to the historical achievements of Great Britain and restricted thereby. As a good patriot he is bound to be more preoccupied with the inherited fabric of national institutions and traditions than he is with the ideal and more than national possibilities of the future. This very loyalty to the national fabric does, indeed, imply an important ideal content; but the national idealism of an Englishman, a German, or even a Frenchman, is heavily mortgaged to his own national history and cannot honestly escape the debt. The good patriot is obliged to offer faithful allegiance to a network of somewhat arbitrary institutions, social forms, and intellectual habits—on the ground that his country is exposed to more serious dangers from premature emancipation than it is from stubborn conservatism. France is the only European country which has sought to make headway towards a better future by means of a revolutionary break with its past, and the results of the French experiment have served for other European countries more as a warning than as an example.

The higher American patriotism, on the other hand, combines loyalty to historical tradition and precedent with the imaginative projection of an ideal national Promise. The Land of Democracy has always appealed to its more enthusiastic children chiefly as a land of wonderful and more than national possibilities. "Neither race nor tradition," says Professor Hugo Münsterberg in his volume on "The Americans," "nor the actual past, binds the American to his countrymen, but rather the future which together they are building." This vision of a better future is not, perhaps, as unclouded for the present generation of Americans as it was for certain former generations; but in spite of a more friendly acquaintance with all sorts of obstacles and pitfalls, our country is still figured in the imagination of its citizens as the Land of Promise. They still believe that somehow and sometime something better will happen to good Americans than has happened to men in any other country; and this belief, vague, innocent, and uninformed though it be, is the expression of an essential constituent in our national ideal. The past should mean less to a European than it does to an American, and the future should mean more. To be sure, American life cannot with impunity be wrenched violently from its moorings any more than the life of a European country can; but our American past, compared to that of any European country, has a character all its own. Its peculiarity consists, not merely in its brevity, but in the fact that from the beginning it has been informed by an idea. From the beginning Americans have been anticipating and projecting a better future. From the beginning the Land of Democracy has been figured as the Land of Promise. Thus the American's loyalty to the national tradition rather affirms than denies the imaginative projection of a better future. An America which was not the Land of Promise, which was not informed by a prophetic outlook and a more or less constructive ideal, would not be the America bequeathed to us by our forefathers. In cherishing the Promise of a better national future the American is fulfilling rather than imperiling the substance of the national tradition.

When, however, Americans talk of their country as the Land of Promise, a question may well be raised as to precisely what they mean. They mean, of course, in general, that the future will have something better in store for them individually and collectively than has the past or the present; but a very superficial analysis of this meaning discloses certain ambiguities. What are the particular benefits which this better future will give to Americans either individually or as a nation? And how is this Promise to be fulfilled? Will it fulfill itself, or does it imply certain responsibilities? If so, what responsibilities? When we speak of a young man's career as promising, we mean that his abilities and opportunities are such that he is likely to become rich or famous or powerful; and this judgment does not of course imply, so far as we are concerned, any responsibility. It is merely a prophecy based upon past performances and proved qualities. But the career, which from the standpoint of an outsider is merely an anticipation, becomes for the young man himself a serious task. For him, at all events, the better future will not merely happen. He will have to do something to deserve it. It may be wrecked by unforeseen obstacles, by unsuspected infirmities, or by some critical error of judgment. So it is with the Promise of American life. From the point of view of an immigrant this Promise may consist of the anticipation of a better future, which he can share merely by taking up his residence on American soil; but once he has become an American, the Promise can no longer remain merely an anticipation. It becomes in that case a responsibility, which requires for its fulfillment a certain kind of behavior on the part of himself and his fellow-Americans. And when we attempt to define the Promise of American life, we are obliged, also, to describe the kind of behavior which the fulfillment of the Promise demands.

The distinction between the two aspects of America as a Land of Promise made in the preceding paragraph is sufficiently obvious, but it is usually slurred by the average good American patriot. The better future, which is promised for himself, his children, and for other Americans, is chiefly a matter of confident anticipation. He looks upon it very much as a friendly outsider might look on some promising individual career. The better future is understood by him as something which fulfills itself. He calls his country, not only the Land of Promise, but the Land of Destiny. It is fairly launched on a brilliant and successful career, the continued prosperity of which is prophesied by the very momentum of its advance. As Mr. H. G. Wells says in "The Future in America," "When one talks to an American of his national purpose, he seems a little at a loss; if one speaks of his national destiny, he responds with alacrity." The great majority of Americans would expect a book written about "The Promise of American Life" to contain chiefly a fanciful description of the glorious American future—a sort of Utopia up-to-date, situated in the land of Good-Enough, and flying the Stars and Stripes. They might admit in words that the achievement of this glorious future implied certain responsibilities, but they would not regard the admission either as startling or novel. Such responsibilities were met by our predecessors; they will be met by our followers. Inasmuch as it is the honorable American past which prophesies on behalf of the better American future, our national responsibility consists fundamentally in remaining true to traditional ways of behavior, standards, and ideals. What we Americans have to do in order to fulfill our national Promise is to keep up the good work—to continue resolutely and cheerfully along the appointed path.

The reader who expects this book to contain a collection of patriotic prophecies will be disappointed. I am not a prophet in any sense of the word, and I entertain an active and intense dislike of the foregoing mixture of optimism, fatalism, and conservatism. To conceive the better American future as a consummation which will take care of itself,—as the necessary result of our customary conditions, institutions, and ideas,—persistence in such a conception is admirably designed to deprive American life of any promise at all. The better future which Americans propose to build is nothing if not an idea which must in certain essential respects emancipate them from their past. American history contains much matter for pride and congratulation, and much matter for regret and humiliation. On the whole, it is a past of which the loyal American has no reason to feel ashamed, chiefly because it has throughout been made better than it was by the vision of a better future; and the American of to-day and to-morrow must remain true to that traditional vision. He must be prepared to sacrifice to that traditional vision even the traditional American ways of realizing it. Such a sacrifice is, I believe, coming to be demanded; and unless it is made, American life will gradually cease to have any specific Promise.

The only fruitful promise of which the life of any individual or any nation can be possessed, is a promise determined by an ideal. Such a promise is to be fulfilled, not by sanguine anticipations, not by a conservative imitation of past achievements, but by laborious, single-minded, clear-sighted, and fearless work. If the promising career of any individual is not determined by a specific and worthy purpose, it rapidly drifts into a mere pursuit of success; and even if such a pursuit is successful, whatever promise it may have had, is buried in the grave of its triumph. So it is with a nation. If its promise is anything more than a vision of power and success, that addition must derive its value from a purpose; because in the moral world the future exists only as a workshop in which a purpose is to be realized. Each of the several leading European nations is possessed of a specific purpose determined for the most part by the pressure of historical circumstances; but the American nation is committed to a purpose which is not merely of historical manufacture. It is committed to the realization of the democratic ideal; and if its Promise is to be fulfilled, it must be prepared to follow whithersoever that ideal may lead.

No doubt Americans have in some measure always conceived their national future as an ideal to be fulfilled. Their anticipations have been uplifting as well as confident and vainglorious. They have been prophesying not merely a safe and triumphant, but also a better, future. The ideal demand for some sort of individual and social amelioration has always accompanied even their vainest flights of patriotic prophecy. They may never have sufficiently realized that this better future, just in so far as it is better, will have to be planned and constructed rather than fulfilled of its own momentum; but at any rate, in seeking to disentangle and emphasize the ideal implications of the American national Promise, I am not wholly false to the accepted American tradition. Even if Americans have neglected these ideal implications, even if they have conceived the better future as containing chiefly a larger portion of familiar benefits, the ideal demand, nevertheless, has always been palpably present; and if it can be established as the dominant aspect of the American tradition, that tradition may be transformed, but it will not be violated.

Furthermore, much as we may dislike the American disposition to take the fulfillment of our national Promise for granted, the fact that such a disposition exists in its present volume and vigor demands respectful consideration. It has its roots in the salient conditions of American life, and in the actual experience of the American people. The national Promise, as it is popularly understood, has in a way been fulfilling itself. If the underlying conditions were to remain much as they have been, the prevalent mixture of optimism, fatalism, and conservatism might retain a formidable measure of justification; and the changes which are taking place in the underlying conditions and in the scope of American national experience afford the most reasonable expectation that this state of mind will undergo a radical alteration. It is new conditions which are forcing Americans to choose between the conception of their national Promise as a process and an ideal. Before, however, the nature of these novel conditions and their significance can be considered, we must examine with more care the relation between the earlier American economic and social conditions and the ideas and institutions associated with them. Only by a better understanding of the popular tradition, only by an analysis of its merits and its difficulties, can we reach a more consistent and edifying conception of the Promise of American life.

II   How the Promise Has Been Realized

All the conditions of American life have tended to encourage an easy, generous, and irresponsible optimism.

As compared to Europeans, Americans have been very much favored by circumstances. Had it not been for the Atlantic Ocean and the virgin wilderness, the United States would never have been the Land of Promise. The European Powers have been obliged from the very conditions of their existence to be more circumspect and less confident of the future. They are always by way of fighting for their national security and integrity. With possible or actual enemies on their several frontiers, and with their land fully occupied by their own population, they need above all to be strong, to be cautious, to be united, and to be opportune in their policy and behavior. The case of France shows the danger of neglecting the sources of internal strength, while at the same time philandering with ideas and projects of human amelioration. Bismarck and Cavour seized the opportunity of making extremely useful for Germany and Italy the irrelevant and vacillating idealism and the timid absolutism of the third Napoleon. Great Britain has occupied in this respect a better situation than has the Continental Powers. Her insular security made her more independent of the menaces and complications of foreign politics, and left her free to be measurably liberal at home and immeasurably imperial abroad. Yet she has made only a circumspect use of her freedom. British liberalism was forged almost exclusively for the British people, and the British peace for colonial subjects. Great Britain could have afforded better than France to tie its national life to an over-national idea, but the only idea in which Britons have really believed was that of British security, prosperity, and power. In the case of our own country the advantages possessed by England have been amplified and extended. The United States was divided from the mainland of Europe not by a channel but by an ocean. Its dimensions were continental rather than insular. We were for the most part freed from alien interference, and could, so far as we dared, experiment with political and social ideals. The land was unoccupied, and its settlement offered an unprecedented area and abundance of economic opportunity. After the Revolution the whole political and social organization was renewed, and made both more serviceable and more flexible. Under such happy circumstances the New World was assuredly destined to become to its inhabitants a Land of Promise,—a land in which men were offered a fairer chance and a better future than the best which the Old World could afford.

No more explicit expression has ever been given to the way in which the Land of Promise was first conceived by its children than in the "Letters of an American Farmer." This book was written by a French immigrant, Hector St. John de Crèvecoeur before the Revolution, and is informed by an intense consciousness of the difference between conditions in the Old and in the New World. "What, then, is an American, this new man?" asks the Pennsylvanian farmer. "He is either a European or the descendant of a European; hence the strange mixture of blood, which you will find in no other country. . . .

"He becomes an American by being received in the broad lap of our great *Alma Mater*. Here individuals of all nations are melted into a new race of men, whose labors and prosperity will one day cause great changes in the world. Here the rewards of his industry follow with equal steps the progress of his labor; this labor is founded on the basis of *self-interest*; can it want a stronger allurement? Wives and children, who before in vain demanded a morsel of bread, now fat and frolicsome, gladly help their father to clear those fields, whence exuberant crops are to arise to feed them all; without any part being claimed either by a despotic prince, a rich abbot, or a mighty lord. . . . The American is a new man, who acts upon new principles; he must therefore

entertain new ideas and form new opinions. From invol-
untary idleness, servile dependence, penury, and useless
labor, he has passed to toils of a very different nature
rewarded by ample subsistence. This is an American."

Although the foregoing is one of the first, it is also
one of the most explicit descriptions of the fundamental American; and it deserves to be analyzed with some
care. According to this French convert the American is
a man, or the descendant of a man, who has emigrated
from Europe chiefly because he expects to be better
able in the New World to enjoy the fruits of his own
labor. The conception implies, consequently, an Old
World, in which the ordinary man cannot become independent and prosperous, and, on the other hand, a
New World in which economic opportunities are much
more abundant and accessible. America has been peo-
pled by Europeans primarily because they expected in
that country to make more money more easily. To the
European immigrant—that is, to the aliens who have
been converted into Americans by the advantages of
American life—the Promise of America has consisted
largely in the opportunity which it offered of economic
independence and prosperity. Whatever else the better
future, of which Europeans anticipate the enjoyment
in America, may contain, these converts will consider
themselves cheated unless they are in a measure relieved
of the curse of poverty.

This conception of American life and its Promise is
as much alive to-day as it was in 1780. Its expression
has no doubt been modified during four generations of
democratic political independence, but the modification
has consisted of an expansion and a development rather
than of a transposition. The native American, like the
alien immigrant, conceives the better future which
awaits himself and other men in America as fundamentally a future in which economic prosperity will

be still more abundant and still more accessible than it has yet been either here or abroad. No alteration or attenuation of this demand has been permitted. With all their professions of Christianity their national idea remains thoroughly worldly. They do not want either for themselves or for their descendants an indefinite future of poverty and deprivation in this world, redeemed by beatitude in the next. The Promise, which bulks so large in their patriotic outlook, is a promise of comfort and prosperity for an ever increasing majority of good Americans. At a later stage of their social development they may come to believe that they have ordered a larger supply of prosperity than the economic factory is capable of producing. Those who are already rich and comfortable, and who are keenly alive to the difficulty of distributing these benefits over a larger social area, may come to tolerate the idea that poverty and want are an essential part of the social order. But as yet this traditional European opinion has found few echoes in America, even among the comfortable and the rich. The general belief still is that Americans are not destined to renounce, but to enjoy.

Let it be immediately added, however, that this economic independence and prosperity has always been absolutely associated in the American mind with free political institutions. The "American Farmer" traced the good fortune of the European immigrant in America, not merely to the abundance of economic opportunity, but to the fact that a ruling class of abbots and lords had no prior claim to a large share of the products of the soil. He did not attach the name of democracy to the improved political and social institutions of America, and when the political differences between Great Britain and her American colonies culminated in the Revolutionary War, the converted "American Farmer" was filled with anguish at this violent assertion of the

"New Americanism." Nevertheless he was fully alive to the benefits which the immigrant enjoyed from a larger dose of political and social freedom; and so, of course, have been all the more intelligent of the European converts to Americanism. A certain number of them, particularly during the early years, came over less for the purpose of making money than for that of escaping from European political and religious persecution. America has always been conventionally conceived, not merely as a land of abundant and accessible economic opportunities, but also as a refuge for the oppressed; and the immigrant ships are crowded both during times of European famine and during times of political revolution and persecution.

Inevitably, however, this aspect of the American Promise has undergone certain important changes since the establishment of our national independence. When the colonists succeeded in emancipating themselves from political allegiance to Great Britain, they were confronted by the task of organizing a stable and efficient government without encroaching on the freedom, which was even at that time traditionally associated with American life. The task was by no means an easy one, and required for its performance the application of other political principles than that of freedom. The men who were responsible for this great work were not, perhaps, entirely candid in recognizing the profound modifications in their traditional ideas which their constructive political work had implied; but they were at all events fully aware of the great importance of their addition to the American idea. That idea, while not ceasing to be at bottom economic, became more than ever political and social in its meaning and contents. The Land of Freedom became in the course of time also the Land of Equality. The special American political system, the construction of which was predicted in the "Farmer's" assertion of the necessary novelty of American modes of thought and action, was made explicitly, if not uncompromisingly, democratic; and the success of this democratic political system was indissolubly associated in the American mind with the persistence of abundant and widely distributed economic prosperity. Our democratic institutions became in a sense the guarantee that prosperity would continue to be abundant and accessible. In case the majority of good Americans were not prosperous, there would be grave reasons for suspecting that our institutions were not doing their duty.

The more consciously democratic Americans became, however, the less they were satisfied with a conception of the Promised Land, which went no farther than a pervasive economic prosperity guaranteed by free institutions. The amelioration promised to aliens and to future Americans was to possess its moral and social aspects. The implication was, and still is, that by virtue of the more comfortable and less trammeled lives which Americans were enabled to lead, they would constitute a better society and would become in general a worthier set of men. The confidence which American institutions placed in the American citizen was considered equivalent to a greater faith in the excellence of human nature. In our favored land political liberty and economic opportunity were by a process of natural education inevitably making for individual and social amelioration. In Europe the people did not have a fair chance. Population increased more quickly than economic opportunities, and the opportunities which did exist were largely monopolized by privileged classes. Power was lodged in the hands of a few men, whose interest depended upon keeping the people in a condition of economic and political servitude; and in this way a divorce was created between individual interest and social stability and welfare. The interests of the privileged rulers demanded the perpetuation of unjust institutions. The interest of the people demanded a revolutionary upheaval. In the absence of such a revolution they had no sufficient inducement to seek their own material and moral improvement. The theory was proclaimed and accepted as a justification for this system of popular oppression that men were not to be trusted to take care of themselves—that they could be kept socially useful only by the severest measures of moral, religious, and political discipline. The theory of the American democracy and its practice was proclaimed to be the antithesis of this European theory and practice. The people were to be trusted rather than suspected and disciplined. They must be tied to their country by the strong bond of self-interest. Give them a fair chance, and the natural goodness of human nature would do the rest. Individual and public interest will, on the whole, coincide, provided no individuals are allowed to have special privileges. Thus the American system will be predestined to success by its own adequacy, and its success will constitute an enormous stride towards human amelioration. Just because our system is at bottom a thorough test of the ability of human nature to respond admirably to a fair chance, the issue of the experiment is bound to be of more than national importance. The American system stands for the highest hope of an excellent worldly life that mankind has yet ventured,—the hope that men can be improved without being fettered, that they can be saved without even vicariously being nailed to the cross.

Such are the claims advanced on behalf of the American system; and within certain limits this system has made good. Americans have been more than usually prosperous. They have been more than usually free. They have, on the whole, made their freedom and prosperity contribute to a higher level of individual and social excellence. Most assuredly the average Americanized American is neither a more intelligent, a wiser, nor a better man than the average European; but he is likely to be a more energetic and hopeful one. Out of a million well-established Americans, taken indiscriminately from all occupations and conditions, compared to a corresponding assortment of Europeans, a larger proportion of the former will be leading alert, active, and useful lives. Within a given social area there will be a smaller amount of social wreckage and a larger amount of wholesome and profitable achievement. The mass of the American people is, on the whole, more deeply stirred, more thoroughly awake, more assertive in their personal demands, and more confident of satisfying them. In a word, they are more alive, and they must be credited with the moral and social benefit attaching to a larger amount of vitality.

Furthermore, this greater individual vitality, although intimately connected with the superior agricultural and industrial opportunities of a new country, has not been due exclusively to such advantages. Undoubtedly the vast areas of cheap and fertile land which have been continuously available for settlement have contributed, not only to the abundance of American prosperity, but also to the formation of American character and institutions; and undoubtedly many of the economic and political evils which are now becoming offensively obtrusive are directly or indirectly derived from the gradual monopolization of certain important economic opportunities. Nevertheless, these opportunities could never have been converted so quickly into substantial benefits had it not been for our more democratic political and social forms. A privileged class does not secure itself in the enjoyment of its advantages merely by legal intrenchments. It depends quite as much upon disqualifying the "lower classes" from utilizing their opportunities by a species of social inhibition. The rail-splitter can be so easily encouraged to believe that rail-splitting is his vocation. The tragedy in the life of Mr. J. M. Barrie's "Admirable Crichton" was not due to any legal prohibition of his conversion in England, as on the tropic island, into a veritable chief, but that on English soil he did not in his own soul want any such elevation and distinction. His very loyalty to the forms and fabric of English life kept him fatuously content with the mean truckling and meaner domineering of his position of butler. On the other hand, the loyalty of an American to the American idea would tend to make him aggressive and self-confident. Our democratic prohibition of any but occasional social distinctions and our democratic dislike to any suggestion of authentic social inferiority have contributed as essentially to the fluid and elastic substance of American life as have its abundant and accessible economic opportunities.

The increased momentum of American life, both in its particles and its mass, unquestionably has a considerable moral and social value. It is the beginning, the only possible beginning, of a better life for the people as individuals and for society. So long as the great majority of the poor in any country are inert and are laboring without any hope of substantial rewards in this world, the whole associated life of that community rests on an equivocal foundation. Its moral and social order is tied to an economic system which starves and mutilates the great majority of the population, and under such conditions its religion necessarily becomes a spiritual drug, administered for the purpose of subduing the popular discontent and relieving the popular misery. The only way the associated life of such a community can be radically improved is by the leavening of the inert popular mass. Their wants must be satisfied, and must be sharpened and increased with the habit of satisfaction. During the past hundred years every European state has made a great stride in the direction of arousing its poorer citizens to be more wholesomely active, discontented, and expectant; but our own country has succeeded in traveling farther in this direction than has any other, and it may well be proud of its achievement. That the American political and economic system has accomplished so much on behalf of the ordinary man does constitute the fairest hope that men have been justified in entertaining of a better worldly order; and any higher social achievement, which America may hereafter reach, must depend upon an improved perpetuation of this process. The mass of mankind must be aroused to still greater activity by a still more abundant satisfaction of their needs, and by a consequent increase of their aggressive discontent.

The most discriminating appreciation, which I have ever read, of the social value of American national achievement has been written by Mr. John B. Crozier; and the importance of the matter is such that it will be well to quote it at length. Says Mr. Crozier in his chapter on "Reconstruction in America," in the third volume of his "History of Intellectual Development": "There [in America] a natural equality of sentiment, springing out of and resting on a broad equality of material and social conditions, has been the heritage of the people from the earliest times. . . . This broad natural equality of sentiment, rooted in equal material opportunities, equal education, equal laws, equal opportunities, and equal access to all positions of honor and trust, has just sufficient inequality mixed with it—in the shape of greater or less mental endowments, higher or lower degrees of culture, larger or smaller material possessions, and so on—to keep it sweet and human; while at the same time it is all so gently graded, and marked by transitions so easy and natural, that no gap was anywhere to be discovered on which to found an order of privilege or caste. Now an equality like this, with the erectness, independence, energy, and initiative it brings with it, in men, sprung from the loins of an imperial race is a possession, not for a nation only, but for civilization itself and for humanity. It is the distinct raising of the entire body of a people to a higher level, and so brings civilization a stage nearer its goal. It is the first successful attempt in recorded history to get a healthy, natural equality which should reach down to the foundations of the state and to the great masses of men; and in its results corresponds to what in other lands (excepting, perhaps, in luxury alone) has been attained only by the few,—the successful and the ruling spirits. To lose it, therefore, to barter it or give it away, would be in the language of Othello 'such deep damnation that nothing else could match,' and would be an irreparable loss to the world and to civilization."

Surely no nation can ask for a higher and more generous tribute than that which Mr. Crozier renders to America in the foregoing quotation, and its value is increased by the source from which it comes. It is written by a man who, as a Canadian, has had the opportunity of knowing American life well without being biased in its favor, and who, as the historian of the intellectual development of our race, has made an exhaustive study of the civilizations both of the ancient and the modern worlds. Nothing can be soberly added to it on behalf of American national achievement, but neither should it be diminished by any important idea and phrase. The American economic, political, and social organization has given to its citizens the benefits of material prosperity, political liberty, and a wholesome natural equality; and this achievement is a gain, not only to Americans, but to the world and to civilization.

III How the Promise Is to Be Realized

In the preceding section I have been seeking to render justice to the actual achievements of the American nation. A work of manifest individual and social value has been wrought; and this work, not only explains the expectant popular outlook towards the future, but it partially determines the character as distinguished from the continued fulfillment of the American national Promise. The better future, whatever else it may bring, must bring at any rate a continuation of the good things of the past. The drama of its fulfillment must find an appropriate setting in the familiar American social and economic scenery. No matter how remote the end may be, no matter what unfamiliar sacrifices may eventually be required on its behalf, the substance of the existing achievement must constitute a veritable beginning, because on no other condition can the attribution of a peculiar Promise to American life find a specific warrant. On no other condition would our national Promise constitute more than an admirable but irrelevant moral and social aspiration.

The moral and social aspiration proper to American life is, of course, the aspiration vaguely described by the word democratic; and the actual achievement of the American nation points towards an adequate and fruitful definition of the democratic ideal. Americans are usually satisfied by a most inadequate verbal description of democracy, but their national achievement implies one which is much more comprehensive and formative. In order to be true to their past, the increasing comfort and economic independence of an ever increasing proportion of the population must be secured, and it must be secured by a combination of individual effort and proper political organization. Above all, however, this economic and political system must be made to secure results of moral and social value. It is the seeking of such results which converts democracy from a political system into a constructive social ideal; and the more the ideal significance of the American national Promise is asserted and emphasized, the greater will become the importance of securing these moral and social benefits.

The fault in the vision of our national future possessed by the ordinary American does not consist in the expectation of some continuity of achievement. It consists rather in the expectation that the familiar benefits will continue to accumulate automatically. In his mind the ideal Promise is identified with the processes and conditions which hitherto have very much simplified its fulfillment, and he fails sufficiently to realize that the conditions and processes are one thing and the ideal Promise quite another. Moreover, these underlying social and economic conditions are themselves changing, in such wise that hereafter the ideal Promise, instead of being automatically fulfilled, may well be automatically stifled. For two generations and more the American people were, from the economic point of view, most happily situated. They were able, in a sense, to slide down hill into the valley of fulfillment. Economic conditions were such that, given a fair start, they could scarcely avoid reaching a desirable goal. But such is no longer the case. Economic conditions have been profoundly modified, and American political and social problems have been modified with them. The Promise of American life must depend less than it did upon the virgin wilderness and the Atlantic Ocean, for the virgin wilderness has disappeared, and the Atlantic Ocean has become merely a big channel. The same results can no longer be achieved by the same easy methods. Ugly obstacles have jumped into view, and ugly obstacles are peculiarly dangerous to a person who is sliding down hill. The man who is clambering up hill is in a much better position to evade or overcome them. Americans will possess a safer as well as a worthier vision of their national Promise as soon as they give it a house on a hill-top rather than in a valley.

The very genuine experience upon which American optimistic fatalism rests, is equivalent, because of its limitations, to a dangerous inexperience, and of late years an increasing number of Americans have been drawing this inference. They have been coming to see themselves more as others see them; and as an introduction to a consideration of this more critical frame of mind, I am going to quote another foreigner's view of American life,—the foreigner in this case being an Englishman and writing in 1893.

"The American note," says Mr. James Muirhead in his "Land of Contrasts," "includes a sense of illimitable expansion and possibility, an almost childlike confidence in human ability and fearlessness of both the present and the future, a wider realization of human brotherhood than has yet existed, a greater theoretical willingness to judge by the individual than by the class, a breezy indifference to authority and a positive predilection for innovation, a marked alertness of mind, and a manifold variety of interest—above all, an inextinguishable hopefulness and courage. It is easy to lay one's finger in America upon almost every one of the great defects of civilization—even those defects which are specially characteristic of the civilization of the Old World. The United States cannot claim to be exempt from manifestations of economic slavery, of grinding the faces of the poor, of exploitation of the weak, of unfair distribution of wealth, of unjust monopoly, of unequal laws, of industrial and commercial chicanery, of disgraceful ignorance, of economic fallacies, of public corruption, of interested legislation, of want of public spirit, of vulgar boasting and chauvinism, of snobbery, of class prejudice, of respect of persons, and of a preference of the material over the spiritual. In a word, America has not attained, or nearly attained, perfection. But below and behind, and beyond all its weakness and evils, there is the grand fact of a noble national theory founded on reason and conscience." The reader will remark in the foregoing quotation that Mr. Muirhead is equally emphatic in his approval and in his disapproval. He generously recognizes almost as much that is good about Americans and their ways as our most vivacious patriotic orators would claim, while at the same time he has marshaled an army of abuses and sins which sound like an echo of the pages of the *London Saturday Review*. In the end he applies a friendly dash of whitewash by congratulating us on the "grand fact of our noble national theory," but to a discerning mind the consolation is not very consoling. The trouble is that the sins with which America is charged by Mr. Muirhead are flagrant violations of our noble national theory. So far as his charges are true, they are a denial that the American political and economic organization is accomplishing the results which its traditional claims require. If, as Mr. Muirhead charges, Americans permit the existence of economic slavery, if they grind the face of the poor, if they exploit the weak and distribute wealth unjustly, if they allow monopolies to prevail and laws to be unequal, if they are disgracefully ignorant, politically corrupt, commercially unscrupulous, socially snobbish, vulgarly boastful, and morally coarse,—if the substance of the foregoing indictment is really true, why, the less that is said about a noble national theory, the better. A man who is a sturdy sinner all the week hardly improves his moral standing by attending church on Sunday and professing a noble Christian theory of life. There must surely be some better way of excusing our sins than by raising aloft a noble theory of which these sins are a glaring violation.

I have quoted from Mr. Muirhead, not because his antithetic characterization of American life is very illuminating, but because of the precise terms of his charges against America. His indictment is practically equivalent to the assertion that the American system is not, or at least is no longer, achieving as much as has been claimed on its behalf. A democratic system may permit undefiled the existence of many sins and abuses, but it cannot permit the exploitation of the ordinary man by means of unjust laws and institutions. Neither can this indictment be dismissed without argument. When Mr. Muirhead's book was written sixteen years ago, the majority of good Americans would assuredly have read the charge with an incredulous smile; but in the year 1909 they might behave differently. The sins of which Mr. Muirhead accused Americans sixteen years ago are substantially the sins of which to-day they are accusing themselves—or rather one another. A numerous and powerful group of reformers has been collecting whose whole political policy and action is based on the conviction that the "common people" have not been getting the Square Deal to which they are entitled under the American system; and these reformers are carrying with them a constantly increasing body of public opinion. A considerable proportion of the American people is beginning to exhibit economic and political, as well as personal, discontent. A generation ago the implication was that if a man remained poor and needy, his poverty was his own fault, because the American system was giving all its citizens a fair chance. Now, however, the discontented poor are beginning to charge their poverty to an unjust political and economic organization, and reforming agitators do not hesitate to support them in this contention. Manifestly a threatened obstacle has been raised against the anticipated realization of our national Promise. Unless the great majority of Americans not only have, but believe they have, a fair chance, the better American future will be dangerously compromised.

The conscious recognition of grave national abuses casts a deep shadow across the traditional American patriotic vision. The sincere and candid reformer can no longer consider the national Promise as destined to automatic fulfillment. The reformers themselves are, no doubt, far from believing that whatever peril there is cannot be successfully averted. They make a point of being as patriotically prophetic as the most "old-fashioned Democrat." They proclaim even more loudly their conviction of an indubitable and a beneficent national future. But they do not and cannot believe that this future will take care of itself. As reformers they are bound to assert that the national body requires for the time being a good deal of medical attendance, and many of them anticipate that even after the doctors have discontinued their daily visits the patient will still need the supervision of a sanitary specialist. He must be persuaded to behave so that he will not easily fall ill again, and so that his health will be permanently improved. Consequently, just in so far as reformers are reformers they are obliged to abandon the traditional American patriotic fatalism. The national Promise has been transformed into a closer equivalent of a national purpose, the fulfillment of which is a matter of conscious work.

The transformation of the old sense of a glorious national destiny into the sense of a serious national purpose will inevitably tend to make the popular realization of the Promise of American life both more explicit and more serious. As long as Americans believed they were able to fulfill a noble national Promise merely by virtue of maintaining intact a set of political institutions and by the vigorous individual pursuit of private ends, their allegiance to their national fulfillment remained more a matter of words than of deeds; but now that they are being aroused from their patriotic slumber, the effect is inevitably to disentangle the national idea and to give it more dignity. The redemption of the national Promise has become a cause for which the good American must fight, and the cause for which a man fights is a cause which he more than ever values. The American idea is no longer to be propagated merely by multiplying the children of the West and by granting ignorant aliens permission to vote. Like all sacred causes, it must be propagated by the Word and by that right arm of the Word, which is the Sword.

The more enlightened reformers are conscious of the additional dignity and value which the popularity of reform has bestowed upon the American idea, but they still fail to realize the deeper implications of their own programme. In abandoning the older conception of an automatic fulfillment of our national destiny, they have abandoned more of the traditional American point of view than they are aware. The traditional American optimistic fatalism was not of accidental origin, and it cannot be abandoned without involving in its fall some other important ingredients in the accepted American tradition. Not only was it dependent on economic conditions which prevailed until comparatively recent times, but it has been associated with certain erroneous but highly cherished political theories. It has been wrought into the fabric of our popular economic and political ideas to such an extent that its overthrow necessitates a partial revision of some of the most important articles in the traditional American creed.

The extent and the character of this revision may be inferred from a brief consideration of the effect upon the substance of our national Promise of an alteration in its proposed method of fulfillment. The substance of our national Promise has consisted, as we have seen, of an improving popular economic condition, guaranteed by democratic political institutions, and resulting in moral and social amelioration. These manifold benefits were to be obtained merely by liberating the enlightened self-interest of the American people. The beneficent result followed inevitably from the action of wholly selfish motives—provided, of course, the democratic political system of equal rights was maintained in its integrity. The fulfillment of the American Promise was considered inevitable because it was based upon a combination of self-interest and the natural goodness of human nature. On the other hand, if the fulfillment of our national Promise can no longer be considered inevitable, if it must be considered as equivalent to a conscious national purpose instead of an inexorable national destiny, the implication necessarily is that the trust reposed in individual self-interest has been in some measure betrayed. No preëstablished harmony can then exist between the free and abundant satisfaction of private needs and the accomplishment of a morally and socially desirable result. The Promise of American life is to be fulfilled—not merely by a maximum amount of economic freedom, but by a certain measure of discipline; not merely by the abundant satisfaction of individual desires, but by a large measure of individual subordination and self-denial. And this necessity of subordinating the satisfaction of individual desires to the fulfillment of a national purpose is attached particularly to the absorbing occupation of the American people,—the occupation, viz.: of accumulating wealth. The automatic fulfillment of the American national Promise is to be abandoned, if at all, precisely because the traditional American confidence in individual freedom has resulted in a morally and socially undesirable distribution of wealth.

In making the concluding statement of the last paragraph I am venturing, of course, upon very debatable ground. Neither can I attempt in this immediate connection to offer any justification for the statement which might or should be sufficient to satisfy a stubborn skeptic. I must be content for the present with the bare assertion that the prevailing abuses and sins, which have made reform necessary, are all of them associated with the prodigious concentration of wealth, and of the power exercised by wealth, in the hands of a few men. I am far from believing that this concentration of economic power is wholly an undesirable thing, and I am also far from believing that the men in whose hands this power is concentrated deserve, on the whole, any exceptional moral reprobation for the manner in which it has been used. In certain respects they have served their country well, and in almost every respect their moral or immoral standards are those of the great majority of their fellow-countrymen. But it is none the less true that the political corruption, the unwise economic organization, and the legal support afforded to certain economic privileges are all under existing conditions due to the malevolent social influence of individual and incorporated American wealth; and it is equally true that these abuses, and the excessive "money power" with which they are associated, have originated in the peculiar freedom which the American tradition and organization have granted to the individual. Up to a certain point that freedom has been and still is beneficial. Beyond that point it is not merely harmful; it is by way of being fatal. Efficient regulation there must be; and it must be regulation which will strike, not at the symptoms of the evil, but at its roots. The existing concentration of wealth and financial power in the hands of a few irresponsible men is the inevitable outcome of the chaotic individualism of our political and economic organization, while at the same time it is inimical to democracy, because it tends to erect political abuses and social inequalities into a system. The inference which follows may be disagreeable, but it is not to be escaped. In becoming re-sponsible for the subordination of the individual to the demand of a dominant and constructive national pur-pose, the American state will in effect be making itself responsible for a morally and socially desirable distribu-tion of wealth.

The consequences, then, of converting our American national destiny into a national purpose are beginning to be revolutionary. When the Promise of American life is conceived as a national ideal, whose fulfillment is a matter of artful and laborious work, the effect thereof is substantially to identify the national purpose with the social problem. What the American people of the present and the future have really been promised by our patriotic prophecies is an attempt to solve that problem. They have been promised on American soil comfort, prosperity, and the opportunity for self-improvement; and the lesson of the existing crisis is that such a Promise can never be redeemed by an indiscriminate individual scramble for wealth. The individual competition, even when it starts under fair conditions and rules, results, not only, as it should, in the triumph of the strongest, but in the attempt to perpetuate the victory; and it is this attempt which must be recognized and forestalled in the interest of the American national purpose. The way to realize a purpose is, not to leave it to chance, but to keep it loyally in mind, and adopt means proper to the importance and the difficulty of the task. No vol-untary association of individuals, resourceful and dis-interested though they be, is competent to assume the responsibility. The problem belongs to the American national democracy, and its solution must be attempted chiefly by means of official national action.

Neither can its attempted solution be escaped. When they are confronted by the individual sacrifices which the fulfillment of their national Promise demands, American political leaders will find many excuses for ignoring the responsibility thereby implied; but the difficulty of such an attempted evasion will consist in the reënforcement of the historical tradition by a logical and a practical necessity. The American problem is the social problem partly because the social problem is the democratic problem. American political and social leaders will find that in a democracy the problem cannot be evaded. The American people have no irremediable political griev- ances. No good American denies the desirability of popular sovereignty and of a government which should somehow represent the popular will. While our national institutions may not be a perfect embodiment of these doctrines, a decisive and a resolute popular majority has the power to alter American institutions and give them a more immediately representative character. Existing political evils and abuses are serious enough; but inas- much as they have come into being, not against the will, but with the connivance of the American people, the lat- ter are responsible for their persistence. In the long run, consequently, the ordinary American will have nothing irremediable to complain about except economic and social inequalities. In Europe such will not be the case. The several European peoples have, and will continue to have, political grievances, because such grievances are the inevitable consequence of their national history and their international situation; and as long as these griev- ances remain, the more difficult social problem will be subordinated to an agitation for political emancipation. But the American people, having achieved democratic institutions, have nothing to do but to turn them to good account. In so far as the social problem is a real problem and the economic grievance a real grievance, they are bound under the American political system to come eventually to the surface and to demand express and intelligent consideration. A democratic ideal makes the social problem inevitable and its attempted solution indispensable.

I am fully aware, as already intimated, that the forgoing interpretation of the Promise of American life will seem fantastic and obnoxious to the great majority of Americans, and I am far from claiming that any reasons as yet alleged afford a sufficient justification for such a radical transformation of the traditional national policy and democratic creed. All that can be claimed is that if a democratic ideal makes an express consideration of the social problem inevitable, it is of the first importance for Americans to realize this truth and to understand the reasons for it. Furthermore, the assumption is worth making, in case the traditional American system is breaking down, because a more highly socialized democracy is the only practical substitute on the part of convinced democrats for an excessively individualized democracy. Of course, it will be claimed that the traditional system is not breaking down, and again no absolute proof of the breakdown has been or can be alleged. Nevertheless, the serious nature of contemporary American political and economic symptoms at least pointedly suggests the existence of some radical disease, and when one assumes such to be the case, one cannot be accused of borrowing trouble. I shall, consequently, start from such an assumption, and make an attempt to explain contemporary American problems as in part the result of the practice of an erroneous democratic theory. The attempt will necessarily involve a brief review of our political and economic history, undertaken for the purpose of tracing the traditional ideas of their origin and testing them by their performances. There will follow a detailed examination of current political and economic problems and conditions—considered in relation both to the American democratic tradition and to the proposed revision thereof. In view of the increasing ferment of American political and economic thought, no apology is necessary for submitting our traditional ideas and practices to an examination from an untraditional point of view. I need scarcely add that the untraditional point of view will contain little or no original matter. The only novelty such an inquiry can claim is the novelty of applying ideas, long familiar to foreign political thinkers, to the subject-matter of American life. When applied to American life, this group of ideas assumes a somewhat new complexion and significance; and the promise of such a small amount of novelty will, I trust, tempt even a disapproving reader to follow somewhat farther the course of the argument.

2.

The Federalists and the Republicans

I

The purpose of the following review of American political ideas and practices is, it must be premised, critical
rather than narrative or expository. I am not seeking
to justify a political and economic theory by an appeal to historical facts. I am seeking, on the contrary, to
place some kind of an estimate and interpretation upon
American political ideas and achievements; and this estimate and interpretation is determined chiefly by a preconceived ideal. The acceptability of such an estimate
and interpretation will, of course, depend at bottom
upon the number of important facts which it explains
and the number which it either neglects or distorts. No
doubt, certain omissions and distortions are inevitable
in an attempt of this kind; but I need scarcely add that
the greatest care has been taken to avoid them. In case
the proposed conception of the Promise of American life
cannot be applied to our political and economic history
without essential perversion, it must obviously fall to
the ground; and as a matter of fact, the ideal itself has
been sensibly modified during the course of this attempt
to give it an historical application. In spite of all these
modifications it remains, however, an extremely controversial review. Our political and economic past is, in
a measure, challenged in order to justify our political
and social future. The values placed upon many political ideas, tendencies, and achievements differ radically

from the values placed upon them either by their originators and partisans or in some cases by the majority
of American historians. The review, consequently, will
meet with a far larger portion of instinctive opposition
and distrust than it will of acquiescence. The whole
traditional set of values which it criticises is almost as
much alive to-day as it was two generations ago, and it
forms a background to the political faith of the great
majority of Americans. Whatever favor a radical criticism can obtain, it must win on its merits both as an
adequate interpretation of our political past and as an
outlook towards the solution of our present and future
political and economic problems.

The material for this critical estimate must be sought,
not so much in the events of our national career, as
in the ideas which have influenced its course. Closely
as these ideas are associated with the actual course of
American development, their meaning and their re-
moter tendencies have not been wholly realized therein,
because beyond a certain point no attempt was made
to think out these ideas candidly and consistently. For
one generation American statesmen were vigorous and
fruitful political thinkers; but the time soon came when
Americans ceased to criticise their own ideas, and since
that time the meaning of many of our fundamental national conceptions has been partly obscured, as well as
partly expressed, by the facts of our national growth.
Consequently we must go behind these facts and scruti-
nize, with more caution than is usually considered necessary, the adequacy and consistency of the underlying
ideas. And I believe that the results of such a scrutiny
will be very illuminating. It will be found that from the
start there has been one group of principles at work
which have made for American national fulfillment, and
another group of principles which has made for American national distraction; and that these principles are as

much alive to-day as they were when Jefferson wrote the Kentucky resolutions or when Jackson, at the dinner of the Jefferson Club, toasted the preservation of the Union. But while these warring principles always have been, and still are, alive, they have never, in my opinion, been properly discriminated one from another; and until such a discrimination is made, the lesson cannot be profitably applied to the solution of our contemporary national problems.

All our histories recognize, of course, the existence from the very beginning of our national career of two different and, in some respects, antagonistic groups of political ideas,—the ideas which were represented by Jefferson, and the ideas which were represented by Hamilton. It is very generally understood, also, that neither the Jeffersonian nor the Hamiltonian doctrine was entirely adequate, and that in order to reach a correct understanding of the really formative constituent in the complex of American national life, a combination must be made of both Republicanism and Federalism. But while the necessity of such a combination is fully realized, I do not believe that it has ever been mixed in just the proper proportions. We are content to say with Webster that the prosperity of American institutions depends upon the unity and inseparability of individual and local liberties and a national union. We are content to declare that the United States must remain somehow a free and a united country, because there can be no complete unity without liberty and no salutary liberty outside of a Union. But the difficulties with this phrase, its implications and consequences, we do not sufficiently consider. It is enough that we have found an optimistic formula wherewith to unite the divergent aspects of the Republican and Federalist doctrines.

We must begin, consequently, with critical accounts of the ideas both of Jefferson and of Hamilton; and we must seek to discover wherein each of these sets of ideas was right, and wherein each was wrong; in what proportions they were subsequently combined in order to form "our noble national theory," and what were the advantages, the limitations, and the effects of this combination. I shall not disguise the fact that, on the whole, my own preferences are on the side of Hamilton rather than of Jefferson. He was the sound thinker, the constructive statesman, the candid and honorable, if erring, gentleman; while Jefferson was the amiable enthusiast, who understood his fellow-countrymen better and trusted them more than his rival, but who was incapable either of uniting with his fine phrases a habit of candid and honorable private dealing or of embodying those phrases in a set of efficient institutions. But although Hamilton is much the finer man and much the sounder thinker and statesman, there were certain limitations in his ideas and sympathies the effects of which have been almost as baleful as the effects of Jefferson's intellectual superficiality and insincerity. He perverted the American national idea almost as much as Jefferson perverted the American democratic idea, and the proper relation of these two fundamental conceptions one to another cannot be completely understood until this double perversion is corrected.

To make Hamilton and Jefferson exclusively responsible for this double perversion is, however, by no means fair. The germs of it are to be found in the political ideas and prejudices with which the American people emerged from their successful Revolutionary War. At that time, indeed, the opposition between the Republican and the Federalist doctrines had not become definite and acute; and it is fortunate that such was the case, because if the opponents of an efficient Federal constitution had been organized and had been possessed of the full courage and consciousness of their convictions, that instrument would never have been accepted, or it would have been accepted only in a much more mutilated and enfeebled condition. Nevertheless, the different political points of view which afterwards developed into Hamiltonian Federalism and Jeffersonian Republicanism were latent in the interests and opinions of the friends and of the opponents of an efficient Federal government; and these interests and opinions were the natural product of contemporary American economic and political conditions.

Both Federalism and anti-Federalism were the mixed issue of an interest and a theory. The interest which lay behind Federalism was that of well-to-do citizens in a stable political and social order, and this interest aroused them to favor and to seek some form of political organization which was capable of protecting their property and promoting its interest. They were the friends of liberty because they were in a position to benefit largely by the possession of liberty; and they wanted a strong central government because only by such means could their liberties, which consisted fundamentally in the ability to enjoy and increase their property, be guaranteed. Their interests were threatened by the disorganized state governments in two different but connected respects. These governments did not seem able to secure either internal order or external peace. In their domestic policy the states threatened to become the prey of a factious radical democracy, and their relations one to another were by way of being constantly embroiled. Unless something could be done, it looked as if they would drift in a condition either of internecine warfare without profit or, at best, of peace without security. A centralized and efficient government would do away with both of these threats. It would prevent or curb all but the most serious sectional disputes, while at the same time it would provide a much stronger guarantee for internal political order and social stability. An equally strong interest lay at the roots of anti-Federalism and it had its theory, though this theory was less mature and definite. Behind the opposition to a centralized government were the interests and the prejudices of the mass of the American people,—the people who were, comparatively speaking, lacking in money, in education, and in experience. The Revolutionary War, while not exclusively the work of the popular element in the community, had undoubtedly increased considerably its power and influence. A large proportion of the well-to-do colonial Americans had been active or passive Tories, and had either been ruined or politically disqualified by the Revolution. Their successful opponents reorganized the state governments in a radical democratic spirit. The power of the state was usually concentrated in the hands of a single assembly, to whom both the executive and the courts were subservient; and this method of organization was undoubtedly designed to give immediate and complete effect to the will of a popular majority. The temper of the local democracies, which, for the most part, controlled the state governments, was insubordinate, factious, and extremely independent. They disliked the idea of a centralized Federal government because a supreme power would be thereby constituted which could interfere with the freedom of local public opinion and thwart its will. No less than the Federalists, they believed in freedom; but the kind of freedom they wanted, was freedom from anything but local interference. The ordinary American democrat felt that the power of *his* personality and *his* point of view would be diminished by the efficient centralization of political authority. He had no definite intention of using the democratic state governments for anti-social or revolutionary purposes, but he was self-willed and unruly in temper; and his savage treatment of the Tories during and after the Revolution had given him a taste of the sweets of confiscation. The spirit of his democracy was self-reliant, undisciplined, suspicious of authority, equalitarian, and individualistic.

With all their differences, however, the Federalists and their opponents had certain common opinions and interests, and it was these common opinions and interests which prevented the split from becoming irremediable. The men of both parties were individualist in spirit, and they were chiefly interested in the great American task of improving their own condition in this world. They both wanted a government which would secure them freedom of action for this purpose. The difference between them was really less a difference of purpose than of the means whereby a purpose should be accomplished. The Federalists, representing as they did chiefly the people of wealth and education, demanded a government adequate to protect existing propertied rights; but they were not seeking any exceptional privileges— except those traditionally associated with the ownership of private property. The anti-Federalists, on the other hand, having less to protect and more to acquire, insisted rather upon being let alone than in being protected. They expressed themselves sometimes in such an extremely insubordinate manner as almost to threaten social disorder, but were very far from being fundamentally anti-social in interest or opinion. They were all by way of being property-owners, and they all expected to benefit by freedom from interference in the acquisition of wealth. It was this community of interest and point of view which prepared the way, not only for the adoption of the Constitution, but for the loyalty it subsequently inspired in the average American.

It remains none the less true, however, that the division of interest and the controversy thereby provoked was sharp and brought about certain very unfortunate consequences. Inasmuch as the anti-Federalists were unruly democrats and were suspicious of any efficient political authority, the Federalists came, justly or unjustly, to identify both anti-Federalism and democracy with political disorder and social instability. They came, that is, to have much the same opinion of radical democracy as an English peer might have had at the time of the French Revolution; and this prejudice, which was unjust but not unnatural, was very influential in determining the character of the Federal Constitution. That instrument was framed, not as the expression of a democratic creed, but partly as a legal fortress against the possible errors and failings of democracy. The federalist point of view resembled that of the later constitutional liberals in France. The political ideal and benefit which they prized most highly was that of liberty, and the Constitution was framed chiefly for the purpose of securing liberty from any possible dangers. Popular liberty must be protected against possible administrative or executive tyranny by free representative institutions. Individual liberty must be protected against the action of an unjust majority by the strongest possible legal guarantees. And above all the general liberties of the community must not be endangered by any inefficiency of the government as a whole. The only method whereby these complicated and, in a measure, conflicting ends could be attained was by a system of checks and balances, which would make the executive, legislative, and judicial departments of the government independent of one another, while at the same time endowing each department with all the essentials of efficient action within its own sphere. But such a method of political organization was calculated to thwart the popular will, just in so far as that will did not conform to what the Federalists believed to be the essentials of a stable political and social order. It was antagonistic to democracy as that word was then, and is still to a large extent, understood.

The extent of this antagonism to democracy, if not in intention at least in effect, is frequently over-rated. The antagonism depends upon the identification of democracy with a political organization for expressing immediately and completely the will of the majority— whatever that will may be; and such a conception of democracy contains only part of the truth. Nevertheless the founders of the Constitution did succeed in giving some effect to their distrust of the democratic principle, no matter how conservatively defined; and this was at once a grave error on their part and a grave misfortune for the American state. Founded as the national government is, partly on a distrust of the American democracy, it has always tended to make the democracy somewhat suspicious of the national government. This mutual suspicion, while it has been limited in scope and diminished by the action of time, constitutes a manifest impediment to the efficient action of the American political system. The great lesson of American political experience, as we shall see, is rather that of interdependence than of incompatibility between an efficient national organization and a group of radical democratic institutions and ideals; and the meaning of this lesson has been obscured, because the Federal organization has not been constituted in a sufficiently democratic spirit, and because, consequently, it has tended to provoke distrust on the part of good democrats. At every stage in the history of American political ideas and practice we shall meet with the unfortunate effects of this partial antagonism.

The error of the Federalists can, however, be excused by many extenuating circumstances. Democracy as an ideal was misunderstood in 1786, and it was possessed of little or no standing in theory or tradition. Moreover, the radical American democrats were doing much to deserve the misgivings of the Federalists. Their ideas were narrow, impracticable, and hazardous; and they were opposed to the essential political need of the time—viz. the constitution of an efficient Federal government. The Federalists may have misinterpreted and perverted the proper purpose of American national organization, but they could have avoided such misinterpretation only by an extraordinary display of political insight and a heroic superiority to natural prejudice. Their error sinks into insignificance compared with the enormous service which they rendered to the American people and the American cause. Without their help there might not have been any American nation at all, or it might have been born under a far darker cloud of political suspicion and animosity. The instrument which they created, with all its faults, proved capable of becoming both the organ of an efficient national government and the fundamental law of a potentially democratic state. It has proved capable of flexible development both in function and in purpose, and it has been developed in both these directions without any sacrifice of integrity.

Its success has been due to the fact that its makers, with all their apprehensions about democracy, were possessed of a wise and positive political faith. They believed in liberty. They believed that the essential condition of fruitful liberty was an efficient central government. They knew that no government could be efficient unless its powers equaled its responsibilities. They were willing to trust to such a government the security and the welfare of the American people. The Constitution has proved capable of development chiefly as the instrument of these positive political ideas. Thanks to the theory of implied powers, to the liberal construction of the Supreme Court during the first forty years of its existence, and to the results of the Civil War the Federal government has, on the whole, become more rather than less efficient as the national political organ of the American people. Almost from the start American life has grown more and more national in substance, in such wise that a rigid constitution which could not have been developed in a national direction would have been an increasing source of irritation and protest. But this reën-forcement of the substance of American national life has, until recently, found an adequate expression in the increasing scope and efficiency of the Federal govern-ment. The Federalists had the insight to anticipate the kind of government which their country needed; and this was a great and a rare achievement—all the more so because they were obliged in a measure to impose it on their fellow-countrymen.

There is, however, another face to the shield. The Con-stitution was the expression not only of a political faith, but also of political fears. It was wrought both as the organ of the national interest and as the bulwark of cer-tain individual and local rights. The Federalists sought to surround private property, freedom of contract, and personal liberty with an impregnable legal fortress; and they were forced by their opponents to amend the origi-nal draft of the Constitution in order to include a still more stringent bill of individual and state rights. Now I am far from pretending that these legal restrictions have not had their value in American national history, and were not the expression of an essential element in the composition and the ideal of the American nation. The security of private property and personal liberty, and a proper distribution of activity between the local and the central governments, demanded at that time, and within limits still demand, adequate legal guarantees. It remains none the less true, however, that every popular government should in the end, and after a necessarily prolonged deliberation, possess the power of taking any action, which, in the opinion of a decisive majority of the people, is demanded by the public welfare. Such is not the case with the government organized under the

Federal Constitution. In respect to certain fundamental provisions, which necessarily receive the most rigid interpretation on the part of the courts, it is practically unmodifiable. A very small percentage of the American people can in this respect permanently thwart the will of an enormous majority, and there can be no justification for such a condition on any possible theory of popular Sovereignty. This defect has not hitherto had very many practical inconveniences, but it is an absolute violation of the theory and the spirit of American democratic institutions. The time may come when the fulfillment of a justifiable democratic purpose may demand the limitation of certain rights, to which the Constitution affords such absolute guarantees; and in that case the American democracy might be forced to seek by revolutionary means the accomplishment of a result which should be attainable under the law.

It was, none the less, a great good thing that the Union under the new Constitution triumphed. Americans have more reason to be proud of its triumph than of any other event in their national history. The formation of an effective nation out of the thirteen original colonies was a political achievement for which there was no historical precedent. Up to that time large countries had been brought, if not held, together by military force or by a long process of gradually closer historical association. Small and partly independent communities had combined one with another only on compulsion. The necessities of joint defense might occasionally drive them into temporary union, but they would not stay united. They preferred a precarious and tumultuous independence to a combination with neighboring communities, which brought security at the price of partial subordination and loyal coöperation. Even the provinces which composed the United Netherlands never submitted to an effective political union during the active and vital period of their history. The small American states had apparently quite as many reasons for separation as the small Grecian and Italian states. The military necessities of the Revolution had welded them only into a loose and feeble confederation, and a successful revolution does not constitute a very good precedent for political subordination. The colonies were divided from one another by difficulties of communication, by variations in economic conditions and social customs, by divergent interests, and above all by a rampant provincial and separatist spirit. On the other hand, they were united by a common language, by a common political and legal tradition, and by the fact that none of them had ever been really independent sovereign states. Nobody dared or cared to object to union in the abstract; nobody advocated the alternative of complete separation; it was only a strong efficient union which aroused the opposition of the Clintons and the Patrick Henrys. Nevertheless, the conditions making for separation have the appearance of being more insistent and powerful than the conditions making for an effective union. Disunion was so easy. Union was so difficult. If the states had only kept on drifting a little longer, they would, at least for a while, inevitably have drifted apart. They were saved from such a fate chiefly by the insight and energy of a few unionist leaders—of whom Washington and Hamilton were the most important.

Perhaps American conditions were such that eventually some kind of a national government was sure to come; but the important point is that when it came, it came as the result of forethought and will rather than of compulsion. "It seems to have been reserved," says Hamilton in the very first number of the *Federalist*, "to the people of this country by their conduct and example, to decide the important question whether societies of men are really capable or not of establishing good government from reflection and choice, or whether they are forever destined to depend for their political constitutions on accident and force." Americans deliberately selected the better part. It is true that the evil effects of a loose union were only too apparent, and that public safety, order, and private property were obviously endangered by the feeble machinery of Federal government. Nevertheless, conditions had not become intolerable. The terrible cost of disunion in money, blood, humiliation, and hatred had not actually been paid. It might well have seemed cheaper to most Americans to drift on a little longer than to make the sacrifices and to undertake the labor demanded by the formation of an effective union. There were plenty of arguments by which a policy of letting things alone could be plausibly defended, and the precedents were all in its favor. Other people had acquired such political experience as they were capable of assimilating, first by drifting into some intolerable excess or some distressing error, and then by undergoing some violent process of purgation or reform. But it is the distinction of our own country that at the critical moment of its history, the policy of drift was stopped before a virulent disease had necessitated a violent and exhausting remedy.

This result was achieved chiefly by virtue of capable, energetic, and patriotic leadership. It is stated that if the Constitution had been subjected to a popular vote as soon as the labors of the Convention terminated, it would probably have been rejected in almost every state in the Union. That it was finally adopted, particularly by certain important states, was distinctly due to the conversion of public opinion, by means of powerful and convincing argument. The American people steered the proper course because their leaders convinced them of the proper course to steer; and the behavior of the many who followed behind is as exemplary as is that of the few who pointed the way. A better example could not be asked of the successful operation of the democratic institutions, and it would be as difficult to find its parallel in the history of our own as in the history of European countries.

II Federalism and Republicanism as Opponents

Fortunately for the American nation the unionists, who wrought the Constitution, were substantially the same body of men as the Federalist party who organized under its provisions an efficient national government. The work of Washington, Hamilton, and their associates during the first two administrations was characterized by the same admirable qualities as the work of the makers of the Constitution, and it is of similar importance. A vigorous, positive, constructive national policy was outlined and carried substantially into effect,—a policy that implied a faith in the powers of an efficient government to advance the national interest, and which justified the faith by actually meeting the critical problems of the time with a series of wise legislative measures. Hamilton's part in this constructive legislation was, of course, more important than it had been in the framing of the Constitution. During Washington's two administrations the United States was governed practically by his ideas, if not by his will; and the sound and unsound parts of his political creed can consequently be more definitely disentangled than they can be during the years when the Constitution was being wrought. The Constitution was in many respects a compromise, whereas the ensuing constructive legislation was a tolerably pure example of Hamiltonian Federalism. It will be instructive, consequently, to examine the trend of this Hamiltonian policy, and seek to discover wherein it started the country on the right path, and wherein it sought to commit the national government to a more dubious line of action.

Hamilton's great object as Secretary of the Treasury was that of making the organization of the national finances serve the cause of a constructive national policy. He wished to strengthen the Federal government by a striking exhibition of its serviceability, and by creating both a strong sentiment and an influential interest in its favor. To this end he committed the nation to a policy of scrupulous financial honesty, which has helped to make it ever since the mainstay of sound American finance. He secured the consent of Congress to the recognition at their face value of the debts incurred during the war both by the Confederacy and by the individual states. He created in the National Bank an efficient fiscal agent for the Treasury Department and a means whereby it could give stability to the banking system of the country. Finally he sought by means of his proposed fiscal and commercial policy to make the central government the effective promoter of a wholesome and many-sided national development. He detected the danger to political stability and self-control which would result from the continued growth of the United States as a merely agricultural and trading community, and he saw that it was necessary to cultivate manufacturing industries and technical knowledge and training, because diversified activity and a well-rounded social and economic life brings with it national balance and security.

Underlying the several aspects of Hamilton's policy can be discerned a definite theory of governmental functions. The central government is to be used, not merely to maintain the Constitution, but to promote the national interest and to consolidate the national organization. Hamilton saw clearly that the American Union was far from being achieved when the Constitution was accepted by the states and the machinery of the Federal government set in motion. A good start had been made, but the way in which to keep what had been gained was to seek for more. Unionism must be converted into a positive policy which labored to strengthen the national interest and organization, discredit possible or actual disunionist ideas and forces, and increase the national spirit. All this implied an active interference with the natural course of American economic and political business and its regulation and guidance in the national direction. It implied a conscious and indefatigable attempt on the part of the national leaders to promote the national welfare. It implied the predominance in American political life of the men who had the energy and the insight to discriminate between those ideas and tendencies which promoted the national welfare, and those ideas and tendencies whereby it was imperiled. It implied, in fine, the perpetuation of the same kind of leadership which had guided the country safely through the dangers of the critical period, and the perpetuation of the purposes which inspired that leadership.

So far I, at least, have no fault to find with implications of Hamilton's Federalism, but unfortunately his policy was in certain other respects tainted with a more doubtful tendency. On the persistent vitality of Hamilton's national principle depends the safety of the American republic and the fertility of the American idea, but he did not seek a sufficiently broad, popular basis for the realization of those ideas. He was betrayed by his fears and by his lack of faith. Believing as he did, and far more than he had any right to believe, that he was still fighting for the cause of social stability and political order against the seven devils of anarchy and dissolution, he thought it necessary to bestow upon the central government the support of a strong special interest. During the Constitutional Convention he had failed to secure the adoption of certain institutions which in his opinion would have established as the guardian of the Constitution an aristocracy of ability; and he now insisted all the more upon the plan of attaching to the Federal government the support of well-to-do people. As we have seen, the Constitution had been framed and its adoption secured chiefly by citizens of education and means; and the way had been prepared, consequently, for the attempt of Hamilton to rally this class as a class more than ever to the support of the Federal government. They were the people who had most to lose by political instability or inefficiency, and they must be brought to lend their influence to the perpetuation of a centralized political authority. Hence he believed a considerable national debt to be a good thing for the Federal national interest, and he insisted strenuously upon the assumption by the Federal government of the state war-debts. He conceived the Constitution and the Union as a valley of peace and plenty which had to be fortified against the marauders by the heavy ramparts of borrowed money and the big guns of a propertied interest.

In so doing Hamilton believed that he was (to vary the metaphor) loading the ship of state with a necessary ballast, whereas in truth he was disturbing its balance and preventing it from sailing free. He succeeded in imbuing both men of property and the mass of the "plain people" with the idea that the well-to-do were the peculiar beneficiaries of the American Federal organization, the result being that the rising democracy came more than ever to distrust the national government. Instead of seeking to base the perpetuation of the Union upon the interested motives of a minority of well-to-do citizens, he would have been far wiser to have frankly intrusted its welfare to the good-will of the whole people. But unfortunately he was prevented from so doing by the limitation both of his sympathies and ideas. He was possessed by the English conception of a national state, based on the domination of special privileged orders and interests; and he failed to understand that the permanent support of the American national organization could not be found in anything less than the whole American democracy. The American Union was a novel and a promising political creation, not because it was a democracy, for there had been plenty of previous democracies, and not because it was a nation, for there had been plenty of previous nations, but precisely and entirely because it was a democratic nation,—a nation committed by its institutions and aspirations to realize the democratic idea.

Much, consequently, as we may value Hamilton's work and for the most part his ideas, it must be admitted that the popular disfavor with which he came to be regarded had its measure of justice. This disfavor was indeed partly the result of his resolute adherence to a wise but an unpopular foreign policy; and the way in which this policy was carried through by Washington, Hamilton, and their followers, in spite of the general dislike which it inspired, deserves the warmest praise. But Hamilton's unpopularity was fundamentally due to deeper causes. He and his fellow-Federalists did not understand their fellow-countrymen and sympathize with their purposes, and naturally they were repaid with misunderstanding and suspicion. He ceased, after Washington's retirement, to be a national leader, and became the leader of a faction; and before his death his party ceased to be the national party, and came to represent only a section and a class. In this way it irretrievably lost public support, and not even the miserable failure of Jefferson's policy of embargo could persuade the American people to restore the Federalists to power. As a party organization they disappeared entirely after the second English war, and unfortunately much that was good in

Hamilton's political point of view disappeared with the bad. But by its failure one good result was finally established. For better or worse the United States had become a democracy as well as a nation, and its national task was not that of escaping the dangers of democracy, but of realizing its responsibilities and opportunities.

It did not take Hamilton's opponents long to discover that his ideas and plans were in some respects inimical to democracy; and the consequence was that Hamilton was soon confronted by one of the most implacable and unscrupulous oppositions which ever abused a faithful and useful public servant. This opposition was led by Jefferson, and while it most unfortunately lacked Hamilton's statesmanship and sound constructive ideas, it possessed the one saving quality which Hamilton himself lacked: Jefferson was filled with a sincere, indiscriminate, and unlimited faith in the American people. He was according to his own lights a radical and unqualified democrat, and as a democrat he fought most bitterly what he considered to be the aristocratic or even monarchic tendency of Hamilton's policy. Much of the denunciation which he and his followers lavished upon Hamilton was unjust, and much of the fight which they put up against his measures was contrary to the public welfare. They absolutely failed to give him credit for the patriotism of his intentions or for the merit of his achievements, and their unscrupulous and unfair tactics established a baleful tradition in American party warfare. But Jefferson was wholly right in believing that his country was nothing, if not a democracy, and that any tendency to impair the integrity of the democratic idea could be productive only of disaster.

Unfortunately Jefferson's conception of democracy was meager, narrow, and self-contradictory; and just because his ideas prevailed, while Hamilton toward the end of his life lost his influence, the consequences of Jefferson's imperfect conception of democracy have been much more serious than the consequences of Hamilton's inadequate conception of American nationality. In Jefferson's mind democracy was tantamount to extreme individualism. He conceived a democratic society to be composed of a collection of individuals, fundamentally alike in their abilities and deserts; and in organizing such a society, politically, the prime object was to provide for the greatest satisfaction of its individual members. The good things of life which had formerly been monopolized by the privileged few, were now to be distributed among all the people. It was unnecessary, moreover, to make any very artful arrangements, in order to effect an equitable distribution. Such distribution would take care of itself, provided nobody enjoyed any special privileges and everybody had equal opportunities. Once these conditions were secured, the motto of a democratic government should simply be "Hands Off." There should be as little government as possible, because persistent governmental interference implied distrust in popular efficiency and good-will; and what government there was, should be so far as possible confided to local authorities. The vitality of a democracy resided in its extremities, and it would be diminished rather than increased by specialized or centralized guidance. Its individual members needed merely to be protected against privileges and to be let alone, whereafter the native goodness of human nature would accomplish the perfect consummation.

Thus Jefferson sought an essentially equalitarian and even socialistic result by means of an essentially individualistic machinery. His theory implied a complete harmony both in logic and in effect between the idea of liberty and the idea of equality; and just in so far as there is any antagonism between those ideas, his whole political system becomes unsound and impracticable. Neither is there any doubt as to which of these ideas Jefferson and his followers really attached the more importance. Their mouths have always been full of the praise of liberty; and unquestionably they have really believed it to be the corner-stone of their political and social structure. None the less, however, is it true that in so far as any antagonism has developed in American life between liberty and equality, the Jeffersonian Democrats have been found on the side of equality. Representing as they did the democratic principle, it is perfectly natural and desirable that they should fight the battle of equality in a democratic state; and their error has been, not their devotion to equality, but their inability to discern wherein any antagonism existed between liberty and equality, and the extent to which they were sacrificing a desirable liberty to an undesirable equality.

On this, as on so many other points, Hamilton's political philosophy was much more clearly thought out than that of Jefferson. He has been accused by his opponents of being the enemy of liberty; whereas in point of fact, he wished, like the Englishman he was, to protect and encourage liberty, just as far as such encouragement was compatible with good order, because he realized that genuine liberty would inevitably issue in fruitful social and economic inequalities. But he also realized that genuine liberty was not merely a matter of a constitutional declaration of rights. It could be protected only by an energetic and clear-sighted central government, and it could be fertilized only by the efficient national organization of American activities. For national organization demands in relation to individuals a certain amount of selection, and a certain classification of these individuals according to their abilities and deserts. It is just this kind or effect of liberty which Jefferson and his followers have always disliked and discouraged.

They have been loud in their praise of legally constituted rights; but they have shown an instinctive and an implacable distrust of intellectual and moral independence, and have always sought to suppress it in favor of intellectual and moral conformity. They have, that is, stood for the sacrifice of liberty—in so far as liberty meant positive intellectual and moral achievement—to a certain kind of equality.

I do not mean to imply by the preceding statement that either Jefferson or his followers were the conscious enemies of moral and intellectual achievement. On the contrary, they appeared to themselves in their amiable credulity to be the friends and guardians of everything admirable in human life; but their good intentions did not prevent them from actively or passively opposing positive intellectual and moral achievement, directed either towards social or individual ends. The effect of their whole state of mind was negative and fatalistic. They approved in general of everything approvable; but the things of which they actively approved were the things which everybody in general was doing. Their point of view implied that society and individuals could be made better without actually planning the improvement or building up an organization for the purpose; and this assertion brings me to the deepest-lying difference between Hamilton and Jefferson. Jefferson's policy was at bottom the old fatal policy of drift, whose distorted body was concealed by fair-seeming clothes, and whose ugly face was covered by a mask of good intentions. Hamilton's policy was one of energetic and intelligent assertion of the national good. He knew that the only method whereby the good could prevail either in individual or social life was by persistently willing that it should prevail and by the adoption of intelligent means to that end. His vision of the national good was limited; but he was absolutely right about the way in which it was to be achieved.

Hamilton was not afraid to exhibit in his own life moral and intellectual independence. He was not afraid to incur unpopularity for pursuing what he believed to be a wise public policy, and the general disapprobation under which he suffered during the last years of his life, while it was chiefly due, as we have seen, to his distrust of the American democracy, was also partly due to his high conception of the duties of leadership. Jefferson, on the other hand, afforded an equally impressive example of the statesman who assiduously and intentionally courted popular favor. It was, of course, easy for him to court popular favor, because he understood the American people extremely well and really sympathized with them; but he never used the influence which he thereby obtained for the realization of any positive or formative purpose, which might be unpopular. His policy, while in office, was one of fine phrases and temporary expedients, some of which necessarily incurred odium, but none of which were pursued by him or his followers with any persistence. Whatever the people demanded, their leaders should perform, including, if necessary, a declaration of war against England. It was to be a government of and by the people, not a government for the people by popular but responsible leaders; and the leaders to whom the people delegated their authority had in theory no right to pursue an unpopular policy. The people were to guide their leaders, not their leaders the people; and any intellectual or moral independence and initiative on the part of the leaders in a democracy was to be condemned as undemocratic. The representatives of a Sovereign people were in the same position as the courtiers of an absolute monarch. It was their business to flatter and obey.

III   Federalism and Republicanism as Allies

It is not surprising, consequently, that Jefferson, who had been a lion in opposition, was transformed by the assumption of power into a lamb. Inasmuch as he had been denouncing every act of the Federalists since the consummation of the Union as dangerous to American liberties or as inimical to the public welfare, it was to be anticipated, when he and his party assumed office, that they would seek both to tear down the Federalist structure and rear in its place a temple of the true Republican faith. Not only did nothing of the kind follow, but nothing of the kind was even attempted. Considering the fulminations of the Republicans during the last ten years of Federalist domination, Jefferson's first Inaugural is a bewildering document. The recent past, which had but lately been so full of dangers, was ignored; and the future, the dangers of which were much more real, was not for the moment considered. Jefferson was sworn in with his head encircled by a halo of beautiful phrases; and he and his followers were so well satisfied with this beatific vision that they entirely overlooked the desirability of redeeming their own past or of providing for their country's future. Sufficient unto the day was the popularity thereof. The Federalists themselves must be conciliated, and the national organization achieved by them is by implication accepted. The Federalist structure, so recently the prison of the free American spirit, becomes itself a large part of the temple of democracy. The Union is no longer inimical to liberty. For the first time we begin to hear from good Republican mouths, some sacred words about the necessary connection of liberty and union. Jefferson celebrated his triumph by adopting the work, if not the creed, of his adversaries.

The adoption by Jefferson and the Republicans of the political structure of their opponents is of an importance hardly inferior to that of the adoption of the Constitution by the states. It was the first practical indication that democracy and Federalism were not as radically antagonistic as their extreme partisans had believed; and it was also the first indication that the interests which were concealed behind the phrases of the two parties were not irreconcilable. When the democracy rallied to the national organization, the American state began to be a democratic nation. The alliance was as yet both fragile and superficial. It was founded on a sacrifice by the two parties, not merely of certain errors and misconceptions, but also of certain convictions, which had been considered essential. The Republicans tacitly admitted the substantial falsity of their attacks upon the Federal organization. The many Federalists who joined their opponents abandoned without scruple the whole spirit and purpose of the Hamiltonian national policy. But at any rate the reconciliation was accomplished. The newly founded American state was for the time being saved from the danger of being torn asunder by two rival factions, each representing irreconcilable ideas and interests. The Union, which had been celebrated in 1789, was consummated in 1801. Its fertility was still to be proved.

When Jefferson and the Republicans rallied to the Union and to the existing Federalist organization, the fabric of traditional American democracy was almost completely woven. Thereafter the American people had only to wear it and keep it in repair. The policy announced in Jefferson's first Inaugural was in all important respects merely a policy of conservatism. The American people were possessed of a set of political institutions, which deprived them of any legitimate grievances and supplied them with every reasonable opportunity; and their political duty was confined to the administration of these institutions in a faithful spirit and their preservation from harm. The future contained only one serious danger. Such liberties were always open to attack, and there would always be designing men whose interest it was to attack them. The great political responsibility of the American democracy was to guard itself against such assaults; and should they succeed in this task they need have no further concern about their future. Their political salvation was secure. They had placed it, as it were, in a good sound bank. It would be sure to draw interest provided the bank were conservatively managed—that is, provided it were managed by loyal Republicans. There was no room or need for any increase in the fund, because it already satisfied every reasonable purpose. But it must not be diminished; and it must not be exposed to any risk of diminution by hazardous speculative investments.

During the next fifty years, the American democracy accepted almost literally this Jeffersonian tradition. Until the question of slavery became acute, they ceased to think seriously about political problems. The lawyers were preoccupied with certain important questions of constitutional interpretation, which had their political implications; but the purpose of these expositions of our fundamental law was the affirmation, the consolidation, and towards the end, the partial restriction of the existing Federalist organization. In this as in other respects the Americans of the second and third generations were merely preserving what their fathers had wrought. Their political institutions were good, in so far as they were not disturbed. They might become bad, only in case they were perverted. The way to guard against such perversion was, of course, to secure the election of righteous democrats. From the traditional American point of view, it was far more important to get the safe candidates elected than it was to use the power so obtained for any useful political achievement. In the hands of unsafe men,—that is, one's political opponents,—the government might be perverted to dangerous uses, whereas in the hands of safe men, it could at best merely be preserved in safety. Misgovernment was a greater danger than good government was a benefit, because good government, particularly on the part of Federal officials, consisted, apart from routine business, in letting things alone. Thus the furious interest, which the good American took in getting himself and his associates elected, could be justified by reasons founded on the essential nature of the traditional political system.

The good American democrat had, of course, another political duty besides that of securing the election of himself and his friends. His political system was designed, not merely to deprive him of grievances, but to offer him superlative opportunities. In taking the utmost advantage of those opportunities, he was not only fulfilling his duty to himself, but he was helping to realize the substantial purpose of democracy. Just as it was the function of the national organization to keep itself undefiled and not to interfere, so it was his personal function to make hay while the sun was shining. The triumph of Jefferson and the defeat of Hamilton enabled the natural individualism of the American people free play. The democratic political system was considered tantamount in practice to a species of vigorous, licensed, and purified selfishness. The responsibilities of the government were negative; those of the individual were positive. And it is no wonder that in the course of time his positive responsibilities began to look larger and larger. This licensed selfishness became more domineering in proportion as it became more successful. If a political question arose, which in any way interfered with his opportunities, the good American began to believe that his democratic political machine was out of gear. Did Abolitionism create a condition of political unrest, and interfere with good business, then Abolitionists were wicked men, who were tampering with the ark of the Constitution; and in much the same way the modern reformer, who proposes policies looking toward a restriction in the activity of corporations and stands in the way of the immediate transaction of the largest possible volume of business, is denounced as un-American. These were merely crude ways of expressing the spirit of traditional American democracy,—which was that of a rampant individualism, checked only by a system of legally constituted rights. The test of American national success was the comfort and prosperity of the individual; and the means to that end,—a system of unrestricted individual aggrandizement and collective irresponsibility.

The alliance between Federalism and democracy on which this traditional system was based, was excellent in many of its effects; but unfortunately it implied on the part of both the allies a sacrifice of political sincerity and conviction. And this sacrifice was more demoralizing to the Republicans than to the Federalists, because they were the victorious party. A central government, constructed on the basis of their democratic creed, would have been a government whose powers were smaller, more rigid, and more inefficiently distributed than those granted under our Federal Constitution—as may be seen from the various state constitutions subsequently written under Jeffersonian influence. When they obtained power either they should have been faithful to their convictions and tried to modify the Federal machinery in accordance therewith, or they should have modified their ideas in order to make them square with their behavior. But instead of seriously and candidly considering the meaning of their own actions, they opened their mouths wide enough to swallow their own past and then deliberately shut their eyes. They accepted the national organization as a fact and as a condition of national safety; but they rejected it as a lesson in political wisdom, and as an implicit principle of political action. By so doing they began that career of intellectual lethargy, superficiality, and insincerity which ever since has been characteristic of official American political thought.

This lack of intellectual integrity on the part of the American democracy both falsified the spirit in which our institutions had originated, and seriously compromised their future success. The Union had been wrought by virtue of vigorous, responsible, and enterprising leadership, and of sound and consistent political thinking. It was to be perpetuated by a company of men, who disbelieved in enterprising and responsible leadership, and who had abandoned and tended to disparage anything but the most routine political ideas. The American people, after passing through a period of positive achievement, distinguished in all history for the powerful application of brains to the solution of an organic political problem—the American people, after this almost unprecedented exhibition of good-will and good judgment, proceeded to put a wholly false interpretation on their remarkable triumph. They proceeded, also, to cultivate a state of mind which has kept them peculiarly liable to intellectual ineptitude and conformity. The mixture of optimism, conservatism, and superficiality, which has until recently characterized their political point of view, has made them almost blind to the true lessons of their own national experience.

The best that can be said on behalf of this traditional American system of political ideas is that it contained the germ of better things. The combination of Federalism and Republicanism which formed the substance of

the system, did not constitute a progressive and formative political principle, but it pointed in the direction of
a constructive formula. The political leaders of the "era
of good feeling" who began to use with some degree of
conviction certain comely phrases about the eternal and
inseparable alliance between "liberty and union" were
looking towards the promised land of American democratic fulfillment. As we shall see, the kind of liberty and
the kind of union which they had in mind were by no
means indissolubly and inseparably united; and both of
these words had to be transformed from a negative and
legal into a positive moral and social meaning before
the boasted alliance could be anything but precarious
and sterile. But if for liberty we substitute the word democracy, which means something more than liberty, and
if for union, we substitute the phrase American nationality, which means so much more than a legal union, we
shall be looking in the direction of a fruitful alliance between two supplementary principles. It can, I believe, be
stated without qualification that wherever the nationalist idea and tendency has been divided from democracy, its achievements have been limited and partially
sterilized. It can also be stated that the separation of the
democratic idea from the national principle and organization has issued not merely in sterility, but in moral
and political mischief. All this must remain mere assertion for the present; but I shall hope gradually to justify
these assertions by an examination of the subsequent
course of American political development.

3.

The Democrats and the Whigs

|

The first phase of American political history was characterized by the conflict between the Federalists and the
Republicans, and it resulted in the complete triumph of
the latter. The second period was characterized by an
almost equally bitter contest between the Democrats
and the Whigs in which the Democrats represented a
new version of the earlier Republican tradition and
the Whigs a resurrected Federalism. The Democracy of
Jackson differed in many important respects from the
Republicanism of Jefferson, and the Whig doctrine of
Henry Clay was far removed from the Federalism of
Alexander Hamilton. Nevertheless, from 1825 to 1850,
the most important fact in American political development continued to be a fight between an inadequate
conception of democracy, represented by Jackson and
his followers, and a feeble conception of American nationality, represented best by Henry Clay and Daniel
Webster; and in this second fight the victory still rested,
on the whole, with the Democrats. The Whigs were not
annihilated as the Federalists had been. In the end they
perished as a party, but not because of the assaults of
their opponents, but because of their impotence in the
face of a grave national crisis. Nevertheless, they were
on all essential issues beaten by the Democrats; and on
the few occasions on which they were victorious, their
victories were both meaningless and fruitless.

The years between 1800 and 1825 were distinguished, so far as our domestic development was concerned, by the growth of the Western pioneer Democracy in power and self-consciousness. It was one of the gravest errors of Hamilton and the Federalists that they misunderstood and suspected the pioneer Democracy, just as it was one of the greatest merits of Jefferson that he early appreciated its importance and used his influence and power to advance its interests. The consequence was that the pioneers became enthusiastic and radical supporters of the Republican party. They repeated and celebrated the Jeffersonian catchwords with the utmost conviction. They became imbued with the spirit of the true Jeffersonian faith. They were, indeed, in many respects more Jeffersonian than Jefferson himself, and sought to realize some of his ideas with more energy and consistency. These ideas expressed and served their practical needs marvelously well, and if the formulas had not already been provided by Jefferson, they would most assuredly have been crystallized by the pioneer politicians of the day. The Jeffersonian creed has exercised a profound influence upon the thought of the American people, not because Jefferson was an original and profound thinker, but because of his ability to formulate popular opinions, prejudices, and interests.

It is none the less true that the pioneer Democracy soon came to differ with Jefferson about some important questions of public policy. They early showed, for instance, a lively disapproval of Jefferson's management of the crisis in foreign affairs, which preceded the War of 1812. Jefferson's policy of commercial embargo seemed pusillanimous to Jackson and the other Western Democrats. They did not believe in peaceful warfare; and their different conception of the effective way of fighting a foreign enemy was symptomatic of a profound difference of opinion and temper. The Western Democracy did not share Jefferson's amiable cosmopolitanism. It was, on the contrary, aggressively resolved to assert the rights and the interests of the United States against any suspicion of European aggrandizement. However much it preferred a let-alone policy in respect to the domestic affairs, all its instincts revolted against a weak foreign policy; and its instincts were outraged by the administration's policy of peaceful warfare, which injured ourselves so much more than it injured England, not only because the pioneers were fighting men by conviction and habit, but because they were much more genuinely national in their feelings than were Jefferson and Madison.

The Western Democrats finally forced Madison and the official Republican leaders to declare war against England, because Madison preferred even a foreign war to the loss of popularity; but Madison, although he accepted the necessity of war, was wholly incompetent to conduct it efficiently. The inadequacy of our national organization and our lack of national cohesion was immediately and painfully exhibited. The Republican superstition about militarism had prevented the formation of a regular army at all adequate to the demands of our national policy, and the American navy, while efficient so far as it went, was very much too small to constitute an effective engine of naval warfare. Moreover, the very Congress that clearly announced an intention of declaring war on Great Britain failed to make any sufficient provision for its energetic prosecution. The consequence of this short-sighted view of our national responsibilities is that the history of the War of 1812 makes painful reading for a patriotic American. The little American navy earned distinction, but it was so small that its successes did not prevent it from being shut off eventually from the high seas. The military operations were a succession of blunders both in strategy and in performance. On the northern frontier a series of incompetent generals led little armies of half-hearted soldiers to unnecessary defeats or at best to ineffectual victories; and the most conspicuous military success was won at New Orleans by the Western pioneers, who had no constitutional scruples about fighting outside of their own states, and who were animated by lively patriotic feelings. On the whole, however, the story makes humiliating reading, not because the national Capital was captured almost without resistance, or because we were so frequently beaten, but because our disorganization, the incompetence of the national government, and the disloyalty of so many Americans made us deserve both a less successful war and a more humiliating peace.

The chief interest of the second English war for the purpose of this book is, however, its clear indication of the abiding-place at that time of the American national spirit. That spirit was not found along the Atlantic coast, whose inhabitants were embittered and blinded by party and sectional prejudices. It was resident in the newer states of the West and the Southwest. A genuine American national democracy was coming into existence in that part of the country—a democracy which was as democratic as it knew how to be, while at the same time loyal and devoted to the national government. The pioneers had in a measure outgrown the colonialism of the thirteen original commonwealths. They occupied a territory which had in the beginning been part of the national domain. Their local commonwealths had not antedated the Federal Union, but were in a way children of the central government; and they felt that they belonged to the Union in a way that was rarely shared by an inhabitant of Massachusetts or South Carolina. Their national feeling did not prevent them from being in some respects extremely local and provincial in their point of view. It did not prevent them from resenting with the utmost energy any interference of the Federal government in what they believed to be their local affairs. But they were none the less, first and foremost, loyal citizens of the American Federal state.

II The New National Democracy

We must consider carefully this earliest combination of the national with the democratic idea. The Western Democracy is important, not only because it played the leading part in our political history down to 1850, but precisely because it does offer, in a primitive but significant form, a combination of the two ideas, which, when united, constitute the formative principle in American political and social development. The way had been prepared for this combination by the Republican acceptance of the Federal organization, after that party had assumed power; but the Western Democrats took this alliance much more innocently than the older Republican leaders. They insisted, as we have seen, on a declaration of war against Great Britain; and humiliating as were the results of that war, this vigorous assertion of the national point of view, both exposed in clear relief the sectional disloyalty of the Federalists of New England and resulted later in an attempted revival of a national constructive policy. It is true that the regeneration of the Hamiltonian spirit belongs rather to the history of the Whigs than to the history of the Democrats. It is true, also, that the attempted revival at once brought out the inadequacy of the pioneer's conceptions both of the national and the democratic ideas. Nevertheless, it was their assertion of the national interest against a foreign enemy which provoked its renewed vitality in relation to our domestic affairs. Whatever the alliance between nationality and democracy, represented by the pioneers, lacked in fruitful understanding of the correlative ideas, at least it was solid alliance. The Western Democrats were suspicious of any increase of the national organization in power and scope, but they were even more determined that it should be neither shattered nor vitally injured. Although they were unable to grasp the meaning of their own convictions, the Federal Union really meant to them something more than an indissoluble legal contract. It was rooted in their life. It was one of those things for which they were willing to fight; and their readiness to fight for the national idea was the great salutary fact. Our country was thereby saved from the consequences of its distracting individualistic conception of democracy, and its merely legal conception of nationality. It was because the followers of Jackson and Douglas did fight for it, that the Union was preserved.

Be it immediately remarked, however, that the pioneer Democrats were obliged to fight for the Union, just because they were not interested in its progressive consummation. They willed at one and the same time that the Union *should* be preserved, but that it *should not* be increased and strengthened. They were national in feeling, but local and individualistic in their ideas; and these limited ideas were associated with a false and inadequate conception of democracy. Jefferson had taught them to believe that any increase of the national organization was inimical to democracy. The limitations of their own economic and social experience and of their practical needs confirmed them in this belief. Their manner of life made them at once thoroughly loyal and extremely insubordinate. They combined the sincerest patriotism with an energetic and selfish individualism; and they failed wholly to realize any discrepancy between these two dominant elements in their life. They were to love their country, but they were to work for themselves; and nothing wrong could happen to their country, provided they preserved its institutions and continued to enjoy its opportunities. Their failure to grasp the idea that the Federal Union would not take care of itself, prevented them from taking disunionist ideas seriously, and encouraged them to provoke a crisis, which, subsequently, their fundamental loyalty to the Union prevented from becoming disastrous. They expected their country to drift to a safe harbor in the Promised Land, whereas the inexorable end of a drifting ship is either the rocks or the shoals.

In their opposition to the consolidation of the national organization, the pioneers believed that they were defending the citadel of their democratic creed. Democracy meant to them, not only equal opportunities secured by law, but an approximately equal standing among individual citizens, and an approximately equal division of the social and economic fruits. They realized vaguely that national consolidation brought with it organization, and organization depended for its efficiency upon a classification of individual citizens according to ability, knowledge, and competence. In a nationalized state, it is the man of exceptional position, power, responsibility, and training who is most likely to be representative and efficient, whereas in a thoroughly democratic state, as they conceived it, the average man was the representative citizen and the fruitful type. Nationalization looked towards the introduction and perpetuation of a political, social, and financial hierarchy. They opposed it consequently, on behalf of the "plain people"; and they even reached the conclusion that the contemporary political system was to some extent organized for the benefit of special interests. They discovered in the fiscal and administrative organization the presence of discrimination against the average man. The National Bank was an example of special economic privileges. The office-holding clique was an example of special political privileges. Jackson and his followers declared war on these sacrilegious anomalies in the temple of democracy. Thus the only innovations which the pioneers sought to impose on our national political system were by way of being destructive. They uprooted a national institution which had existed, with but one brief interruption, for more than forty years; and they entirely altered the tradition of appointment in the American civil service. Both of these destructive achievements throw a great deal of light upon their unconscious tendencies and upon their explicit convictions, and will help us to understand the value and the limitation of the positive contribution which the pioneers made to the fullness of the American democratic idea.

The National Bank was the institution by virtue of which Hamilton sought to secure a stable national currency and an efficient national fiscal agent; and the Bank, particularly under its second charter, had undoubtedly been a useful and economical piece of financial machinery. The Republicans had protested against it in the beginning, but they had later come to believe in its necessity; and at the time Benton and Jackson declared war upon it, the Bank was, on the whole, and in spite of certain minor and local grievances, a popular institution. If the question of the re-charter of the National Bank had been submitted to popular vote in 1832, a popular majority would probably have declared in its favor. Jackson's victory was due partly to his personal popularity, partly to the unwise manner in which the Bank was defended, but chiefly to his success in convincing public opinion that the Bank was an institution whose legal privileges were used to the detriment of the American people. As a matter of fact, such was not the case. The Bank was a semi-public corporation, upon which certain exceptional privileges had been conferred, because the enjoyment of such privileges was inseparable from the services it performed and the responsibilities it assumed. When we consider how important those services were, and how difficult it has since been to substitute any arrangement, which provides as well both a flexible and a stable currency and for the articulation of the financial operations of the Federal Treasury with those of the business of the country, it does not look as if the emoluments and privileges of the Bank were disproportionate to its services. But Jackson and his followers never even considered whether its services and responsibilities were proportionate to its legal privileges. The fact that any such privilege existed, the fact that any legal association of individuals should enjoy such exceptional opportunities, was to their minds a violation of democratic principles. It must consequently be destroyed, no matter how much the country needed its services, and no matter how difficult it was to establish in its place any equally efficient institution.

The important point is, however, that the campaign against the National Bank uncovered a latent socialism, which lay concealed behind the rampant individualism of the pioneer Democracy. The ostensible grievance against the Bank was the possession by a semi-public corporation of special economic privileges; but the anti-Bank literature of the time was filled half unconsciously with a far more fundamental complaint. What the Western Democrats disliked and feared most of all was the possession of any special power by men of wealth. Their crusade against the "Money Power" meant that in their opinion money must not become a power in a democratic state. They had no objection, of course, to certain inequalities in the distribution of wealth; but they fiercely resented the idea that such inequalities should give a group of men any special advantages which were inaccessible to their fellow-countrymen. The full meaning of their complaint against the Bank was left vague and ambiguous, because the Bank itself possessed special legal privileges; and the inference was that when these privileges were withdrawn, the "Money Power" would disappear with them. The Western Democrat devoutly believed that an approximately equal division of the good things of life would result from the possession by all American citizens of equal legal rights and similar economic opportunities. But the importance of this result in their whole point of view was concealed by the fact that they expected to reach it by wholly negative means—that is, by leaving the individual alone. The substantially equal distribution of wealth, which was characteristic of the American society of their own day, was far more fundamental in their system of political and social ideas than was the machinery of liberty whereby it was to be secured. And just as soon as it becomes apparent that the proposed machinery does as a matter of fact accomplish a radically unequal result, their whole political and economic creed cries loudly for revision.

The introduction of the spoils system was due to the perverted application of kindred ideas. The emoluments of office loomed large among the good things of life to the pioneer Democrat; and such emoluments differed from other economic rewards, in that they were necessarily at the disposal of the political organization. The public offices constituted the tangible political patrimony of the American people. It was not enough that they were open to everybody. They must actually be shared by almost everybody. The terms of all elected officials must be short, so that as many good democrats as possible could occupy an easy chair in the house of government; and officials must for similar reasons be appointed for only short terms. Traditional practice at Washington disregarded these obvious inferences from the principles of true democracy. Until the beginning of

Jackson's first administration the offices in the government departments had been appropriated by a few bureaucrats who had grown old at their posts; and how could such a permanent appropriation be justified? The pioneer Democrat believed that he was as competent to do the work as any member of an office-holding clique, so that when he came into power, he corrected what seemed to him to be a genuine abuse in the traditional way of distributing the American political patrimony. He could not understand that training, special ability, or long experience constituted any special claim upon a public office, or upon any other particular opportunity or salary. One democrat was as good as another, and deserved his share of the rewards of public service. The state could not undertake to secure a good living to all good democrats, but, when properly administered, it could prevent any appropriation by a few people of the public pay-roll.

In the long run the effect of the spoils system was, of course, just the opposite of that anticipated by the early Jacksonian Democrats. It merely substituted one kind of office-holding privilege for another. It helped to build up a group of professional politicians who became in their turn an office-holding clique—the only difference being that one man in his political life held, not one, but many offices. Yet the Jacksonian Democrat undoubtedly believed, when he introduced the system into the Federal civil service, that he was carrying out a desirable reform along strictly democratic lines. He was betrayed into such an error by the narrowness of his own experience and of his intellectual outlook. His experience had been chiefly that of frontier life, in which the utmost freedom of economic and social movement was necessary; and he attempted to apply the results of this limited experience to the government of a complicated social organism whose different parts had very different needs. The direct results of the attempt were very mischievous. He fastened upon the American public service a system of appointment which turned political office into the reward of partisan service, which made it unnecessary for the public officials to be competent and impossible for them to be properly experienced, and which contributed finally to the creation of a class of office-holding politicians. But the introduction of the spoils system had a meaning superior to its results. It was, after all, an attempt to realize an ideal, and the ideal was based on a genuine experience. The "Virginian Oligarchy," although it was the work of Jefferson and his followers, was an anachronism in a state governed in the spirit of Jeffersonian Democratic principles. It was better for the Jacksonian Democrats to sacrifice what they believed to be an obnoxious precedent to their principles than to sacrifice their principles to mere precedent. If in so doing they were making a mistake, that was because their principles were wrong. The benefit which they were temporarily conferring on themselves, as a class in the community, was sanctioned by the letter and the spirit of their creed.

Closely connected with their perverted ideas and their narrow view of life, we may discern a leaven of new and useful democratic experience. The new and useful experience which they contributed to our national stock was that of homogeneous social intercourse. I have already remarked that the Western pioneers were the first large body of Americans who were genuinely national in feeling. They were also the first large body of Americans who were genuinely democratic in feeling. Consequently they imparted a certain emotional consistency to the American democracy, and they thereby performed a social service which was in its way quite as valuable as their political service. Democracy has always been stronger as a political than it has as a social force. When adopted as a political ideal of the American people, it was very far from possessing any effective social vitality; and until the present day it has been a much more active force in political than in social life. But whatever traditional social force it has obtained, can be traced directly to the Western pioneer Democrat. His democracy was based on genuine good-fellowship. Unlike the French Fraternity, it was the product neither of abstract theories nor of a disembodied humanitarianism. It was the natural issue of their interests, their occupations, and their manner of life. They felt kindly towards one another and communicated freely with one another because they were not divided by radical differences in class, standards, point of view, and wealth. The social aspect of their democracy may, in fact, be compared to the sense of good-fellowship which pervades the rooms of a properly constituted club.

Their community of feeling and their ease of communication had come about as the result of pioneer life in a self-governing community. The Western Americans were confronted by a gigantic task of overwhelming practical importance,—the task of subduing to the needs of complicated and civilized society a rich but virgin wilderness. This task was one which united a desirable social purpose with a profitable individual interest. The country was undeveloped, and its inhabitants were poor. They were to enrich themselves by the development of the country, and the two different aspects of their task were scarcely distinguished. They felt themselves authorized by social necessity to pursue their own interests energetically and unscrupulously, and they were not either hampered or helped in so doing by the interference of the local or the national authorities. While the only people the pioneer was obliged to consult were his neighbors, all his surroundings tended to make his neighbors like himself—to bind them together by common interests, feelings, and ideas. These surroundings called for practical, able, flexible, alert, energetic, and resolute men, and men of a different type had no opportunity of coming to the surface. The successful pioneer Democrat was not a pleasant type in many respects, but he was saved from many of the worst aspects of his limited experience and ideas by a certain innocence, generosity, and kindliness of spirit. With all his willful aggressiveness he was a companionable person who meant much better towards his fellows than he himself knew.

We need to guard scrupulously against the undervaluation of the advance which the pioneers made towards a genuine social democracy. The freedom of intercourse and the consistency of feeling which they succeeded in attaining is an indispensable characteristic of a democratic society. The unity of such a state must lie deeper than any bond established by obedience to a single political authority, or by the acceptance of common precedents and ideas. It must be based in some measure upon an instinctive familiarity of association, upon a quick communicability of sympathy, upon the easy and effortless sense of companionship. Such familiar intercourse is impossible, not only in a society with aristocratic institutions, but it can with difficulty be attained in a society that has once had aristocratic institutions. A century more or less of political democracy has not introduced it into France, and in 1830 it did not exist along the Atlantic seaboard at all to the same extent that it did in the newer states of the West. In those states the people, in a sense, really lived together. They were divided by fewer barriers than have been any similarly numerous body of people in the history of the world; and it was this characteristic which made them so efficient and so easily directed by their natural leaders. No doubt it would be neither possible nor desirable to reproduce a precisely similar consistency of feeling over a social area in which there was a greater diversity of manners, standards, and occupations; but it remains true that the American democracy will lose its most valuable and promising characteristic in case it loses the homogeneity of feeling which the pioneers were the first to embody.

It is equally important to remember, however, that the social consistency of the pioneer communities should under different conditions undergo a radical transformation. Neither the pioneers themselves nor their admirers and their critics have sufficiently understood how much individual independence was sacrificed in order to obtain this consistency of feeling, or how completely it was the product, in the form it assumed, of temporary economic conditions. If we study the Western Democrats as a body of men who, on the whole, responded admirably to the conditions and opportunities of their time, but who were also very much victimized and impoverished by the limited nature of these conditions and opportunities—if we study the Western Democrat from that point of view, we shall find him to be the most significant economic and social type in American history. On the other hand, if we regard him in the way that he and his subsequent prototypes wish to be regarded, as the example of all that is permanently excellent and formative in American democracy, he will be, not only entirely misunderstood, but transformed from an edifying into a mischievous type.

Their peculiar social homogeneity, and their conviction that one man was as good as another, was the natural and legitimate product of contemporary economic conditions. The average man, without any special bent or qualifications, was in the pioneer states the useful man. In that country it was sheer waste to spend much energy upon tasks which demanded skill, prolonged experience, high technical standards, or exclusive devotion. The cheaply and easily made instrument was the efficient instrument, because it was adapted to a year or two of use and then for supersession by a better instrument; and for the service of such tools one man was as likely to be good as another. No special equipment was required. The farmer was obliged to be all kinds of a rough mechanic. The business man was merchant, manufacturer, and storekeeper. Almost everybody was something of a politician. The number of parts which a man of energy played in his time was astonishingly large. Andrew Jackson was successively a lawyer, judge, planter, merchant, general, politician, and statesman; and he played most of these parts with conspicuous success. In such a society a man who persisted in one job, and who applied the most rigorous and exacting standards to his work, was out of place and was really inefficient. His finished product did not serve its temporary purpose much better than did the current careless and hasty product, and his higher standards and peculiar ways constituted an implied criticism upon the easy methods of his neighbors. He interfered with the rough good-fellowship which naturally arises among a group of men who submit good-naturedly and uncritically to current standards.

It is no wonder, consequently, that the pioneer Democracy viewed with distrust and aversion the man with a special vocation and high standards of achievement. Such a man did insist upon being in certain respects better than the average; and under the prevalent economic social conditions he did impair the consistency of feeling upon which the pioneers rightly placed such a high value. Consequently they half unconsciously sought to suppress men with special vocations. For the most part this suppression was easily accomplished by the action of ordinary social and economic motives. All the industrial, political, and social rewards went to the man who pursued his business, professional, or political career along regular lines; and in this way an ordinary task and an interested motive were often imposed on men who were better qualified for special tasks undertaken from disinterested motives. But it was not enough to suppress the man with a special vocation by depriving him of social and pecuniary rewards. Public opinion must be taught to approve of the average man as the representative type of the American democracy, so that the man with a special vocation may be deprived of any interest or share in the American democratic tradition; and this attempt to make the average man the representative American democrat has persisted to the present day—that is, to a time when the average man is no longer, as in 1830, the dominant economic factor.

It is in this way, most unfortunately, that one of the leading articles in the American popular creed has tended to impair American moral and intellectual integrity. If the man with special standards and a special vocation interfered with democratic consistency of feeling, it was chiefly because this consistency of feeling had been obtained at too great a sacrifice—at the sacrifice of a higher to a lower type of individuality. In all civilized communities the great individualizing force is the resolute, efficient, and intense pursuit of special ideals, standards, and occupations; and the country which discourages such pursuits must necessarily put up with an inferior quality and a less varied assortment of desirable individual types. But whatever the loss our country has been and is suffering from this cause, our popular philosophers welcome rather than deplore it. We adapt our ideals of individuality to its local examples. When orators of the Jacksonian Democratic tradition begin to glorify the superlative individuals developed by the freedom of American life, what they mean by individuality is an unusual amount of individual energy successfully spent in popular and remunerative occupations. Of the individuality which may reside in the gallant and exclusive devotion to some disinterested, and perhaps unpopular moral, intellectual, or technical purpose, they have not the remotest conception; and yet it is this kind of individuality which is indispensable to the fullness and intensity of American national life.

III   The Whig Failure

The Jacksonian Democrats were not, of course, absolutely dominant during the Middle Period of American history. They were persistently, and on a few occasions successfully, opposed by the Whigs. The latter naturally represented the political, social, and economic ideas which the Democrats under-valued or disparaged. They were strong in those Northern and border states, which had reached a higher stage of economic and social development, and which contained the mansions of contemporary American culture, wealth, and intelligence. It is a significant fact that the majority of Americans of intelligence during the Jacksonian epoch were opponents of Jackson, just as the majority of educated Americans of intelligence have always protested against the national political irresponsibility and the social equalitarianism characteristic of our democratic tradition; but unfortunately they have always failed to make their protests effective. The spirit of the times was against them. The Whigs represented the higher standards, the more definite organization, and the social inequalities of the older states, but when they attempted to make their ideas good, they were faced by a dilemma either horn of which was disastrous to their interests. They were compelled either to sacrifice their standards to the conditions of popular efficiency or the chance of success to the integrity of their standards. In point of fact they pursued precisely the worst course of all. They abandoned their standards, and yet they failed to achieve success. Down to the Civil War the fruits of victory and the prestige of popularity were appropriated by the Democrats.

The Whigs, like their predecessors, the Federalists, were ostensibly the party of national ideas. Their association began with a group of Jeffersonian Republicans who, after the second English war, sought to resume the interrupted work of national consolidation. The results of that war had clearly exposed certain grave deficiencies in the American national organization; and these deficiencies a group of progressive young men, under the lead of Calhoun and Clay, proposed to remedy. One of the greatest handicaps from which the military conduct of the war had suffered was the lack of any sufficient means of internal communication; and the construction of a system of national roads and waterways became an important plank in their platform. There was also proposed a policy of industrial protection which Calhoun supported by arguments so national in import and scope that they might well have been derived from Hamilton's report. Under the influence of similar ideas the National Bank was rechartered; and as the correlative of this constructive policy, a liberal nationalistic interpretation of the Constitution was explicitly advocated. As one reads the speeches delivered by some of these men, particularly by Calhoun, during the first session of Congress after the conclusion of peace, it seems as if a genuine revival had taken the place of Hamiltonian nationalism, and that this revival was both by way of escaping Hamilton's fatal distrust of democracy and of avoiding the factious and embittered opposition of the earlier period.

The Whigs made a fair start, but unfortunately they ran a poor race and came to a bad end. No doubt they were in a way an improvement on the Federalists, in that they, like their opponents, the Democrats, stood for a combination between democracy and nationalism. They believed that the consolidation and the development of the national organization was contributory rather than antagonistic to the purpose of the American political system. Yet they made no conquests on behalf of their convictions. The Federalists really accomplished a great and necessary task of national organization and founded a tradition of constructive national achievement. The Whigs at best kept this tradition alive. They were on the defensive throughout, and they accomplished nothing at all in the way of permanent constructive legislation. Their successes were merely electioneering raids, whereas their defeats were wholly disastrous in that they lost, not only all of their strongholds, but most of their military reputation and good name. Their final disappearance was wholly the result of their own incapacity. They were condemned somehow to inefficiency, defeat, and dishonor.

Every important article in their programme went astray. The policy of internal improvements in the national interest and at the national expense was thwarted by the Constitutional scruples of such Presidents as Monroe and Jackson, and for that reason it could never be discussed on its merits. The Cumberland Road was the only great national highway constructed, and remains to this day a striking symbol of what the Federal government might have accomplished towards the establishment of an efficient system of inter-state communication. The re-charter of the National Bank which was one of the first fruits of the new national movement, proved in the end to be the occasion of its most flagrant failure. The Bank was the national institution for the perpetuation of which the Whig leaders fought most persistently and loyally. They began the fight with the support of public opinion, and with the prestige of an established and useful institution in their favor; but the campaign was conducted with such little skill that in the end they were utterly beaten. Far from being able to advance the policy of national consolidation, they were unable even to preserve existing national institutions, and their conspicuous failure in this crucial instance was due to their inability to keep public opinion convinced of the truth that the Bank was really organized and maintained in the national interest. Their policy of protection met in the long run with a similar fate. In the first place, the tariff schedules which they successively placed upon the statute books were not drawn up in Hamilton's wise and moderate national spirit. They were practically dictated by the special interests which profited from the increases in duties. The Whig leaders accepted a retainer from the manufacturers of the North, and by legislating exclusively in their favor almost drove South Carolina to secession. Then after accomplishing this admirable feat, they agreed to placate the disaffected state by the gradual reduction in the scale of duties until there was very little protection left. In short, they first perverted the protectionist system until it ceased to be a national policy; and then compromised it until it ceased to be any policy at all.

Perhaps the Whigs failed and blundered most completely in the fight which they made against the Federal executive and in the interest of the Federal legislature. They were forced into this position, because for many years the Democrats, impersonated by Jackson, occupied the Presidential chair, while the Whigs controlled one or both of the Congressional bodies; but the attitude of the two opposing parties in respect to the issue corresponded to an essential difference of organization and personnel. The Whigs were led by a group of brilliant orators and lawyers, while the Democrats were dominated by one powerful man, who held the

Presidential office. Consequently the Whigs proclaimed a Constitutional doctrine which practically amounted to Congressional omnipotence, and for many years assailed Jackson as a military dictator who was undermining the representative institutions of his country. The American people, however, appraised these fulminations at their true value. While continuing for twelve years to elect to the Presidency Jackson or his nominee, they finally dispossessed the Whigs from the control of Congress; and they were right. The American people have much more to fear from Congressional usurpation than they have from executive usurpation. Both Jackson and Lincoln somewhat strained their powers, but for good purposes, and in essentially a moderate and candid spirit; but when Congress attempts to dominate the executive, its objects are generally bad and its methods furtive and dangerous. Our legislatures were and still are the strongholds of special and local interests, and anything which undermines executive authority in this country seriously threatens our national integrity and balance. It is to the credit of the American people that they have instinctively recognized this fact, and have estimated at their true value the tirades which men no better than Henry Clay level against men no worse than Andrew Jackson.

The reason for the failure of the Whigs was that their opponents embodied more completely the living forces of contemporary American life. Jackson and his followers prevailed because they were simple, energetic, efficient, and strong. Their consistency of feeling and their mutual loyalty enabled them to form a much more effective partisan organization than that of the Whigs. It is one of those interesting paradoxes, not uncommon in American history, that the party which represented official organization and leadership was loosely organized and unwisely led, while the party which distrusted official organization and surrounded official leadership with rigid restraints was most efficiently organized and was for many years absolutely dominated by a single man. At bottom, of course, the difference between the two parties was a difference in vitality. All the contemporary conditions worked in favor of the strong narrow man with prodigious force of will like Andrew Jackson, and against men like Henry Clay and Daniel Webster who had more intelligence, but were deficient in force of character and singleness of purpose. The former had behind him the impulse of a great popular movement which was sweeping irresistibly towards wholly unexpected results; and the latter, while ostensibly trying to stem the tide, were in reality carried noisily along on its flood.

Daniel Webster and Henry Clay were in fact faced by an alternative similar to that which sterilized the lives of almost all their contemporaries who represented an intellectual interest. They were men of national ideas but of something less than national feeling. Their interests, temperament, and manner of life prevented them from instinctively sympathizing with the most vital social and political movement of their day. If they wanted popularity, they had to purchase it by compromises, whereas Andrew Jackson obtained a much larger popular following by acting strictly in accordance with the dictates of his temperament and ideas. He was effective and succeeded because his personality was representative of the American national democracy, whereas they failed, on the whole, because the constituency they represented concealed limited sympathies and special interests under words of national import. Jackson, who in theory was the servant and mouthpiece of his followers, played the part of a genuine leader in his campaign against the National Bank; while the Whigs, who should have been able to look ahead and educate their fellow-countrymen

up to the level of their presumably better insight, strag-
gled along in the rear of the procession.

The truth is that the Democrats, under the lead of
Jackson, were temporarily the national party, although
they used their genuinely national standing to impose in
certain respects a group of anti-national ideas on their
country. The Whigs, on the other hand, national as they
might be in ideas and aspirations, were in effect not
much better than a faction. Finding that they could not
rally behind their ideas an effective popular following,
they were obliged to seek support, partly at the hands
of special interests and partly by means of the sacrifice
of their convictions. Under their guidance the national
policy became a policy of conciliation and compromise
at any cost, and the national idea was deprived of consistency and dignity. It became equivalent to a hodge-
podge of policies and purposes, the incompatibility of
whose ingredients was concealed behind a smooth crust
of constitutional legality and popular acquiescence. The
national idea and interest, that is, was not merely disarmed and ignored, as it had been by Jefferson. It was
mutilated and distorted in obedience to an erroneous
democratic theory; and its friends, the Whigs, deluded
themselves with the belief that in draining the national
idea of its vitality they were prolonging its life. But if its
life was saved, its safety was chiefly due to its ostensible
enemies. While the Whigs were less national in feeling
and purpose than their ideas demanded, the Democrats were more national than they knew. From 1830
to 1850 American nationality was being attenuated as
a conscious idea, but the great unconscious forces of
American life were working powerfully and decisively
in its favor.

Most assuredly the failure of the Whigs is susceptible
of abundant explanation. Prevailing conditions were
inimical to men whose strength lay more in their intel-

ligence than in their will. It was a period of big phrases, of personal motives and altercations, of intellectual attenuation, and of narrow, moral commonplaces,—all of which made it very difficult for any statesman to see beyond his nose, or in case he did, to act upon his knowledge. Yet in spite of all this, it does seem as if some Whig might have worked out the logic of the national idea with as much power and consistency as Calhoun worked out the logic of his sectional idea. That no Whig rose to the occasion is an indication that in sacrificing their ideas they were sacrificing also their personal integrity. Intellectual insincerity and irresponsibility was in the case of the Democrats the outcome of their lives and their point of view; but on the part of the Whigs it was equivalent to sheer self-prostitution. Jefferson's work had been done only too well. The country had become so entirely possessed by a system of individual aggrandizement, national drift, and mental torpor that the men who for their own moral and intellectual welfare should have opposed it, were reduced to the position of hangers-on; and the dangers of the situation were most strikingly revealed by the attitude which contemporary statesmen assumed towards the critical national problem of the period,—the problem of the existence of legalized slavery in a democratic state.

4.

Slavery and American Nationality

I

Both the Whig and the Democratic parties betrayed the
insufficiency of their ideas by their behavior towards the
problem of slavery. Hitherto I have refrained from comment on the effect which the institution of slavery was
coming to have upon American politics because the increasing importance of slavery, and of the resulting anti-
slavery agitation, demand for the purpose of this book
special consideration. Such a consideration must now
be undertaken. The bitter personal and partisan controversies of the Whigs and the Democrats were terminated
by the appearance of a radical and a perilous issue; and
in the settlement of this question the principles of both
of these parties, in the manner in which they had been
applied, were of no vital assistance.

The issue was created by the legal existence in the
United States of an essentially undemocratic institution.
The United States was a democracy, and however much
or little this phrase means, it certainly excludes any
ownership of one man by another. Yet this was just what
the Constitution sanctioned. Its makers had been confronted by the legal existence of slavery in nearly all of
the constituent states; and a refusal to recognize the institution would have resulted in the failure of the whole
scheme of Constitutional legislation. Consequently they
did not seek to forbid negro servitude; and inasmuch
as it seemed at that time to be on the road to extinc-

tion through the action of natural causes, the makers of the Constitution had a good excuse for refusing to sacrifice their whole project to the abolition of slavery, and in throwing thereby upon the future the burden of dealing with it in some more radical and consistent way. Later, however, it came to pass that slavery, instead of being gradually extinguished by economic causes, was fastened thereby more firmly than ever upon one section of the country. The whole agricultural, political, and social life of the South became dominated by the existence of negro slavery; and the problem of reconciling the expansion of such an institution with the logic of our national idea was bound to become critical. Our country was committed by every consideration of national honor and moral integrity to make its institutions thoroughly democratic, and it could not continue to permit the aggressive legal existence of human servitude without degenerating into a glaring example of political and moral hypocrisy.

The two leading political parties deliberately and persistently sought to evade the issue. The Western pioneers were so fascinated with the vision of millions of pale-faced democrats, leading free and prosperous lives as the reward for virtuously taking care of their own business, that the Constitutional existence of negro slavery did not in the least discommode them. Disunionism they detested and would fight to the end; but to waste valuable time in bothering about a perplexing and an apparently irremediable political problem was in their eyes the worst kind of economy. They were too optimistic and too superficial to anticipate any serious trouble in the Promised Land of America; and they were so habituated to inconsistent and irresponsible political thinking, that they attached no importance to the moral and intellectual turpitude implied by the existence of slavery in a democratic nation. The responsibility of the Whigs for evading the issue is more serious than that of the Democrats. Their leaders were the trained political thinkers of their generation. They were committed by the logic of their party platform to protect the integrity of American national life and to consolidate its organization. But the Whigs, almost as much as the Democrats, refused to take seriously the legal existence of slavery. They shirked the problem whenever they could and for as long as they could; and they looked upon the men who persisted in raising it aloft as perverse fomenters of discord and trouble. The truth is, of course, that both of the dominant parties were merely representing the prevailing attitude towards slavery of American public opinion. That attitude was characterized chiefly by moral and intellectual cowardice. Throughout the whole of the Middle Period the increasing importance of negro servitude was the ghost in the house of the American democracy. The good Americans of the day sought to exorcise the ghost by many amiable devices. Sometimes they would try to lock him up in a cupboard; sometimes they would offer him a soothing bribe; more often they would be content with shutting their eyes and pretending that he was not present. But in proportion as he was kindly treated he persisted in intruding, until finally they were obliged to face the alternative, either of giving him possession of the house or taking possession of it themselves.

Foreign commentators on American history have declared that a peaceable solution of the slavery question was not beyond the power of wise and patriotic statesmanship. This may or may not be true. No solution of the problem could have been at once final and peaceable, unless it provided for the ultimate extinction of slavery without any violation of the Constitutional rights of the Southern states; and it may well be that the Southern planters could never have been argued or persuaded into abolishing an institution which they eventually came to believe was a righteous method of dealing with an inferior race. Nobody can assert with any confidence that they could have been brought by candid, courageous, and just negotiation and discussion into a reasonable frame of mind; but what we do know and can assert is that during the three decades from 1820 to 1850, the national political leaders made absolutely no attempt to deal resolutely, courageously, or candidly with the question. On those occasions when it *would* come to the surface, they contented themselves and public opinion with meaningless compromises. It would have been well enough to frame compromises suited to the immediate occasion, provided the problem of ultimately extinguishing slavery without rending the Union had been kept persistently on the surface of political discussion: but the object of these compromises was not to cure the disease, but merely to allay its symptoms. They would not admit that slavery was a disease; and in the end this habit of systematic drifting and shirking on the part of moderate and sensible men threw the national responsibility upon Abolitionist extremists, in whose hands the issue took such a distorted emphasis that gradually a peaceable preservation of American national integrity became impossible.

The problem of slavery was admirably designed to bring out the confusion of ideas and the inconsistency resident in the traditional American political system. The groundwork of that system consisted, as we have seen, in the alliance between democracy, as formulated in the Jeffersonian creed, and American nationality, as embodied in the Constitutional Union; and the two dominant political parties of the Middle Period, the Whigs and the Jacksonian Democrats, both believed in the necessity of such an alliance. But negro slavery, just in so far as it became an issue, tended to make the alliance precarious. The national organization embodied in the Constitution authorized not only the existence of negro slavery, but its indefinite expansion. American democracy, on the other hand, as embodied in the Declaration of Independence and in the spirit and letter of the Jeffersonian creed, was hostile from certain points of view to the institution of negro slavery. Loyalty to the Constitution meant disloyalty to democracy, and an active interest in the triumph of democracy seemed to bring with it the condemnation of the Constitution. What, then, was a good American to do who was at once a convinced democrat and a loyal Unionist?

The ordinary answer to this question was, of course, expressed in the behavior of public opinion during the Middle Period. The thing to do was to shut your eyes to the inconsistency, denounce anybody who insisted on it as unpatriotic, and then hold on tight to both horns of the dilemma. Men of high intelligence, who really loved their country, and believed in the democratic idea, persisted in this attitude, whose ablest and most distinguished representative was Daniel Webster. He is usually considered as the most eloquent and effective expositor of American nationalism who played an important part during the Middle Period; and unquestionably he came nearer to thinking nationally than did any American statesman of his generation. He defended the Union against the Nullifiers as decisively in one way as Jackson did in another. Jackson flourished his sword, while Webster taught American public opinion to consider the Union as the core and the crown of the American political system. His services in giving the Union a more impressive place in the American political imagination can scarcely be over-estimated. Had the other Whig leaders joined him in refusing to compromise with the Nullifiers and in strengthening by legislation the Federal government as an expression of an indestructible American national unity, a precedent might have been established which would have increased the difficulty of a subsequent secessionist outbreak. But Henry Clay believed in compromises (particularly when his own name was attached to them) as the very substance of a national American policy; and Webster was too much of a Presidential candidate to travel very far on a lonely path. Moreover, there was a fundamental weakness in Webster's own position, which was gradually revealed as the slavery crisis became acute. He could be bold and resolute, when defending a nationalistic interpretation of the Constitution against the Nullifiers or the Abolitionists; but when the slaveholders themselves became aggressive in policy and separatist in spirit, the courage of his convictions deserted him. If an indubitably Constitutional institution, such as slavery, could be used as an ax with which to hew at the trunk of the Constitutional tree, his whole theory of the American system was undermined, and he could speak only halting and dubious words. He was as much terrorized by the possible consequences of any candid and courageous dealing with the question as were the prosperous business men of the North; and his luminous intelligence shed no light upon a question, which evaded his Constitutional theories, terrified his will, and clouded the radiance of his patriotic visions.

The patriotic formula, of which Webster was the ablest and most eloquent expositor, was fairly torn to pieces by the claws of the problem of slavery. The formula triumphantly affirmed the inseparable relation between individual liberty and the preservation of the Federal Union; but obviously such a formula could have no validity from the point of view of a Southerner. The liberties which men most cherish are those which are guaranteed to them by law—among which one of the most important from the Southerner's point of view was the right to own negro bondsmen. As soon as it began to appear that the perpetuation of the Union threatened this right, they were not to be placated with any glowing proclamation about the inseparability of liberty in general from an indestructible union. From the standpoint of their own most cherished rights, they could put up a very strong argument on behalf of disunion; and they had as much of the spirit of the Constitution on their side as had their opponents. That instrument was intended not only to give legal form to the Union of the American commonwealths and the American people, but also to guarantee certain specified rights and liberties. If, on the one hand, negro slavery undermined the moral unity and consequently the political integrity of the American people, and if on the other, the South stubbornly insisted upon its legal right to property in negroes, the difficulty ran too deep to be solved by peaceable Constitutional means. The legal structure of American nationality became a house divided against itself, and either the national principle had to be sacrificed to the Constitution or the Constitution to the national principle.

The significance of the whole controversy does not become clear, until we modify Webster's formula about the inseparability of liberty and union, and affirm in its place the inseparability of American nationality and American democracy. The Union had come to mean something more to the Americans of the North than loyalty to the Constitution. It had come to mean devotion to a common national idea,—the idea of democracy; and while the wiser among them did not want to destroy the Constitution for the benefit of democracy, they insisted that the Constitution should be officially stigmatized as in this respect an inadequate expression of the national idea. American democracy and American nationality are inseparably related, precisely because democracy means very much more than liberty or liberties, whether natural or legal, and nationality very much more than an indestructible legal association. Webster's formula counseled an evasion of the problem of slavery. From his point of view it was plainly insoluble. But an affirmation of an inseparable relationship between American nationality and American democracy would just as manifestly have demanded its candid, courageous, and persistent agitation.

The slavery question, when it could no longer be avoided, gradually separated the American people into five different political parties or factions—the Abolitionists, the Southern Democrats, the Northern Democrats, the Constitutional Unionists, and the Republicans. Each of these factions selected one of the several alternative methods of solution or evasion, to which the problem of negro slavery could be reduced, and each deserves its special consideration.

Of the five alternatives, the least substantial was that of the Constitutional Unionists. These well-meaning gentlemen, composed for the most part of former Whigs, persisted in asserting that the Constitution was capable of solving every political problem generated under its protection; and this assertion, in the teeth of the fact that the Union had been torn asunder by means of a Constitutional controversy, had become merely an absurdity. Up to 1850 the position of such Constitutional Unionists as Webster and Clay could be plausibly defended; but after the failure of that final compromise, it was plain that a man of any intellectual substance must seek support for his special interpretation of the Constitution by means of a special interpretation of the national idea. That slavery was Constitutional nobody could deny, any more than they could deny the Constitutionality of anti-slavery agitation. The real question, to which the controversy had been reduced, had become, Is slavery consistent with the principle which

constitutes the basis of American national integrity—
the principle of democracy?

Each of the four other factions answered this question in a different way; and every one of these answers
was derived from different aspects of the system of traditional American ideas. The Abolitionists believed that
a democratic state, which ignored the natural rights
proclaimed by the Declaration of Independence, was a
piece of organized political hypocrisy,—worthy only of
destruction. The Southerners believed that democracy
meant above all the preservation of recognized Constitutional rights in property of all kinds, and freedom
from interference in the management of their local affairs. The Northern Democrats insisted just as strenuously as the South on local self-government, and tried
to erect it into the constituent principle of democracy;
but they were loyal to the Union and would not admit
either that slavery could be nationalized, or that secession had any legal justification. Finally the Republicans
believed with the Abolitionists that slavery was wrong;
while they believed with the Northern Democrats that
the Union must be preserved; and it was their attempt to
de-nationalize slavery as undemocratic and at the same
time to affirm the indestructibility of the Union, which
proved in the end to be salutary.

Surely never was there a more distressing example
of confusion of thought in relation to a "noble national
theory." The traditional democratic system of ideas
provoked fanatical activity on the part of the Abolitionists, as the defenders of "natural rights," a kindred
fanaticism in the Southerners as the defenders of legal
rights, and moral indifference and lethargy on the part
of the Northern Democrat for the benefit of his own
local interests. The behavior of all three factions was
dictated by the worship of what was called liberty; and
the word was as confidently and glibly used by Calhoun

and Davis as it was by Garrison, Webster, and Douglas. The Western Democrat, and indeed the average American, thought of democratic liberty chiefly as individual freedom from legal discrimination and state interference in doing some kind of a business. The Abolitionist was even more exclusively preoccupied with the liberty which the Constitution denied to the negro. The Southerners thought only of the Constitutional rights, which the Abolitionists wished to abolish, and the Republicans to restrict. Each of the contending parties had some justification in dwelling exclusively upon the legal or natural rights, in which they were most interested, because the system of traditional American ideas provided no positive principle, in relation to which these conflicting liberties could be classified and valued. It is in the nature of liberties and rights, abstractly considered, to be insubordinate and to conflict both one with another and, perhaps, with the common weal. If the chief purpose of a democratic political system is merely the preservation of such rights, democracy becomes an invitation to local, factional, and individual ambitions and purposes. On the other hand, if these Constitutional and natural rights are considered a temporary philosophical or legal machinery, whereby a democratic society is to reach a higher moral and social consummation, and if the national organization is considered merely as an effective method of keeping the legal and moral machinery adjusted to the higher democratic purpose, then no individual or faction or section could claim the benefit of a democratic halo for its distracting purposes and ambitions. Instead of subordinating these conflicting rights and liberties to the national idea, and erecting the national organization into an effective instrument thereof, the national idea and organization was subordinated to individual local and factional ideas and interests. No one could or would recognize the constructive relation between the democratic purpose and the process of national organization and development. The men who would rend the national body in order to protect their property in negro slaves could pretend to be as good democrats as the men who would rend in order to give the negro his liberty. And if either of these hostile factions had obtained its way, the same disastrous result would have been accomplished. American national integrity would have been destroyed, and slavery on American soil, in a form necessarily hostile to democracy, would have been perpetuated.

II   Slavery as a Democratic Institution

I have already suggested that it was the irresponsibility and the evasions of the party politicians, which threw upon the Abolitionists the duty of fighting slavery as an undemocratic institution. They took up the cause of the negro in a spirit of religious self-consecration. The prevalence of irresolution and timidity in relation to slavery among the leaders of public opinion incited the Abolitionists to a high degree of courage and exclusive devotion; and unfortunately, also, the conciliating attitude of the official leaders encouraged on the part of the Abolitionists an outburst of fanaticism. In their devotion to their adopted cause they lost all sense of proportion, all balance of judgment, and all justice of perception; and their narrowness and want of balance is in itself a sufficient indication that they were possessed of a half, instead of a whole, truth.

The fact that the Abolitionists were disinterested and for a while persecuted men should not prevent the present generation from putting a just estimate on their work. While they redeemed the honor of their country by assuming a grave and hard national responsibility, they sought to meet that responsibility in a way that would have destroyed their country. The Abolitionists, no less than the Southerners, were tearing at the fabric of American nationality. They did it, no doubt, in the name of democracy; but of all perverted conceptions of democracy, one of the most perverted and dangerous is that which identifies it exclusively with a system of natural rights. Such a conception of democracy is in its effect inevitably revolutionary, and merely loosens the social and national bond. In the present instance they were betrayed into one of the worst possible sins against the national bond—into the sin of doing a gross personal injustice to a large group of their fellow-countrymen. Inasmuch as the Southerners were willfully violating a Divine law, they became in the eyes of the Abolitionists, not merely misguided, but wicked, men; and the Abolitionists did not scruple to speak of them as unclean beasts, who were fattening on the fruits of an iniquitous institution. But such an inference was palpably false. The Southern slave owners were not unclean beasts; and any theory which justified such an inference must be erroneous. They were, for the most part, estimable if somewhat quick-tempered and irascible gentlemen, who did much to mitigate the evils of negro servitude, and who were on the whole liked rather than disliked by their bondsmen. They were right, moreover, in believing that the negroes were a race possessed of moral and intellectual qualities inferior to those of the white men; and, however much they overworked their conviction of negro inferiority, they could clearly see that the Abolitionists were applying a narrow and perverted political theory to a complicated and delicate set of economic and social conditions. It is no wonder, consequently, that they did not submit tamely to the abuse of the Abolitionists; and that they in their turn lost their heads. Unfortunately, however, the consequence of their wrong-headedness was more disastrous than it was in

the case of the Abolitionists, because they were powerful and domineering, as well as angry and unreasonable.
They were in a position, if they so willed, to tear the
Union to pieces, whereas the Abolitionists could only
talk and behave as if any legal association with such
sinners ought to be destroyed.

The Southern slaveholders, then, undoubtedly had
a grievance. They were being abused by a faction of
their fellow-countrymen, because they insisted on enjoying a strictly legal right; and it is no wonder that
they began to think of the Abolitionists very much as
the Abolitionists thought of them. Moreover, their anger
was probably increased by the fact that the Abolitionists could make out some kind of a case against them.
Property in slaves was contrary to the Declaration of
Independence, and had been denounced in theory by the
earlier American democrats. So long as a conception of
democracy, which placed natural above legal rights was
permitted to obtain, their property in slaves would be
imperiled: and it was necessary, consequently, for the
Southerners to advance a conception of democracy,
which would stand as a fortress around their "peculiar"
institution. During the earlier days of the Republic no
such necessity had existed. The Southerners had merely
endeavored to protect their negro property by insisting
on an equal division of the domain out of which future states were to be carved, and upon the admission
into the Union of a slave state to balance every new free
commonwealth. But the attempt of the Abolitionists to
identify the American national idea with a system of
natural rights, coupled with the plain fact that the national domain contained more material for free than it
did for slave states, provoked the Southerners into taking more aggressive ground. They began to identify the
national idea exclusively with a system of legal rights;
and it became from their point of view a violation of

national good faith even to criticise any rights enjoyed under the Constitution. They advanced a conception of American democracy, which defied the Constitution in its most rigid interpretation,—which made Congress incompetent to meddle with any rights enjoyed under the Constitution, which converted any protest against such rights into national disloyalty, and which in the end converted secession into a species of higher Constitutional action.

Calhoun's theory of Constitutional interpretation was ingeniously wrought and powerfully argued. From an exclusively legal standpoint, it was plausible, if not convincing; but it was opposed by something deeper than counter-theories of Constitutional law. It was opposed to the increasingly national outlook of a large majority of the American people. They would not submit to a conception of the American political system, designed exclusively to give legal protection to property in negroes, and resulting substantially in the nationalization of slavery. They insisted upon a conception of the Constitution, which made the national organization the expression of a democratic idea, more comprehensive and dignified than that of existing legal rights; and in so doing the Northerners undoubtedly had behind them, not merely the sound political idea, but also a fair share of the living American tradition. The Southerners had pushed the traditional worship of Constitutional rights to a point which subordinated the whole American legal system to the needs of one peculiar and incongruous institution, and such an innovation was bound to be revolutionary. But when the North proposed to put its nationalistic interpretation of the Constitution into effect, and to prevent the South by force from seceding, the South could claim for its resistance a larger share of the American tradition than could the North for its coercion. To insist that the Southern states remain in the

Union was assuredly an attempt to govern a whole society without its consent; and the fact that the Southerners rather than the Northerners were technically violators of the law, did not prevent the former from going into battle profoundly possessed with the conviction that they were fighting for an essentially democratic cause.

The aggressive theories and policy of the Southerners made the moderate opponents of slavery realize that the beneficiaries of that institution would, unless checked, succeed eventually in nationalizing slavery by appropriating on its behalf the national domain. A body of public opinion was gradually formed, which looked in the direction merely of de-nationalizing slavery by restricting its expansion. This body of public opinion was finally organized into the Republican party; and this party has certain claims to be considered the first genuinely national party which has appeared in American politics. The character of being national has been denied to it, because it was, compared to the old Whig and Democratic parties, a sectional organization; but a party becomes national, not by the locus of its support, but by the national import of its idea and its policy. The Republican party was not entirely national, because it had originated partly in embittered sectional feeling, but it proclaimed a national idea and a national policy. It insisted on the responsibility of the national government in relation to the institution of slavery, and it insisted also that the Union should be preserved. But before the Republicanism could be recognized as national even in the North, it was obliged to meet and vanquish one more proposed treatment of the problem of slavery— founded on an inadequate conception of democracy. In this case, moreover, the inadequate conception of democracy was much more traditionally American than was an exclusive preoccupation either with natural or legal rights; and according to its chief advocate it would have the magical result of permitting the expansion of slavery, and of preserving the Constitutional Union, without doing any harm to democracy.

This was the theory of Popular Sovereignty, whose ablest exponent was Stephen Douglas. About 1850, he became the official leader of the Western Democracy. This section of the party no longer controlled the organization as it did in the days of Jackson; but it was still powerful and influential. It persisted in its loyalty to the Union coupled with its dislike of nationalizing organization; and it persisted, also, in its dislike of any interference with the individual so long as he was making lawful money. The legal right to own slaves was from their point of view a right like another; and not only could it not be taken away from the Southern states, but no individual should be deprived of it by the national government. When a state came to be organized, such a right might be denied by the state constitution; but the nation should do nothing to prejudice the decision. The inhabitants of the national domain should be allowed to own slaves or not to own them, just as they pleased, until the time came for the adoption of a state constitution; and any interference with this right violated democratic principles by an unjustifiable restriction upon individual and local action. Thus was another kind of liberty invoked in order to meet the new phase of the crisis; and if it had prevailed, the United States would have become a legal union without national cohesion, and a democracy which issued, not illogically, in human servitude.

Douglas was sincere in his belief that the principle of local or Popular Sovereignty supplied a strictly democratic solution of the slavery problem, and it was natural that he should seek to use this principle for the purpose of reaching a permanent settlement. When with the assistance of the South he effected the repeal of the

Missouri Compromise, he honestly thought that he was replacing an arbitrary and unstable territorial division of the country into slave and free states, by a settlement which would be stable, because it was the logical product of the American democratic idea. The interpretation of democracy which dictated the proposed solution was sufficiently perverted; but it was nevertheless a faithful reflection of the traditional point of view of the Jacksonian Democratic party, and it deserves more respectful historical treatment than it sometimes receives. It was, after all, the first attempt which had been made to legislate in relation to slavery on the basis of a principle, and the application of any honest idea to the subject-matter of the controversy served to clear an atmosphere which for thirty years had been clouded by unprincipled compromises. The methods and the objects of the several different parties were made suddenly definite and unmistakable; and their representatives found it necessary for the first time to stand firmly upon their convictions instead of sacrificing them in order to maintain an appearance of peace. It soon became apparent that not even this erection of national irresponsibility into a principle would be sufficient to satisfy the South, because the interests of the South had come to demand the propagation of slavery as a Constitutional right, and if necessary in defiance of local public opinion. Unionists were consequently given to understand that the South was offering them a choice between a divided Union and the nationalization of slavery; and they naturally drew the conclusion that they must de-nationalize slavery in order to perpetuate the Union. The repeal, consequently, hastened the formation of the Republican party, whose object it was to prevent the expansion of slavery and to preserve the Union, without violating the Constitutional rights of the South. Such a policy could no longer prevail without a war. The Southerners had no faith in the fair intentions of their opponents. They worked themselves into the belief that the whole anti-slavery party was Abolitionist, and the whole anti-slavery agitation national disloyalty. But the issue had been so shaped that the war could be fought for the purpose of preserving American national integrity; and that was the only issue on which a righteous war could be fought.

Thus the really decisive debates which preceded the Civil War were not those which took place in Congress over states-rights, but rather the discussion in Illinois between Lincoln and Douglas as to whether slavery was a local or a national issue. The Congressional debates were on both sides merely a matter of legal special pleading for the purpose of justifying a preconceived decision. What it was necessary for patriotic American citizens and particularly for Western Democrats to understand was, not whether the South possessed a dubious right of secession, because that dispute, in case it came to a head, could only be settled by war; but whether a democratic nation could on democratic principles continue to shirk the problem of slavery by shifting the responsibility for it to individuals and localities. As soon as Lincoln made it plain that a democratic nation could not make local and individual rights an excuse for national irresponsibility, then the Unionist party could count upon the support of the American conscience. The former followers of Douglas finally rallied to the man and to the party which stood for a nationalized rather than a merely localized democracy; and the triumph of the North in the war, not only put an end to the legal right of secession, but it began to emancipate the American national idea from an obscurantist individualism and provincialism. Our current interpretation of democracy still contains much dubious matter derived from the Jacksonian epoch; but no American statesmen can hereafter follow Douglas in making the democratic principle equivalent to utter national incoherence and irresponsibility.

Mr. Theodore Roosevelt in his addresses to the veterans of the Civil War has been heard to assert that the crisis teaches us a much-needed lesson as to the supreme value of moral energy. It would have been much pleasanter and cheaper to let the South secede, but the people of the North preferred to pay the cost of justifiable coercion in blood and treasure than to submit to the danger and humiliation of peaceable rebellion. Doubtless the foregoing is sometimes a wholesome lesson on which to insist, but it is by no means the only lesson suggested by the event. The Abolitionists had not shirked their duty as they understood it. They had given their property and their lives to the anti-slavery agitation. But they were as willing as the worst Copperheads to permit the secession of the South, because of the erroneous and limited character of their political ideas. While the crisis had undoubtedly been, in a large measure, brought about by moral lethargy, and it could only be properly faced by a great expenditure of moral energy, it had also been brought about quite as much by political unintelligence; and the salvation of the Union depended primarily and emphatically upon a better understanding on the part of Northern public opinion of the issues involved. Confused as was the counsel offered to them, and distracting as were their habits of political thought, the people of the North finally disentangled the essential question, and then supported loyally the man who, more than any other single political leader, had properly defined the issue.

That man was Abraham Lincoln. Lincoln's peculiar service to his countrymen before the war was that of seeing straighter and thinking harder than did his contemporaries. No doubt he must needs have courage, also, for in the beginning he acted against the advice of his Republican associates. But in 1858 there were plenty of men who had the courage, whereas there were very few who had Lincoln's disciplined intelligence and his just and penetrating insight. Lincoln's vision placed every aspect of the situation in its proper relations; and he was as fully competent to detect the logical weakness of his opponent's position as he was to explain his own lucidly, candidly, and persuasively. It so happened that the body of public opinion which he particularly addressed was that very part of the American democracy most likely to be deluded into allowing the Southern leaders to have their will, yet whose adhesion to the national cause was necessary to the preservation of the Union. It was into this mass of public opinion, after the announcement of his senatorial candidacy, that he hammered a new and a hard truth. He was the first responsible politician to draw the logical inference from the policy of the Republican party. The Constitution was inadequate to cure the ills it generated. By its authorization of slavery it established an institution whose legality did not prevent it from being anti-national. That institution must either be gradually reduced to insignificance, or else it must transform and take possession of the American national idea. The Union had become a house divided against itself; and this deep-lying division could not be bridged merely by loyal Constitutionalism or by an anti-national interpretation of democracy. The legal Union was being threatened precisely because American national integrity was being gutted by an undemocratic institution. The house must either fall or else cease to be divided. Thus for the first time it was clearly proclaimed by a responsible politician that American nationality was a living principle rather than a legal bond; and Lincoln's service to his country in making the Western Democracy understand that living Americans were responsible for their national integrity can scarcely be over-valued. The ground was cut from under the traditional point of view of the pioneer—which had been to feel patriotic and national, but to plan and to agitate only for the fulfillment of local and individual ends.

The virtue of Lincoln's attitude may seem to be as much a matter of character as of intelligence; and such, indeed, is undoubtedly the case. My point is, not that Lincoln's greatness was more a matter of intellect than of will, but that he rendered to his country a peculiar service, because his luminous and disciplined intelligence and his national outlook enabled him to give each aspect of a complicated and confused situation its proper relative emphasis. At a later date, when he had become President and was obliged to take decisive action in order to prevent the House from utterly collapsing, he showed an inflexibility of purpose no less remarkable than his previous intellectual insight. For as long as he had not made up his mind, he hesitated firmly and patiently; but when he had made up his mind, he was not to be confused or turned aside. Indeed, during the weeks of perplexity which preceded the bombardment of Fort Sumter, Lincoln sometimes seems to be the one wise and resolute man among a group of leaders who were either resolute and foolish or wise (after a fashion) and irresolute. The amount of bad advice which was offered to the American people at this moment is appalling, and is to be explained only by the bad moral and intellectual habits fastened upon our country during forty years of national turpitude. But Lincoln never for an instant allowed his course to be diverted. If the Union was attacked, he was prepared actively to defend it. If it was let alone, he was prepared to do what little he could towards the de-nationalization of slavery. But he refused absolutely to throw away the fruits of Republican victory by renewing the policy of futile and unprincipled compromises. Back of all his opinions there was an ultimate stability of purpose which was the result both of sound mental discipline and of a firm will. His was a mind, unlike that of Clay, Seward, or even Webster, which had never been cheapened by its own exercise. During his mature years he rarely, if ever, proclaimed an idea which he had not mastered, and he never abandoned a truth which he had once thoroughly achieved.

III Lincoln as More Than an American

Lincoln's services to his country have been rewarded with such abundant appreciation that it may seem superfluous to insist upon them once again; but I believe that from the point of view of this book an even higher value may be placed, if not upon his patriotic service, at least upon his personal worth. The Union might well have been saved and slavery extinguished without his assistance; but the life of no other American has revealed with anything like the same completeness the peculiar moral promise of genuine democracy. He shows us by the full but unconscious integrity of his example the kind of human excellence which a political and social democracy may and should fashion; and its most grateful and hopeful aspect is, not merely that there is something partially American about the manner of his excellence, but that it can be fairly compared with the classic types of consummate personal distinction.

To all appearance nobody could have been more than Abraham Lincoln a man of his own time and place. Until 1858 his outer life ran much in the same groove as that of hundreds of other Western politicians and lawyers. Beginning as a poor and ignorant boy, even less provided with props and stepping-stones than were his associates, he had worked his way to a position of ordinary professional and political distinction.

He was not, like Douglas, a brilliant success. He was not, like Grant, an apparently hopeless failure. He had achieved as much and as little as hundreds of others had achieved. He was respected by his neighbors as an honest man and as a competent lawyer. They credited him with ability, but not to any extraordinary extent. No one would have pointed him out as a remarkable and distinguished man. He had shown himself to be desirous of recognition and influence; but ambition had not been the compelling motive in his life. In most respects his ideas, interests, and standards were precisely the same as those of his associates. He accepted with them the fabric of traditional American political thought and the ordinary standards of contemporary political morality. He had none of the moral strenuousness of the reformer, none of the exclusiveness of a man, whose purposes and ideas were consciously perched higher than those of his neighbors. Probably the majority of his more successful associates classed him as a good and able man who was somewhat lacking in ambition and had too much of a disposition to loaf. He was most at home, not in his own house, but in the corner grocery store, where he could sit with his feet on the stove swapping stories with his friends; and if an English traveler of 1850 had happened in on the group, he would most assuredly have discovered another instance of the distressing vulgarity to which the absence of an hereditary aristocracy and an established church condemned the American democracy. Thus no man could apparently have been more the average product of his day and generation. Nevertheless, at bottom, Abraham Lincoln differed as essentially from the ordinary Western American of the Middle Period as St. Francis of Assisi differed from the ordinary Benedictine monk of the thirteenth century.

The average Western American of Lincoln's generation was fundamentally a man who subordinated his intelligence to certain dominant practical interests and purposes. He was far from being a stupid or slow-witted man. On the contrary, his wits had been sharpened by the traffic of American politics and business, and his mind was shrewd, flexible, and alert. But he was wholly incapable either of disinterested or of concentrated intellectual exertion. His energies were bent in the conquest of certain stubborn external forces, and he used his intelligence almost exclusively to this end. The struggles, the hardships, and the necessary self-denial of pioneer life constituted an admirable training of the will. It developed a body of men with great resolution of purpose and with great ingenuity and fertility in adapting their insufficient means to the realization of their important business affairs. But their almost exclusive preoccupation with practical tasks and their failure to grant their intelligence any room for independent exercise bent them into exceedingly warped and one-sided human beings.

Lincoln, on the contrary, much as he was a man of his own time and people, was precisely an example of high and disinterested intellectual culture. During all the formative years in which his life did not superficially differ from that of his associates, he was in point of fact using every chance which the material of Western life afforded to discipline and inform his mind. These materials were not very abundant; and in the use which he proceeded to make of them Lincoln had no assistance, either from a sound tradition or from a better educated master. On the contrary, as the history of the times shows, there was every temptation for a man with a strong intellectual bent to be betrayed into mere extravagance and aberration. But with the sound instinct of a well-balanced intelligence Lincoln seized upon the three available books, the earnest study of which might best help to develop harmoniously a strong and many-sided intelligence. He seized, that is, upon the Bible, Shakespeare, and Euclid. To his contemporaries the Bible was for the most part a fountain of fanatic revivalism, and Shakespeare, if anything, a mine of quotations. But in the case of Lincoln, Shakespeare and the Bible served, not merely to awaken his taste and fashion his style, but also to liberate his literary and moral imagination. At the same time he was training his powers of thought by an assiduous study of algebra and geometry. The absorbing hours he spent over his Euclid were apparently of no use to him in his profession; but Lincoln was in his way an intellectual gymnast and enjoyed the exertion for its own sake. Such a use of his leisure must have seemed a sheer waste of time to his more practical friends, and they might well have accounted for his comparative lack of success by his indulgence in such secret and useless pastimes. Neither would this criticism have been beside the mark, for if Lincoln's great energy and powers of work had been devoted exclusively to practical ends, he might well have become in the early days a more prominent lawyer and politician than he actually was. But he preferred the satisfaction of his own intellectual and social instincts, and so qualified himself for achievements beyond the power of a Douglas.

In addition, however, to these private gymnastics Lincoln shared with his neighbors a public and popular source of intellectual and human insight. The Western pioneers, for all their exclusive devotion to practical purposes, wasted a good deal of time on apparently useless social intercourse. In the Middle Western towns of that day there was, as we have seen, an extraordinary amount of good-fellowship, which was quite the most wholesome and humanizing thing which entered into the lines of these hard-working and hard-featured men. The whole male countryside was in its way a club; and when the presence of women did not make them awkward and sentimental, the men let themselves loose in an amount of rough pleasantry and free conversation, which added the one genial and liberating touch to their lives. This club life of his own people Lincoln enjoyed and shared much more than did his average neighbor. He passed the greater part of what he would have called his leisure time in swapping with his friends stories, in which the genial and humorous side of Western life was embodied. Doubtless his domestic unhappiness had much to do with his vagrancy; but his native instinct for the wholesome and illuminating aspect of the life around him brought him more frequently than any other cause to the club of loafers in the general store. And whatever the promiscuous conversation and the racy yarns meant to his associates, they meant vastly more to Lincoln. His hours of social vagrancy really completed the process of his intellectual training. It relieved his culture from the taint of bookishness. It gave substance to his humor. It humanized his wisdom and enabled him to express it in a familiar and dramatic form. It placed at his disposal, that is, the great classic vehicle of popular expression, which is the parable and the spoken word.

Of course, it was just because he shared so completely the amusements and the occupations of his neighbors that his private personal culture had no embarrassing effects. Neither he nor his neighbors were in the least aware that he had been placed thereby in a different intellectual class. No doubt this loneliness and sadness of his personal life may be partly explained by a dumb sense of difference from his fellows; and no doubt this very loneliness and sadness intensified the mental pre-occupation which was both the sign and the result of his personal culture. But his unconsciousness of his own distinction, as well as his regular participation in political and professional practice, kept his will as firm and vigorous as if he were really no more than a man of action. His natural steadiness of purpose had been toughened in the beginning by the hardships and struggles which he shared with his neighbors; and his self-imposed intellectual discipline in no way impaired the stability of his character, because his personal culture never alienated him from his neighbors and threw him into a consciously critical frame of mind. The time which he spent in intellectual diversion may have diminished to some extent his practical efficiency previous to the gathering crisis. It certainly made him less inclined to the aggressive self-assertion which a successful political career demanded. But when the crisis came, when the minds of Northern patriots were stirred by the ugly alternative offered to them by the South, and when Lincoln was by the course of events restored to active participation in politics, he soon showed that he had reached the highest of all objects of personal culture. While still remaining one of a body of men who, all unconsciously, impoverished their minds in order to increase the momentum of their practical energy, he none the less achieved for himself a mutually helpful relation between a firm will and a luminous intelligence. The training of his mind, the awakening of his imagination, the formation of his taste and style, the humorous dramatizing of his experience,—all this discipline had failed to pervert his character, narrow his sympathies, or undermine his purposes. His intelligence served to enlighten his will, and his will, to establish the mature decisions of his intelligence. Late in life the two faculties became in their exercise almost indistinguishable. His judgments, in so far as they were decisive, were charged with momentum, and his actions were instinct with sympathy and understanding.

Just because his actions were instinct with sympathy and understanding, Lincoln was certainly the most humane statesman who ever guided a nation through a great crisis. He always regarded other men and acted towards them, not merely as the embodiment of an erroneous or harmful idea, but as human beings, capable of better things; and consequently all of his thoughts and actions looked in the direction of a higher level of human association. It is this characteristic which makes him a better and, be it hoped, a more prophetic democrat than any other national American leader. His peculiar distinction does not consist in the fact that he was a "Man of the People" who passed from the condition of splitting rails to the condition of being President. No doubt he was in this respect as good a democrat as you please, and no doubt it was desirable that he should be this kind of a democrat. But many other Americans could be named who were also men of the people, and who passed from the most insignificant to the most honored positions in American life. Lincoln's peculiar and permanent distinction as a democrat will depend rather upon the fact that his thoughts and his actions looked towards the realization of the highest and most edifying democratic ideal. Whatever his theories were, he showed by his general outlook and behavior that democracy meant to him more than anything else the spirit and principle of brotherhood. He was the foremost to deny liberty to the South, and he had his sensible doubts about the equality between the negro and the white man; but he actually treated everybody—the Southern rebel, the negro slave, the Northern deserter, the personal enemy—in a just and kindly spirit. Neither was this kindliness merely an instance of ordinary American amiability and good nature. It was the result, not of superficial feeling which could be easily ruffled, but of his personal, moral, and intellectual discipline. He had made for himself a second nature, compact of insight and loving-kindness.

It must be remembered, also, that this higher human-ity resided in a man who was the human instrument partly responsible for an awful amount of slaughter and human anguish. He was not only the commander-in-chief of a great army which fought a long and bloody war, but he was the statesman who had insisted that, if necessary, the war should be fought. His mental attitude was dictated by a mixture of practical common sense with genuine human insight, and it is just this mixture which makes him so rare a man and, be it hoped, so pro-phetic a democrat. He could at one and the same mo-ment order his countrymen to be killed for seeking to destroy the American nation and forgive them for their error. His kindliness and his brotherly feeling did not lead him, after the manner of Jefferson, to shirk the ne-cessity and duty of national defense. Neither did it lead him, after the manner of William Lloyd Garrison, to ad-vocate non-resistance, while at the same time arousing in his fellow-countrymen a spirit of fratricidal warfare. In the midst of that hideous civil contest which was pro-voked, perhaps unnecessarily, by hatred, irresponsibility, passion, and disloyalty, and which has been the fruitful cause of national disloyalty down to the present day, Lincoln did not for a moment cherish a bitter or unjust feeling against the national enemies. The Southerners, filled as they were with a passionate democratic devo-tion to their own interests and liberties, abused Lincoln until they really came to believe that he was a military tyrant, yet he never failed to treat them in a fair and forgiving spirit. When he was assassinated, it was the South, as well as the American nation, which had lost its best friend, because he alone among the Republican leaders had the wisdom to see that the divided House could only be restored by justice and kindness; and if there are any defects in its restoration to-day, they are chiefly due to the baleful spirit of injustice and hatred which the Republicans took over from the Abolitionists.

His superiority to his political associates in constructive statesmanship is measured by his superiority in personal character. There are many men who are able to forgive the enemies of their country, but there are few who can forgive their personal enemies. I need not rehearse the well-known instances of Lincoln's magnanimity. He not only cherished no resentment against men who had intentionally and even maliciously injured him, but he seems at times to have gone out of his way to do them a service. This is, perhaps, his greatest distinction. Lincoln's magnanimity is the final proof of the completeness of his self-discipline. The quality of being magnanimous is both the consummate virtue and the one which is least natural. It was certainly far from being natural among Lincoln's own people. Americans of his time were generally of the opinion that it was dishonorable to overlook a personal injury. They considered it weak and unmanly not to quarrel with another man a little harder than he quarreled with you. The pioneer was good-natured and kindly; but he was aggressive, quick-tempered, unreasonable, and utterly devoid of personal discipline. A slight or an insult to his personality became in his eyes a moral wrong which must be cherished and avenged, and which relieved him of any obligation to be just or kind to his enemy. Many conspicuous illustrations of this quarrelsome spirit are to be found in the political life of the Middle Period, which, indeed, cannot be understood without constantly falling back upon the influence of lively personal resentments. Every prominent politician cordially disliked or hated a certain number of his political adversaries and associates; and his public actions were often dictated by a purpose either to injure these men or to get ahead of them. After the retirement of Jackson these enmities and resentments came to have a smaller influence; but a man's right and duty to quarrel with anybody who, in his opinion, had done him an injury was unchallenged, and was generally considered to be the necessary accompaniment of American democratic virility.

As I have intimated above, Andrew Jackson was the most conspicuous example of this quarrelsome spirit, and for this reason he is wholly inferior to Lincoln as a type of democratic manhood. Jackson had many admirable qualities, and on the whole he served his country well. He also was a "Man of the People" who understood and represented the mass of his fellow-countrymen, and who played the part, according to his lights, of a courageous and independent political leader. He also loved and defended the Union. But with all his excellence he should never be held up as a model to American youth. The world was divided into his personal friends and followers and his personal enemies, and he was as eager to do the latter an injury as he was to do the former a service. His quarrels were not petty, because Jackson was, on the whole, a big rather than a little man, but they were fierce and they were for the most part irreconcilable. They bulk so large in his life that they cannot be overlooked. They stamp him a type of the vindictive man without personal discipline, just as Lincoln's behavior towards Stanton, Chase, and others stamps him a type of the man who has achieved magnanimity. He is the kind of national hero the admiring imitation of whom can do nothing but good.

Lincoln had abandoned the illusion of his own peculiar personal importance. He had become profoundly and sincerely humble, and his humility was as far as possible from being either a conventional pose or a matter of nervous self-distrust. It did not impair the firmness of his will. It did not betray him into shirking responsibilities. Although only a country lawyer without executive experience, he did not flinch from assuming the leadership of a great nation in one of the gravest crises of its national history, from becoming commander-in-chief of an army of a million men, and from spending $3,000,000,000 in the prosecution of a war. His humility, that is, was precisely an example of moral vitality and insight rather than of moral awkwardness and enfeeblement. It was the fruit of reflection on his own personal experience—the supreme instance of his ability to attain moral truth both in discipline and in idea; and in its aspect of a moral truth it obtained a more explicit expression than did some other of his finer personal attributes. His practice of cherishing and repeating the plaintive little verses which inquire monotonously whether the spirit of mortal has any right to be proud indicates the depth and the highly conscious character of this fundamental moral conviction. He is not only humble himself, but he feels and declares that men have no right to be anything but humble; and he thereby enters into possession of the most fruitful and the most universal of all religious ideas.

Lincoln's humility, no less than his liberal intelligence and his magnanimous disposition, is more democratic than it is American; but in this, as in so many other cases, his personal moral dignity and his peculiar moral insight did not separate him from his associates. Like them, he wanted professional success, public office, and the ordinary rewards of American life; and like them, he bears no trace of political or moral purism. But, unlike them, he was not the intellectual and moral victim of his own purposes and ambitions; and unlike them, his life is a tribute to the sincerity and depth of his moral insight. He could never have become a national leader by the ordinary road of insistent and clamorous self-assertion. Had he not been restored to public life by the crisis, he would have remained in all probability a comparatively

obscure and a wholly under-valued man. But the political ferment of 1856 and the threat of ruin overhanging
the American Union pushed him again on to the political highway; and once there, his years of intellectual
discipline enabled him to play a leading and a decisive
part. His personality obtained momentum, direction,
and increasing dignity from its identification with great
issues and events. He became the individual instrument
whereby an essential and salutary national purpose was
fulfilled; and the instrument was admirably effective,
precisely because it had been silently and unconsciously
tempered and formed for high achievement. Issue as
he was of a society in which the cheap tool, whether
mechanical or personal, was the immediately successful
tool, he had none the less labored long in the making of
a consummate individual instrument.

Some of my readers may protest that I have over-
emphasized the difference between Lincoln and his
contemporary fellow-countrymen. In order to exalt the
leader have I not too much disparaged the followers?
Well, a comparison of this kind always involves the risk
of unfairness; but if there is much truth in the foregoing estimate of Lincoln, the lessons of the comparison
are worth its inevitable risk. The ordinary interpretation
of Lincoln as a consummate democrat and a "Man of
the People" has implied that he was, like Jackson, simply a bigger and a better version of the plain American
citizen; and it is just this interpretation which I have
sought to deny and to expose. In many respects he was,
of course, very much like his neighbors and associates.
He accepted everything wholesome and useful in their
life and behavior. He shared their good-fellowship, their
strength of will, their excellent faith, and above all their
innocence; and he could never have served his country
so well, or reached as high a level of personal dignity, in
case he had not been good-natured and strong and in-

nocent. But, as all commentators have noted, he was not only good-natured, strong and innocent; he had made himself intellectually candid, concentrated, and disinterested, and morally humane, magnanimous, and humble. All these qualities, which were the very flower of his personal life, were not possessed either by the average or the exceptional American of his day; and not only were they not possessed, but they were either wholly ignored or consciously under-valued. Yet these very qualities of high intelligence, humanity, magnanimity and humility are precisely the qualities which Americans, in order to become better democrats, should add to their strength, their homogeneity, and their innocence; while at the same time they are just the qualities which Americans are prevented by their individualistic practice and tradition from attaining or properly valuing. Their deepest convictions make the average unintelligent man the representative democrat, and the aggressive successful individual, the admirable national type; and in conformity with these convictions their uppermost ideas in respect to Lincoln are that he was a "Man of the People" and an example of strong will. He was both of these things, but his great distinction is that he was also something vastly more and better. He cannot be fully understood and properly valued as a national hero without an implicit criticism of those traditional convictions. Such a criticism he himself did not and could not make. In case he had made it, he could never have achieved his great political task and his great personal triumph. But other times bring other needs. It is as desirable to-day that the criticism should be made explicit as it was that Lincoln himself in his day should preserve the innocence and integrity of a unique unconscious example.

5.

The Contemporary Situation
and Its Problems

|

It is important to recognize that the anti-slavery agitation, the secession of the South, and the Civil War were,
after all, only an episode in the course of American national development. The episode was desperately serious. Like the acute illness of a strong man, it almost
killed its victim; and the crisis exposed certain weaknesses in our political organism, in the absence of which
the illness would never have become acute. But the roots
of our national vitality were apparently untouched by
the disease. When the crisis was over, the country resumed with astonishing celerity the interrupted process
of economic expansion. The germs of a severe disease,
to which the Fathers of the Republic had given a place
in the national Constitution, and which had been allowed to flourish, because of the lack of wholesome
cohesion in the body politic—this alien growth had
been cut out by a drastic surgical operation, and the
robust patient soon recovered something like his normal health. Indeed, being in his own opinion even more
robust than he was before the crisis, he was more eager
than ever to convert his good health into the gold of
satisfied desire. The ghost of slavery had been banished
from our national banquet: and, relieved of this terror,
the American people began to show, more aggressively
than ever before, their ability to provide and to consume

a bountiful feast. They were no longer children, grasping at the first fruits of a half-cultivated wilderness. They were adults, beginning to plan the satisfaction of an appetite which had been sharpened by self-denial, and made self-conscious by maturity.

The North, after the war was over, did not have much time for serious reflection upon its meaning and consequences. The Republican leaders did just enough thinking to carry them through the crisis; but once the rebellion was suppressed and the South partly de-nationalized in the name of reconstruction, the need and desire was for action rather than for thought. The anti-slavery agitation and the war had interrupted the process, which from the public point of view, was described as the economic development of the country, and which from an individual standpoint meant the making of money. For many years Americans had been unable, because of the ghost of slavery, to take full advantage of their liberties and opportunities; and now that the specter was exorcised, they gladly put aside any anxious political preoccupations. Politics could be left to the politicians. It was about time to get down to business. In this happiest of all countries, and under this best of all governments, which had been preserved at such an awful cost, the good American was entitled to give his undivided attention to the great work of molding and equipping the continent for human habitation, and incidentally to the minor task of securing his share of the rewards. A lively, even a frenzied, outburst of industrial, commercial, and speculative activity followed hard upon the restoration of peace. This activity and its effects have been the most important fact in American life during the forty years which have supervened; and it has assumed very different characteristics from those which it had assumed previous to the War. We must now consider the circumstances, the consequences, and the meaning of this economic revolution.

Although nobody in 1870 suspected it, the United States was entering upon a new phase of its economic career; and the new economy was bringing with it radical social changes. Even before the outbreak of the Civil War the rich and fertile states of the Middle West had become well populated. They had passed from an almost exclusively agricultural economy to one which was much more largely urban and industrial. The farms had become well-equipped; large cities were being built up; factories of various kinds were being established; and most important of all, the whole industrial organization of the country was being adjusted to transportation by means of the railroad. An industrial community, which was, comparatively speaking, well-organized and well-furnished with machinery, was taking the place of the agricultural community of 1830-1840, which was incoherent and scattered and which lacked everything except energy and opportunity. Such an increase of organization, capital, and equipment necessarily modified the outlook and interests of the people of the Middle West. While still retaining many of their local traits, their point of view had been approaching in certain respects that of the inhabitants of the East. They had ceased to be pioneers.

During the two decades after the Civil War, the territory, which was still in the early stage of agricultural development, was the first and second tier of states west of the Mississippi River. Missouri, Iowa, and Minnesota, Kansas, Nebraska, and finally the Dakotas were being opened for settlement; but in their case the effect and symptoms of this condition were not the same as they had been with the earlier pioneer states. Their economy was from the beginning adjusted to the railroad; and the railroad had made an essential difference. It worked in favor of a more comprehensive and definite organization and a more complete equipment. While the business

interests of the new states were and still are predominantly agricultural, the railroads had transformed the
occupation of farming. After 1870, the pioneer farmer
was much less dependent than he had been upon local
conditions and markets, and upon the unaided exertions of himself and his neighbors. He bought and sold
in the markets of the world. He needed more capital and
more machinery. He had to borrow money and make
shrewd business calculations. From every standpoint his
economic environment had become more complicated
and more extended, and his success depended much
more upon conditions which were beyond his control.
He never was a pioneer in the sense that the early inhabitants of the Middle West and South had been pioneers;
and he has never exercised any corresponding influence
upon the American national temper. The pioneer had
enjoyed his day, and his day was over. The Jack-of-all-
trades no longer possessed an important economic function. The average farmer was, of course, still obliged to
be many kinds of a rough mechanic, but for the most
part he was nothing more than a farmer. Unskilled labor
began to mean labor which was insignificant and badly
paid. Industrial economy demanded the expert with his
high and special standards of achievement. The railroads and factories could not be financed and operated
without the assistance of well-paid and well-trained
men, who could do one or two things remarkably well,
and who did not pretend to do much of anything else.
These men had to retain great flexibility and an easy
adaptability of intelligence, because American industry
and commerce remained very quick in its movements.
The machinery which they handled was less permanent,
and was intended to be less permanent than the machinery which was considered economical in Europe. But
although they had to avoid routine and business rigidity
on the penalty of utter failure, still they belonged essen-

tially to a class of experts. Like all experts, they had to depend, not upon mere energy, untutored enthusiasm, and good-will, but upon careful training and single-minded devotion to a special task, and at the same time proper provision had to be made for coördinating the results of this highly specialized work. More complete organization necessarily accompanied specialization. The expert became a part of a great industrial machine. His individuality tended to disappear in his work. His interests became those of a group. Imperative economic necessities began to classify the individuals composing American society in the same way, if not to the same extent, that they had been classified in Europe.

This was a result which had never entered into the calculations of the pioneer Democrat. He had disliked specialization, because, as he thought, it narrowed and impoverished the individual; and he distrusted perma-nent and official forms of organization, because, as he thought, they hampered the individual. His whole polit-ical, social, and economic outlook embodied a society of energetic, optimistic, and prosperous democrats, united by much the same interests, occupations, and point of view. Each of these democrats was to be essentially an all-round man. His conception of all-round manhood was somewhat limited; but it meant at least a person who was expansive in feeling, who was enough of a business man successfully to pursue his own interests, and enough of a politician to prevent any infringement or perversion of his rights. He never doubted that the desired combination of business man, politician, and good fellow constituted an excellent ideal of democratic individuality, that it was sufficiently realized in the aver-age Western American of the Jacksonian epoch, that it would continue to be the type of admirable manhood, and that the good democrats embodying this type would continue to merit and to obtain substantial and approximately equal pecuniary rewards. Moreover, for a long time the vision remained sufficiently true. The typical American democrat described by De Tocqueville corresponded very well with the vision of the pioneer; and he did not disappear during the succeeding generation. For many years millions of Americans of much the same pattern were rewarded for their democratic virtue in an approximately similar manner. Of course some people were poor, and some people were rich; but there was no class of the very rich, and the poverty of the poor was generally their own fault. Opportunity knocked at the door of every man, and the poor man of to-day was the prosperous householder of to-morrow. For a long time American social and economic conditions were not merely fluid, but consistent and homogeneous, and the vision of the pioneer was fulfilled. Nevertheless, this condition was essentially transient. It contained within itself the seeds of its own dissolution and transformation; and this transformation made headway just as soon as, and just as far as, economic conditions began to prefer the man who was capable of specializing his work, and of organizing it with the work of his fellows.

The dominant note, consequently, of the pioneer period was an unformed national consistency, reached by means of a natural community of feeling and a general similarity of occupation and well-being. On the other hand, the dominant note of the period from 1870 until the present day has been the gradual disintegration of this early national consistency, brought about by economic forces making for specialization and organization in all practical affairs, for social classification, and finally for greater individual distinction. Moreover, the tendency towards specialization first began to undermine the very corner-stone of the pioneer's democratic edifice. If private interest and public weal were to be as harmonious as the pioneer assumed, every economic producer must be a practical politician, and there must be no deep-lying division between these primary activities. But the very first result of the specializing tendency was to send the man of business, the politician, and the lawyer off on separate tacks. Business interests became so absorbing that they demanded all of a man's time and energy; and he was obliged to neglect politics except in so far as politics affected business. In this same way, the successful lawyers after the War were less apt than formerly to become politicians and statesmen. They left public affairs largely to the unsuccessful lawyers. Politics itself became an occupation which made very exacting demands upon a man's time and upon his conscience. Public service or military success were no longer the best roads to public distinction. Men became renowned and distinguished quite as much, if not more, for achievements in their private and special occupations. Along with leadership of statesmen and generals, the American people began to recognize that of financiers, "captains of industry," corporation lawyers, political and labor "bosses," and these gentlemen assumed extremely important parts in the direction of American affairs. Officially, the new leaders were just like any other American citizen. No titles could be conferred upon them, and their position brought with it no necessary public responsibilities. Actually, however, they exercised in many cases more influence upon American social and political economy than did the official leaders. They were an intrusion, into the traditional economic political and social system, for which no provision had been made. Their special interests, and the necessities of their special tasks, made their manner of life different from that of other American citizens, and their peculiar opportunities enabled them to appropriate an unusually large share of the fruits of American economic development. Thus they seriously impaired the social and economic homogeneity, which the pioneer believed to be the essential quality of fruitful Americanism.

II The Development of the Business Specialist

Before seeking to trace the consequences and the significance of this specialized organization of American practical affairs, we must examine its origin with some care. An exact and complete understanding thereof will in itself afford an unmistakable hint of the way in which its consequences are to be appraised, and wherever necessary, corrected. The great and increasing influence of the new unofficial leaders has been due not only to economic conditions and to individual initiative, but to the nature of our political ideas and institutions. The traditional American theory was that the individual should have a free hand. In so far as he was subject to public regulation and control such control should be exercised by local authorities, whereof the result would be a happy combination of individual prosperity and public weal. But this expectation, as we have seen, has proved to be erroneous. While it has, indeed, resulted in individual prosperity, the individual who has reaped most of the prosperity is not the average, but the special man; and however the public may have benefited from the process, the benefit is mixed with so many drawbacks that, even if it may not be wholly condemned, it certainly cannot be wholly approved. The plain fact is that the individual in freely and energetically pursuing his own private purposes has not been the inevitable public benefactor assumed by the traditional American interpretation of democracy. No doubt he has incidentally accomplished, in the pursuit of his own aggrandizement, certain manifest public benefits; but wherever public and private advantages have conflicted, he has naturally preferred the latter. And under our traditional political system there was, until recently, no effective way of correcting his preference.

As long as the economic opportunities of American life consisted chiefly in the appropriation and improvement of uncultivated land, the average energetic man had no difficulty in obtaining his fair share of the increasing American economic product; but the time came when such opportunities, although still important, were dwarfed by other opportunities, incident to the development of a more mature economic system. These opportunities, which were, of course, connected with the manufacturing, industrial, and technical development of the country, demanded under American conditions a very special type of man—the man who would bring to his task not merely energy, but unscrupulous devotion, originality, daring, and in the course of time a large fund of instructive experience. The early American industrial conditions differed from those of Europe in that they were fluid, and as a result of this instability, extremely precarious. Rapid changes in markets, business methods, and industrial machinery made it very difficult to build up a safe business. A manufacturer or a merchant could not secure his business salvation, as in Europe, merely by the adoption of sound conservative methods. The American business man had greater opportunities and a freer hand than his European prototype; but he was also beset by more severe, more unscrupulous, and more dangerous competition. The industrious and thrifty farmer could be tolerably sure of a modest competence, due partly to his own efforts, and partly to the increased value of his land in a more populous community; but the business man had no such security. In his case it was war to the knife. He was presented with a choice between aggressive daring business operations, and financial insignificance or ruin.

No doubt this situation was due as much to the temper of the American business man as to his economic environment. American energy had been consecrated to economic development. The business man in seeking to realize his ambitions and purposes was checked neither by government control nor social custom. He had nothing to do and nothing to consider except his own business advancement and success. He was eager, strenuous, and impatient. He liked the excitement and the risk of large operations. The capital at his command was generally too small for the safe and conservative conduct of his business; and he was consequently obliged to be adventurous, or else to be left behind in the race. He might well be earning enormous profits one year and skirting bankruptcy the next. Under such a stress conservatism and caution were suicidal. It was the instinct of self-preservation, as well as the spirit of business adventure, which kept him constantly seeking for larger markets, improved methods, or for some peculiar means of getting ahead of his competitors. He had no fortress behind which he could hide and enjoy his conquests. Surrounded as he was by aggressive enemies and undefended frontiers, his best means of security lay in a policy of constant innovation and expansion. Moreover, even after he had obtained the bulwark of sufficient capital and more settled industrial surroundings, he was under no temptation to quit and enjoy the spoils of his conquests. The social, intellectual, or even the more vulgar pleasures, afforded by leisure and wealth, could bring him no thrill, which was anything like as intense as that derived from the exercise of his business ability and power. He could not conquer except by virtue of a strong, tenacious, adventurous, and unscrupulous will; and after he had conquered, this will had him in complete possession. He had nothing to do but to play the game to the end—

even though his additional profits were of no living use to him.

If, however, the fluid and fluctuating nature of American economic conditions and the fierceness of American competitive methods turned business into a state of dangerous and aggressive warfare, the steady and enormous expansion of the American markets made the rewards of victory correspondingly great. Not only was the population of the country increasing at an enormous rate, but the demand for certain necessary products, services, and commodities was increasing at a higher rate than the population. The American people were still a most homogeneous collection of human beings. They wanted very much the same things; they wanted more of these things year after year; and they immediately rewarded any cheapening of the product by buying it in much larger quantities. The great business opportunities of American life consisted, consequently, in supplying some popular or necessary article or service at a cheaper price than that at which any one else could furnish it; and the great effort of American business men was, of course, to obtain some advantage over their competitors in producing such an article or in supplying such a service. The best result of this condition was a constant improvement in the mechanism of production. Cheapness was found to depend largely upon the efficient use of machinery, and the efficient use of machinery was found to depend upon constant wear and quick replacement by a better machine. But while the economic advantage of the exhausting use and the constant improvement of machinery was the most important economic discovery of the American business man, he was also encouraged by his surroundings to seek economies in other and less legitimate ways. It was all very well to multiply machines and make them more efficient, but similar improvements were open to competitors. The great object was to obtain some advantage which was denied to your competitors. Then the business man could not only secure his own position, but utterly rout and annihilate his adversaries.

At this point the railroads came to the assistance of the aggressive and unscrupulous business man. They gave such men an advantage over their competitors by granting them special rates; and inasmuch as this practice has played a decisive part in American business development, its effect and its meaning, frequently as they have been pointed out, must be carefully traced.

The railroads themselves are, perhaps, the most perfect illustration of the profits which accrue in a rapidly growing country from the possession of certain advantages in supplying to the public an indispensable service. They were not built, as in most European states, under national supervision and regulation, or according to a general plan which prevented unnecessary competition. Their routes and their methods were due almost entirely to private enterprise and to local economic necessities. They originated in local lines radiating from large cities; and only very slowly did their organization come to correspond with the great national routes of trade. The process of building up the leading systems was in the beginning a process of combining the local roads into important trunk lines. Such combinations were enormously profitable, because the business of the consolidated roads increased in a much larger proportion than did the cost of financing and operating the larger mileage; and after the combinations were made the owners of the consolidated road were precisely in the position of men who had obtained a certain strategic advantage in supplying a necessary service to their fellow-countrymen. Their terminals, rights of way, and machinery could not be duplicated except at an increased cost, and their owners were in a position necessarily to benefit from the growth of the country in industry and population. No doubt their economic position was in certain respects precarious. They did not escape the necessity, to which other American business enterprises had to submit, of fighting for a sufficient share of the spoils. But in making the fight, they had acquired certain advantages which, if they were intelligently used, would necessarily result in victory; and as we all know, these advantages have proved to be sufficient. The railroads have been the greatest single source of large American fortunes, and the men who control the large railroad systems are the most powerful and conspicuous American industrial leaders.

Important, however, as has been the direct effect of big railroad systems on the industrial economy of the country, their indirect effects have probably been even more important. In one way or another, they have been the most effective of all agencies working for the larger organization of American industries. Probably such an organization was bound to have come in any event, because the standard economic needs of millions of thrifty democrats could in the long run be most cheaply satisfied by means of well-situated and fully equipped industrial plants of the largest size; but the railroad both hastened this result and determined its peculiar character. The population of the United States is so scattered, its distances so huge, and its variations in topographical level so great, that its industries would necessarily have remained very local in character, as long as its system of transportation depended chiefly upon waterways and highways. Some kind of quick transportation across country was, consequently, an indispensable condition of the national organization of American industry and commerce. The railroad not only supplied this need, but coming as it did pretty much at the beginning of our industrial development, it largely modified and determined the character thereof. By considerably increasing the area within which the products of any one locality could be profitably sold, it worked naturally in favor of the concentration of a few large factories in peculiarly favorable locations; and this natural process was accelerated by the policy which the larger companies adopted in the making of their rates. The rapid growth of big producing establishments was forced, because of the rebates granted to them by the railroads. Without such rebates the large manufacturing corporation controlled by a few individuals might still have come into existence; but these individuals would have been neither as powerful as they now are, nor as opulent, nor as much subject to suspicion.

It is peculiarly desirable to understand, consequently, just how these rebates came to be granted. It was, apparently, contrary to the interest of the railroad companies to cut their rates for the benefit of any one class of customers; and it was, also, an illegal practice, which had to be carried on by secret and underhand methods. Almost all the state laws under which corporations engaged in transportation had been organized, had defined railways, like highways, as public necessities. Such corporations had usually been granted by the states the power to condemn land,—and the delegation of such a power to a private company meant, of course, that it owed certain responsibilities to the public as a common carrier, among which the responsibility of not allowing special privileges to any one customer was manifestly to be included. When the railroad managers have been asked why they cut their published rates and evaded the laws, they have always contended that they were forced to do so; and whatever may be thought of the plea, it cannot be lightly set aside. As we have seen, the trunk lines leading from Chicago to the coast were the result of the consolidation of local roads. After the consolidations had taken place, these companies began to compete fiercely for through freight, and the rebates were an incident in this competition. The trunk lines in the early years of their existence were in the position of many other American business enterprises. For the time being, they were more than competent to carry all the freight offered at competitive points. Inasmuch as there was not enough to go around, they fought mercilessly for what business there was. When a large individual shipper was prepared to guarantee them a certain amount of freight in return for special rates, they were obliged either to grant the rates or to lose the business. Of course they submitted, and defended their submission as a measure of self-preservation.

No great intelligence is required to detect in this situation the evidence of a vicious circle. The absorption of Americans in business affairs, and the free hand which the structure and ideals of American life granted them, had made business competition a fierce and merciless affair; while at the same time the fluid nature of American economic conditions made success very precarious. Every shrewd and resolute man would seek to secure himself against the dangers of this situation by means of special advantages, and the most effective of all special advantages would, of course, be special railroad rates. But a shipper such as John D. Rockefeller could obtain special rates only because the railroads were in a position similar to his own, and were fighting strenuously for supremacy. The favored shipper and the railroad both excused themselves on the ground of self-preservation, and sometimes even claimed that it was just for a large shipper to obtain better rates than a small one. This was all very well for the larger shipper and the railroad, but in the meantime what became of the small shipper, whom Mr. Rockefeller was enabled to annihilate by means of his contracts with the railroad companies? The small shipper saw himself forced out of business, because corporations to whom the state had granted special privileges as common carriers, had a private interest in doing business with his bigger, more daring, and unscrupulous competitors.

Of course no such result could have happened, if at any point in this vicious circle of private interests, there had been asserted a dominant public interest; and there are several points at which such an interest might well have been intruded. The circle would have been broken, if, for instance, the granting of illegal rebates had been effectively prohibited; but as a matter of fact they could not be effectively prohibited by the public authorities, to whom either the railroads or the large shippers were technically responsible. A shipper of oil in Cleveland, Ohio, would have a difficult time in protesting against illegal discrimination on the part of a railroad conducting an inter-state business and organized under the laws of New York. No doubt he could appeal to the Federal government; but the Federal government had been, for the time being, disqualified by many different causes from effective interference. In the first place there was to be overcome the conventional democratic prejudice against what was called centralization. A tradition of local control over the machinery of transit and transportation was dominant during the early period of railroad construction. The fact that railways would finally become the all-important vehicles of inter-state commerce was either overlooked or considered unimportant. The general government did not interfere—except when, as in the case of the Pacific lines, its interference and assistance were solicited by private interests. For a long time the idea that the Federal government had any general responsibility in respect to the national transportation system was devoid of practical consequences.

In the end an Inter-state Commerce law was passed, in which the presence of a national interest in respect to the American system of transportation was recognized. But this law, like our tariff laws, was framed for the benefit chiefly of a combination of local and special interests; and it served little to advance any genuine national interest in relation to the railroads. To be sure it did forbid rebates, but the machinery for enforcing the prohibition was inefficient, and during another twenty years the prohibition remained substantially a dead letter. The provisions of the law forbidding rebates were in truth merely a bit of legal hypocrisy. Rebates could not be openly defended; but the business of the country was honeycombed with them, and the majority of the shippers in whose interest the law was passed did not want the prohibition enforced. Their influence at Washington was sufficiently powerful to prevent the adoption of any effective measures for the abatement of the evil. The Federal Inter-state Commerce Commission, unlike the local authorities, would have been fully competent to abolish rebates; but the plain truth was that the effective public opinion in the business world either supported the evil or connived at it. The private interests at stake were, for the time being, too strong for the public interest. The whole American business tradition was opposed to government interference with prevailing business practices; and in view of this fact the responsibility for the rebates cannot be fixed merely upon the railroads and the trusts. The American system had licensed energetic and unscrupulous individual aggrandizement as the best means of securing a public benefit; and rebates were merely a flagrant instance of the extent to which public opinion permitted the domination of private interests.

The failure of the Federal government to protect the public interest in a matter over which the state governments had no effective control, has greatly accelerated the organization of American industries on a national scale, but for private and special purposes. Certain individuals controlling certain corporations were enabled to obtain a decided advantage in supplying certain services and products to the enormously increasing American market; and once those individuals and corporations had obtained dominant positions, it was in their interest to strengthen one another's hands in every possible way. One big corporation has as a rule preferred to do business with another big corporation. They were all of them producing some standard commodity or service, and it is part of the economical conduct of such businesses to buy and sell so far as possible in large quantities and under long contracts. Such contracts reduced to a comparatively low level the necessary uncertainties of business. It enabled the managers of these corporations to count upon a certain market for their product or a certain cost for part of their raw material; and it must be remembered that the chief object of this whole work of industrial organization was to diminish the hazards of unregulated competition and to subject large business operations to effective control. A conspicuous instance of the effect of such interests and motives may be seen in the lease of the ore lands belonging to the Great Northern Railroad to the United States Steel Corporation. The railroad company owned the largest body of good ore in the country outside of the control of the Steel Corporation, and if these lands had been leased to many small companies, the ability of the independent steel manufacturers to compete with the big steel company would have been very much increased. But the Great Northern Railroad Company found it simpler and more secure to do business with one large than a number of small companies; and in this way the Steel Corporation has obtained almost a monopoly of the raw material most necessary to the production of finished steel. It will be understood, consequently, how inevitably these big corporations strengthen one another's hands; and it must be added that they had political as well as economic motives for so doing. Although the big fellows sometimes indulge in the luxury of fierce fighting, such fights are always the prelude to still closer agreements. They are all embarked in the same boat; and surrounded as they are by an increasing amount of enmity, provoked by their aggrandizement, they have every reason to lend one another constant and effective support.

There may be discerned in this peculiar organization of American industry an entangling alliance between a wholesome and a baleful tendency. The purpose which prompted men like John D. Rockefeller to escape from the savage warfare in which so many American business men were engaged, was in itself a justifiable and ameliorating purpose. Competition in American business was insufficiently moderated either by the state or by the prevailing temper of American life. No sensible and resourceful man will submit to such a precarious existence without making some attempt to escape from it; and if the means which Mr. Rockefeller and others took to secure themselves served to make the business lives of their competitors still more precarious, such a result was only the expiation which American business men were obliged to pay for their own excesses. The concentrated leadership, the partial control, the thorough organization thereby effected, was not necessarily a bad thing. It was in some respects a decidedly good thing, because leadership of any kind has certain intrinsic advantages. The trusts have certainly succeeded in reducing the amount of waste which was necessitated by the earlier condition of wholly unregulated competition. The competitive methods of nature have been, and still are, within limits indispensable; but the whole effort of civilization has been to reduce the area within which they are desirably effective; and it is entirely possible that in the end the American system of industrial organization will constitute a genuine advance in industrial economy. Large corporations, which can afford the best machinery, which control abundant capital, and which can plan with scrupulous economy all the details of producing and selling an important product or service, are actually able to reduce the cost of production to a minimum; and in the cases of certain American corporations such results have actually been achieved. The new organization of American industry has created an economic mechanism which is capable of being wonderfully and indefinitely serviceable to the American people.

On the other hand, its serviceability is much diminished by the special opportunities it gives a few individuals. These opportunities do not amount in any case to a monopoly, but they do amount to a species of economic privilege which enable them to wring profits from the increasing American market disproportionate to the value of their economic services. What is still more unfortunate, however, is the equivocal position of these big corporations in respect to the laws under which they are organized, and in respect to the public authorities which are supposed to control them. Many of the large railway and industrial corporations have reached their present size partly by an evasion or a defiance of the law. Their organizers took advantage of the American system of local self-government and the American disposition to reduce the functions of the Federal government to a minimum—they took advantage of these legal conditions and political ideas to organize an industrial machinery which cannot be effectively reached by local statutes and officials. The favorable corporation laws of some states have been used as a means of preying upon the whole country; and the unfavorable corporation laws of other states have been practically nullified. The big corporations have proved to be too big and powerful for the laws and officials to which the American political system has subjected them; and their equivocal legal position has resulted in the corruption of American public life and in the serious deterioration of our system of local government.

The net result of the industrial expansion of the United States since the Civil War has been the establishment in the heart of the American economic and social system of certain glaring inequalities of condition and power. The greater American railroad and industrial corporations control resources and conduct operations on a scale unprecedented in the economic history of the world. The great American industrial leaders have accumulated fortunes for which there is also no precedent on the part of men who exercise no official political power. These inequalities are the result of the organization of American industry on almost a national scale,—an organization which was brought about as a means of escape from the intolerable evils of unregulated competition. Every aspect of American business methods has helped to make them inevitable, and the responsibility for them must be distributed over the whole business and social fabric. But in spite of the fact that they have originated as the inevitable result of American business methods and political ideas and institutions, they constitute a serious problem for a democracy to face; and this problem has many different aspects. Its most serious aspect is constituted by the sheer size of the resulting inequalities. The rich men and the big corporations have become too wealthy and powerful for their official standing in American life. They have not obeyed the laws. They have attempted to control the official makers, administrators, and expounders of the law. They have done little to allay and much to excite the resentment and

suspicion. In short, while their work has been constructive from an economic and industrial standpoint, it has
made for political corruption and social disintegration.
Children, as they are, of the traditional American individualistic institutions, ideas, and practices, they have
turned on their parents and dealt them an ugly wound.
Either these economic monsters will destroy the system
of ideas, institutions, and practices out of which they
have issued or else be destroyed by them.

III   The Development of the Political Specialist

The corporations were able to secure and to exercise an
excessive and corrupt influence on legislation, because
their aggrandizement coincided with a process of deterioration in our local political institutions. We have seen
that the stress of economic competition had specialized the American business man and made him almost
exclusively preoccupied with the advancement of his
own private interests; and one of the first results of this
specialization was an alteration in his attitude towards
the political welfare of his country. Not only did he no
longer give as much time to politics as he formerly did,
but as his business increased in size and scope, he found
his own interests by way of conflicting at many points
with the laws of his country and with its well-being. He
did not take this conflict very seriously. He was still reflected in the mirror of his own mind as a patriotic and
a public-spirited citizen; but at the same time his ambition was to conquer, and he did not scruple to sacrifice
both the law and the public weal to his own prosperity.
All unknowingly he began to testify to a growing and
a decisive division between the two primary interests of
American life,—between the interest of the individual
business man and the interest of the body politic; and
he became a living refutation of the amiable theories of

the Jacksonian Democrat that the two must substantially coincide. The business man had become merely a business man, and the conditions which had made him less of a politician had also had its effect upon the men whose business was that of politics. Just as business had become specialized and organized, so politics also became subject to specialization and organization. The appearance of the "Captain of Industry" was almost coincident with the appearance of the "Boss."

There has been a disposition to treat the "Boss" chiefly as the political creature of the corrupt corporation; and it is undoubtedly true that one of the most important functions of the municipal and state "Bosses" has been that of conducting negotiations with the corporations. But to consider the specialized organization of our local politics as the direct result of specialized organization of American business is wholly to misunderstand its significance. The two processes are the parallel effects of the same conditions and ideas working in different fields. Business efficiency under the conditions prevailing in our political and economic fabric demanded the "Captain of Industry." Political efficiency under our system of local government demanded the "Boss." The latter is an independent power who has his own special reasons for existence. He put in an embryonic appearance long before the large corporations had obtained anything like their existing power in American politics; and he will survive in some form their reduction to political insignificance. He has been a genuine and within limits a useful product of the American democracy; and it would be fatal either to undervalue or to misunderstand him.

The American system of local self-government encouraged the creation of the political "Boss," because it required such an enormous amount of political business. Some one was needed to transact this business, and the professional politician was developed to supply the need. There was no reason why such a need should have existed; because the amount of political business incident to state government could have been very much economized by a simpler method of organization. But American democratic ideas during the years when the state governments took form were wholly opposed to simplicity of organization. The state constitutions adopted during the period of Jacksonian supremacy seem designed to make local government costly in time and energy and irresponsible in action; and they provided the legal scenery in the midst of which the professional politician became the only effective hero.

The state constitutions were all very much influenced by the Federal instrument, but in the copies many attempts were made to improve upon the model. The Democracy had come to believe that the Federal Constitution tended to encourage independence and even special efficiency on the part of Federal officials; and it proposed to correct such an erroneous tendency in the more thoroughly democratic state governments. No attempt was, indeed, made to deprive the executive and the judicial officials of independence by making them the creatures of the legislative branch; for such a change, although conforming to earlier democratic ideas, would have looked in the direction of a concentration of responsibility. The far more insidious course was adopted of keeping the executive, the judicial, and the legislative branches of the government technically separate, while at the same time depriving all three of any genuine independence and efficiency. The term of the executive, for instance, was not allowed to exceed one or two years. The importance of his functions was diminished. His power of appointment was curtailed. Many of his most important executive assistants were elected by popular vote and made independent of him. In some few instances he was even deprived of a qualified veto upon legislation. But the legislature itself was not treated much better. Instead of deriving its power from a short constitution which conferred upon it full legislative responsibilities and powers, the tendency has been to incorporate an enormous mass of special and detailed legislation in the fundamental law, and so to diminish indefinitely the power of the legislative branch either to be useful or dangerous. Finally state judges instead of being appointed for life were usually elected for limited terms, so that they could scarcely avoid being more "amenable to public opinion." The tendency in every respect was to multiply elections and elective officials, divide responsibility and power, and destroy independence. The more "democratic" these constitutions became, the more clearly the Democracy showed its disposition to distrust its own representatives, and to deprive them of any chance of being genuinely representative.

The object of the Jacksonion Democrat in framing constitutions of this kind was to keep political power in the hands of the "plain people," and to forestall the domination of administrative and legislative specialists. The effect was precisely the opposite. They afforded the political specialist a wonderful opportunity. The ordinary American could not pretend to give as much time to politics as the smooth operation of this complicated machine demanded; and little by little there emerged in different parts of the country a class of politicians who spent all their time in nominating and electing candidates to these numerous offices. The officials so elected, instead of being responsible to the people, were responsible to the men to whom they owed their offices; and their own individual official power was usually so small that they could not put what little independence they possessed to any good use. As a matter of fact, they used their official powers chiefly for the benefit of their creators. They appointed to office the men whom the "Bosses" selected. They passed the measures which the machine demanded. In this way the professional politician gradually obtained a stock of political goods wherewith to maintain and increase his power. Reënforced by the introduction of the spoils system first into the state and then into the Federal civil services, a process of local political organization began after 1830 to make rapid headway. Local leaders appeared in different parts of the country who little by little relieved the farmer and the business man of the cares and preoccupations of government. In the beginning the most efficient of these politicians were usually Jacksonian Democrats, and they ruled both in the name of the people and by virtue of a sturdy popular following. They gradually increased in power, until in the years succeeding the war they became the dominant influence in local American politics, and had won the right to be called something which they would never have dared to call themselves, viz. a governing class.

While the local "Boss" nearly always belonged to the political party dominant in his neighborhood, so that he could in ordinary elections depend upon the regular party vote, still the real source of his power consisted in a band of personal retainers; and the means by which such groups were collected and held together contain a curious mixture of corruption and democracy. In the first place the local leader had to be a "good fellow" who lived in the midst of his followers and knew all about them. His influence was entirely dependent upon personal kindliness, loyalty, and good-comradeship. He was socially the playmate and the equal of his followers, and the relations among them were characterized by many admirable qualities. The group was within limits a genuine example of social democracy, and was founded on mutual understanding, good-will, and assistance. The leader used his official and unofficial power to obtain jobs for his followers. He succored them when in need; he sometimes protected them against the invidious activity of the police or the prosecuting attorneys; he provided excursions and picnics for them in hot weather; he tied them to himself by a thousand bonds of interest and association; he organized them into a clan, who supported him blindly at elections in return for a deal of personal kindliness and a multitude of small services; he became their genuine representative, whether official or not, because he represented their most vital interests and satisfied their most pressing and intimate needs.

The general method of political organization indicated above was perfected in the two decades succeeding the Civil War. The American democracy was divided politically into a multitude of small groups, organized chiefly for the purpose of securing the local and individual interests of these groups and their leaders, and supported by local and personal feeling, political patronage, and petty "graft." These groups were associated with both parties, and merely made the use of partisan ties and cries to secure the coöperation of more disinterested voters. The result was that so far as American political representation was merely local, it was generally corrupt, and it was always selfish. The leader's power depended absolutely on an appeal to the individual, neighborhood, and class interests of his followers. They were the "people"; he was the popular tribune. He could not retain his power for a month, in case he failed to subordinate every larger interest to the flattery, cajolery, and nourishment of his local clan. Thus the local representative system was poisoned at its source. The alderman, the assemblyman, or the congressman, even if he were an honest man, represented little more than the political powers controlling his district; and to be disinterested in local politics was usually equivalent to being indifferent.

Although these local clans were the basis of American political organization, they were not, of course, its ultimate fruit. In many of the cities, large and small, and in some of the states the leaders of the local groups were subordinated to one of their number who became the real "Boss" and who strengthened the district organizations by using for their benefit the municipal, state, and Federal patronage. The relation of the municipal or state "Boss" to the district leaders was similar to the relation which the district leader bore to his more important retainers. The "Boss" first obtained his primacy by means of diplomatic skill or force of character; and his ability to retain it depended upon his ability to satisfy the demands of the district leaders for patronage, while at the same time leading the organization to victory in the local elections. His special duties as "Boss" required personal prestige, strength of will, power of persuasive talking, good judgment of men, loyalty to his promises and his followers, and a complete lack of scruple. Unlike the district leader, however, the municipal "Boss" has tended to become a secretive and somewhat lonely person, who carried on his business behind closed doors, and on whom was visited the odium incurred by this whole system of political organization. The district leader either does not incur or is less affected by this odium, because his social status is precisely that of his followers. The "Boss," on the other hand, by this wealth and public position would naturally be an important member of the society in which he lives, whereas as a matter of fact he has come to be ostracized because of the source of his power and wealth. His leadership overreached the district clan, which was real social basis; and the consequence was that the "Boss" became, to all appearances, a very unpopular man in the democracy which he ruled.

His secretiveness and his unpopularity point to one of the most important functions of the municipal and state "Bosses," to which as yet only incidental reference has been made. The "Boss" became the man who negotiated with the corporations, and through whom they obtained what they wanted. We have already seen that the large corporation, particularly those owning railroad and municipal franchises, have found that the purchase of a certain amount of political power was a necessary consequence of their dubious legal position. A traffic of this kind was not one, of course, to which many people could be admitted. It must be transmitted in secret, and by people who possessed full authority. An agreement to secure certain franchises or certain needed legislation in return for certain personal or party favors was not an agreement which could be made between a board of directors and a group of district leaders. If a large number of people were familiar with the details of such negotiations, something more than a hint thereof would be sure to leak out; and unquestionably the fact that a traffic of this kind was part of the political game had much to do with the ability of the municipal or state "Boss" to obtain and to keep his power. The profits not only enabled him to increase party funds and to line his own pockets, but it also furnished him with a useful and abundant source of patronage. He could get positions for the political henchmen of his district leaders, not only with the local and state governments, but with the corporations. Thus every "Boss," even those whose influence did not extend beyond an election district, was more or less completely identified with the corporations who occupied within his bailiwick any important relation to the state.

This alliance between the political machines and the big corporations—particularly those who operate railroads or control municipal franchises—was an alliance between two independent and coördinate powers in the kingdom of American practical affairs. The political "Boss" did not create the industrial leader for his own good purposes. Neither did the industrial leader create the machine and its "Boss," although he has done much to confirm the latter's influence. Each of them saw an opportunity to turn to his own account the individualistic "freedom" of American politics and industry. Each of them was enabled by the character of our political traditions to obtain an amount of power which the originators of those political ideas never anticipated, and which, if not illegal, was entirely outside the law. It so happened that the kind of power which each obtained was very useful to the other. A corporation which derived its profits from public franchises, or from a business transacted in many different states, found the purchase of a local or state machine well within its means and well according to its interests. The professional politicians who had embarked in politics as a business and who were making what they could out of it for themselves and their followers, could not resist this unexpected and lucrative addition to their market. But it must be remembered that the alliance was founded on interest rather than association, on mutual agreement rather than on any effective subordination one to another. A certain change in conditions might easily make their separate interests diverge, and abstract all the profits from their traffic. If anything happened, for instance, to make inter-state railroad corporations less dependent on the state governments, they would no longer need the expense of subsidizing the state machines. There are signs at the present time that these interests are diverging, and that such alliances will be less dangerous in the future than they have been in the past. But even if the alliance is broken, the peculiar unofficial organization of American industry and politics will persist, and will constitute, both in its consequences and its significance, two of our most important national problems.

It would be as grave a mistake, however, absolutely to condemn this process of political organization as it would absolutely to condemn the process of industrial organization. The huge corporation and the political machine were both created to satisfy a real and a permanent need—the needs of specialized leadership and associated action in these two primary American activities. That in both of these cases the actual method of organization has threatened vital public interests, and even the very future of democracy has been due chiefly to the disregard by the official American political system of the necessity and the consequences of specialized leadership and associated action. The political system was based on the assumption that the individualism it encouraged could be persuaded merely by the power of words to respect the public interest, that public officials could be deprived of independence and authority for the real benefit of the "plain people," and that the "plain people" would ask nothing from the government but their legal rights. These assumptions were all erroneous; and when associated action and specialized leadership became necessary in local American politics, the leaders and their machine took advantage of the defective official system to build up an unofficial system, better suited to actual popular needs. The "people" wanted the government to do something for them, and the politicians made their living and served their country by satisfying the want. To be sure, the "people" they benefited were a small minority of the whole population whose interests were far from being the public interest; but it was none the less natural that the people, whoever they were, should want the government to do more for them than to guarantee certain legal rights, and it was inevitable that they should select leaders who could satisfy their positive, if selfish, needs.

The consequence has been, however, a separation of actual political power from official political responsibility. The public officers are still technically responsible for the good government of the states, even if, as individuals, they have not been granted the necessary authority effectively to perform their task. But their actual power is even smaller than their official authority. They are almost completely controlled by the machine which secures their election or appointment. The leader or leaders of that machine are the rulers of the community, even though they occupy no offices and cannot be held in any way publicly responsible. Here, again, as in the case of the multi-millionaire, we have an example of a dangerous inequality in the distribution of power, and one which tends to maintain and perpetuate itself. The professional politician is frequently beaten and is being vigorously fought; but he himself understands how necessary he is under the existing local political organization, and how difficult it will be to dislodge him. Beaten though he be again and again, he constantly recovers his influence, because he is performing a necessary political task and because he is genuinely representative of the needs of his followers. Organizations such as Tammany in New York City are founded on a deeply rooted political tradition, a group of popular ideas, prejudices, and interests, and a species of genuine democratic association which are a guarantee of a long and tenacious life. They will survive much of the reforming machinery which is being created for their extirpation.

IV   The Labor Union and the Democratic Tradition

One other decisive instance of this specialized organization of American activity remains to be considered—
that of the labor unions. The power which the unions
have obtained in certain industrial centers and the tight-
ness of their organization would have seemed anomalous to the good Jacksonian Democrat. From his point
of view the whole American democracy was a kind of
labor union whose political constitution provided for
a substantially equal division of the products of labor;
and if the United States had remained as much of an agricultural community as it was in 1830, the Jacksonian
system would have preserved a much higher degree of
serviceability.

Except in the case of certain local Granger and Popu-
list movements, the American farmers have never felt
the necessity of organization to advance either their economic or their political interests. But when the mechanic
or the day-laborer gathered into the cities, he soon discovered that life in a democratic state by no means deprived him of special class interests. No doubt he was at
worst paid better than his European analogues, because
the demand for labor in a new country was continually
outrunning the supply; but on occasions he was, like
his employer, threatened with merciless competition.
The large and continuous stream of foreign immigrants,
whose standards of living were in the beginning lower
than those which prevailed in this country, were, particularly in hard times, a constant menace not merely to
his advancement, but to the stability of his economic situation; and he began to organize partly for the purpose
of protecting himself against such competition. During
the past thirty years the work of organization has made
enormous strides; and it has been much accelerated by

the increasing industrial power of huge corporations. The mechanic and the laborer have come to believe that they must meet organization with organization, and discipline with discipline. Their object in forming trade associations has been militant. Their purpose has been to conquer a larger share of the economic product by aggressive associated action.

They have been very successful in accomplishing their object. In spite of the flood of alien immigration the American laborer has been able to earn an almost constantly increasing wage, and he devoutly thinks that his unions have been the chief agency of his stronger economic position. He believes in unionism, consequently, as he believes in nothing else. He is, indeed, far more aggressively preoccupied with his class, as contrasted with his individual interests, than are his employers. He has no respect for the traditional American individualism as applied to his own social and economic standing. Whenever he has had the power, he has suppressed competition as ruthlessly as have his employers. Every kind of contumelious reproach is heaped on the heads of the working men who dare to replace him when he strikes; and he does not scruple to use under such conditions weapons more convincing than the most opprobrious epithets. His own personality is merged in that of the union. No individual has any rights as opposed to the interests of the union. He fully believes, of course, in competition among employers, just as the employers are extremely enthusiastic over the individual liberty of the working man. But in his own trade he has no use for individuality of any kind. The union is to be composed of so many equal units who will work the same number of hours for the some wages, and no one of whom is to receive more pay even for more work. The unionist, that is, has come to depend upon his union for that material prosperity and advancement which, according to the American tradition, was to be the inevitable result of American political ideas and institutions. His attachment to his union has come to be the most important attachment of his life—more important in most cases than his attachment to the American ideal and to the national interest.

Some of the labor unions, like some of the corporations, have taken advantage of the infirmities of local and state governments to become arrogant and lawless. On the occasion of a great strike the strikers are often just as disorderly as they are permitted to be by the local police. When the police prevent them from resisting the employment of strike-breakers by force, they apparently believe that the political system of the country has been pressed into the service of their enemies; and they begin to wonder whether it will not be necessary for them to control such an inimical political organization. The average union laborer, even though he might hesitate himself to assault a "scab," warmly sympathizes with such assaults, and believes that in the existing state of industrial warfare they are morally justifiable. In these and in other respects he places his allegiance to his union and to his class above his allegiance to his state and to his country. He becomes in the interests of his organization a bad citizen, and at times an inhuman animal, who is ready to maim or even to kill another man and for the supposed benefit of himself and his fellows.

The most serious danger to the American democratic future which may issue from aggressive and unscrupulous unionism consists in the state of mind of which mob-violence is only one expression. The militant unionists are beginning to talk and believe as if they were at war with the existing social and political order—as if the American political system was as inimical to their interests as would be that of any European monarchy or aristocracy. The idea is being systematically propagated that the American government is one which favors the millionaire rather than the wage-earner; and the facts which either superficially or really support this view are sufficiently numerous to win for it an apparently increasing number of adherents. The union laborer is tending to become suspicious, not merely of his employer, but of the constitution of American society. His morals are becoming those of men engaged in a struggle for life. The manifestations of this state of mind in notion are not very numerous, although on many occasions they have worn a sufficiently sinister aspect. But they are numerous enough to demand serious attention, for the literature popular among the unionists is a literature, not merely of discontent, but sometimes of revolt.

Whether this aggressive unionism will ever become popular enough to endanger the foundations of the American political and social order, I shall not pretend to predict. The practical dangers resulting from it at any one time are largely neutralized by the mere size of the country and its extremely complicated social and industrial economy. The menace it contains to the nation as a whole can hardly become very critical as long as so large a proportion of the American voters are land-owning farmers. But while the general national well-being seems sufficiently protected for the present against the aggressive assertion of the class interests of the unionists, the legal public interest of particular states and cities cannot be considered as anywhere near so secure; and in any event the existence of aggressive discontent on that part of the unionists must constitute a serious problem for the American legislator and statesman. Is there any ground for such aggressive discontent? How has it come to pass that the American political system, which was designed to guarantee the welfare and prosperity of the people, is the subject of such violent popular suspicion? Can these suspicions be allayed merely by curbing the somewhat excessive opportunities of the rich man and by the diminution of his influence upon the government? Or does the discontent indicate the existence of more radical economic evils or the necessity of more radical economic reforms?

However the foregoing questions ought to be answered, there can be no doubt as to the nature of the answers, proposed by the unionists themselves. The unionist leaders frequently offer verbal homage to the great American principle of equal rights, but what they really demand is the abandonment of that principle. What they want is an economic and political order which will discriminate in favor of union labor and against non-union labor; and they want it on the ground that the unions have proved to be the most effective agency on behalf of economic and social amelioration of the wage-earner. The unions, that is, are helping most effectively to accomplish the task, traditionally attributed to the American democratic political system—the task of raising the general standard of living; and the unionists claim that they deserve on this ground recognition by the state and active encouragement. Obviously, however, such encouragement could not go very far without violating both the Federal and many state constitutions—the result being that there is a profound antagonism between our existing political system and what the unionists consider to be a perfectly fair demand. Like all good Americans, while verbally asking for nothing but equal rights, they interpret the phrase so that equal rights become equivalent to special rights.

Of all the hard blows which the course of American political and economic development has dealt the traditional system of political ideas and institutions, perhaps the hardest is this demand for discrimination on behalf of union labor. It means that the more intelligent and progressive American workingmen are coming to believe that the American political and economic organization does not sufficiently secure the material improvement of the wage-earner. This conviction may be to a large extent erroneous. Certain it is that the wages of unorganized farm laborers have been increasing as rapidly during the past thirty years as have the wages of the organized mechanics. But whether erroneous or not, it is widespread and deep-rooted; and whatever danger it possesses is derived from the fact that it affords to a substantially revolutionary purpose a large and increasing popular following. The other instances of organization for special purposes which have been remarked, have superficially, at least, been making for conservatism. The millionaire and the professional politician want above all things to be let alone, and to be allowed to enjoy the benefit of their conquests. But the labor organizations cannot exercise the power necessary in their opinion to their interests without certain radical changes in the political and economic order; and inasmuch as their power is likely to increase rather than diminish, the American people are confronted with the prospect of persistent, unscrupulous, and increasing agitation on behalf of an economic and political reorganization in favor of one class of citizens.

The large corporations and the unions occupy in certain respects a similar relation to the American political system. Their advocates both believe in associated action for themselves and in competition for their adversaries. They both demand governmental protection and recognition, but resent the notion of efficient governmental regulation. They have both reached their existing power, partly because of the weakness of the state governments, to which they are legally subject, and they both are opposed to any interference by the Federal government—except exclusively on their own behalf.

Yet they both have become so very powerful that they are frequently too strong for the state governments, and in different ways they both traffic for their own benefit with the politicians, who so often control those governments. Here, of course, the parallelism ends and the divergence begins. The corporations have apparently the best of the situation because existing institutions are more favorable to the interests of the corporations than to the interests of the unionists; but on the other hand, the unions have the immense advantage of a great and increasing numerical strength. They are beginning to use the suffrage to promote a class interest, though how far they will travel on this perilous path remains doubtful. In any event, it is obvious that the development in this country of two such powerful and unscrupulous and well-organized special interests has created a condition which the founders of the Republic never anticipated, and which demands as a counterpoise a more effective body of national opinion, and a more powerful organization of the national interest.

V   Government by Lawyers

The corporation, the politician, and the union laborer are all illustrations of the organization of men representing fundamental interests for special purposes. The specialization of American society has not, however, stopped with its specialized organization. A similar process has been taking place in the different professions, arts, and trades; and of these much the most important is the gradual transformation of the function of the lawyer in the American political system. He no longer either performs the same office or occupies the same place in the public mind as he did before the Civil War; and the nature and meaning of this change cannot be understood without some preliminary consideration of the important part which American lawyers have played in American political history.

The importance of that part is both considerable and peculiar—as is the debt of gratitude which the American people owe to American lawyers. They founded the Republic, and they have always governed it. Some few generals, and even one colonel, have been elected to the Presidency of the United States; and occasionally business men of one kind or another have prevailed in local politics; but really important political action in our country has almost always been taken under the influence of lawyers. On the whole, American laws have been made by lawyers; they have been executed by lawyers; and, of course, they have been expounded by lawyers. Their predominance has been practically complete; and so far as I know, it has been unprecedented. No other great people, either in classic, mediæval, or modern times, has ever allowed such a professional monopoly of governmental functions. Certain religious bodies have submitted for a while to the dominion of ecclesiastical lawyers; but the lawyer has rarely been allowed to interfere either in the executive or the legislative branches of the government. The lawyer phrased the laws and he expounded them for the benefit of litigants. The construction which he has placed upon bodies of customary law, particularly in England, has sometimes been equivalent to the most permanent and fruitful legislation. But the people responsible for the government of European countries have rarely been trained lawyers, whereas American statesmen, untrained in the law, are palpable exceptions. This dominion of lawyers is so defiant of precedent that it must be due to certain novel and peremptory American conditions.

The American would claim, of course, that the unprecedented prominence of the lawyer in American politics is to be explained on the ground that the American government is a government by law. The lawyer is necessarily of subordinate importance in any political system tending towards absolutism. He is even of subordinate importance in a liberal system such as that of Great Britain, where Crown and Parliament, acting together, have the power to enact any desired legislation. The Federal Constitution, on the other hand, by establishing the Supreme Court as the interpreter of the Fundamental Law, and as a separate and independent department of the government, really made the American lawyer responsible for the future of the country. In so far as the Constitution continues to prevail, the Supreme Court becomes the final arbiter of the destinies of the United States. Whenever its action can be legally invoked, it can, if necessary, declare the will of either or both the President and Congress of no effect; and inasmuch as almost every important question of public policy raises corresponding questions of Constitutional interpretation, its possible or actual influence dominates American political discussion. Thus the lawyer, when consecrated as Justice of the Supreme Court, has become the High Priest of our political faith. He sits in the sanctuary and guards the sacred rights which have been enshrined in the ark of the Constitution.

The importance of lawyers as legislators and executives in the actual work of American government has been an indirect consequence of the peculiar function of the Supreme Court in the American political system. The state constitutions confer a corresponding function on the highest state courts, although they make no similar provision for the independence of the state judiciary. The whole business of American government is so entangled in a network of legal conditions that a training in the law is the best education which an American public man can receive. The first question asked of any important legislative project, whether state or Federal, concerns its constitutionality; and the question of its wisdom is necessarily subordinate to these fundamental legal considerations. The statesman, who is not a lawyer, suffers under many disadvantages—not the least of which is the suspicion wherewith he is regarded by his legal fellow-statesmen. When they talk about a government by law, they really mean a government by lawyers; and they are by way of believing that government by anybody but lawyers is really unsafe.

The Constitution bestowed upon the American lawyer a constructive political function; and this function has been confirmed and even enlarged by American political custom and practice. The work of finally interpreting the Federal Constitution has rarely been either conceived or executed in a merely negative spirit. The construction, which successive generations of Supreme Court Justices have placed upon the instrument, has tended to enlarge its scope, and make it a legal garment, which was being better cut to fit the American political and economic organism. In its original form, and to a certain extent in its present form, the Constitution was in many respects an ambiguous document which might have been interpreted along several different lines; and the Supreme Court in its official expositions has been influenced by other than strictly legal and verbal reasons—by considerations of public welfare or by general political ideas. But such constructive interpretations have been most cautiously and discreetly admitted. In proclaiming them, the Supreme Court has usually represented a substantial consensus of the better legal opinion of the time; and constructions of this kind are accepted and confirmed only when any particular decision is the expression of some permanent advance or achievement in political thinking by the American lawyer. It becomes consequently of the utmost importance that American lawyers should really represent the current of national political opinion. The Supreme Court has been, on the whole, one of the great successes of the American political system, because the lawyers, whom it represented, were themselves representative of the ideas and interests of the bulk of their fellow-countrymen; and if for any reason they become less representative, a dangerous division would be created between the body of American public opinion and its official and final legal expositors. If the lawyers have any reason to misinterpret a serious political problem, the difficulty of dealing therewith is much increased, because in addition to the ordinary risks of political therapeutics there will be added that of a false diagnosis by the family doctor. The adequacy of the lawyers' training, the disinterestedness of their political motives, the fairness of their mental outlook, and the closeness of their contact with the national public opinion—all become matters of grave public concern.

It can be fairly asserted that the qualifications of the American lawyer for his traditional task as the official interpreter and guide of American constitutional democracy have been considerably impaired. Whatever his qualifications have been for the task (and they have, perhaps, been overestimated) they are no longer as substantial as they were. Not only has the average lawyer become a less representative citizen, but a strictly legal training has become a less desirable preparation for the candid consideration of contemporary political problems.

Since 1870 the lawyer has been traveling in the same path as the business man and the politician. He has tended to become a professional specialist, and to give all his time to his specialty. The greatest and most successful American lawyers no longer become legislators and statesmen as they did in the time of Daniel Webster. They no longer obtain the experience of men and affairs which an active political life brings with it. Their professional practice, whenever they are successful, is so remunerative and so exacting that they cannot afford either the time or the money which a political career demands. The most eminent American lawyers usually remain lawyers all their lives; and if they abandon private practice at all, it is generally for the purpose of taking a seat on the Bench. Like nearly all other Americans they have found rigid specialization a condition of success.

A considerable proportion of our legislators and executives continue to be lawyers, but the difference is that now they are more likely to be less successful lawyers. Knowledge of the law and a legal habit of mind still have a great practical value in political work; and the professional politicians, who are themselves rarely men of legal training, need the services of lawyers whose legal methods are not attenuated by scruples. Lawyers of this class occupy the same relation to the local political "Bosses" as the European lawyer used to occupy in the court of the absolute monarch. He phrases the legislation which the ruler decides to be of private or public benefit; and he acts frequently as his employer's official mouthpiece and special pleader.

No doubt many excellent and even eminent lawyers continue to play an important and an honorable part in American politics. Mr. Elihu Root is a conspicuous example of a lawyer, who has sacrificed a most lucrative private practice for the purpose of giving his country the benefit of his great abilities. Mr. Taft was, of course, a lawyer before he was an administrator, though he had made no professional success corresponding to that of Mr. Root. Mr. Hughes, also, was a successful lawyer. The reform movement has brought into prominence many public-spirited lawyers, who, either as attorney-generals or as district attorneys, have sought vigorously to enforce the law and punish its violators. The lawyers, like every class of business and professional men, have felt the influence of the reforming ideas, which have become so conspicuous in American practical politics, and they have performed admirable and essential work on behalf of reform.

But it is equally true that the most prominent and thorough-going reformers, such as Roosevelt, Bryan, and Hearst, are not lawyers by profession, and that the majority of prominent American lawyers are not reformers. The tendency of the legally trained mind is inevitably and extremely conservative. So far as reform consists in the enforcement of the law, it is, of course, supported by the majority of successful lawyers; but so far as reform has come to mean a tendency to political or economic reorganization, it has to face the opposition of the bulk of American legal opinion. The existing political order has been created by lawyers; and they naturally believe somewhat obsequiously in a system for which they are responsible, and from which they benefit. This government by law, of which they boast, is not only a government by lawyers, but is a government in the interest of litigation. It makes legal advice more constantly essential to the corporation and the individual than any European political system. The lawyer, just as much as the millionaire and the politician, has reaped a bountiful harvest from the inefficiency and irresponsibility of American state governments, and from the worship of individual rights.

They have corporations in Europe, but they have nothing corresponding to the American corporation lawyer. The ablest American lawyers have been retained by the special interests. In some cases they have been retained to perform tasks which must have been repugnant to honest men; but that is not the most serious aspect of the situation. The retainer which the American legal profession has accepted from the corporations inevitably increases its natural tendency to a blind conservatism; and its influence has been used not for the purpose of extricating the large corporations from their dubious and dangerous legal situation, but for the purpose of keeping them entangled in its meshes. At a time when the public interest needs a candid reconsideration of the basis and the purpose of the American legal system, they have either opposed or contributed little to the essential work, and in adopting this course they have betrayed the interests of their more profitable clients—the large corporations themselves—whose one chance of perpetuation depends upon political and legal reconstruction.

The conservative believer in the existing American political system will doubtless reply that the lawyer, in so far as he opposes radical reform or reorganization, is merely remaining true to his function as the High Priest of American constitutional democracy. And no doubt it is begging the question at the present stage of this discussion, to assert that American lawyers as such are not so well qualified as they were to guide American political thought and action. But it can at least be maintained that, assuming some radical reorganization to be necessary, the existing prejudices, interests, and mental outlook of the American lawyer disqualify him for the task. The legal profession is risking its traditional position as the mouthpiece of the American political creed and faith upon the adequacy of the existing political system. If there is any thorough-going reorganization needed, it will be brought about in spite of the opposition of the legal profession. They occupy in relation to the modern economic and political problem a position similar to that of the Constitutional Unionists previous to the Civil War. Those estimable gentlemen believed devoutly that the Constitution, which created the problem of slavery and provoked the anti-slavery agitation, was

adequate to its solution. In the same spirit learned lawyers now affirm that the existing problems can easily be
solved, if only American public opinion remain faithful
to the Constitution. But it may be that the Constitution, as well as the system of local political government
built up around the Federal Constitution, is itself partly
responsible for some of the existing abuses, evils, and
problems; and if so, the American lawyer may be useful, as he was before the Civil War, in evading our difficulties; but he will not be very useful in settling them.
He may try to settle them by decisions of the Supreme
Court; but such decisions,—assuming, of course, that
the problem is as inexorable as was that of the legal
existence of slavery in a democratic nation,—such decisions would have precisely the same effect on public
opinion as did the Dred Scott decision. They would
merely excite a crisis, which they were intended to allay,
and strengthen the hands of the more radical critics of
the existing political system.

VI American Democracy and the Social Problem

The changes which have been taking place in industrial
and political and social conditions have all tended to impair the consistency of feeling characteristic of the first
phase of American national democracy. Americans are
divided from one another much more than they were
during the Middle Period by differences of interest, of
intellectual outlook, of moral and technical standards,
and of manner of life. Grave inequalities of power
and deep-lying differences of purpose have developed
in relation of the several primary American activities.
The millionaire, the "Boss," the union laborer, and the
lawyer, have all taken advantage of the loose American
political organization to promote somewhat unscrupulously their own interests, and to obtain special sources

of power and profit at the expense of a wholesome national balance. But the foregoing examples of specialized
organization and purposes do not stand alone. They are
the most conspicuous and the most troublesome because
of the power wielded by those particular classes, and because they can claim for their purposes the support of
certain aspects of the American national tradition. Yet
the same process has been taking place in all the other
departments of American social and intellectual life.
Technical experts of all kinds—engineers, men of letters,
and artists—have all of them been asserting much more
vigorously their own special interests and purposes. In
so asserting themselves they cannot claim the support of
the American national democratic convention. On the
contrary, the proclamation of high technical standards
and of insistent individual purposes is equivalent to a
revolt from the traditions of the Middle Period, which
were all in favor of cheap work and the average worker.
But different as is the situation of these technical experts, the fundamental meaning of their self-assertion
is analogous to that of the millionaire and the "Boss."
The vast incoherent mass of the American people is falling into definite social groups, which restrict and define
the mental outlook and social experience of their members. The all-round man of the innocent Middle Period
has become the exception. The earlier homogeneity of
American society has been impaired, and no authoritative and edifying, but conscious, social ideal has as yet
taken its place.

The specialized organization of American industry,
politics, and labor, and the increasingly severe special
discipline imposed upon the individual, are not to be
considered as evils. On the contrary, they are indications of greater practical efficiency, and they contain a
promise of individual moral and intellectual emancipation. But they have their serious and perilous aspects,

because no sufficient provision has been made for them in the national democratic tradition. What it means is that the American nation is being confronted by a problem which the earlier national democracy expected to avoid—the social problem. By the social problem is usually meant the problem of poverty; but grave inequalities of wealth are merely the most dangerous and distressing expression of fundamental differences among the members of a society of interest and of intellectual and moral standards. In its deepest aspect, consequently, the social problem is the problem of preventing such divisions from dissolving the society into which they enter—of keeping such a highly differentiated society fundamentally sound and whole.

In this country the solution of the social problem demands the substitution of a conscious social ideal for the earlier instinctive homogeneity of the American nation. That homogeneity has disappeared never to return. We should not want it to return, because it was dependent upon too many sacrifices of individual purpose and achievement. But a democracy cannot dispense with the solidarity which it imparted to American life, and in one way or another such solidarity must be restored. There is only one way in which it can be restored, and that is by means of a democratic social ideal, which shall give consistency to American social life, without entailing any essential sacrifice of desirable individual and class distinctions. I have used the word "restoration" to describe this binding and healing process; but the consistency which would result from the loyal realization of a comprehensive coherent democratic social ideal would differ radically from the earlier American homogeneity of feeling. The solidarity which it would impart to American society would have its basis in feeling and its results in good fellowship; but it must always remain a promise and constructive ideal rather than a finished

performance. The social problem must, as long as societies continue to endure, be solved afresh by almost every
generation; and the one chance of progress depends
both upon an invincible loyalty to a constructive social
ideal and upon a current understanding by the new generation of the actual experience of its predecessors.

6.

Reform and the Reformers

I

Sensible and patriotic Americans have not, of course, tamely and ignobly submitted to the obvious evils of their political and economic condition. There was, indeed, a season when the average good American refused to take these evils seriously. He was possessed by the idea that American life was a stream, which purified itself in the running, and that reformers and critics were merely men who prevented the stream from running free. He looked upon the first spasmodic and ineffective protests with something like contempt. Reformers he appraised as busybodies, who were protesting against the conditions of success in business and politics. He nicknamed them "mugwumps" and continued to vote the regular tickets of his party. There succeeded to this phase of contemptuous dislike a few years, in which he was somewhat bewildered by the increasing evidences of corruption in American politics and lawlessness in American business methods, and during which he occasionally supported some favorite among the several reforming movements. Then a habit of criticism and reform increased with the sense that the evils were both more flagrant and more stubborn than he imagined, until at the present time average well-intentioned Americans are likely to be reformers of one kind or another, while the more intelligent and disinterested of them are pretty sure to vote a "reform" ticket. To stand for a programme of reform has become one of the recognized roads to popularity. The political leaders with the largest personal followings are some kind of reformers. They sit in presidential chairs; they occupy executive mansions; they extort legislation from unwilling politicians; they regulate and abuse the erring corporations; they are coming to control the press; and they are the most aggressive force in American public opinion. The supporters and beneficiaries of existing abuses still control much of the official and practically all the unofficial political and business machinery; but they are less domineering and self-confident than they were. The reformers have both scared and bewildered them. They begin to realize that reform has come to stay, and perhaps even to conquer, while reform itself is beginning to pay the penalty of success by being threatened with deterioration. It has had not only its hero in Theodore Roosevelt, but its specter in William R. Hearst.

In studying the course of the reforming movement during the last twenty-five years, it appears that, while reform has had a history, this history is only beginning. Since 1880, or even 1895 or 1900, it has been transformed in many significant ways. In the beginning it was spasmodic in its outbursts, innocent in its purposes, and narrow in its outlook. It sprang up almost spontaneously in a number of different places and in a number of different detached movements; and its adherents did not look much beyond a victory at a particular election, or the passage of a few remedial laws. Gradually, however, it increased in definiteness, persistence, and comprehensiveness of purpose. The reformers found the need of permanent organization, of constant work, and even within limits, of a positive programme. Their success and their influence upon public opinion increased just in proportion as they began to take their job seriously. Indeed, they have become extremely self-conscious in

relation to their present standing and their future responsibilities. They are beginning to predict the most
abundant results from the "uplift" movement, of which
they are the leaders. They confidently anticipate that
they are destined to make a much more salient and significant contribution to the history of their country than
has been made by any group of political leaders since
the Civil War.

It is in a sense a misnomer to write of "Reform" as
a single thing. Reform is, as a matter of fact, all sorts
of things. The name has been applied to a number of
separate political agitations, which have been started by
different people at different times in different parts of
the country, and these separate movements have secured
very different kinds of support, and have run very different courses. Tariff reform, for instance, was an early
and popular agitation whose peculiarity has consisted in
securing the support of one of the two national parties,
but which in spite of that support has so far made little
substantial progress. Civil service reform, on the other
hand, was the first agitation looking in the direction of
political purification. The early reformers believed that
the eradication of the spoils system would deal a deadly
blow at political corruption and professional politics.
But although they have been fairly successful in establishing the "merit" system in the various public offices,
the results of the reform have not equaled the promises
of its advocates. While it is still an important part of the
programme of reform from the point of view of many
reformers, it has recently been over-shadowed by other
issues. It does not provoke either as much interest as it
did or as much opposition. Municipal reform has, of
course, almost as many centers of agitation as there are
centers of corruption—that is, large municipalities in the
United States. It began as a series of local non-partisan
movements for the enforcement of the laws, the dispos-

session of the "rascals," and the businesslike, efficient administration of municipal affairs; but the reformers discovered in many cases that municipal corruption could not be eradicated without the reform of state politics, and without some drastic purging of the local public service corporations. They have consequently in many cases enlarged the area of their agitation; but in so doing they have become divided among themselves, and their agitation has usually lost its non-partisan character. Finally the agitation against the trusts has developed a confused hodge-podge of harmless and deadly, overlapping and mutually exclusive, remedies, which are the cause of endless disagreements. Of course they are all for the People and against the Octopus, but beyond this precise and comprehensive statement of the issue, the reformers have endlessly different views about the nature of the disease and the severity of the necessary remedy.

If reform is an ambiguous and many-headed thing, the leading reformers are as far as possible from being a body of men capable of mutual coöperation. They differ almost as widely among themselves as they do from the beneficiaries or supporters of the existing abuses. William R. Hearst, William Travers Jerome, Seth Low, and George B. McClellan are all in their different ways reformers; but they would not constitute precisely a happy family. Indeed, Mr. Hearst, who in his own opinion is the only immaculate reformer, is, in the eyes of his fellow-reformers, as dangerous a public enemy as the most corrupt politician or the most unscrupulous millionaire. Any reformer who, like Mr. William Jennings Bryan, proclaims views which are in some respects more than usually radical, comes in for heartier denunciation from his brothers in reform than he does from the conservatives. Each of our leading reformers is more or less a man on horseback, who is seeking to popularize a particular brand of reform, and who is inclined to doubt whether the other brands are available for public consumption without rigid inspection. Consequently, the party of reform is broken up into a number of insurgent personalities. "The typical reformer," says the late Alfred Hodder in a book written in praise of Mr. William Travers Jerome, "The typical reformer is a 'star,' and a typical reform administration is usually a company of stars," and a most amusing piece of special pleading is the reasoning whereby the same author seeks to prove that Mr. Jerome himself is or was not a "star" performer. The preference which individual performers have shown for leading parts is in itself far from being a bad thing, but the lack of "team play" has none the less diminished the efficiency of reform as a practical and prosperous political agitation.

These disagreements are the more significant, because the different "star" reformers are sufficiently united upon their statement of fundamental principles. They all of them agree to conceive of reform as at bottom a moral protest and awakening, which seeks to enforce the violated laws and to restore the American political and economic system to its pristine purity and vigor. From their point of view certain abuses have become unwholesomely conspicuous, because the average American citizen has been a little lethargic, and allowed a few of his more energetic and unscrupulous fellow-citizens to exploit for selfish purposes the opportunities of American business and politics. The function of reform, consequently, is to deprive these parasites of their peculiar opportunities. Few reformers anticipate now that this task will be easily or quickly accomplished. They are coming to realize that the abuses are firmly intrenched, and a prolonged siege as well as constant assaults are necessary for final success. Some reformers are even tending to the opinion that a tradition of reform and succession of reformers will be demanded for the vigilant protection of the American political and economic system against abuse. But the point is the agreement among practical reformers that reform means at bottom no more than moral and political purification. It may, indeed, bring with it the necessity of a certain amount of reorganization; but such reorganization will aim merely at the improvement of the existing political and economic machinery. Present and future reformers must cleanse, oil, and patch a piece of economic and political machinery, which in all essentials is adequate to its purpose. The millionaire and the trust have appropriated too many of the economic opportunities formerly enjoyed by the people. The corrupt politician has usurped too much of the power which should be exercised by the people. Reform must restore to the people the opportunities and power of which they have been deprived.

An agitation of this kind, deriving as it does its principles and purposes from the very source of American democracy, would seem to deserve the support of all good Americans: and such support was in the beginning expected. Reformers have always tended to believe that their agitation ought to be and essentially was non-partisan. They considered it inconceivable either that patriotic American citizens should hesitate about restoring the purity and vigor of American institutions, or such an object should not appeal to every disinterested man, irrespective of party. It was a fight between the law and its violators, between the Faithful and the Heretic, between the Good and the Wicked. In such a fight there was, of course, only one side to take. It was not to be doubted that the honest men, who constitute, of course, an enormous majority of the "plain people," would rally to the banners of reform. The rascals would be turned out; the people would regain their economic opportunities and political rights; and the American democracy would pursue undefiled its triumphant career of legalized prosperity.

These hopes have never been realized. Reform has rarely been non-partisan—except in the minds of its more innocent advocates. Now and then an agitation for municipal reform in a particular city will suffer a spasm of non-partisanship; but the reformers soon develop such lively differences among themselves, that they separate into special groups or else resume their regular party ties. Their common conception of reform as fundamentally a moral awakening, which seeks to restore the American political and economic system to its early purity and vigor, does not help them to unity of action or to unity in the framing of a remedial policy. Different reformers really mean something very different by the traditional system, from which American practice has departed and which they propose to restore. Some of them mean thereby a condition of spiritual excellence, which will be restored by a sort of politico-moral revivalism and which will somehow make the results of divine and popular election coincide. Others mean nothing more than the rigid enforcement of existing laws. Still others mean a new legal expression of the traditional democratic principle, framed to meet the new political and social conditions; but the reformers who agree upon this last conception of reform disagree radically as to what the new legal expression should be. The traditional system, which they seek to restore, assumes almost as many shapes as there are leading reformers; and as the reforming movement develops, the disagreements among the reformers become more instead of less definite and acute.

The inability of the reformers to coöperate in action or to agree as to the application of their principles is in part merely a natural result of their essential work.

Reformers are primarily protestants; and protestants are naturally insubordinate. They have been protesting against the established order in American business and politics. Their protest implies a certain degree of moral and intellectual independence, which makes them dislike to surrender or subordinate their own personal opinions and manner of action. Such independence is a new and refreshing thing, which has suddenly made American politics much more interesting and significant than it has been at any time since the Civil War. It has a high value wholly apart from its immediate political results. It means that the American people are beginning a new phase of their political experience,—a phase in which there will be room for a much freer play of individual ability and character. Inevitably the sudden realization by certain exceptional politicians that they have a right to be individuals, and that they can take a strong line of their own in politics without being disqualified for practical political association with their fellow-countrymen—such a new light could hardly break without tempting the performers to over-play the part. The fact that they have over-played their parts, and have wasted time and energy over meaningless and unnecessary disagreements is not in itself a matter of much importance. The great majority of them are disinterested and patriotic men, who will not allow in the long run either personal ambition or political crotchets to prevent them from coöperating for the good of the cause.

Unfortunately, however, neither public spirit nor patriotism will be sufficient to bring them effectively together—any more than genuine excellence of intention and real public spirit enabled patriotic Americans to coöperate upon a remedial policy during the years immediately preceding the Civil War. The plain fact is that the traditional American political system, which so many good reformers wish to restore by some sort of reforming revivalism, is just as much responsible for the existing political and economic abuses as the Constitution was responsible for the evil of slavery. As long, consequently, as reform is considered to be a species of higher conservatism, the existing abuses can no more be frankly faced and fully understood than the Whig leaders were able to face and understand the full meaning and consequences of any attempt on the part of a democracy to keep house with slavery. The first condition of a better understanding and a more efficient coöperation among the reforming leaders is a better understanding of the meaning of reform and the function of reformers. They will never be united on the basis of allegiance to the traditional American political creed, because that creed itself is overflowing with inconsistencies and ambiguities, which afford a footing for almost every extreme of radicalism and conservatism; and in case they persist in the attempt to reform political and economic abuses merely by a restoration of earlier conditions and methods, they will be compromising much that is good in the present economic and political organization without recovering that which was good in the past.

II   The Logic of Reform

The prevailing preconception of the reformers, that the existing evils and abuses have been due chiefly to the energy and lack of scruple with which business men and politicians have taken advantage of the good but easy-going American, and that a general increase of moral energy, assisted by some minor legal changes, will restore the balance,—such a conception of the situation is less than half true. No doubt, the "plain people" of the United States have been morally indifferent, and have allowed unscrupulous special interests to usurp too much power; but that is far from being the whole story. The unscrupulous energy of the "Boss" or the "tainted" millionaire is vitally related to the moral indifference of the "plain people." Both of them have been encouraged to believe by the nature of our traditional ideas and institutions that a man could be patriotic without being either public-spirited or disinterested. The democratic state has been conceived as a piece of political machinery, which existed for the purpose of securing certain individual rights and opportunities—the expectation being that the greatest individual happiness would be thereby promoted, and one which harmonized with the public interest. Consequently when the "Boss" and the "tainted" millionaire took advantage of this situation to secure for themselves an unusually large amount of political and economic power, they were putting into practice an idea which traditionally had been entirely respectable, and which during the pioneer period had not worked badly. On the other hand, when, the mass of American voters failed to detect the danger of such usurpation until it had gone altogether too far, they, too, were not without warrant for their lethargy and callousness. They, too, in a smaller way had considered the American political and economic system chiefly as a system framed for their individual benefit, and it did not seem sportsmanlike to turn and rend their more successful competitors, until they were told that the "trusts" and the "Bosses" were violating the sacred principle of equal rights. Thus the abuses of which we are complaining are not weeds which have been allowed to spring up from neglect, and which can be eradicated by a man with a hoe. They are cultivated plants, which, if not precisely specified in the plan of the American political and economic garden, have at least been encouraged by traditional methods of cultivation.

The fact that this dangerous usurpation of power has been accomplished partly by illegal methods has blinded many reformers to two considerations, which have a vital relation to both the theory and the practice of reform. Violation of the law was itself partly the result of conflicting and unwise state legislation, and for this reason did not seem very heinous either to its perpetrators or to public opinion. But even if the law had not been violated, similar results would have followed. Under the traditional American system, with the freedom permitted to the individual, with the restriction placed on the central authority, and with its assumption of a substantial identity between the individual and the public interest—under such a system unusually energetic and unscrupulous men were bound to seize a kind and an amount of political and economic power which was not entirely wholesome. They had a license to do so; and if they had failed to take advantage thereof, their failure would have been an indication, not of disinterestedness or moral impeccability, but of sheer weakness and inefficiency.

How utterly confusing it is, consequently, to consider reform as equivalent merely to the restoration of the American democracy to a former condition of purity and excellence! Our earlier political and economic condition was not at its best a fit subject for any great amount of complacency. It cannot be restored, even if we would; and the public interest has nothing to gain by its restoration. The usurpation of power by "trusts" and "Bosses" is more than anything else an expression of a desirable individual initiative and organizing ability—which have been allowed to become dangerous and partly corrupt, because of the incoherence and the lack of purpose and responsibility in the traditional American political and economic system. A "purification" might well destroy the good with the evil; and even if it were successful in eradicating certain abuses, would only prepare the way for the outbreak in another form of the tendency towards individual aggrandizement and social classification. No amount of moral energy, directed merely towards the enforcement of the laws, can possibly avail to accomplish any genuine or lasting reform. It is the laws themselves which are partly at fault, and still more at fault is the group of ideas and traditional practices behind the laws.

Reformers have failed for the most part to reach a correct diagnosis of existing political and economic abuses, because they are almost as much the victim of perverted, confused, and routine habits of political thought as is the ordinary politician. They have eschewed the tradition of partisan conformity in reference to controverted political questions, but they have not eschewed a still more insidious tradition of conformity—the tradition that a patriotic American citizen must not in his political thinking go beyond the formulas consecrated in the sacred American writings. They adhere to the stupefying rule that the good Fathers of the Republic relieved their children from the necessity of vigorous, independent, or consistent thinking in political matters,—that it is the duty of their loyal children to repeat the sacred words and then await a miraculous consummation of individual and social prosperity. Accordingly, all the leading reformers begin by piously reiterating certain phrases about equal rights for all and special privileges for none, and of government of the people, by the people, and for the people. Having in this way proved their fundamental political orthodoxy, they proceed to interpret the phrases according to their personal, class, local, and partisan preconceptions and interests. They have never stopped to inquire whether the principle of equal rights in its actual embodiment in American institutional and political practice has not been partly responsible for some of the existing abuses, whether it is either a safe or sufficient platform for a reforming movement, and whether its continued proclamation as the fundamental political principle of a democracy will help or hinder the higher democratic consummation. Their unquestioning orthodoxy in this respect has made them faithless both to their own personal interest as reformers and to the cause of reform. Reform exclusively as a moral protest and awakening is condemned to sterility. Reformers exclusively as moral protestants and purifiers are condemned to misdirected effort, to an illiberal puritanism, and to personal self-stultification. Reform must necessarily mean an intellectual as well as a moral challenge; and its higher purposes will never be accomplished unless it is accompanied by a masterful and jubilant intellectual awakening.

All Americans, whether they are professional politicians or reformers, "predatory" millionaires or common people, political philosophers or schoolboys, accept the principle of "equal rights for all and special privileges for none" as the absolutely sufficient rule of an American democratic political system. The platforms of both parties testify on its behalf. Corporation lawyers and their clients appear frequently to believe in it. Tammany offers tribute to it during every local political campaign in New York. A Democratic Senator, in the intervals between his votes for increased duties on the products of his state, declares it to be the summary of all political wisdom. The fact that Mr. Bryan incorporates it in most of his speeches does not prevent Mr. Hearst from keeping it standing in type for the purpose of showing how very American the *American* can be. The fact that Mr. Hearst has appropriated it with the American flag as belonging peculiarly to himself has not prevented Mr. Roosevelt from explaining the whole of his policy of reform as at the bottom an attempt to restore a "Square Deal"—that is, a condition of equal rights and non-existing privileges. More radical reformers find the same principle equally useful for their own purposes. Mr. Frederic C. Howe, in his "Hope of Democracy," bases an elaborate scheme of municipal socialism exclusively upon it. Mr. William Smythe, in his "Constructive Democracy," finds warrant in the same principle for the immediate purchase by the central government of the railway and "trust" franchises. Mr. Henry George, Jr., in his "Menace of Privilege," asserts that the plain American citizen can never enjoy equality of rights as long as land, mines, railroad rights of way and terminals, and the like remain in the hands of private owners. The collectivist socialists are no less certain that the institution of private property necessarily gives some men an unjust advantage over others. There is no extreme of radicalism or conservatism, of individualism or socialism, of Republicanism or Democracy, which does not rest its argument on this one consummate principle.

In this respect, the good American finds himself in a situation similar to that with which he was confronted before the Civil War. At that time, also, Abolitionist and slave-holder, Republican and pioneer Democrat, each of them declared himself to be the interpreter of the true democratic doctrine; and no substantial progress could be made towards the settlement of the question, until public opinion had been instructed as to the real meaning of democracy in relation to the double-headed problem of slavery and states' rights. It required the utmost intellectual courage and ability to emancipate the conception of democracy from the illusions and confusions of thought which enabled Davis, Douglas, and Garrison all to pose as impeccable democrats; and at the present time reformers need to devote as much ability and more courage to the task of framing a fitting creed for a reformed and reforming American democracy.

The political lessons of the anti-slavery and states' rights discussions may not be of much obvious assistance in thinking out such a creed; but they should at least help the reformers to understand the methods whereby the purposes of a reformed democracy can be achieved. No progress was made towards the solution of the slavery question until the question itself was admitted to be national in scope, and its solution a national responsibility. No substantial progress had been made in the direction of reform until it began to be understood that here, also, a national responsibility existed, which demanded an exercise of the powers of the central government. Reform is both meaningless and powerless unless the Jeffersonian principle of non-interference is abandoned. The experience of the last generation plainly shows that the American economic and social system cannot be allowed to take care of itself, and that the automatic harmony of the individual and the public interest, which is the essence of the Jeffersonian democratic creed, has proved to be an illusion. Interference with the natural course of individual and popular action there must be in the public interest; and such interference must at least be sufficient to accomplish its purposes. The house of the American democracy is again by way of being divided against itself, because the national interest has not been consistently asserted as against special and local interests; and again, also, it can be reunited only by being partly reconstructed on better foundations. If reform does not and cannot mean restoration, it is bound to mean reconstruction.

The reformers have come partly to realize that the Jeffersonian policy of drift must be abandoned. They no longer expect the American ship of state by virtue of its own righteous framework to sail away to a safe harbor in the Promised Land. They understand that there must be a vigorous and conscious assertion of the public as opposed to private and special interests, and that the American people must to a greater extent than they have in the past subordinate the latter to the former. They behave as if the American ship of state will hereafter require careful steering; and a turn or two at the wheel has given them some idea of the course they must set. On the other hand, even the best of them have not learned the name of its ultimate destination, the full difficulties of the navigation, or the stern discipline which may eventually be imposed upon the ship's crew. They do not realize, that is, how thoroughly Jeffersonian individualism must be abandoned for the benefit of a genuinely individual and social consummation; and they do not realize how dangerous and fallacious a chart their cherished principle of equal rights may well become. In reviving the practice of vigorous national action for the achievement of a national purpose, the better reformers have, if they only knew it, been looking in the direction of a much more trustworthy and serviceable political principle. The assumption of such a responsibility implies the rejection of a large part of the Jeffersonian creed, and a renewed attempt to establish in its place the popularity of its Hamiltonian rival. On the other hand, it involves no less surely the transformation of Hamiltonianism into a thoroughly democratic political principle. None of these inferences have, however, as yet been generally drawn, and no leading reformer has sought to give reform its necessary foundation of positive, political principle.

Only a very innocent person will expect reformers to be convinced of such a novel notion of reform by mere assertion, no matter how emphatic, or by argument, no matter how conclusive. But if, as I have said, reform actually implies a criticism of traditional American ideas, and a more responsible and more positive conception of democracy, these implications will necessarily be revealed in the future history of the reforming agitation. The reformers who understand will be assisted by the logic of events, whereas those who cannot and will not understand will be thwarted by the logic of events. Gradually (it may be anticipated) reformers, who dare to criticise and who are not afraid to reconstruct will be sharply distinguished from reformers who believe reform to be a species of higher conservatism. The latter will be forced where they belong into the ranks of the supporters and beneficiaries of the existing system; and the party of genuine reform will be strengthened by their departure. On the other hand, the sincere and thorough-going reformers can hardly avoid a division into two divergent groups. One of these groups will stick faithfully to the principle of equal rights and to the spirit of the true Jeffersonian faith. It will seek still further to undermine the representative character of American institutions, to deprive official leadership of any genuine responsibility, and to cultivate individualism at the expense of individual and national integrity. The second group, on the other hand, may learn from experience that the principle of equal rights is a dangerous weapon in the hands of factious and merely revolutionary agitators, and even that such a principle is only a partial and poverty-stricken statement of the purpose of a democratic polity. The logic of its purposes will compel it to favor the principle of responsible representative government, and it will seek to forge institutions which will endow responsible political government with renewed life. Above all, it may discover that the attempt to unite the Hamiltonian principle of national political responsibility and efficiency with a frank democratic purpose will give a new meaning to the Hamiltonian system of political ideas and a new power to democracy.

III William J. Bryan as a Reformer

One would hardly dare to assert that such a future for the reforming agitation is already prophesied by the history of reform; but the divergence between different classes of the reformers is certainly widening, and some such alignment can already be distinguished. Hitherto I have been classing reformers together and have been occupied in pointing out the merits and failings which they possess in common. Such a method of treatment hardly does justice to the significance of their mutual disagreements, or to the individual value of their several personalities and points of view. In many instances their disagreements are meaningless, and are not the result of any genuine conviction; but in other instances they do represent a relevant and significant conflict of ideas. It remains to be seen, consequently, what can be made out of their differences of opinion and policy, and whether they point in the direction of a gradual transformation of the agitation for reform. For this purpose I shall select a number of leading reformers whose work has been most important, and whose individual opinions are most significant, and seek some sort of an appraisal both of the comparative value of their work and of the promise of their characteristic ideas. The men who naturally suggest themselves for this purpose are William J. Bryan, William Travers Jerome, William Randolph Hearst, and Theodore Roosevelt. Each of these gentlemen throughout his public life has consistently stood for reform of one kind or another; and together they include almost every popular brand or phase thereof. Reform as a practical agitation is pretty well exhausted by the points of view of these four gentlemen. They exhibit its weakness and its strength, its illusions and its good intentions, its dangerous and its salutary tendencies.

Be it remarked at the outset that three of these gentle-men call themselves Democrats, while the fourth has been the official leader of the Republican party. The distinction to be made on this ground is sufficiently obvious, but it is also extremely important. The three Democrats differ among themselves in certain very im-portant respects, and these differences will receive their full share of attention. Nevertheless the fact that under ordinary circumstances they affiliate with the Demo-cratic party and accept its traditions gives them certain common characteristics, and (it must be added) subjects them to certain common disabilities. On the other hand the fact that Theodore Roosevelt, although a reformer from the very beginning of his public life, has resolutely adhered to the Republican partisan organization and has accepted its peculiar traditions,—this fact, also, has largely determined the character and the limits of his work. These limits are plainly revealed in the opin-ions, the public policy, and the public action of the four typical reformers; and attempt to appraise the value of their individual opinions and their personalities must be constantly checked by a careful consideration of the ad-vantages or disadvantages which they have enjoyed or suffered from their partisan ties.

Mr. William J. Bryan is a fine figure of a man—amiable, winning, disinterested, courageous, enthusi-astic, genuinely patriotic, and after a fashion liberal in spirit. Although he hails from Nebraska, he is in temper-ament a Democrat of the Middle Period—a Democrat of the days when organization in business and politics did not count for as much as it does to-day, and when excellent intentions and noble sentiments embodied in big flowing words were the popular currency of Ameri-can democracy. But while an old-fashioned Democrat in temperament, he has become in ideas a curious mixture

of traditional democracy and modern Western radicalism; and he can, perhaps, be best understood as a Democrat of both Jeffersonian and Jacksonian tendencies,
who has been born a few generations too late. He is
honestly seeking to deal with contemporary American
political problems in the spirit, if not according to the
letter, of traditional democracy; but though he is making
a gallant fight and a brave show, his efforts are not being
rewarded with any conspicuous measure of success.

Mr. Bryan has always been a reformer, but his programme of reform has always been ill conceived. His
first conspicuous appearance in public life in the Democratic Convention of 1806 was occasioned by the acute
and widespread economic distress among his own people west of the Mississippi; and the means whereby he
sought to remedy that distress, viz. by a change in the
currency system, which would enable the Western debt-
ors partly to repudiate their debts, was a genuine result
of Jacksonian economic ideas. The Jacksonian Democracy, being the product of agricultural life, and being inexperienced in the complicated business of finance, has
always relished financial heresies. Bryan's first campaign
was, consequently, a new assertion of a time-honored
tendency of his party; and in other respects, also, he
exhibited a lingering fealty to its older traditions. Reformer though he be, he has never been much interested
in civil service reform, or in any agitations looking in
the direction of the diminution of the influence of the
professional politician. The reforms for which he has
stood have been economic, and he has had little sympathy with any thorough-going attempt to disturb even
such an equivocally Democratic institution as the spoils
system. Yet his lack of sympathy with this aspect of reform was not due to any preference for corruption. It
must be traced to a persistence of the old Democratic
prejudice that administrative specialization, like other

kinds of expert service, implied a discrimination against the average Democrat.

After the revival of prosperity among his own people had shown that partial repudiation was not the only cure for poverty, Mr. Bryan fought his second campaign chiefly on the issue of imperialism, and again met with defeat. But in this instance his platform was influenced more by Jeffersonian than Jacksonian ideas. The Jacksonian Democracy had always been expansionist in disposition and policy, and under the influence of their nationalism they had lost interest in Jefferson's humanitarianism. In this matter, however, Mr. Bryan has shown more sympathy with the first than with the second phase of the Democratic tradition; and in making this choice he was undoubtedly more faithful to the spirit and the letter of the Democratic creed than were the expansionist Democrats of the Middle Period. The traditional American democracy has frequently been national in feeling, but it has never been national in idea and purpose. In the campaign of 1900 Mr. Bryan committed himself and his party to an anti-national point of view; and no matter how well intentioned and consistent he was in so doing, he made a second mistake, even more disastrous than the first. In seeking to prevent his countrymen from asserting their national interest beyond their own continent, he was also opposing in effect the resolute assertion of the national interest in domestic affairs. He stamped himself, that is, as an anti-nationalist, and his anti-nationalism has disqualified him for effective leadership of the party of reform.

Mr. Bryan's anti-nationalism is peculiarly embarrassing to his political efficiency just because he is, as I have indicated, in many of his ideas an advanced contemporary radical. He is, indeed, more of a radical than any other political leader of similar prominence; and his radicalism is the result of a sincere and a candid attempt to think out a satisfactory solution of the contemporary economic and political problems. As a result of these reflections he dared to advocate openly and unequivocally the public ownership of the railway system of the country; and he has proposed, also, a measure of Federal regulation of corporations, conducting an inter-state business, much more drastic than that of Mr. Roosevelt. These proposed increases of Federal responsibility and power would have been considered outrageous by an old-fashioned Democrat; and they indicate on the part of Mr. Bryan an unusually liberal and courageous mind. But the value and effect of his radicalism is seriously impaired by the manner in which it is qualified. He proposes in one breath enormous increases of Federal power and responsibility, and in the next betrays the old Democratic distrust of effective national organization. He is willing to grant power to the Federal authorities, but he denies them any confidence, because of the democratic tradition of an essential conflict between political authority, particularly so far as it is centralized, and the popular interest. He is incapable of adapting his general political theories to his actual political programme; and, consequently, the utmost personal enthusiasm on his part and great power of effective political agitation cannot give essential coherence, substantial integrity, or triumphant effect to his campaigns.

The incoherence of his political thinking is best exemplified by the way in which he proposed to nationalize the American railway system. His advocacy of public ownership was the most courageous act of his political career; but he soon showed that he was prepared neither to insist upon such a policy nor even to carry it to a logical conclusion. Almost as soon as the words were out of his mouth, he became horrified at his own audacity and sought to mitigate its effects. He admitted that the centralization of so much power was dangerous, and he sought to make these dangers less by proposing that the states appropriate the railroads operating within the boundaries of one state, and the central government, only the large inter-state systems. But this qualification destroyed the effect of his Federalist audacity. The inter-state railroads constitute such an enormous percentage of the total mileage of the country that if centralized governmental control was dangerous for all the railroads of the country, it would be almost equally dangerous for that proportion of the railway mileage operated as part of inter-state systems. In the one and the same speech, that is, Mr. Bryan placed himself on record as a radical centralizer of economic and political power and as a man who was on general principles afraid of centralization and opposed to it. No wonder public opinion did not take his proposal seriously, and no wonder he himself has gradually dropped it out of his practical programme.

The confusion and inconsistency of Mr. Bryan's own thinking is merely the reflection of the confusion and inconsistency resident in the creed of his party. It is particularly conspicuous in his case, because he is, as I have intimated, a sincere and within limits a candid thinker; but Jeffersonian and Jacksonian Democrats alike have always distrusted and condemned the means whereby alone the underlying purposes of democracy can be fulfilled. Mr. Bryan is in no respect more genuinely Democratic than in his incoherence. The remedial policy which he proposes for the ills of the American political body are meaningless, unless sustained by faith in the ability of the national political organization to promote the national welfare. He needs for the success and integrity of his own policy a conviction which his traditions prevent him from entertaining. He is possessed by the time-honored Democratic dislike of organization and of the faith in expert skill, in specialized training, and in large personal opportunities and responsibilities which are implied by a trust in organization. Of course he himself would deny that he was the enemy of anything which made towards human betterment, for it is characteristic of the old-fashioned Democrats verbally to side with the angels, but at the same time to insist on clipping their wings. His fundamental prejudice against efficient organization and personal independence is plainly betrayed by his opinions in relation to institutional reform—which are absolutely those of a Democrat of the Middle Period. He is on record in favor of destroying the independence of the Federal judiciary by making it elective, of diminishing the authority of the President by allowing him only a suspensive veto on legislation, and of converting representative assemblies into a machinery, like that of the old French Parliaments, for merely registering the Sovereign will. Faith in the people and confidence in popular government means to Mr. Bryan an utter lack of faith in those personal instruments whereby such rule can be endowed with foresight, moderation, and direction. Confidence in the average man, that is, means to him distrust in the exceptional man, or in any sort of organization which bestows on the exceptional man an opportunity equal to his ability and equipment. He stands for the sacrifice of the individual to the popular average; and the perpetuation of such a sacrifice would mean ultimate democratic degeneration.

IV William Travers Jerome as a Reformer

Mr. William Travers Jerome has not so assured a rank in the hierarchy of reformers as he had a few years ago, but his work and his point of view remain typical and significant. Unlike Mr. Bryan, he is in temperament and sympathies far from being an old-fashioned Democrat.

He is, as his official expositor, the late Mr. Alfred Hodder, says, "a typical American of the new time." No old-fashioned Democrat would have smoked cigarettes, tossed dice in public for drinks, and "handed out" slang to his constituents; and his unconventionality in these respects is merely an occasional expression of a novel, individual, and refreshing point of view. Mr. Jerome alone among American politicians has made a specialty of plain speaking. He has revolted against the tradition in our politics which seeks to stop every leak with a good intention and plaster every sore with a "decorative phrase." He has, says Mr. Hodder, "a partly Gallic passion for intellectual veracity, for a clear recognition of the facts before him, however ugly, and a wholly Gallic hatred of hypocrisy." It is Mr. Jerome's intellectual veracity, his somewhat conscious and strenuous ideal of plain speaking, which has been his personal contribution to the cause of reform; and he is right in believing it to be a very important contribution. The effective work of reform, as has already been pointed out, demands on the part of its leaders the intellectual virtues of candor, consistency, and a clear recognition of facts. In Mr. Jerome's own case his candor and his clear recognition of facts have been used almost exclusively in the field of municipal reform. He has vigorously protested against existing laws which have been passed in obedience to a rigorous puritanism, which, because of their defiance of stubborn facts, can scarcely be enforced, and whose statutory existence merely provides an opportunity for the "grafter." He has clearly discerned that in seeking the amendment of such laws he is obliged to fight, not merely an unwise statute, but an erroneous, superficial, and hypocritical state of mind. Although it may have been his own official duty as district attorney to see that certain laws are enforced and to prosecute the law breakers, he fully realizes that municipal reform at least will never attain its ends until the public—the respect-able, well-to-do, church-going public—is converted to an abandonment of what Mr. Hodder calls admin-istrative lying. Consequently his intellectual candor is more than a personal peculiarity—more even than an extremely effective method of popular agitation. It is the expression of a deeper aspect of reform, which many respectable reformers, not merely ignore, but fear and reprobate,—an aspect of reform which can never pre-vail until the reformers themselves are subjected to a process of purgation and education.

It has happened, however, that Mr. Jerome's reputa-tion and successes have been won in the field of local politics; and, unfortunately, as soon as he transgressed the boundaries of that field, he lost his efficiency, his insight, and, to my mind, his interest. Only a year after he was elected to the district attorneyship of New York County, in spite of the opposition both of Tammany and William R. Hearst, he offered himself as a candidate for the Democratic gubernatorial nomination of New York on the comprehensive platform of his oath of office; but in the larger arena his tactics proved to be ineffective, and his recent popularity of small avail. He cut no figure at all in the convention, and a very insignificant one out-side. Neither was there any reason to be surprised at this result. In municipal politics he stood for an ideal and a method of agitation which was both individual and of great value. In state and national politics he stood for nothing individual, for nothing of peculiar value, for no specific group of ideas or scheme of policy. The an-nouncement that a candidate's platform consists of his oath of office doubtless has a full persuasive sound to many Americans; but it was none the less on Mr. Je-rome's part an inept and meaningless performance. He was bidding for support merely on the ground that he was an honest man who proposed to keep his word; but honesty and good faith are qualities which the public have a right to take for granted in their officials, and no candidate can lay peculiar claim to them without becoming politically sanctimonious. Mr. Hearst's strength consisted in the fact that he had for years stood for a particular group of ideas and a particular attitude of mind towards the problems of state and national politics, while Mr. Jerome's weakness consisted in the fact that he had never really tried to lead public opinion in relation to state and national political problems, and that he was obliged to claim support on the score of personal moral superiority to his opponent. The moral superiority may be admitted; but alone it never would and never should contribute to his election. In times like these a reformer must identify a particular group of remedial measures with his public personality. The public has a right to know in what definite ways a reformer's righteousness is to be made effective; and Mr. Jerome has never taken any vigorous and novel line in relation to the problems of state and national politics. When he speaks on those subjects, he loses his vivacity, and betrays in his thinking a tendency to old-fashioned Democracy far beyond that of Mr. Bryan. He becomes in his opinions eminently respectable and tolerably dull, which is, as the late Mr. Alfred Hodder could have told him, quite out of keeping with the part of a "New American."

Mr. Jerome has never given the smallest evidence of having taken serious independent thought on our fundamental political problems. In certain points of detail respecting general political questions he has shown a refreshing freedom from conventional illusions; but, so far as I know, no public word has ever escaped him, which indicates that he has applied his "ideal of intellectual veracity," "his Gallic instinct for consistency," to the creed of his own party. When confronted by the fabric of traditional Jeffersonian Democracy, his mind, like that of so many other Democrats, is immediately lulled into repose. In one of his speeches, for instance, he has referred to his party as essentially the party of "liberal ideas," and he was much praised by the anti-Hearst newspapers for this consoling description; but it can hardly be considered as an illustration of Mr. Jerome's "intellectual veracity." If by "liberal ideas" one means economic and political heresies, such as nullification, "squatter" sovereignty, secession, free silver, and occasional projects of repudiation, then, indeed, the Democracy has been a party of "liberal ideas." But heresies of this kind are not the expression of liberal thought; they are the result of various phases of local political and economic discontent. When a group of Democrats become "liberal," it usually means that they are doing a bad business, or are suffering from a real or supposed injury. But if by "liberal" we mean, not merely radical and subversive, but progressive national ideas, the application of the adjective to the Democratic party is attended with certain difficulties. In the course of American history what measure of legislation expressive of a progressive national idea can be attributed to the Democratic party? At times it has been possessed by certain revolutionary tendencies; at other times it has been steeped in Bourbon conservatism. At present it is alternating between one and the other, according to the needs and opportunities of the immediate political situation. It is trying to find room within its hospitable folds for both Alton B. Parker and William J. Bryan, and it has such an appetite for inconsistencies that it may succeed. But in that event one would expect some symptoms of uneasiness on the part of a Democratic reformer with "Gallic clearness and consistency of mind, with an instinct for consistency, and a hatred of hypocrisy."

V William R. Hearst as a Reformer

The truth is that Mr. William R. Hearst offers his countrymen a fair expression of the kind of "liberal ideas"
proper to the creed of democracy. In respect to patriotism and personal character Mr. Bryan is a better
example of the representative Democrat than is Mr.
Hearst; but in the tendency and spirit of his agitation for
reform Hearst more completely reveals the true nature
of Democratic "liberalism." When Mr. Lincoln Steffens
asserts on the authority of the "man of mystery" himself that one of Hearst's mysterious actions has been a
profound and searching study of Jeffersonian doctrine,
I can almost bring myself to believe the assertion. The
radicalism of Hearst is simply an unscrupulous expression of the radical element in the Jeffersonian tradition.
He bases his whole agitation upon the sacred idea of
equal rights for all and special privileges for none, and
he indignantly disclaims the taint of socialism. His specific remedial proposals do not differ essentially from
those of Mr. Bryan. His methods of agitation and his
popular catch words are an ingenious adaptation of Jefferson to the needs of political "yellow journalism." He
is always an advocate of the popular fact. He always
detests the unpopular word. He approves expansion,
but abhors imperialism. He welcomes any opportunity
for war, but execrates militarism. He wants the Federal
government to crush the trusts by the most drastic legislation, but he is opposed to centralization. The institutional reforms which he favors all of them look in the
direction of destroying what remains of judicial, executive, or legislative independence. The whole programme
is as incoherent as is that of Mr. Bryan; but incoherence
is the least of his faults. Mr. Bryan's inconsistencies are
partly redeemed by his genuine patriotism. The distract-

ing effect of Hearst's inconsistencies is intensified by his factiousness. He is more and less than a radical. He is in temper a revolutionist. The disgust and distrust which he excites is the issue of a wholesome political and social instinct, for the political instincts of the American people are often much sounder than their ideas. Hearst and Hearstism is a living menace to the orderly process of reform and to American national integrity.

Hearst is revolutionary in spirit, because the principle of equal rights itself, in the hand either of a fanatic or a demagogue, can be converted into a revolutionary principle. He considers, as do all reformers, the prevalent inequalities of economic and political power to be violations of that principle. He also believes in the truth of American political individualism, and in the adequacy, except in certain minor respects, of our systems of inherited institutions. How, then, did these inequalities come about? How did the Democratic political system of Jefferson and Jackson issue in undemocratic inequalities? The answer is obviously (and it is an answer drawn by other reformers) that these inequalities are the work of wicked and unscrupulous men. Financial or political pirates of one kind or another have been preying on the guileless public, and by means of their aggressions have perversely violated the supreme law of equal rights. These men must be exposed; they must be denounced as enemies of the people; they must be held up to public execration and scorn; they must become the objects of a righteous popular vengeance. Such are the feelings and ideas which possess the followers of Hearst, and on the basis of which Hearst himself acts and talks. An apparent justification is reached for a systematic vilification of the trusts, the "predatory" millionaires and their supporters; and such vilification has become Hearst's peculiar stock in trade. In effect he treats his opponents very much as the French revolutionary leaders treated

their opponents, so that in case the conflict should become still more embittered, his "reformed" democracy
may resemble the purified republic of which Robespierre
and St. Just dreamed when they sent Desmoulins
and Danton to the guillotine. When he embodies such
ideas and betrays such a spirit, the disputed point as
to Hearst's sincerity sinks into insignificance. A fanatic
sincerely possessed by these ideas is a more dangerous
menace to American national integrity and the Promise
of American democracy than the sheerest demagogue.

The logic of Hearst's agitation is analogous to the
logic of the anti-slavery agitation in 1830, and Hearstism is merely Abolitionism applied to a new material
and translated into rowdy journalism. The Abolitionists, believing as they did, that the institution of slavery
violated an abstract principle of political justice, felt
thereby fully authorized to vilify the Southern slaveholders as far as the resources of the English language
would permit. They attempted to remedy one injustice
by committing another injustice; and by the violence of
their methods they almost succeeded in tearing apart the
good fabric of our national life. Hearst is headed in precisely the same direction. He is doing a radical injustice
to a large body of respectable American citizens who,
like Hearst himself, have merely shown a certain lack of
scruple in taking advantage of the opportunities which
the American political and economic system offers, and
who have been distinguished rather by peculiar ability
and energy than by peculiar selfishness. On a rigid interpretation of the principle of equal rights he may be
justified in holding them up to public execration, just
as the Abolitionists, on the principle that the right to
freedom was a Divine law, might be justified in vilifying
the Southerners. But as a matter of fact we know that
personally neither the millionaire nor the slave-holder
deserves such denunciation; and we ought to know that

the prejudices and passions provoked by language of this kind violate the essential principle both of nationality and democracy. The foundation of nationality is mutual confidence and fair dealing, and the aim of democracy is a better quality of human nature effected by a higher type of human association. Hearstism, like Abolitionism, is the work of unbalanced and vindictive men, and increases enormously the difficulty of the wise and effective cure of the contemporary evils.

Yet Hearst, as little as the millionaires he denounces, is not entirely responsible for himself. Such a responsibility would be too heavy for the shoulders of one man. He has been given to the American people for their sins in politics and economics. His opponents may scold him as much as they please. They may call him a demagogue and a charlatan; they may accuse him of corrupting the public mind and pandering to degrading passions; they may declare that his abusive attacks on the late Mr. McKinley were at least indirectly the cause of that gentleman's assassination; they may, in short, behave and talk as if he were a much more dangerous public enemy than the most "tainted" millionaire or the most corrupt politician. Nevertheless they cannot deprive him or his imitators of the standing to be obtained from the proclamation of a rigorous interpretation of the principle of equal rights. Hearst has understood that principle better than the other reformers, or the conservatives who claim its authority. He has exhibited its disintegrating and revolutionary implications; and he has convinced a large, though fluctuating, following that he is only fighting for justice. He personally may or may not have run his course, but it is manifest that his peculiar application of the principle of equal rights to our contemporary economic and political problems has come to stay. As long as that principle keeps its present high position in the hierarchy of American political ideas, just so long will it afford authority and countenance to agitators like Hearst. He is not a passing danger, which will disappear in case the truly Herculean efforts to discredit him personally continue to be successful. Just as slavery was the ghost in the House of the American Democracy during the Middle Period, so Hearstism is and will remain the ghost in the House of Reform. And the incantation by which it will be permanently exorcised has not yet been publicly phrased.

VI Theodore Roosevelt as a Reformer

It is fortunate, consequently, that one reformer can be named whose work has tended to give reform the dignity of a constructive mission. Mr. Theodore Roosevelt's behavior at least is not dictated by negative conception of reform. During the course of an extremely active and varied political career he has, indeed, been all kinds of a reformer. His first appearance in public life, as a member of the Legislature of New York, coincided with an outbreak of dissatisfaction over the charter of New York City; and Mr. Roosevelt's name was identified with the bills which began the revision of that very much revised instrument. Somewhat later, as one of the Federal Commissioners, Mr. Roosevelt made a most useful contribution to the more effective enforcement of the Civil Service Law. Still later, as Police Commissioner of New York City, he had his experience of reform by means of unregenerate instruments and administrative lies. Then, as Governor of the State of New York, he was instrumental in securing the passage of a law taxing franchises as real property and thus faced for the first time and in a preliminary way the many-headed problem of the trusts. Finally, when an accident placed him in the Presidential chair, he consistently used the power of the Federal government and his own influence and popularity for the purpose of regulating the corporations in what he believed to be the public interest. No other American has had anything like so varied and so intimate an acquaintance with the practical work of reform as has Mr. Roosevelt; and when, after more than twenty years of such experience, he adds to the work of administrative reform the additional task of political and economic reconstruction, his originality cannot be considered the result of innocence. Mr. Roosevelt's reconstructive policy does not go very far in purpose or achievement, but limited as it is, it does tend to give the agitation for reform the benefit of a much more positive significance and a much more dignified task.

Mr. Roosevelt has imparted a higher and more positive significance to reform, because throughout his career he has consistently stood for an idea, from which the idea of reform cannot be separated—namely, the national idea. He has, indeed, been even more of a nationalist than he has a reformer. His most important literary work was a history of the beginning of American national expansion. He has treated all public questions from a vigorous, even from an extreme, national standpoint. No American politician was more eager to assert the national interest against an actual or a possible foreign enemy; and not even William R. Hearst was more resolute to involve his country in a war with Spain. Fortunately, however, his aggressive nationalism did not, like that of so many other statesmen, faint from exhaustion as soon as there were no more foreign enemies to defy. He was the first political leader of the American people to identify the national principle with an ideal of reform. He was the first to realize that an American statesman could no longer really represent the national interest without becoming a reformer. Mr. Grover Cleveland showed a glimmering of the necessity of this affiliation; but he could not carry it far, because, as a sincere traditional Democrat, he could not reach a clear understanding of the meaning either of reform or of nationality. Mr. Roosevelt, however, divined that an American statesman who eschewed or evaded the work of reform came inevitably to represent either special and local interests or else a merely Bourbon political tradition, and in this way was disqualified for genuinely national service. He divined that the national principle involved a continual process of internal reformation; and that the reforming idea implied the necessity of more efficient national organization. Consequently, when he became President of the United States and the official representative of the national interest of the country, he attained finally his proper sphere of action. He immediately began the salutary and indispensable work of nationalizing the reform movement.

The nationalization of reform endowed the movement with new vitality and meaning. What Mr. Roosevelt really did was to revive the Hamiltonian ideal of constructive national legislation. During the whole of the nineteenth century that ideal, while by no means dead, was disabled by associations and conditions from active and efficient service. Not until the end of the Spanish War was a condition of public feeling created, which made it possible to revive Hamiltonianism. That war and its resulting policy of extra-territorial expansion, so far from hindering the process of domestic amelioration, availed, from the sheer force of the national aspirations it aroused, to give a tremendous impulse to the work of national reform. It made Americans more sensitive to a national idea and more conscious of their national responsibilities, and it indirectly helped to place in the Presidential chair the man who, as I have said, represented both the national idea and the spirit of reform. The sincere and intelligent combination of those two ideas is bound to issue in the Hamiltonian practice of constructive national legislation.

Of course Theodore Roosevelt is Hamiltonian with a difference. Hamilton's fatal error consisted in his attempt to make the Federal organization not merely the effective engine of the national interest, but also a bulwark against the rising tide of democracy. The new Federalism or rather new Nationalism is not in any way inimical to democracy. On the contrary, not only does Mr. Roosevelt believe himself to be an unimpeachable democrat in theory, but he has given his fellow-countrymen a useful example of the way in which a college-bred and a well-to-do man can become by somewhat forcible means a good practical democrat. The whole tendency of his programme is to give a democratic meaning and purpose to the Hamiltonian tradition and method. He proposes to use the power and the resources of the Federal government for the purpose of making his countrymen a more complete democracy in organization and practice; but he does not make these proposals, as Mr. Bryan does, gingerly and with a bad conscience. He makes them with a frank and full confidence in an efficient national organization as the necessary agent of the national interest and purpose. He has completely abandoned that part of the traditional democratic creed which tends to regard the assumption by the government of responsibility, and its endowment with power adequate to the responsibility as inherently dangerous and undemocratic. He realizes that any efficiency of organization and delegation of power which is necessary to the promotion of the American national interest must be helpful to democracy. More than any other American political leader, except Lincoln, his devotion both to the national and to the democratic ideas is thorough-going and absolute.

As the founder of a new national democracy, then, his influence and his work have tended to emancipate American democracy from its Jeffersonian bondage. They have tended to give a new meaning to popular government by endowing it with larger powers, more positive responsibilities, and a better faith in human excellence. Jefferson believed theoretically in human goodness, but in actual practice his faith in human nature was exceedingly restricted. Just as the older aristocratic theory had been to justify hereditary political leadership by considering the ordinary man as necessarily irresponsible and incapable, so the early French democrats, and Jefferson after them, made faith in the people equivalent to a profound suspicion of responsible official leadership. Exceptional power merely offered exceptional opportunities for abuse. He refused, as far as he could, to endow special men, even when chosen by the people, with any opportunity to promote the public welfare proportionate to their abilities. So far as his influence has prevailed the government of the country was organized on the basis of a cordial distrust of the man of exceptional competence, training, or independence as a public official. To the present day this distrust remains the sign by which the demoralizing influence of the Jeffersonian democratic creed is most plainly to be traced. So far as it continues to be influential it destroys one necessary condition of responsible and efficient government, and it is bound to paralyze any attempt to make the national organization adequate to the promotion of the national interest. Mr. Roosevelt has exhibited his genuinely national spirit in nothing so clearly as in his endeavor to give to men of special ability, training, and eminence a better opportunity to serve the public. He has not only appointed such men to office, but he has tried to supply them with an administrative machinery which would enable them to use their abilities to the best public advantage; and he has thereby shown a faith in human nature far more edifying and far more genuinely democratic than that of Jefferson or Jackson.

Mr. Roosevelt, however, has still another title to distinction among the brethren of reform. He has not only nationalized the movement, and pointed it in the direction of a better conception of democracy, but he has rallied to its hammer the ostensible, if not the very enthusiastic, support of the Republican party. He has restored that party to some sense of its historic position and purpose. As the party which before the War had insisted on making the nation answerable for the solution of the slavery problem, it has inherited the tradition of national responsibility for the national good; but it was rapidly losing all sense of its historic mission, and, like the Whigs, was constantly using its principle and its prestige as a cloak for the aggrandizement of special interests. At its worst it had, indeed, earned some claim on the allegiance of patriotic Americans by its defense of the fiscal system of the country against Mr. Bryan's well-meant but dangerous attack, and by its acceptance after the Spanish War of the responsibilities of extra-territorial expansion; but there was grave danger that its alliance with the "vested" interests would make it unfaithful to its past as the party of responsible national action. It escaped such a fate only by an extremely narrow margin; and the fact that it did escape is due chiefly to the personal influence of Theodore Roosevelt. The Republican party is still very far from being a wholly sincere agent of the national reform interest. Its official leadership is opposed to reform; and it cannot be made to take a single step in advance except under compulsion. But Mr. Roosevelt probably prevented it from drifting into the position of an anti-reform party—which if it had happened would have meant its ruin, and would have damaged the cause of national reform. A Republican party which was untrue to the principle of national responsibility would have no reason for existence; and the Democratic party, as we have seen, cannot become the party of national responsibility without being faithless to its own creed.

VII The Reformation of Theodore Roosevelt

Before finishing this account of Mr. Roosevelt's services as a reformer, and his place in the reforming movement, a serious objection on the score of consistency must be fairly faced. Even admitting that Mr. Roosevelt has dignified reform by identifying it with a programme of constructive national legislation, does the fundamental purpose of his reforming legislation differ essentially from that of Mr. Bryan or Mr. Hearst? How can he be called the founder of a new national democracy when the purpose of democracy from his point of view remains substantially the Jeffersonian ideal of equal rights for all and special privileges for none? If, in one respect, he has been emancipating American democracy from the Jeffersonian bondage, he has in another respect been tightening the bonds, because he has continued to identify democracy with the legal constitution of a system of insurgent, ambiguous, and indiscriminate individual rights.

The validity of such a criticism from the point of view of this book cannot be disputed. The figure of the "Square Deal," which Mr. Roosevelt has flourished so vigorously in public addresses, is a translation into the American vernacular of the Jeffersonian principle of equal rights; and in Mr. Roosevelt's dissertations upon the American ideal he has expressly disclaimed the notion of any more positive definition of the purpose of American democracy. Moreover, his favorite figure gives a sinister application to his assertions that the principle of equal rights is being violated. If the American people are not getting a "Square Deal," it must mean that they are having the cards stacked against them; and in that case the questions of paramount importance are: Who are stacking the cards? And how can they be punished? These are precisely the questions which Hearst is always asking and Hearstism is seeking to answer. Neither has Mr. Roosevelt himself entirely escaped the misleading effects of his own figure. He has too frequently talked as if his opponents deserved to be treated as dishonest sharpers; and he has sometimes behaved as if his suspicions of unfair play on their part were injuring the coolness of his judgment. But at bottom and in the long run Mr. Roosevelt is too fair-minded a man and too patriotic a citizen to become much the victim of his dangerous figure of the "Square Deal." He inculcates for the most part in his political sermons a spirit, not of suspicion and hatred, but of mutual forbearance and confidence; and his programme of reform attaches more importance to a revision of the rules of the game than to the treatment of the winners under the old rules as one would treat a dishonest gambler.

In truth, Mr. Roosevelt has been building either better than he knows or better than he cares to admit. The real meaning of his programme is more novel and more radical than he himself has publicly proclaimed. It implies a conception of democracy and its purpose very different from the Jeffersonian doctrine of equal rights. Evidences of deep antagonism can be discerned between the Hamiltonian method and spirit, represented by Mr. Roosevelt, and a conception of democracy which makes it consist fundamentally in the practical realization of any system of equal rights. The distrust with which thorough-going Jeffersonians regard Mr. Roosevelt's nationalizing programme is a justifiable distrust, because efficient and responsible national organization

would be dangerous either to or in the sort of democracy which the doctrine of equal rights encourages—a
democracy of suspicious discontent, of selfish claims, of
factious agitation, and of individual and class aggression. A thoroughly responsible and efficient national
organization would be dangerous in such a democracy,
because it might well be captured by some combination
of local individual or class interests; and the only effective way to guard against such a danger is to substitute for the Jeffersonian democracy of individual rights
a democracy of individual and social improvement. A
democracy of individual rights, that is, must either suffer reconstruction by the logic of a process of efficient
national organization, or else it may pervert that organization to the service of its own ambiguous, contradictory, and in the end subversive political purposes. A
better justification for these statements must be reserved
for the succeeding chapter; but in the meantime I will
take the risk asserting that Mr. Roosevelt's nationalism
really implies a democracy of individual and social improvement. His nationalizing programme has in effect
questioned the value of certain fundamental American
ideas, and if Mr. Roosevelt has not himself outgrown
these ideas, his misreading of his own work need not be
a matter of surprise. It is what one would expect from
the prophet of the Strenuous Life.

Mr. Roosevelt has done little to encourage candid
and consistent thinking. He has preached the doctrine
that the paramount and almost the exclusive duty of the
American citizen consists in being a sixty-horse-power
moral motor-car. In his own career his intelligence has
been the handmaid of his will; and the balance between
those faculties, so finely exemplified in Abraham Lincoln, has been destroyed by sheer exuberance of moral
energy. But although his intelligence is merely the servant of his will, it is at least the willing and competent

servant of a single-minded master. If it has not been leavened by the rigorous routine of its work, neither has it been cheapened; and the service has constantly been growing better worth while. During the course of his public career, his original integrity of character has been intensified by the stress of his labors, his achievements, his experiences, and his exhortations. An individuality such as his—wrought with so much consistent purpose out of much variety of experience—brings with it an intellectual economy of its own and a sincere and useful sort of intellectual enlightenment. He may be figured as a Thor wielding with power and effect a sledge-hammer in the cause of national righteousness; and the sympathetic observer, who is not stunned by the noise of the hammer, may occasionally be rewarded by the sight of something more illuminating than a piece of rebellious metal beaten into shape. He may be rewarded by certain unexpected gleams of insight, as if the face of the sledge-hammer were worn bright by hard service and flashed in the sunlight. Mr. Roosevelt sees as far ahead and as much as he needs to see. He has an almost infallible sense of where to strike the next important blow, and even during the ponderous labors of the day he prudently and confidently lays out the task of to-morrow. Thus while he has contributed to the liberation of American intelligence chiefly in the sense that he has given his fellow-countrymen something to think about, he is very far from being a blind, narrow, or unenlightened leader.

Doubtless the only practical road of advance at present is laborious, slow, and not too enlightened. For the time being the hammer is a mightier weapon than the sword or the pen. Americans have the habit of action rather than of thought. Like their forbears in England, they begin to do things, because their common sense tells them that such things have to be done, and then at a later date think over the accomplished fact. A man in public life who told them that their "noble national theory" was ambiguous and distracting, and that many of their popular catchwords were false and exercised a mischievous influence on public affairs, would do so at his own personal risk and cost. The task of plain speaking must be suggested and justified by the achievement of a considerable body of national reconstructive legislation, and must even then devolve largely upon men who have from the political point of view little to gain or to lose by their apparent heresies. The fact, however, that a responsible politician like Mr. Roosevelt must be an example more of moral than of intellectual independence, increases rather than diminishes the eventual importance of consistent thinking and plain speaking as essential parts of the work of political reform. A reforming movement, whose supporters never understand its own proper meaning and purpose, is sure in the end to go astray. It is all very well for Englishmen to do their thinking after the event, because tradition lies at the basis of their national life. But Americans, as a nation, are consecrated to the realization of a group of ideas; and ideas to be fruitful must square both with the facts to which they are applied and with one another. Mr. Roosevelt and his hammer must be accepted gratefully, as the best available type of national reformer; but the day may and should come when a national reformer will appear who can be figured more in the guise of St. Michael, armed with a flaming sword and winged for flight.

7.

Reconstruction: Its Conditions and Purposes

I

The best method of approaching a critical reconstruction of American political ideas will be by means of an analysis of the meaning of democracy. A clear popular understanding of the contents of the democratic principle is obviously of the utmost practical political importance to the American people. Their loyalty to the idea of democracy, as they understand it, cannot be questioned. Nothing of any considerable political importance is done or left undone in the United States, unless such action or inaction can be plausibly defended on democratic grounds; and the only way to secure for the American people the benefit of a comprehensive and consistent political policy will be to derive it from a comprehensive and consistent conception of democracy.

Democracy as most frequently understood is essentially and exhaustively defined as a matter of popular government; and such a definition raises at once a multitude of time-honored, but by no means superannuated, controversies. The constitutional liberals in England, in France, and in this country have always objected to democracy as so understood, because of the possible sanction it affords for the substitution of a popular despotism in the place of the former royal or oligarchic despotisms. From their point of view individual liberty is the greatest blessing which can be secured to a people by a government; and individual liberty can be permanently guaranteed only in case political liberties are in theory and practice subordinated to civil liberties. Popular political institutions constitute a good servant, but a bad master. When introduced in moderation they keep the government of a country in close relation with well-informed public opinion, which is a necessary condition of political sanitation; but if carried too far, such institutions compromise the security of the individual and the integrity of the state. They erect a power in the state, which in theory is unlimited and which constantly tends in practice to dispense with restrictions. A power which is theoretically absolute is under no obligation to respect the rights either of individuals or minorities; and sooner or later such power will be used for the purpose of opposing the individual. The only way to secure individual liberty is, consequently, to organize a state in which the Sovereign power is deprived of any national excuse or legal opportunity of violating certain essential individual rights.

The foregoing criticism of democracy, defined as popular government, may have much practical importance; but there are objections to it on the score of logic. It is not a criticism of a certain conception of democracy, so much as of democracy itself. Ultimate responsibility for the government of a community must reside somewhere. If the single monarch is practically dethroned, as he is by these liberal critics of democracy, some Sovereign power must be provided to take his place. In England Parliament, by means of a steady encroachment on the royal prerogatives, has gradually become Sovereign; but other countries, such as France and the United States, which have wholly dispensed with royalty, cannot, even if they would, make a legislative body Sovereign by the simple process of allowing it to usurp power once enjoyed by the Crown. France did, indeed, after it had finally dispensed with Legitimacy, make two attempts to found governments in which the theory of popular Sovereignty was evaded. The Orleans monarchy, for instance, through the mouths of its friends, denied Sovereignty to the people, without being able to claim it for the King; and this insecurity of its legal framework was an indirect cause of a violent explosion of effective popular Sovereignty in 1848. The apologists for the Second Empire admitted the theory of a Sovereign people, but claimed that the Sovereign power could be safely and efficiently used only in case it were delegated to one Napoleon III—a view the correctness of which the results of the Imperial policy eventually tended to damage. There is in point of fact no logical escape from a theory of popular Sovereignty—once the theory of divinely appointed royal Sovereignty is rejected. An escape can be made, of course, as in England, by means of a compromise and a legal fiction; and such an escape can be fully justified from the English national point of view; but countries which have rejected the royal and aristocratic tradition are forbidden this means of escape—if escape it is. They are obliged to admit the doctrine of popular Sovereignty. They are obliged to proclaim a theory of unlimited popular powers.

To be sure, a democracy may impose rules of action upon itself—as the American democracy did in accepting the Federal Constitution. But in adopting the Federal Constitution the American people did not abandon either its responsibilities or rights as Sovereign. Difficult as it may be to escape from the legal framework defined in the Constitution, that body of law in theory remains merely an instrument which was made for the people and which if necessary can and will be modified. A people, to whom was denied the ultimate responsibility for its welfare, would not have obtained the prime condition of genuine liberty. Individual freedom is important, but more important still is the freedom of a whole people to dispose of its own destiny; and I do not see how the existence of such an ultimate popular political freedom and responsibility can be denied by any one who has rejected the theory of a divinely appointed political order. The fallibility of human nature being what it is, the practical application of this theory will have its grave dangers; but these dangers are only evaded and postponed by a failure to place ultimate political responsibility where it belongs. While a country in the position of Germany or Great Britain may be fully justified from the point of view of its national tradition, in merely compromising with democracy, other countries, such as the United States and France, which have earned the right to dispense with these compromises, are at least building their political structure on the real and righteous source of political authority. Democracy may mean something more than a theoretically absolute popular government, but it assuredly cannot mean anything less.

If, however, democracy does not mean anything less than popular Sovereignty, it assuredly does mean something more. It must at least mean an expression of the Sovereign will, which will not contradict and destroy the continuous existence of its own Sovereign power. Several times during the political history of France in the nineteenth century, the popular will has expressed itself in a manner adverse to popular political institutions. Assemblies have been elected by universal suffrage, whose tendencies have been reactionary and undemocratic, and who have been supported in this reactionary policy by an effective public opinion. Or the French people have by means of a plebiscite delegated their Sovereign power to an Imperial dictator, whose whole political system was based on a deep suspicion of the source of his own authority. A particular group of political institutions or course of political action may, then, be representative of the popular will, and yet may be undemocratic. Popular Sovereignty is self-contradictory, unless it is expressed in a manner favorable to its own perpetuity and integrity.

The assertion of the doctrine of popular Sovereignty is, consequently, rather the beginning than the end of democracy. There can be no democracy where the people do not rule; but government by the people is not necessarily democratic. The popular will must in a democratic state be expressed somehow in the interest of democracy itself; and we have not traveled very far towards a satisfactory conception of democracy until this democratic purpose has received some definition. In what way must a democratic state behave in order to contribute to its own integrity?

The ordinary American answer to this question is contained in the assertion of Lincoln, that our government is "dedicated to the proposition that all men are created equal." Lincoln's phrasing of the principle was due to the fact that the obnoxious and undemocratic system of negro slavery was uppermost in his mind when he made his Gettysburg address; but he meant by his assertion of the principle of equality substantially what is meant to-day by the principle of "equal rights for all and special privileges for none." Government by the people has its natural and logical complement in government for the people. Every state with a legal framework must grant certain rights to individuals; and every state, in so far as it is efficient, must guarantee to the individual that his rights, as legally defined, are secure. But an essentially democratic state consists in the circumstance that all citizens enjoy these rights equally. If any citizen or any group of citizens enjoys by virtue of the law any advantage over their fellow-citizens, then the most sacred principle of democracy is violated. On the other hand, a community in which no man or no group of men are granted by law any advantage over their fellow-citizens is the type of the perfect and fruitful democratic state. Society is organized politically for the benefit of all the people. Such an organization may permit radical differences among individuals in the opportunities and possessions they actually enjoy; but no man would be able to impute his own success or failure to the legal framework of society. Every citizen would be getting a "Square Deal."

Such is the idea of the democratic state, which the majority of good Americans believe to be entirely satisfactory. It should endure indefinitely, because it seeks to satisfy every interest essential to associated life. The interest of the individual is protected, because of the liberties he securely enjoys. The general social interest is equally well protected, because the liberties enjoyed by one or by a few are enjoyed by all. Thus the individual and the social interests are automatically harmonized. The virile democrat in pursuing his own interest "under the law" is contributing effectively to the interest of society, while the social interest consists precisely in the promotion of these individual interests, in so far as they can be equally exercised. The divergent demands of the individual and the social interest can be reconciled by grafting the principle of equality on the thrifty tree of individual rights, and the ripe fruit thereof can be gathered merely by shaking the tree.

It must be immediately admitted, also, that the principle of equal rights, like the principle of ultimate popular political responsibility is the expression of an essential aspect of democracy. There is no room for permanent legal privileges in a democratic state. Such privileges may be and frequently are defended on many excellent grounds. They may unquestionably contribute for a time to social and economic efficiency and to individual independence. But whatever advantage may be derived from such permanent discriminations must be abandoned by a democracy. It cannot afford to give any one class of its citizens a permanent advantage or to others a permanent grievance. It ceases to be a democracy, just as soon as any permanent privileges are conferred by its institutions or its laws; and this equality of right and absence of permanent privilege is the expression of a fundamental social interest.

But the principle of equal rights, like the principle of ultimate popular political responsibility, is not sufficient; and because of its insufficiency results in certain dangerous ambiguities and self-contradictions. American political thinkers have always repudiated the idea that by equality of rights they meant anything like equality of performance or power. The utmost varieties of individual power and ability are bound to exist and are bound to bring about many different levels of individual achievement. Democracy both recognizes the right of the individual to use his powers to the utmost, and encourages him to do so by offering a fair field and, in cases of success, an abundant reward. The democratic principle requires an equal start in the race, while expecting at the same time an unequal finish. But Americans who talk in this way seem wholly blind to the fact that under a legal system which holds private property sacred there may be equal rights, but there cannot possibly be any equal opportunities for exercising such rights. The chance which the individual has to compete with his fellows and take a prize in the race is vitally affected by material conditions over which he has no control. It is as if the competitor in a Marathon cross country run were denied proper nourishment or proper training, and was obliged to toe the mark against rivals who had every benefit of food and discipline. Under such conditions he is not as badly off as if he were en-

tirely excluded from the race. With the aid of exceptional strength and intelligence he may overcome the
odds against him and win out. But it would be absurd to
claim, because all the rivals toed the same mark, that a
man's victory or defeat depended exclusively on his own
efforts. Those who have enjoyed the benefits of wealth
and thorough education start with an advantage which
can be overcome only in very exceptional men,—men so
exceptional, in fact, that the average competitor without
such benefits feels himself disqualified for the contest.

Because of the ambiguity indicated above, different
people with different interests, all of them good patriotic
Americans, draw very different inferences from the doctrine of equal rights. The man of conservative ideas and
interests means by the rights, which are to be equally
exercised, only those rights which are defined and protected by the law—the more fundamental of which are
the rights to personal freedom and to private property.
The man of radical ideas, on the other hand, observing,
as he may very clearly, that these equal rights cannot
possibly be made really equivalent to equal opportunities, bases upon the same doctrine a more or less drastic
criticism of the existing economic and social order and
sometimes of the motives of its beneficiaries and conser-
vators. The same principle, differently interpreted, is the
foundation of American political orthodoxy and American political heterodoxy. The same measure of reforming legislation, such as the new Inter-state Commerce
Law, seems to one party a wholly inadequate attempt
to make the exercise of individual rights a little more
equal, while it seems to others an egregious violation of
the principle itself. What with reforming legislation on
the one hand and the lack of it on the other, the once
sweet air of the American political mansion is soured by
complaints. Privileges and discriminations seem to lurk
in every political and economic corner. The "people" are

appealing to the state to protect them against the usur-
pations of the corporations and the Bosses. The government is appealing to the courts to protect the shippers
against the railroads. The corporations are appealing
to the Federal courts to protect them from the unfair
treatment of state legislatures. Employers are fighting
trades-unionism, because it denies equal rights to their
employers. The unionists are entreating public opinion
to protect them against the unfairness of "government
by injunction." To the free trader the whole protectionist system seems a flagrant discrimination on behalf of a
certain portion of the community. Everybody seems to
be clamoring for a "Square Deal" but nobody seems to
be getting it.

The ambiguity of the principle of equal rights and
the resulting confusion of counsel are so obvious that
there must be some good reason for their apparently
unsuspected existence. The truth is that Americans have
not readjusted their political ideas to the teaching of
their political and economic experience. For a couple
of generations after Jefferson had established the doctrine of equal rights as the fundamental principle of
the American democracy, the ambiguity resident in the
application of the doctrine was concealed. The Jacksonian Democrats, for instance, who were constantly nos-
ing the ground for a scent of unfair treatment, could
discover no example of political privileges, except the
continued retention of their offices by experienced public servants; and the only case of economic privilege
of which they were certain was that of the National
Bank. The fact is, of course, that the great majority of
Americans were getting a "Square Deal" as long as the
economic opportunities of a new country had not been
developed and appropriated. Individual and social interest did substantially coincide as long as so many opportunities were open to the poor and untrained man,

and as long as the public interest demanded first of all the utmost celerity of economic development. But, as we have seen in a preceding chapter, the economic development of the country resulted inevitably in a condition which demanded on the part of the successful competitor either increasing capital, improved training, or a larger amount of ability and energy. With the advent of comparative economic and social maturity, the exercise of certain legal rights became substantially equivalent to the exercise of a privilege; and if equality of opportunity was to be maintained, it could not be done by virtue of non-interference. The demands of the "Higher Law" began to diverge from the results of the actual legal system.

Public opinion is, of course, extremely loth to admit that there exists any such divergence of individual and social interest, or any such contradiction in the fundamental American principle. Reformers no less than conservatives have been doggedly determined to place some other interpretation upon the generally recognized abuses; and the interpretation on which they have fastened is that some of the victors have captured too many prizes, because they did not play fair. There is just enough truth in this interpretation to make it plausible, although, as we have seen, the most flagrant examples of apparent cheating were due as much to equivocal rules as to any fraudulent intention. But orthodox public opinion is obliged by the necessities of its own situation to exaggerate the truth of its favorite interpretation; and any such exaggeration is attended with grave dangers, precisely because the ambiguous nature of the principle itself gives a similar ambiguity to its violations. The cheating is understood as disobedience to the actual law, or as violation of a Higher Law, according to the interests and preconceptions of the different reformers; but however it is understood, they believe themselves to be upholding some kind of a Law, and hence endowed with some kind of a sacred mission.

Thus the want of integrity in what is supposed to be the formative principle of democracy results, as it did before the Civil War, in a division of the actual substance of the nation. Men naturally disposed to be indignant at people with whom they disagree come to believe that their indignation is comparable to that of the Lord. Men naturally disposed to be envious and suspicious of others more fortunate than themselves come to confuse their suspicions with a duty to the society. Demagogues can appeal to the passions aroused by this prevailing sense of unfair play for the purpose of getting themselves elected to office or for the purpose of passing blundering measures of repression. The type of admirable and popular democrat ceases to be a statesman, attempting to bestow unity and health on the body politic by prescribing more wholesome habits of living. He becomes instead a sublimated District Attorney, whose duty it is to punish violations both of the actual and the "Higher Law." Thus he is figured as a kind of an avenging angel; but (as it happens) he is an avenging angel who can find little to avenge and who has no power of flight. There is an enormous discrepancy between the promises of these gentlemen and their performances, no matter whether they occupy an executive office, the editorial chairs of yellow journals, or merely the place of public prosecutor; and it sometimes happens that public prosecutors who have played the part of avenging angels before election, are, as Mr. William Travers Jerome knows, themselves prosecuted after a few years of office by their aggrieved constituents. The truth is that these gentlemen are confronted by a task which is in a large measure impossible, and which, so far as possible, would be either disappointing or dangerous in its results.

Hence it is that continued loyalty to a contradictory principle is destructive of a wholesome public sentiment and opinion. A wholesome public opinion in a democracy is one which keeps a democracy sound and whole; and it cannot prevail unless the individuals composing it recognize mutual ties and responsibilities which lie deeper than any differences of interest and idea. No formula whose effect on public opinion is not binding and healing and unifying has any substantial claim to consideration as the essential and formative democratic idea. Belief in the principle of equal rights does not bind, heal, and unify public opinion. Its effect rather is confusing, distracting, and at worst, disintegrating. A democratic political organization has no immunity from grievances. They are a necessary result of a complicated and changing industrial and social organism. What is good for one generation will often be followed by consequences that spell deprivation for the next. What is good for one man or one class of men will bring ills to other men or classes of men. What is good for the community as a whole may mean temporary loss and a sense of injustice to a minority. All grievances from any cause should receive full expression in a democracy, but, inasmuch as the righteously discontented must be always with us, the fundamental democratic principle should, above all, counsel mutual forbearance and loyalty. The principle of equal rights encourages mutual suspicion and disloyalty. It tends to attribute individual and social ills, for which general moral, economic, and social causes are usually in large measure responsible, to individual wrong-doing; and in this way it arouses and intensifies that personal and class hatred, which never in any society lies far below the surface. Men who have grievances are inflamed into anger and resentment. In claiming what they believe to be their rights, they are in their own opinion acting on behalf not merely of their interests, but of an absolute democratic principle. Their angry resentment becomes transformed in their own minds into righteous indignation; and there may be turned loose upon the community a horde of self-seeking fanatics—like unto those soldiers in the religious wars who robbed and slaughtered their opponents in the service of God.

II Democracy and Discrimination

The principle of equal rights has always appealed to its more patriotic and sensible adherents as essentially an impartial rule of political action—one that held a perfectly fair balance between the individual and society, and between different and hostile individual and class interests. But as a fundamental principle of democratic policy it is as ambiguous in this respect as it is in other respects. In its traditional form and expression it has concealed an extremely partial interest under a formal proclamation of impartiality. The political thinker who popularized it in this country was not concerned fundamentally with harmonizing the essential interest of the individual with the essential popular or social interest. Jefferson's political system was intended for the benefit only of a special class of individuals, viz., those average people who would not be helped by any really formative rule or method of discrimination. In practice it has proved to be inimical to individual liberty, efficiency, and distinction. An insistent demand for equality, even in the form of a demand for equal rights, inevitably has a negative and limiting effect upon the free and able exercise of individual opportunities. From the Jeffersonian point of view democracy would incur a graver danger from a violation of equality than it would profit from a triumphant assertion of individual liberty. Every opportunity for the edifying exercise of power, on the part either of an individual, a group of individuals, or the state is by its very nature also an opportunity for its evil exercise. The political leader whose official power depends upon popular confidence may betray the trust. The corporation employing thousands of men and supplying millions of people with some necessary service or commodity may reduce the cost of production only for its own profit. The state may use its great authority chiefly for the benefit of special interests. The advocate of equal rights is preoccupied by these opportunities for the abusive exercise of power, because from his point of view rights exercised in the interest of inequality have ceased to be righteous. He distrusts those forms of individual and associated activity which give any individual or association substantial advantages over their associates. He becomes suspicious of any kind of individual and social distinction with the nature and effects of which he is not completely familiar.

A democracy of equal rights may tend to encourage certain expressions of individual liberty; but they are few in number and limited in scope. It rejoices in the freedom of its citizens, provided this freedom receives certain ordinary expressions. It will follow a political leader, like Jefferson or Jackson, with a blind confidence of which a really free democracy would not be capable, because such leaders are, or claim to be in every respect, except their prominence, one of the "people." Distinction of this kind does not separate a leader from the majority. It only ties them together more firmly. It is an acceptable assertion of individual liberty, because it is liberty converted by its exercise into a kind of equality. In the same way the American democracy most cordially admired for a long time men, who pursued more energetically and successfully than their fellows, ordinary business occupations, because they believed that such familiar expressions of individual liberty really tended towards social and industrial homogeneity. Herein they were mistaken; but the supposition was made in good faith, and it constitutes the basis of the Jeffersonian Democrat's illusion in reference to his own interest in liberty. He dislikes or ignores liberty, only when it looks in the direction of moral and intellectual emancipation. In so far as his influence has prevailed, Americans have been encouraged to think those thoughts and to perform those acts which everybody else is thinking and performing.

The effect of a belief in the principle of "equal rights" on freedom is, however, most clearly shown by its attitude toward Democratic political organization and policy. A people jealous of their rights are not sufficiently afraid of special individual efficiency and distinction to take very many precautions against it. They greet it oftener with neglect than with positive coercion. Jeffersonian Democracy is, however, very much afraid of any examples of associated efficiency. Equality of rights is most in danger of being violated when the exercise of rights is associated with power, and any unusual amount of power is usually derived from the association of a number of individuals for a common purpose. The most dangerous example of such association is not, however, a huge corporation or a labor union; it is the state. The state cannot be bound hand and foot by the law, as can a corporation, because it necessarily possesses some powers of legislation; and the power to legislate inevitably escapes the limitation of the principle of equal rights. The power to legislate implies the power to discriminate; and the best way consequently for a good democracy of equal rights to avoid the danger of discrimination will be to organize the state so that its power for ill will be rigidly restricted. The possible preferential interference on the part of a strong and efficient government must be checked by making the government feeble and devoid of independence. The less independent and efficient the several departments of the government are permitted to become, the less likely that the government as a whole will use its power for anything but a really popular purpose.

In the foregoing type of political organization, which has been very much favored by the American democracy, the freedom of the official political leader is sacrificed for the benefit of the supposed freedom of that class of equalized individuals known as the "people," but by the "people" Jefferson and his followers have never meant all the people or the people as a whole. They have meant a sort of apotheosized majority—the people in so far as they could be generalized and reduced to an average. The interests of this class were conceived as inimical to any discrimination which tended to select peculiarly efficient individuals or those who were peculiarly capable of social service. The system of equal rights, particularly in its economic and political application *has* worked for the benefit of such a class, but rather in its effect upon American intelligence and morals, than in its effect upon American political and economic development. The system, that is, has only partly served the purpose of its founder and his followers, and it has failed because it did not bring with it any machinery adequate even to its own insipid and barren purposes. Even the meager social interest which Jefferson concealed under cover of his demand for equal rights could not be promoted without some effective organ of social responsibility; and the Democrats of to-day are obliged, as we have seen, to invoke the action of the central government to destroy those economic discriminations which its former inaction had encouraged. But even so the traditional democracy still retains its dislike of centralized and socialized responsibility. It consents to use the machinery of the government only for a negative or destructive object. Such must always be the case as long as it remains true to its fundamental principle. That principle defines the social interest merely in the terms of an indiscriminate individualism—which is the one kind of individualism murderous to both the essential individual and the essential social interest.

The net result has been that wherever the attempt to discriminate in favor of the average or indiscriminate individual has succeeded, it has succeeded at the expense of individual liberty, efficiency, and distinction; but it has more often failed than succeeded. Whenever the exceptional individual has been given any genuine liberty, he has inevitably conquered. That is the whole meaning of the process of economic and social development traced in certain preceding chapters. The strong and capable men not only conquer, but they seek to perpetuate their conquests by occupying all the strategic points in the economic and political battle-field—whereby they obtain certain more or less permanent advantages over their fellow-democrats. Thus in so far as the equal rights are freely exercised, they are bound to result in inequalities; and these inequalities are bound to make for their own perpetuation, and so to provoke still further discrimination. Wherever the principle has been allowed to mean what it seems to mean, it has determined and encouraged its own violation. The marriage which it is supposed to consecrate between liberty and equality gives birth to unnatural children, whose nature it is to devour one or the other of their parents.

The only way in which the thorough-going adherent of the principle of equal rights can treat these tendencies to discrimination, when they develop, is rigidly to repress them; and this tendency to repression is now beginning to take possession of those Americans who represent the pure Democratic tradition. They propose to crush out the chief examples of effective individual and associated action, which their system of democracy has encouraged to develop. They propose frankly to destroy, so far as possible, the economic organization which has been built up under stress of competitive conditions; and by assuming such an attitude they have fallen away even from the pretense of impartiality, and have come out as frankly representative of a class interest. But even to assert this class interest efficiently they have been obliged to abandon, in fact if not in word, their correlative principle of national irresponsibility. Whatever the national interest may be, it is not to be asserted by the political practice of non-interference. The hope of automatic democratic fulfillment must be abandoned. The national government must stop in and discriminate; but it must discriminate, not on behalf of liberty and the special individual, but on behalf of equality and the average man.

Thus the Jeffersonian principle of national irresponsibility can no longer be maintained by those Democrats who sincerely believe that the inequalities of power generated in the American economic and political system are dangerous to the integrity of the democratic state. To this extent really sincere followers of Jefferson are obliged to admit the superior political wisdom of Hamilton's principle of national responsibility, and once they have made this admission, they have implicitly abandoned their contention that the doctrine of equal rights is a sufficient principle of democratic political action. They have implicitly accepted the idea that the public interest is to be asserted, not merely by equalizing individual rights, but by controlling individuals in the exercise of those rights. The national public interest has to be affirmed by positive and aggressive fiction. The nation has to have a will and a policy as well as the individual; and this policy can no longer be confined to the merely negative task of keeping individual rights from becoming in any way privileged.

The arduous and responsible political task which a nation in its collective capacity must seek to perform is that of selecting among the various prevailing ways of exercising individual rights those which contribute to national perpetuity and integrity. Such selection implies some interference with the natural course of popular notion; and that interference is always costly and may be harmful either to the individual or the social interest must be frankly admitted. He would be a foolish Hamiltonian who would claim that a state, no matter how efficiently organized and ably managed, will not make serious and perhaps enduring mistakes; but he can answer that inaction and irresponsibility are more costly and dangerous than intelligent and responsible interference. The practice of non-interference is just as selective in its effects as the practice of state interference. It means merely that the nation is willing to accept the results of natural selection instead of preferring to substitute the results of artificial selection. In one way or another a nation is bound to recognize the results of selection. The Hamiltonian principle of national responsibility recognizes the inevitability of selection; and since it is inevitable, is not afraid to interfere on behalf of the selection of the really fittest. If a selective policy is pursued in good faith and with sufficient intelligence, the nation will at least be learning from its mistakes. It should find out gradually the kind and method of selection, which is most desirable, and how far selection by non-interference is to be preferred to active selection.

As a matter of fact the American democracy both in its central and in its local governments has always practiced both methods of selection. The state governments have sedulously indulged in a kind of interference conspicuous both for its activity and its inefficiency. The Federal government, on the other hand, has been permitted to interfere very much less; but even during the palmiest days of national irresponsibility it did not altogether escape active intervention. A protective tariff is, of course, a plain case of preferential class legislation, and so was the original Inter-state Commerce Act. They were designed to substitute artificial preferences for those effected by unregulated individual action, on the ground that the proposed modification of the natural course of trade would contribute to the general economic prosperity. No less preferential in purpose are the measures of reform recently enacted by the central government. The amended Inter-state Commerce Law largely increases the power of possible discrimination possessed by the Federal Commission. The Pure Food Bill forbids many practices, which have arisen in connection with the manufacture of food products, and discriminates against the perpetrators of such practices. Factory legislation or laws regulating the hours of labor have a similar meaning and justification. It is not too much to say that substantially all the industrial legislation, demanded by the "people" both here and abroad and passed in the popular interest, has been based essentially on class discrimination.

The situation which these laws are supposed to meet is always the same. A certain number of individuals enjoy, in the beginning, equal opportunities to perform certain acts; and in the competition resulting there from some of these individuals or associations obtain advantages over their competitors, or over their fellow-citizens whom they employ or serve. Sometimes these advantages and the practices whereby they are obtained are profitable to a larger number of people than they injure. Sometimes the reverse is true. In either event the state is usually asked to interfere by the class whose economic position has been compromised. It by no means follows that the state should acquiesce in this demand. In many cases interference may be more costly than beneficial.

Each case must be considered on its merits. But whether in any particular case the state takes sides or remains impartial, it most assuredly has a positive function to perform on the promises. If it remains impartial, it simply agrees to abide by the results of natural selection. If it interferes, it seeks to replace natural with artificial discrimination. In both cases it authorizes discriminations which in their effect violate the doctrine of "equal rights." Of course, a reformer can always claim that any particular measure of reform proposes merely to restore to the people a "Square Deal"; but that is simply an easy and thoughtless way of concealing novel purposes under familiar formulas. Any genuine measure of economic or political reform will, of course, give certain individuals better opportunities than those they have been recently enjoying, but it will reach this result only by depriving other individuals of advantages which they have earned.

Impartiality is the duty of the judge rather than the statesman, of the courts rather than the government. The state which proposes to draw a ring around the conflicting interests of its citizens and interfere only on behalf of a fair fight will be obliged to interfere constantly and will never accomplish its purpose. In economic warfare, the fighting can never be fair for long, and it is the business of the state to see that its own friends are victorious. It holds, if you please, itself a hand in the game. The several players are playing, not merely with one another, but with the political and social bank. The security and perpetuity of the state and of the individual in so far an he is a social animal, depend upon the victory of the national interest—as represented both in the assurance of the national profit and in the domination of the nation's friends. It is in the position of the bank at Monte Carlo, which does not pretend to play fair, but which frankly promulgates rules advantageous to itself. Considering the percentage in its favor and the length of its purse, it cannot possibly lose. It is not really gambling; and it does not propose to take any unnecessary risks. Neither can a state, democratic or otherwise, which believes in its own purpose. While preserving at times an appearance of impartiality so that its citizens may enjoy for a while a sense of the reality of their private game, it must on the whole make the rules in its own interest. It must help those men to win who are most capable of using their winnings for the benefit of society.

III Constructive Discrimination

Assuming, then, that a democracy cannot avoid the constant assertion of national responsibility for the national welfare, an all-important question remains as to the way in which and the purpose for which this interference should be exercised. Should it be exercised on behalf of individual liberty? Should it be exercised on behalf of social equality? Is there any way in which it can be exercised on behalf both of liberty and equality?

Hamilton and the constitutional liberals asserted that the state should interfere exclusively on behalf of individual liberty; but Hamilton was no democrat and was not outlining the policy of a democratic state. In point of fact democracies have never been satisfied with a definition of democratic policy in terms of liberty. Not only have the particular friends of liberty usually been hostile to democracy, but democracies both in idea and behavior have frequently been hostile to liberty; and they have been justified in distrusting a political régime organized wholly or even chiefly for its benefit. "La Liberté," says Mr. Emile Faguet, in the preface to his "Politiques et Moralistes du Dix-Neuvième Siècle"—"La Liberté s'oppose à l'Égalité, car La Liberté est aristocratique par essence. La Liberté ne se donne jamais, ne s'octroie jamais; elle se conquiert. Or ne peuvent la conquérir que des groupes sociaux qui out su se donne la cohérence, l'organisation et la discipline et qui par conséquent, sont des groupes aristocratiques." The fact that states organized exclusively or largely for the benefit of liberty are essentially aristocratic explains the hostile and suspicious attitude of democracies towards such a principle of political action.

Only a comparatively small minority are capable at any one time of exercising political, economic, and civil liberties in an able, efficient, or thoroughly worthy manner; and a régime wrought for the benefit of such a minority would become at best a state, in which economic, political, and social power would be very unevenly distributed—a state like the Orleans Monarchy in France of the "Bourgeoisie" and the "Intellectuals." Such a state might well give its citizens fairly good government, as did the Orleans Monarchy; but just in so far as the mass of the people had any will of its own, it could not arouse vital popular interest and support; and it could not contribute, except negatively, to the fund of popular good sense and experience. The lack of such popular support caused the death of the French liberal monarchy; and no such régime can endure, save, as in England, by virtue of a somewhat abject popular acquiescence. As long as it does endure, moreover, it tends to undermine the virtue of its own beneficiaries. The favored minority, feeling as they do tolerably sure of their position, can scarcely avoid a habit of making it somewhat too easy for one another. The political, economic, and intellectual leaders begin to be selected without any sufficient test of their efficiency. Some sort of a test continues to be required; but the standards which determine it drift into a condition of being narrow, artificial, and lax. Political, intellectual, and social leadership, in order to preserve its vitality needs a feeling of effective responsibility to a body of public opinion as wide, as varied, and as exacting as that of the whole community.

The desirable democratic object, implied in the traditional democratic demand for equality, consists precisely in that of bestowing a share of the responsibility and the benefits, derived from political and economic association, upon the whole community. Democracies have assumed and have been right in assuming that a proper diffusion of effective responsibility and substantial benefits is the one means whereby a community can be supplied with an ultimate and sufficient bond of union. The American democracy has attempted to manufacture a sufficient bond out of the equalization of rights: but such a bond is, as we have seen, either a rope of sand or a link of chains. A similar object must be achieved in some other way; and the ultimate success of democracy depends upon its achievement.

The fundamental political and social problem of a democracy may be summarized in the following terms. A democracy, like every political and social group, is composed of individuals, and must be organized for the benefit of its constituent members. But the individual has no chance of effective personal power except by means of the secure exercise of certain personal rights. Such rights, then, must be secured and exercised; yet when they are exercised, their tendency is to divide the community into divergent classes. Even if enjoyed with some equality in the beginning, they do not continue to be equally enjoyed, but make towards discriminations advantageous to a minority. The state, as representing the common interest, is obliged to admit the inevitability of such classifications and divisions, and has itself no alternative but to exercise a decisive preference on behalf of one side or the other. A well-governed state will use its power to promote edifying and desirable discriminations. But if discriminations tend to divide the

community, and the state itself cannot do more than select among the various possible cases of discrimination
those which it has some reason to prefer, how is the
solidarity of the community to be preserved? And above
all, how is a democratic community, which necessarily
includes everybody in its benefits and responsibilities, to
be kept well united? Such a community must retain an
ultimate bond of union which counteracts the divergent
effect of the discriminations, yet which at the same time
is not fundamentally hostile to individual liberties.

The clew to the best available solution of the problem
is supplied by a consideration of the precise manner, in
which the advantages derived from the efficient exercise
of liberties become inimical to a wholesome social condition. The hostility depends, not upon the existence of
such advantageous discriminations for a time, but upon
their persistence for too long a time. When, either from
natural or artificial causes, they are properly selected,
they contribute at the time of their selection both to individual and to social efficiency. They have been earned,
and it is both just and edifying that, in so far as they
have been earned, they should be freely enjoyed. On the
other hand, they should not, so far as possible, be allowed to outlast their own utility. They must continue
to be earned. It is power and opportunity enjoyed without being earned which help to damage the individual—
both the individuals who benefit and the individuals
who consent—and which tend to loosen the ultimate
social bond. A democracy, no less than a monarchy or
an aristocracy, must recognize political, economic, and
social discriminations, but it must also manage to with-
draw its consent whenever these discriminations show
any tendency to excessive endurance. The essential
wholeness of the community depends absolutely on the
ceaseless creation of a political, economic, and social aristocracy and their equally incessant replacement.

Both in its organization and in its policy a democratic state has consequently to seek two different but supplementary objects. It is the function of such a state to represent the whole community; and the whole community includes the individual as well as the mass, the many as well as the few. The individual is merged in the mass, unless he is enabled to exercise efficiently and independently his own private and special purposes. He must not only be permitted, he must be encouraged to earn distinction; and the best way in which he can be encouraged to earn distinction is to reward distinction both by abundant opportunity and cordial appreciation. Individual distinction, resulting from the efficient performance of special work, is not only the foundation of all genuine individuality, but is usually of the utmost social value. In so far as it is efficient, it has a tendency to be constructive. It both inserts some member into the social edifice which forms for the time being a desirable part of the whole structure, but it tends to establish a standard of achievement which may well form a permanent contribution to social amelioration. It is useful to the whole community, not because it is derived from popular sources or conforms to popular standards, but because it is formative and so helps to convert the community into a well-formed whole.

Distinction, however, even when it is earned, always has a tendency to remain satisfied with its achievements, and to seek indefinitely its own perpetuation. When such a course is pursued by an efficient and distinguished individual, he is, of course, faithless to the meaning and the source of his own individual power. In abandoning and replacing him a democracy is not recreant to the principle of individual liberty. It is merely subjecting individual liberty to conditions which promote and determine its continued efficiency. Such conditions never have been and never will be imposed for long by individuals or classes of individuals upon themselves. They must be imposed by the community, and nothing less than the whole community. The efficient exercise of individual power is necessary to form a community and make it whole, but the duty of keeping it whole rests with the community itself. It must consciously and resolutely preserve the social benefit, derived from the achievements of its favorite sons; and the most effective means thereto is that of denying to favoritism of all kinds the opportunity of becoming a mere habit.

The specific means whereby this necessary and formative favoritism can be prevented from becoming a mere habit vary radically among the different fields of personal activity. In the field of intellectual work the conditions imposed upon the individual must for the most part be the creation of public opinion; and in its proper place this aspect of the relation between individuality and democracy will receive special consideration. In the present connection, however, the relation of individual liberty to democratic organization and policy can be illustrated and explained most helpfully by a consideration of the binding and formative conditions of political and economic liberty. Democracies have always been chiefly preoccupied with the problems raised by the exercise of political and economic opportunities, because success in politics and business implies the control of a great deal of physical power and the consequent possession by the victors in a peculiar degree of both the motive and the means to perpetuate their victory.

The particular friends of freedom, such as Hamilton and the French "doctrinaires," have always believed that both civil and political liberty depended on the denial of popular Sovereignty and the rigid limitation of the suffrage. Of course, a democrat cannot accept such a conclusion. He should doubtless admit that the possession of absolute Sovereign power is always liable to abuse; and if he is candid, he can hardly fail to add that democratic favoritism is subject to the same weakness as aristocratic or royal favoritism. It tends, that is, to make individuals seek distinction not by high individual efficiency, but by compromises in the interest of useful popularity. It would be vain to deny the gravity of this danger or the extent to which, in the best of democracies, the seekers after all kinds of distinction have been hypnotized by an express desire for popularity. But American statesmen have not always been obliged to choose between Hamilton's unpopular integrity and Henry Clay's unprincipled bidding for popular favor. The greatest American political leaders have been popular without any personal capitulation; and their success is indicative of what is theoretically the most wholesome relation between individual political liberty and a democratic distribution of effective political power. The highest and most profitable individual political distinction is that which is won from a large field and from a whole people. Political, even more than other kinds of distinction, should not be the fruit of a limited area of selection. It must be open to everybody, and it must be acceptable to the community as a whole. In fact, the concession of substantially equal political rights is an absolute condition of any fundamental political bond. Grave as are the dangers which a democratic political system incurs, still graver ones are incurred by a rigidly limited electoral organization. A community, so organized, betrays a fundamental lack of confidence in the mutual loyalty and good faith of its members, and such a community can remain well united only at the cost of a mixture of patronage and servility.

The limitation of the suffrage to those who are individually capable of making the best use of it has the appearance of being reasonable; and it has made a strong appeal to those statesmen and thinkers who believed in the political leadership of intelligent and educated men. Neither can it be denied that a rigidly restricted suffrage might well make in the beginning for administrative efficiency and good government. But it must never be forgotten that a limited suffrage confines ultimate political responsibility, not only to a number of peculiarly competent individuals, but to a larger or smaller class; and in the long run a class is never to be trusted to govern in the interest of the whole community. A democracy should encourage the political leadership of experienced, educated, and well-trained men, but only on the express condition that their power is delegated and is to be used, under severe penalties, for the benefit of the people as a whole. A limited suffrage secures governmental efficiency, if at all, at the expense of the political education and training of the disfranchised class, and at the expense, also, of a permanent and radical popular political grievance. A substantially universal suffrage merely places the ultimate political responsibility in the hands of those for whose benefit governments are created; and its denial can be justified only on the ground that the whole community is incapable of exercising the responsibility. Such cases unquestionably exist. They exist wherever the individuals constituting a community, as at present in the South, are more divided by social or class ambitions and prejudices than they are united by a tradition of common action and mutual loyalty. But wherever the whole people are capable of thinking, feeling, and acting as if they constituted a whole, universal suffrage, even if it costs something in temporary efficiency, has a tendency to be more salutary and more formative than a restricted suffrage.

The substantially equal political rights enjoyed by the American people for so many generations have not proved dangerous to the civil liberties of the individual and, except to a limited extent, not to his political liberty. Of course, the American democracy has been absolutely opposed to the delegation to individuals of official political power, except under rigid conditions both as to scope and duration; and the particular friends of liberty have always claimed that such rigid conditions destroyed individual political independence and freedom. Hamilton, for instance, was insistent upon the necessity of an upper house consisting of life-members who would not be dependent on popular favor for their retention of office. But such proposals have no chance of prevailing in a sensible democracy. A democracy is justified in refusing to bestow permanent political power upon individuals, because such permanent tenure of office relaxes oftener than it stimulates the efficiency of the favored individual, and makes him attach excessive importance to mere independence. The official leaders of a democracy should, indeed, hold their offices under conditions which will enable them to act and think independently; but independence is really valuable only when the officeholder has won it from his own followers. Under any other conditions it is not only peculiarly liable to abuse, but it deprives the whole people of that ultimate responsibility for their own welfare, without which democracy is meaningless. A democracy is or should be constantly delegating an effective share in this responsibility to its official leaders, but only on condition that the power and responsibility delegated is partial and is periodically resumed.

The only Americans who hold important official positions for life are the judges of the Federal courts. Radical democrats have always protested against this exception, which, nevertheless, can be permitted without any infringement of democratic principles. The peculiar position of the Federal judge is symptomatic of the peculiar importance in the American system of the Federal Constitution. A senator would be less likely to be an efficient and public-spirited legislator, in case he were not obliged at regular intervals to prove title to his distinction. A justice of the Supreme Court, on the other hand, can the better perform his special task, provided he has a firm and permanent hold upon his office. He cannot, to be sure, entirely escape responsibility to public opinion, but his primary duty is to expound the Constitution as he understands it; and it is a duty which demands the utmost personal independence. The fault with the American system in this respect consists not in the independence of the Federal judiciary, but in the practical immutability of the Constitution. If the instrument which the Supreme Court expounds could be altered whenever a sufficiently large body of public opinion has demanded a change for a sufficiently long time, the American democracy would have much more to gain than to fear from the independence of the Federal judiciary.

The interest of individual liberty in relation to the organization of democracy demands simply that the individual officeholder should possess an amount of power and independence adequate to the efficient performance of his work. The work of a justice of the Supreme Court demands a power that is absolute for its own special work, and it demands technically complete independence. An executive should, as a rule, serve for a longer term, and hold a position of greater independence than a legislator, because his work of enforcing the laws and attending to the business details of government demands continuity, complete responsibility within its own sphere, and the necessity occasionally of braving adverse currents of public opinion. The term of service and the technical independence of a legislator might well be more restricted than that of an executive; but even a legislator should be granted as much power and independence as he may need for the official performance of his public duty. The American democracy has shown its enmity to individual political liberty, not because it has required its political favorites constantly to seek reëlection, but because it has since 1800 tended to refuse to its favorites during their official term as much power and independence as is needed for administrative, legislative, and judicial efficiency. It has been jealous of the power it delegated, and has tried to take away with one hand what it gave with the other.

Taking American political traditions, ideals, institutions, and practices as a whole, there is no reason to believe that the American democracy cannot and will not combine sufficient opportunities for individual political distinction with an effective ultimate popular political responsibility. The manner in which the combination has been made hitherto is far from flawless, and the American democracy has much to learn before it reaches an organization adequate to its own proper purposes. It must learn, above all, that the state, and the individuals who are temporarily responsible for the action of the state, must be granted all the power necessary to redeem that responsibility. Individual opportunity and social welfare both depend upon the learning of this lesson; and while it is still very far from being learned, the obstacles in the way are not of a disheartening nature.

With the economic liberty of the individual the case is different. The Federalists refrained from protecting individual political rights by incorporating in the Constitution any limitation of the suffrage; but they sought to protect the property rights of the individual by the most absolute constitutional guarantees. Moreover, American practice has allowed the individual a far larger measure of economic liberty than is required by the Constitution; and this liberty was granted in the expectation that it would benefit, not the individual as such, but the great mass of the American people. It has undoubtedly benefited the great mass of the American people; but it has been of far more benefit to a comparatively few individuals. Americans are just beginning to learn that the great freedom which the individual property-owner has enjoyed is having the inevitable result of all unrestrained exercise of freedom. It has tended to create a powerful but limited class whose chief object it is to hold and to increase the power which they have gained; and this unexpected result has presented the American democracy with the most difficult and radical of its problems. Is it to the interest of the American people as a democracy to permit the increase or the perpetuation of the power gained by this aristocracy of money?

A candid consideration of the foregoing question will, I believe, result in a negative answer. A democracy has as much interest in regulating for its own benefit the distribution of economic power as it has the distribution of political power, and the consequences of ignoring this interest would be as fatal in one case as in the other. In both instances regulation in the democratic interest is as far as possible from meaning the annihilation of individual liberty; but in both instances individual liberty should be subjected to conditions which will continue to keep it efficient and generally serviceable. Individual economic power is not any more dangerous than individual political power—provided it is not held too absolutely and for too long a time. But in both cases the interest of the community as a whole should be dominant; and the interest of the whole community demands a considerable concentration of economic power and responsibility, but only for the ultimate purpose of its more efficient exercise and the better distribution of its fruits.

That certain existing American fortunes have in their making been of the utmost benefit to the whole economic organism is to my mind unquestionably the fact.

Men like Mr. J. Pierpont Morgan, Mr. Andrew Carnegie, Mr. James J. Hill, and Mr. Edward Harriman have in the course of their business careers contributed enormously to American economic efficiency. They have been overpaid for their services, but that is irrelevant to the question immediately under consideration. It is sufficient that their economic power has been just as much earned by substantial service as was the political power of a man like Andrew Jackson; and if our country is to continue its prosperous economic career, it must retain an economic organization which will offer to men of this stamp the opportunity and the inducement to earn distinction. The rule which has already been applied to the case of political power applies, also, to economic power. Individuals should enjoy as much freedom from restraint, as much opportunity, and as much responsibility as is necessary for the efficient performance of their work. Opinions will differ as to the extent of this desirable independence and its associated responsibility. The American millionaire and his supporters claim, of course, that any diminution of opportunity and independence would be fatal. To dispute this inference, however, does not involve the abandonment of the rule itself. A democratic economic system, even more than a democratic political system, must delegate a large share of responsibility and power to the individual, but under conditions, if possible, which will really make for individual efficiency and distinction.

The grievance which a democrat may feel towards the existing economic system is that it makes only partially for genuine individual economic efficiency and distinction. The political power enjoyed by an individual American rarely endures long enough to survive its own utility. But economic power can in some measure at least be detached from its creator. Let it be admitted that the man who accumulates $50,000,000 in part earns it, but how about the man who inherits it? The inheritor of such a fortune, like the inheritor of a ducal title, has an opportunity thrust upon him. He succeeds to a colossal economic privilege which he has not earned and for which he may be wholly incompetent. He rarely inherits with the money the individual ability possessed by its maker, but he does inherit a "money power" wholly independent of his own qualifications or deserts. By virtue of that power alone he is in a position in some measure to exploit his fellow-countrymen. Even though a man of very inferior intellectual and moral caliber, he is able vastly to increase his fortune through the information and opportunity which that fortune bestows upon him, and without making any individual contribution to the economic organization of the country. His power brings with it no personal dignity or efficiency; and for the whole material and meaning of his life he becomes as much dependent upon his millions as a nobleman upon his title. The money which was a source of distinction to its creator becomes in the course of time a source of individual demoralization to its inheritor. His life is organized for the purpose of spending a larger income than any private individual can really need; and his intellectual point of view is bounded by his narrow experience and his class interests.

No doubt the institution of private property, necessitating, as it does, the transmission to one person of the possessions and earnings of another, always involves the inheritance of unearned power and opportunity. But the point is that in the case of very large fortunes the inherited power goes far beyond any legitimate individual needs, and in the course of time can hardly fail to corrupt its possessors. The creator of a large fortune may well be its master; but its inheritor will, except in the case of exceptionally able individuals, become its victim, and most assuredly the evil social effects are as bad as the evil individual effects. The political bond which a democracy seeks to create depends for its higher value upon an effective social bond. Gross inequalities in wealth, wholly divorced from economic efficiency on the part of the rich, as effectively loosen the social bond as do gross inequalities of political and social standing. A wholesome social condition in a democracy does not imply uniformity of wealth any more than it implies uniformity of ability and purpose, but it does imply the association of great individual economic distinction with responsibility and efficiency. It does imply that economic leaders, no less than political ones, should have conditions imposed upon them which will force them to recognize the responsibilities attached to so much power. Mutual association and confidence between the leaders and followers is as much a part of democratic economic organization as it is of democratic political organization; and in the long run the inheritance of vast fortunes destroys any such relation. They breed class envy on one side, and class contempt on the other; and the community is either divided irremediably by differences of interest and outlook, or united, if at all, by snobbish servility.

If the integrity of a democracy is injured by the perpetuation of unearned economic distinctions, it is also injured by extreme poverty, whether deserved or not. A democracy which attempted to equalize wealth would incur the same disastrous fate as a democracy which attempted to equalize political power; but a democracy can no more be indifferent to the distribution of wealth than it can to the distribution of the suffrage. In a wholesome democracy every male adult should participate in the ultimate political responsibility, partly because of the political danger of refusing participation to the people, and partly because of the advantages to be derived from the political union of the whole people.

So a wholesome democracy should seek to guarantee to every male adult a certain minimum of economic power and responsibility. No doubt it is much easier to confer the suffrage on the people than it is to make poverty a negligible social factor; but the difficulty of the task does not make it the less necessary. It stands to reason that in the long run the people who possess the political power will want a substantial share of the economic fruits. A prudent democracy should anticipate this demand. Not only does any considerable amount of grinding poverty constitute a grave social danger in a democratic state, but so, in general, does a widespread condition of partial economic privation. The individuals constituting a democracy lack the first essential of individual freedom when they cannot escape from a condition of economic dependence.

The American democracy has confidently believed in the fatal prosperity enjoyed by the people under the American system. In the confidence of that belief it has promised to Americans a substantial satisfaction of their economic needs; and it has made that promise an essential part of the American national idea. The promise has been measurably fulfilled hitherto, because the prodigious natural resources of a new continent were thrown open to anybody with the energy to appropriate them. But those natural resources have now in large measure passed into the possession of individuals, and American statesmen can no longer count upon them to satisfy the popular hunger for economic independence. An ever larger proportion of the total population of the country is taking to industrial occupations, and an industrial system brings with it much more definite social and economic classes, and a diminution of the earlier social homogeneity. The contemporary wage-earner is no longer satisfied with the economic results of being merely an American citizen. His union is usually of

more obvious use to him than the state, and he is tending to make his allegiance to his union paramount to his
allegiance to the state. This is only one of many illustrations that the traditional American system has broken
down. The American state can regain the loyal adhesion
of the economically less independent class only by positive service. What the wage-earner needs, and what it is
to the interest of a democratic state he should obtain,
is a constantly higher standard of living. The state can
help him to conquer a higher standard of living without
doing any necessary injury to his employers and with
a positive benefit to general economic and social efficiency. If it is to earn the loyalty of the wage-earners,
it must recognize the legitimacy of his demand, and
make the satisfaction of it an essential part of its public
policy.

The American state is dedicated to such a duty, not
only by its democratic purpose, but by its national tradition. So far as the former is concerned, it is absurd
and fatal to ask a popular majority to respect the rights
of a minority, when those rights are interpreted so as
seriously to hamper, if not to forbid, the majority from
obtaining the essential condition of individual freedom
and development—viz. the highest possible standard
of living. But this absurdity becomes really critical and
dangerous, in view of the fact that the American people,
particularly those of alien birth and descent, have been
explicitly promised economic freedom and prosperity.
The promise was made on the strength of what was believed to be an inexhaustible store of natural opportunities; and it will have to be kept even when those natural
resources are no longer to be had for the asking. It is
entirely possible, of course, that the promise can never
be kept,—that its redemption will prove to be beyond
the patience, the power, and the wisdom of the American people and their leaders; but if it is not kept, the

American commonwealth will no longer continue to be a democracy.

IV   The Bridge between Democracy and Nationality

We are now prepared, I hope, to venture upon a more fruitful definition of democracy. The popular definitions err in describing it in terms of its machinery or of some partial political or economic object. Democracy does not mean merely government by the people, or majority rule, or universal suffrage. All of these political forms or devices are a part of its necessary organization; but the chief advantage such methods of organization have is their tendency to promote some salutary and formative purpose. The really formative purpose is not exclusively a matter of individual liberty, although it must give individual liberty abundant scope. Neither is it a matter of equal rights alone, although it must always cherish the social bond which that principle represents. The salutary and formative democratic purpose consists in using the democratic organization for the joint benefit of individual distinction and social improvement.

To define the really democratic organization as one which makes expressly and intentionally for individual distinction and social improvement is nothing more than a translation of the statement that such an organization should make expressly and intentionally for the welfare of the whole people. The whole people will always consist of individuals, constituting small classes, who demand special opportunities, and the mass of the population who demand for their improvement more generalized opportunities. At any particular time or in any particular case, the improvement of the smaller classes may conflict with that of the larger class, but the conflict becomes permanent and irreconcilable only when it is intensified by the lack of a really binding and

edifying public policy, and by the consequent stimula-
tion of class and factional prejudices and purposes. A
policy, intelligently informed by the desire to maintain
a joint process of individual and social amelioration,
should be able to keep a democracy sound and whole
both in sentiment and in idea. Such a democracy would
not be dedicated either to liberty or to equality in their
abstract expressions, but to liberty and equality, in so
far as they made for human brotherhood. As M. Faguet
says in the introduction to his "Politiques et Moralistes
du Dix-Neuvième Siècle," from which I have already
quoted: "Liberté et Égalité sont donc contradictoires
et exclusives l'une et l'autre; mais la Fraternité les concilierait. La Fraternité non seulement concilierait la Liberté et l'Égalité, mais elle les ferait gêneratrices l'une et
l'autre." The two subordinate principles, that is, one representing the individual and the other the social interest,
can by their subordination to the principle of human
brotherhood, be made in the long run mutually helpful.

The foregoing definition of the democratic purpose
is the only one which can entitle democracy to an essential superiority to other forms of political organization. Democrats have always tended to claim some such
superiority for their methods and purposes, but in case
democracy is to be considered merely as a piece of political machinery, or a partial political idea, the claim
has no validity. Its superiority must be based upon the
fact that democracy is the best possible translation into
political and social terms of an authoritative and comprehensive moral idea; and provided a democratic state
honestly seeks to make its organization and policy contribute to a better quality of individuality and a higher
level of associated life, it can within certain limits claim
the allegiance of mankind on rational moral grounds.

The proposed definition may seem to be both vague
and commonplace; but it none the less brings with it

practical consequences of paramount importance. The subordination of the machinery of democracy to its purpose and the comprehension within that purpose of the higher interests both of the individual and society, is not only exclusive of many partial and erroneous ideas, but demands both a reconstructive programme and an efficient organization. A government by the people, which seeks an organization and a policy beneficial to the individual and to society, is confronted by a task as responsible and difficult as you please; but it is a specific task which demands the adoption of certain specific and positive means. Moreover it is a task which the American democracy has never sought consciously to achieve. American democrats have always hoped for individual and social amelioration as the result of the operation of their democratic system; but if any such result was to follow, its achievement was to be a happy accident. The organization and policy of a democracy should leave the individual and society to seek their own amelioration. The democratic state should never discriminate in favor of anything or anybody. It should only discriminate against all sorts of privilege. Under the proposed definition, on the other hand, popular government is to make itself expressly and permanently responsible for the amelioration of the individual and society; and a necessary consequence of this responsibility is an adequate organization and a reconstructive policy.

The majority of good Americans will doubtless consider that the reconstructive policy, already indicated, is flagrantly socialistic both in its methods and its objects; and if any critic likes to fasten the stigma of socialism upon the foregoing conception of democracy, I am not concerned with dodging the odium of the word. The proposed definition of democracy is socialistic, if it is socialistic to consider democracy inseparable from a candid, patient, and courageous attempt to advance the social problem towards a satisfactory solution. It is also socialistic in case socialism cannot be divorced from the use, wherever necessary, of the political organization in all its forms to realize the proposed democratic purpose. On the other hand, there are some doctrines frequently associated with socialism, to which the proposed conception of democracy is wholly inimical; and it should be characterized not so much socialistic, as unscrupulously and loyally nationalistic.

A democracy dedicated to individual and social betterment is necessarily individualist as well as socialist. It has little interest in the mere multiplication of average individuals, except in so far as such multiplication is necessary to economic and political efficiency; but it has the deepest interest in the development of a higher quality of individual self-expression. There are two indispensable economic conditions of qualitative individual self-expression. One is the preservation of the institution of private property in some form, and the other is the radical transformation of its existing nature and influence. A democracy certainly cannot fulfill its mission without the eventual assumption by the state of many functions now performed by individuals, and without becoming expressly responsible for an improved distribution of wealth; but if any attempt is made to accomplish these results by violent means, it will most assuredly prove to be a failure. An improvement in the distribution of wealth or in economic efficiency which cannot be accomplished by purchase on the part of the state or by a legitimate use of the power of taxation, must be left to the action of time, assisted, of course, by such arrangements as are immediately practical. But the amount of actual good to the individual and society which can be effected *at any one time* by an alteration in the distribution of wealth is extremely small; and the same statement is true of any proposed state action in the interest of the democratic purpose. Consequently, while responsible state action is an essential condition of any steady approach to the democratic consummation, such action will be wholly vain unless accompanied by a larger measure of spontaneous individual ameliora-tion. In fact, one of the strongest arguments on behalf of a higher and larger conception of state responsibilities in a democracy is that the candid, courageous, patient, and intelligent attempt to redeem those responsibilities provides one of the highest types of individuality—viz. the public-spirited man with a personal opportunity and a task which should be enormously stimulating and edifying.

The great weakness of the most popular form of so-cialism consists, however, in its mixture of a revolution-ary purpose with an international scope. It seeks the abolition of national distinctions by revolutionary re-volts of the wage-earner against the capitalist; and in so far as it proposes to undermine the principle of national cohesion and to substitute for it an international orga-nization of a single class, it is headed absolutely in the wrong direction. Revolutions may at times be necessary and on the whole helpful, but not in case there is any other practicable method of removing grave obstacles to human amelioration; and in any event their tendency is socially disintegrating. The destruction or the weak-ening of nationalities for the ostensible benefit of an in-ternational socialism would in truth gravely imperil the bond upon which actual human association is based. The peoples who have inherited any share in Christian civilization are effectively united chiefly by national habits, traditions, and purposes; and perhaps the most effective way of bringing about an irretrievable division of purpose among them would be the adoption by the class of wage-earners of the programme of international socialism. It is not too much to say that no permanent good can, under existing conditions, come to the individual and society except through the preservation and the development of the existing system of nationalized states.

Radical and enthusiastic democrats have usually failed to attach sufficient importance to the ties whereby civilized men are at the present time actually united. Inasmuch as national traditions are usually associated with all sorts of political, economic, and social privileges and abuses, they have sought to identify the higher social relation with the destruction of the national tradition and the substitution of an ideal bond. In so doing they are committing a disastrous error; and democracy will never become really constructive until this error is recognized and democracy abandons its former alliance with revolution. The higher human relation must be brought about chiefly by the improvement and the intensification of existing human relations. The only possible foundation for a better social structure is the existing order, of which the contemporary system of nationalized states forms the foundation.

Loyalty to the existing system of nationalized states does not necessarily mean loyalty to an existing government merely because it exists. There have been, and still are, governments whose ruin is a necessary condition of popular liberation; and revolution doubtless still has a subordinate part to play in the process of human amelioration. The loyalty which a citizen owes to a government is dependent upon the extent to which the government is representative of national traditions and is organized in the interest of valid national purposes. National traditions and purposes always contain a large infusion of dubious ingredients; but loyalty to them does not necessarily mean the uncritical and unprotesting acceptance of the national limitations and abuses. Nationality is a political and social ideal as well as the great contemporary political fact. Loyalty to the national interest implies devotion to a progressive principle. It demands, to be sure, that the progressive principle be realized without any violation of fundamental national ties. It demands that any national action taken for the benefit of the progressive principle be approved by the official national organization. But it also serves as a ferment quite as much as a bond. It bids the loyal national servants to fashion their fellow-countrymen into more of a nation; and the attempt to perform this bidding constitutes a very powerful and wholesome source of political development. It constitutes, indeed, a source of political development which is of decisive importance for a satisfactory theory of political and social progress, because a people which becomes more of a nation has a tendency to become for that very reason more of a democracy.

The assertion that a people which becomes more of a nation becomes for that very reason more of a democracy, is, I am aware, a hazardous assertion, which can be justified, if at all, only at a considerable expense. As a matter of fact, the two following chapters will be devoted chiefly to this labor of justification. In the first of these chapters I shall give a partly historical and partly critical account of the national principle in its relation to democracy; and in the second I shall apply the results, so achieved, to the American national principle in its relation to the American democratic idea. But before starting this complicated task, a few words must be premised as to the reasons which make the attempt well worth the trouble.

If a people, in becoming more of a nation, become for that very reason more of a democracy, the realization of the democratic purpose is not rendered any easier, but democracy is provided with a simplified, a consistent, and a practicable programme. An alliance is established thereby between the two dominant political and social forces in modern life. The suspicion with which aggressive advocates of the national principle have sometimes regarded democracy would be shown to have only a conditional justification; and the suspicion with which many ardent democrats have regarded aggressive nationalism would be similarly disarmed. A democrat, so far as the statement is true, could trust the fate of his cause in each particular state to the friends of national progress. Democracy would not need for its consummation the ruin of the traditional political fabrics; but so far as those political bodies were informed by genuinely national ideas and aspirations, it could await confidently the process of national development. In fact, the first duty of a good democrat would be that of rendering to his country loyal patriotic service. Democrats would abandon the task of making over the world to suit their own purposes, until they had come to a better understanding with their own countrymen. One's democracy, that is, would begin at home and it would for the most part stay at home; and the cause of national well-being would derive invaluable assistance from the loyal coöperation of good democrats.

A great many obvious objections will, of course, be immediately raised against any such explanation of the relation between democracy and nationality; and I am well aware that these objections demand the most serious consideration. A generation or two ago the European democrat was often by way of being an ardent nationalist; and a constructive relation between the two principles was accepted by many European political reformers. The events of the last fifty years have, however, done much to sever the alliance, and to make European patriots suspicious of democracy, and European democrats suspicious of patriotism. To what extent these suspicions are justified, I shall discuss in the next chapter; but that discussion will be undertaken almost exclusively for obtaining, if possible, some light upon our domestic situation. The formula of a constructive relation between the national and democratic principles has certain importance for European peoples, and particularly for Frenchmen: but, if true, it is of a far superior importance to Americans. It supplies a constructive form for the progressive solution of their political and social problems; and while it imposes on them responsibilities which they have sought to evade, it also offers compensations, the advantage of which they have scarcely expected.

Americans have always been both patriotic and democratic, just as they have always been friendly both to liberty and equality, but in neither case have they brought the two ideas or aspirations into mutually helpful relations. As democrats they have often regarded nationalism with distrust, and have consequently deprived their patriotism of any sufficient substance and organization. As nationalists they have frequently regarded essential aspects of democracy with a wholly unnecessary and embarrassing suspicion. They have been after a fashion Hamiltonian, and Jeffersonian after more of a fashion; but they have never recovered from the initial disagreement between Hamilton and Jefferson. If there is any truth in the idea of a constructive relation between democracy and nationality this disagreement must be healed. They must accept both principles loyally and unreservedly; and by such acceptance their "noble national theory" will obtain a wholly unaccustomed energy and integrity. The alliance between the two principles will not leave either of them intact; but it will necessarily do more harm to the Jeffersonian group of political ideas than it will to the Hamiltonian. The latter's nationalism can be adapted to democracy without an essential injury to itself, but the former's democracy cannot be nationalized without being transformed. The manner of its transformation has already been discussed in detail. It must cease to be a democracy of indiscriminate individualism, and become one of selected individuals who are obliged constantly to justify their selection; and its members must be united not by a sense of joint irresponsibility, but by a sense of joint responsibility for the success of their political and social ideal. They must become, that is, a democracy devoted to the welfare of the whole people by means of a conscious labor of individual and social improvement; and that is precisely the sort of democracy which demands for its realization the aid of the Hamiltonian nationalistic organization and principle.

8.

Nationality and Democracy: National Origins

I

Whatever the contemporary or the logical relation between nationality and democracy as ideas and as political forces, they were in their origin wholly independent one of the other. The Greek city states supplied the first examples of democracy; but their democracy brought with it no specifically national characteristics. In fact, the political condition and ideal implied by the word nation did not exist in the ancient world. The actual historical process, which culminated in the formation of the modern national state, began some time in the Middle Ages—a period in which democracy was almost an incredible form of political association. Some of the mediæval communes were not without traces of democracy; but modern nations do not derive from those turbulent little states. They derive from the larger political divisions into which Europe drifted during the Dark Ages; and they have grown with the gradually prospering attempt to bestow on the government of these European countries the qualities of efficiency and responsibility.

A complete justification of the foregoing statements would require a critical account of the political development of Western Europe since 400 B.C.; but within the necessary limits of the present discussion, we shall have to be satisfied with the barest summary of the way in which the modern national states originated, and of the relation to democracy which has gradually resulted from their own proper development. A great deal of misunderstanding exists as to the fundamental nature of a national as compared to a city or to an imperial state, because the meaning of the national idea has been obscured by the controversies which its militant assertion has involved. It has been identified both with a revolutionary and a racial political principle, whereas its revolutionary or racial associations are essentially occasional and accidental. The modern national state is at bottom the most intelligent and successful attempt which has yet been made to create a comparatively stable, efficient, and responsible type of political association.

The primary objects sought in political association are internal order, security from foreign attack, the authoritative and just adjustment of domestic differences and grievances, and a certain opportunity for individual development; and these several objects are really reducible to two, because internal order cannot be preserved among a vigorous people, in case no sufficient opportunity is provided for individual development or for the adjustment of differences and grievances. In order that a state may be relatively secure from foreign attack, it must possess a certain considerable area, population, and military efficiency. The fundamental weakness of the commune or city state has always been its inability to protect itself from the aggressions of larger or more warlike neighbors, and its correlative inability to settle its own domestic differences without foreign interference. On the other hand, when a state became sufficiently large and well organized to feel safe against alien aggression, it inevitably became the aggressor itself; and it inevitably carried the conquest of its neighbors just as far as it was able. But domestic security, which is reached by constant foreign aggression, results inevitably in a huge unwieldy form of imperial political organization which is obliged by the logic of its situation to seek universal dominion. The Romans made the great attempt to establish a dominion of this kind; and while their Empire could not endure, because their military organization destroyed in the end the very foundation of internal order, they bequeathed to civilization a political ideal and a legal code of inestimable subsequent value.

As long as men were obliged to choose between a communal or an imperial type of political organization,—which was equivalent merely to a choice between anarchy and despotism,—the problem of combining internal order with external security seemed insoluble. They needed a form of association strong enough to defend their frontiers, but not sufficiently strong to attack their neighbors with any chance of continued success; and such a state could not exist unless its unity and integrity had some moral basis, and unless the aggressions of exceptionally efficient states were checked by some effective inter-state organization. The coexistence of such states demanded in its turn the general acceptance of certain common moral ties and standards among a group of neighboring peoples; and such a tie was furnished by the religious bond with which Catholic Christianity united the peoples of Western Europe—a bond whereby the disorder and anarchy of the early Middle Ages was converted into a vehicle of political and social education. The members of the Christian body had much to fear from their fellow-Christians, but they also had much to gain. They shared many interesting and vital subjects of consultation; and even when they fought, as they usually did, they were likely to fight to some purpose. But beyond their quarrels Catholic Christians comprised one universe of discourse. They were somehow responsible one to another; and their mutual ties and responsibilities were most clearly demonstrated whenever a peculiarly unscrupulous and insistent attempt was made to violate them. As new and comparatively strong states began to emerge from the confusion of the early Middle Ages, it was soon found that under the new conditions states which were vigorous enough to establish internal peace and to protect their frontiers were not vigorous enough to conquer their neighbors. Political efficiency was brought to a much better realization of its necessary limits and responsibilities, because of the moral and intellectual education which the adoption of Christianity had imposed upon the Western peoples.

One of the earliest examples of political efficiency in mediæval Europe was the England of Edward I, which had begun to exhibit certain characteristics of a national state. Order was more than usually well preserved. It was sheltered by the Channel from foreign attack. The interest both of the nobles and of the people had been considered in its political organization. A fair balance was maintained among the leading members of the political body, so that the English kings could invade France with united national armies which easily defeated the incoherent rabble of knights and serfs whereby they were opposed. Nevertheless, when the English, after the manner of other efficient states, tried to conquer France, they were wholly unable to extinguish French resistance, as the similar resistance of conquered peoples had so frequently been extinguished in classic times. The French people rallied to a king who united them in their resistance to foreign domination; and the ultimate effect of the prolonged English aggression was merely the increasing national efficiency and the improving political organization of the French people.

The English could not extinguish the resistance of the French people, because their aggression aroused in

Frenchmen latent power of effective association. Notwithstanding the prevalence of a factious minority, and the lack of any habit or tradition of national association, the power of united action for a common purpose was stimulated by the threat of alien domination; and this latent power was unquestionably the result in some measure of the discipline of Christian ideas to which the French, in common with the other European peoples, had been subjected. That discipline had, as has already been observed, increased men's capacity for fruitful association one with another. It had stimulated a social relationship much superior to the prevailing political relationship. It had enabled them to believe in an idea and to fight devotedly on its behalf. It is no accident, consequently, that the national resistance took on a religious character, and in Jeanne d'Arc gave birth to one of the most fragrant figures in human history. Thus the French national resistance, and the national bond thereby created, was one political expression of the power of coöperation developed in the people of Europe by the acceptance of a common religious bond. On the other hand, the use which the English had made of their precocious national organization weakened its foundations. The aggressive exercise of military force abroad for an object which it was incompetent to achieve disturbed the domestic balance of power on which the national organization of the English people rested. English political efficiency was dependent partly upon its responsible exercise; and it could not survive the disregard of domestic responsibilities entailed by the expense in men and money of futile external aggression.

The history of Europe as it emerged from the Middle Ages affords a continuous illustration of the truth that the increasing political efficiency of the several states was proportioned to the exercise of their powers in a responsible manner. The national development of the several states was complicated in the beginning by the religious wars; but those peoples suffered least from the wars of religion who did not in the end allow them to interfere with their primary political responsibilities. Spain, for instance, whose centuries of fighting with the Moors had enormously developed her military efficiency, used this military power solely for the purpose of pursuing political and religious objects antagonistic or irrelevant to the responsibilities of the Spanish kings towards their own subjects. The Spanish monarchy proclaimed as its dominant political object the maintenance by force of the Catholic faith throughout Europe; and for three generations it wasted the superb military strength and the economic resources of the Spanish people in an attempt to crush out Protestantism in Holland and England and to reinforce militant Catholicism in France. Upon Germany, divided into a number of petty states, partly Protestant, and partly Catholic, but with the Imperial power exerted on behalf of a Catholic and anti-national interest, the religious wars laid a heavy hand. Her lack of political cohesion made her the prey of neighboring countries whose population was numerically smaller, but which were better organized; and the end of the Thirty Years' War left her both despoiled and exhausted, because her political organization was wholly incapable of realizing a national policy or of meeting the national needs. Great Britain during all this period was occupied with her domestic problems and interfered comparatively little in continental affairs; and the result of this discreet and sensible effort to adapt her national organization to her peculiar domestic needs was in the eighteenth century an extraordinary increase of national efficiency. France also emerged from the religious wars headed by a dynasty which really represented national aspirations, and which was alive in some respects to its responsibilities toward the

French people. The Bourbon monarchy consolidated the French national organization, encouraged French intellectual and religious life, and at times sought in an intelligent manner to improve the economic conditions of the country. For the first time in the history of continental Europe something resembling a genuinely national state was developed. Differences of religious opinion had been subordinated to the political and social interests of the French people. The crown, with the aid of a succession of able ministers, suppressed a factious nobility at home, and gradually made France the dominant European Power. A condition of the attainment of both of these objects was the loyal support of the French people, and the alliance with the monarchy, as the embodiment of French national life, of Frenchmen of ability and purpose.

The French monarchy, however, after it had become the dominant power in Europe, followed the bad example of previous states, and aroused the fear of its neighbors by a policy of excessive aggression. In this instance French domineering did not stimulate the national development of any one neighbor, because it was not concentrated upon any one or two peoples. But it did threaten the common interests of a number of European states; and it awakened an unprecedented faculty of inter-state association for the protection of these interests. The doctrine of the Balance of Power waxed as the result of this experience into a living principle in European politics; and it imposed an effective check upon the aggression of any single state. France was unable to retain the preponderant position which she had earned during the early years of the reign of Louis XIV; and this mistake of the Bourbon monarchy was the cause of its eventual downfall. The finances of the country were wrecked by its military efforts and failures, the industrial development of the people checked, and their loyalty to the Bourbons undermined. A gulf was gradually created between the French nation and its official organization and policy.

England, on the other hand, was successfully pursuing the opposite work of national improvement and consolidation. She was developing a system of government which, while preserving the crown as the symbol of social order, combined aristocratic leadership with some measure of national representation. For the first time in centuries the different members of her political body again began to function harmoniously; and she used the increasing power of aggression thereby secured with unprecedented discretion and good sense. She had learned that her military power could not be used with any effect across the Channel, and that under existing conditions her national interests in relation to the other European Powers were more negative than positive. Her expansive energy was concentrated on the task of building up a colonial empire in Asia and America; and in this task her comparative freedom from continental entanglements enabled her completely to vanquish France. Her success in creating a colonial empire anticipated with extraordinary precision the course during the nineteenth century of European national development.

In contemplating the political situation of Europe towards the end of the eighteenth century the student of the origin of the power and principle of nationality will be impressed by its two divergent aspects. The governments of the several European states had become tolerably efficient for those purposes in relation to which, during the sixteenth century and before, efficiency had been most necessary. They could keep order. Their citizens were protected to some extent in the enjoyment of their legal rights. The several governments were closely associated chiefly for the purpose of preventing excessive aggression on the part of any one state and of preserving the Balance of Power. Unfortunately, however, these governments had acquired during the turbulent era an unlimited authority which was indispensable to the fundamental task of maintaining order, but which, after order had been secured, was sufficient to encourage abuse. Their power was in theory absolute. It was an imitation of Roman Imperialism, and made no allowance for those limitations, both in its domestic and foreign expressions, which existed as a consequence of national growth and the international system. Their authority at all times was keyed up to the pitch of a great emergency. It was supposed to be the immediate expression of the common weal. The common weal was identified with the security of society and the state. The security of the state dictated the supreme law. The very authority, consequently, which was created to preserve order and the Balance of Power gradually became an effective cause of internal and external disorder. It became a source not of security, but of individual and social insecurity, because a properly organized machinery for exercising such a power and redeeming such a vast responsibility had not as yet been wrought.

The rulers of the continental states in the eighteenth century explained and excused every important action they took by what was called "La Raison d'État"—that is, by reasons connected with the public safety which justified absolute authority and extreme measures. But as a matter of fact this absolute authority, instead of being confined in its exercise to matters in which the public safety was really concerned, was wasted and compromised chiefly for the benefit of a trivial domestic policy and a merely dynastic foreign policy. At home the exercise of absolute authority was not limited to matters and occasions which really raised questions of public safety. In their foreign policies the majority of the states had little idea of the necessary and desirable limits of their own aggressive power. Those limits were imposed from without; and when several states could combine in support of an act of international piracy, as in the case of the partition of Poland, Europe could not be said to have any effective system of public law. The partition of Poland, which France could and should have prevented, was at once a convincing exposure of the miserable international position to which France had been reduced by the Bourbons, and the best possible testimony to the final moral bankruptcy of the political system of the eighteenth century.

II   The Implications of National Development

In 1789 the bombshell of the French Revolution exploded under this fabric of semi-national and semi-despotic, but wholly royalist and aristocratic, European political system. For the first time in the history of European nations a national organization and tradition was confronted by a radical democratic purpose and faith. The two ideas have been face to face ever since; and European history thereafter may, in its broadest aspect, be considered as an attempt to establish a fruitful relation between them. In the beginning it looked as if democracy would, so far as it prevailed, be wholly destructive of national institutions and the existing international organization. The insurgent democrats sought to ignore and to eradicate the very substance of French national achievement. They began by abolishing all social and economic privileges and by framing a new polity based in general upon the English idea of a limited monarchy, partial popular representation, and equal civil rights; but, carried along by the momentum of their ideas and incensed by the disloyalty of the king and his advisers and the threat of invasion they ended by abolishing royalty, establishing universal suffrage and declaring war upon every embodiment, whether at home or abroad, of the older order. The revolutionary French democracy proclaimed a creed, not merely subversive of all monarchical and aristocratic institutions, but inimical to the substance and the spirit of nationality. Indeed it did not perceive any essential distinction between the monarchical or legitimist and the national principles; and the error was under the circumstances not unnatural. In the European political landscape of 1793 despotic royalty was a much more conspicuous fact than the centuries of political association in which these monarchies had been developed. But the eyes of the French democrats had been partially blinded by their own political interests and theories. Their democracy was in theory chiefly a matter of abstract political rights which remitted logically in a sort of revolutionary anarchy. The actual bonds whereby men were united were ignored. All traditional authority fell under suspicion. Frenchmen, in their devotion to their ideas and in their distrust of every institution, idea, or person associated with the Old Régime, hacked at the roots of their national cohesion and undermined the foundations of social order.

To a disinterested political philosopher of that day the antagonism between the principle of political authority and cohesion, as represented by the legitimate monarchies, and the principle of popular Sovereignty represented by the French democracy, may well have looked irretrievable. But events soon proved that such an inference could not be drawn too quickly. It is true that the French democracy, by breaking so violently the bonds of national association, perpetuated a division between their political organization and the substance of their national life, which was bound in the end to constitute a source of weakness. Yet the revolutionary democracy succeeded, nevertheless, in releasing sources of national energy, whose existence had never before been suspected, and in uniting the great body of the French people for the performance of a great task. Even though French national cohesion had been injured in one respect, French national efficiency was temporarily so increased that the existing organization and power of the other continental countries proved inadequate to resist it. When the French democracy was attacked by its monarchical neighbors, the newly aroused national energy of the French people was placed enthusiastically at the service of the military authorities. The success of the French armies, even during the disorders of the Convention and the corruption of the Directory, indicated that revolutionary France possessed possibilities of national efficiency far superior to the France of the Old Régime.

Neither the democrats nor Napoleon had, in truth, broken as much as they themselves and their enemies believed with the French national tradition; but unfortunately that aspect of the national tradition perpetuated by them was by no means its best aspect. The policy, the methods of administration, and the actual power of the Committee of Public Safety and of Napoleon were all inherited from the Old Régime. Revolutionary France merely adapted to new conditions the political organization and policy to which Frenchmen had been accustomed; and the most serious indictment to be made against it is that its excesses prevented it from dispensing with the absolutism which social disorder and unwarranted foreign aggression always necessitate. The Revolution made France more of a nation than it had been in the eighteenth century, because it gave to the French people the civil freedom, the political experience, and the economic opportunities which they needed, but it did not heal the breach which the Bourbons had made between the political organization of France and its legitimate national interests and aspirations. France in 1815, like France in 1789, remained a nation divided against itself,—a nation which had perpetuated during a democratic revolution a part of its national tradition most opposed to the logic of its new political and social ideas. It remained, that is, a nation whose political organization and policy had not been adapted to its domestic needs, and one which occupied on anomalous and suspected position in the European international system.

On the other hand, French democracy and Imperialism had directly and indirectly instigated the greater national efficiency of the neighboring European states. Alliances among European monarchs had not been sufficient to check the Imperial ambitions of Napoleon, as they had been sufficient to check the career of Louis XIV, because behind a greater general was the loyal devotion and the liberated energy of the French people; but when outrages perpetrated on the national feelings of Germans and Spaniards added an enthusiastic popular support to the hatred which the European monarchs cherished towards a domineering upstart, the fall of Napoleon became only a question of time. The excess and the abuse of French national efficiency and energy, consequent upon its sudden liberation and its perpetuation of an illogical but natural policy of national aggression, had the same effect upon Europe as English aggression had upon the national development of France. Napoleon was crushed under a popular uprising, comparable to that of the French people, which had been the condition of his own aggrandizement. Thus, in spite of the partial antagonism between the ideas of the French Revolutionary democracy and the principle of nationality the ultimate effect of the Revolution both in France and in Europe was to increase the force and to enlarge the area of the national movement. English national sentiment was enormously stimulated by the strenuous wars of the Revolutionary epoch. The embers of Spanish national feeling were blown into spasmodic life. The peoples of Italy and Germany had been possessed by the momentum of a common political purpose, and had been stirred by promises of national representation. Even France, unstable though its political condition was, had lost none of the results of the Revolution for which it had fought in the beginning; and if the Bourbons were restored, it was only on the implicit condition that the monarchy should be nationalized. The Revolutionary democracy, subversive as were its ideas, had started a new era for the European peoples of national and international construction.

Of course, it was by no means obvious in 1815 that a constructive national and international principle had come to dominate the European political system. The Treaty of Vienna was an unprincipled compromise among the divergent interests and claims of the dominant Powers, and the triumphant monarchs ignored their promises of national reform or representation. For one whole generation they resolutely suppressed, so far as they were able, every symptom of an insurgent democratic or national idea. They sought persistently and ingeniously to identify in Europe the principle of political integrity and order with the principle of the legitimate monarchy. But obscurantist as were the ideas and the policy of the Holy Alliance, the political system it established was an enormous improvement upon that of the eighteenth century. Not only was the sense of responsibility of the governing classes very much quickened, but the international system was based on a comparatively moral and rational idea. For the first time in European history a group of rulers, possessing in theory absolute authority and forming an apparently irresistible combination, exercised this power with moderation. They did not combine, as in the case of the partition of Poland, to break the peace and prey upon a defenseless neighbor, but to keep the peace; and if to keep the peace meant the suppression wherever possible of liberal political ideas, it meant also the renunciation of aggressive foreign policies. In this way Europe obtained the rest which was necessary after the havoc of the Revolutionary wars, while at the same time the principle on which the Holy Alliance was based was being put to the test of experience. Such a test it could not stand. The people of Europe were not content to identify the principle of political order, whether in domestic or foreign affairs, with that of legitimate monarchy and with the arbitrary political alignments of the Treaty of Vienna. Such a settlement ignored the political forces and ideas which, while originating in Revolutionary France, had none the less saved Europe from the consequences of French Revolutionary and Imperial aggression.

Beginning in 1848, Europe entered upon another period of revolutionary disturbance, which completely destroyed the political system of the Holy Alliance. At the outset these revolutions were no more respectful of national traditions than was the French Revolution; and as long as they remained chiefly subversive in idea and purpose, they accomplished little. But after some unsuccessful experimentation, the new revolutionary movement gradually adopted a national programme; and thereafter, its triumphs were many and varied. For the first time in political history the meaning of the national principle began to be understood; and it became in the most explicit manner a substantial and a formative political idea.

The revolutionary period taught European statesmen and political thinkers that political efficiency and responsibility both implied some degree of popular representation. Such representation did not necessarily go as far as thorough-going democrats would like. It did not necessarily transfer the source of political authority from the crown to the people. It did not necessarily bring with it, as in France, the overthrow of those political and social institutions which constituted the traditional structure of the national life. But it did imply that the government should make itself expressly responsible to public opinion, and should consult public opinion about all important questions of public policy. A certain amount of political freedom was shown to be indispensable to the making of a nation, and the granting of this amount of political freedom was no more than a fulfillment of the historical process in which the nations of Europe had originated.

The people of Europe had drifted into groups, the members of which, for one reason or another, were capable of effective political association. This association was not based at bottom on physical conditions. It was not dependent on a blood bond, because as a matter of fact the racial composition of the European peoples is exceedingly mixed. It was partly conditioned on geographical continuity without being necessarily caused thereby, and was wholly independent of any uniformity of climate. The association was in the beginning largely a matter of convenience or a matter of habit. Those associations endured which proved under stress of historical vicissitudes to be worthy of endurance. The longer any particular association endured, the more firm it became in political structure and the more definite in policy. Its citizens became accustomed to association one with another, and they became accustomed to those political and social forms which supplied the machinery of joint action. Certain institutions and ideas were selected by the pressure of historical events and were capitalized into the effective local political and social traditions. These traditions constituted the substance of the political and social bond. They provided the forms which enabled the people of any group to realize a joint purpose or, if necessary, to discuss serious differences. In their absence the very foundation of permanent political cohesion was lacking. For a while the protection of these groups against domestic and foreign enemies demanded, as we have seen, the exercise of an absolute political authority and the severe suppression of any but time-honored individual or class interests; but when comparative order had been secured, a higher standard of association gradually came to prevail. Differences of conviction and interest among individuals and classes, which formerly were suppressed or ignored, could no longer be considered either as so dangerous to public safety as to demand suppression or as so insignificant as to justify indifference. Effective association began to demand, that is, a new adjustment among the individual and class interests, traditions, and convictions which constituted the substance of any particular state; and such an adjustment could be secured only by an adequate machinery of consultation and discussion. Cohesion could no longer be imposed upon a people, because they no longer had any sufficient reason to submit to the discipline of such an imposition. It had to be reached by an enlarged area of political association, by the full expression of individual and class differences, and finally by the proper adjustment of those differences in relation to the general interest of the whole community.

As soon as any European state attained, by whatever means, a representative government, it began to be more of a nation, and to obtain the advantages of a more nationalized political organization. England's comparative domestic security enabled her to become more of a nation sooner than any of her continental neighbors; and her national efficiency forced the French to cultivate their latent power of national association. In France the government finally succeeded in becoming nationally representative without much assistance from any regular machinery of representation; but under such conditions it could not remain representative. One of its defects as a nation to-day is its lack of representative institutions to which Frenchmen have been long accustomed and which command some instinctive loyalty. Stimulated by French and English example, the other European states finally understood that some form or degree of popular representation was essential to national cohesion; and little by little they have been grafting representative institutions upon their traditional political structures. Thus the need of political and social cohesion was converted into a principle of constructive national reform. A nation is more or less of a nation according as its members are more or less capable of effective association; and the great object of a genuinely national domestic policy is that of making such association candid, loyal, and fruitful. Loyal and fruitful association is far from demanding mere uniformity of purpose and conviction on the part of those associated. On the contrary it gains enormously from a wide variety of individual differences,—but with the essential condition that such differences do not become factious in spirit and hostile to the utmost freedom of intercourse. But the only way of mitigating factiousness and misunderstanding is by means of some machinery of mutual consultation, which may help to remedy grievances and whose decision shall determine the political action taken in the name of the whole community. The national principle, that is, which is precisely the principle of loyal and fruitful political association, depends for its vitality upon the establishment and maintenance of a constructive relation between the official political organization and policy and the interests, the ideas, and the traditions of the people as a whole. The nations of Europe, much as they suffered from the French Revolution and disliked it, owe to the insurgent French democracy their effective instruction in this political truth.

It follows, however, that there is no universal and perfect machinery whereby loyal and fruitful national association can be secured. The nations of Europe originated in local political groups, each of which possessed its own peculiar interests, institutions, and traditions. Their power of fruitful national association depended more upon loyalty to their particular local political tradition and habits than upon any ideal perfection in their new and experimental machinery for distributing political responsibility and securing popular representation. A national policy and organization is, consequently, essentially particular; and, what is equally important, its particular character is partly determined by the similarly special character of the policy and organization of the surrounding states. The historical process in which each of the European nations originated included, as an essential element, the action and reaction of these particular states one upon the other. Each nation was formed, that is, as part of a political system which included other nations. As any particular state became more of a nation, its increasing power of effective association forced its neighbors either into submission or into an equally efficient exercise of national resistance. Little by little it has been discovered that any increase in the loyalty and fertility of a country's domestic life was contingent upon the attainment of a more definite position in the general European system; and that, on the other hand, any attempt to escape from the limitations imposed upon a particular state by the general system was followed by a diminished efficiency in its machinery of national association.

The full meaning of these general principles can, perhaps, be best explained by the consideration in re-

lation thereto of the existing political condition of the
foremost European nations—Great Britain, France, and
Germany. Each of these special cases will afford an opportunity of exhibiting a new and a significant varia-
tion of the relation between the principles of nationality and the principles of democracy; and together they
should enable us to reach a fairly complete definition
of the extent to which, in contemporary Europe, any
fruitful relation can be established between them. What
has already been said sufficiently indicates that the effective realization of a national principle, even in Europe, demands a certain infusion of democracy; but it
also indicates that this democratic infusion cannot at
any one time be carried very far without impairing the
national integrity. How far, then, in these three decisive
cases has the democratic infusion been carried and what
are the consequences, the promise, and the dangers of
each experiment?

III   Nationality and Democracy in England

It has already been observed that England was the first
European state both in mediæval and modern times
to reach a high degree of national efficiency. At a period when the foreign policies of the continental states
were exclusively but timidly dynastic, and when their
domestic organizations illustrated the disadvantages
of a tepid autocracy, Great Britain had entered upon a
foreign policy of national colonial expansion and was
building up a representative national domestic organization. After several centuries of revolutionary disturbance the English had regained their national balance,
without sacrificing any of the time-honored elements in
their national life. The monarchy was reconstituted as
the symbol of the national integrity and as the crown of
the social system. The hereditary aristocracy, which was

kept in touch with the commoners because its younger sons were not noble and which was national, if not liberal, in spirit, became the real rulers of England; but its role was supplemented by an effective though limited measure of general representation. This organization was perfected in the nineteenth century. Little by little the area of popular representation was enlarged, until it included almost the whole adult male population; and the government became more and more effectively controlled by national public opinion. As a result of this slowly gathering but comprehensive plan of national organization, the English have become more completely united in spirit and purpose than are the people of any other country. The crown and the aristocracy recognize the limitations of their positions and their inherited responsibilities to the gentry and the people. The commoners on their side are proud of their lords and of the monarchy and grant them full confidence. It is a unique instance of mutual loyalty and well-distributed responsibility among social classes, differing widely in station, occupations, and wealth; and it is founded upon habit of joint consultation, coupled, as the result of the long persistence of this habit, with an unusual similarity of intellectual and moral outlook.

The result, until recently, was an exceptional degree of national efficiency; and in scrutinizing this national efficiency the fact must be faced that the political success of Great Britain has apparently been due, not merely to her adoption of the practice of national representation, but to her abhorrence of any more subversive democratic ideas. On the one hand, the British have organized a political system which is probably more sensitively and completely responsive to a nationalized public opinion than is the political system of the American democracy. On the other hand, this same nationalized political organization is aristocratic to the core—aristocratic without scruple or qualification. What is the effect of this aristocratic organization upon the efficiency and fertility of the English political system? Has it contributed in the past to such efficiency? Does it still contribute? And if so, how far?

The power of the English aristocracy is no doubt to be justified, in part, by the admirable service which has been rendered to the country by the nobility and the gentry. During the eighteenth and a part of the nineteenth centuries the political leadership of the English people was on the whole both efficient and edifying. During all this period their continental competitors were either burdened with autocratic obscurantism or else were weakened by civil struggles and the fatal consequences of military aggression. In the meantime Great Britain pursued a comparatively tranquil course of domestic reform and colonial and industrial expansion. She was the European Power whose political and industrial energies were most completely liberated and most successfully used; and as a consequence she naturally drifted into an extremely self-satisfied state of mind in respect to her political and economic organization and policy. But during the last quarter of the nineteenth century political and economic conditions both began to change. The more important competing nations had by that time overcome their internal disorders, and by virtue of their domestic reforms had released new springs of national energy. Great Britain had to face much severer competition in the fields both of industrial and colonial expansion; and during all of these years she has been losing ground. Her expansion has not entirely ceased; but industrially she is being left behind by Germany and by the United States, and her recent colonial acquisitions have been attained only at an excessive cost. Inasmuch as she has succeeded in retaining her relative superiority on the sea, she has maintained her special position in the European political system; but the relatively greater responsibilities of the future coupled with her relatively smaller resources make her future international standing dubious. It looks as if there might be something lacking in the national organization and policy with which Great Britain has been so completely content.

Many Englishmen recognize that their national organization has diminished in efficiency, and they are considering various methods of meeting the emergency. But to an outsider it does not look as if any remedy, as yet seriously proposed, was really adequate. The truth is, that the existing political, social, and economic organization of Great Britain both impairs and misleads the energy of the people. It was adequate to the economic and political conditions of two generations ago, but it is at the present time becoming more and more inadequate. It is inferior in certain essential respects to the economic and political organization of Great Britain's two leading competitors—Germany and the United States. It is lacking in purpose. It is lacking in brains. It is lacking in faith.

Just as Great Britain benefited enormously during a century and a half from her political precocity, so she is now suffering from the consequences thereof. The political temperament of her people, their method of organization, and their national ideals all took form at a time when international competition for colonies and trade was not very sharp, and when democracy had no philosophic or moral standing. At the beginning of the eighteenth century the country was longing for domestic peace, and it was willing to secure peace at any price save that of liberty. The leadership of the landed aristocracy and gentry secured to the British people domestic peace and civil liberty, and in return for these very great blessings they sold themselves to the privileged classes. These privileged classes have probably deserved their privileges more completely than has the aristocracy of any other country. They have been patriotic; they have shed their blood and spent their money on what they believed to be the national welfare; they introduced an honorable and an admirable *esprit de corps* into the English public service; and they have been loyal to the great formative English political idea—the idea of liberty. They have granted to the people from time to time as much liberty as public opinion demanded, and have in this way maintained to the present day their political and social prestige. But although they have been, on the whole, individually disinterested, they have not been and they could not be disinterested as a class. Owning as they did much of the land, they had as a class certain economic interests. Possessing as they did certain special privileges, they had as a class certain political interests. These interests have been scrupulously preserved, no matter whether they did or did not conflict with the national interest. Their landed proprietorship has resulted in certain radical inequalities of taxation and certain grave economic drawbacks. Their position as a privileged class made them hospitable only to those reforms which spared their privileges. But their privileges could not be spared, provided Englishmen allowed rational ideas any decisive influence in their political life; and the consequence of this abstention from ideas was the gradual cultivation of a contempt for intelligence, an excessive worship of tradition, and a deep-rooted faith in the value of compromise. In the interest of domestic harmony they have identified complacent social subserviency with the virtue of loyalty, and have erected compromise into an ultimate principle of political action.

The landed aristocracy and gentry of England have been obliged to face only one serious crisis—the prolonged crisis occasioned by the transformation of Great Britain from an agricultural to an industrial community.

The way the English privileged classes preserved their political leadership during a period, in which land was ceasing to be the source of Great Britain's economic prosperity, is an extraordinary illustration of their political tact and social prestige. But it must be added that their leadership has been preserved more in name than in substance. The aristocracy managed to keep its prestige and its apparent power during the course of the industrial revolution, but only on condition of the abandonment of the substance thereof. The nobility and the gentry became the privileged servants of the rising middle class. They bought off their commercial and industrial conquerors with the concession of free trade, because at the time such a concession did not seem to injure their own interests; and they agreed to let the English business man practically dictate the national policy. In this way they preserved their political and social privileges and have gradually so identified the interests of the well-to-do middle class with their interest that the two have become scarcely distinguishable. The aristocracy of privilege and the aristocracy of wealth are absolutely united in their devotion to the existing political organization and policy of the United Kingdom.

This bargain appeared to work very well for a while; but indications are accumulating that a let-alone economic policy has not preserved the vitality of the British economic system. The English farmer has lost ambition, and has been sacrificed to the industrial growth of the nation, while the industrial growth itself no longer shows its former power of expansion. The nation passed the responsibility for its economic welfare on to the individual; and the individual with all his energy and initiative seems unable to hold his own against better organized competition. Its competitors have profited by the very qualities which Great Britain renounced when she accepted the anti-national liberalism of the Manchester school. They have shown under widely different conditions the power of nationalizing their economic organization; and in spite of the commission of many errors, particularly in this country, a system of national economy appears to make for a higher level of economic vitality than a system of international economy. "At the present time," says Mr. O. Elzbacher in his "Modern Germany," "when other nations are no longer divided against themselves, but have become homogeneous unified nations in fact and nations in organization, and when the most progressive nations have become gigantic institutions for self-improvement and gigantic business concerns on coöperative principles, the spasmodic individual efforts of patriotic and energetic Englishmen and their unorganized individual action prove less efficient for the good of their country than they were formerly." The political leaders of England abandoned, that is, all leadership in economic affairs and allowed a merely individualistic liberalism complete control of the fiscal and economic policy of the country. The government resigned economic responsibility at the very time when English economic interests began to need vigilant protection and promotion; and as a consequence of this resignation the English governing class practically surrendered its primary function. What seemed to be an easy transferal to more competent shoulders of the national responsibility for the economic welfare of the country has proved to be a betrayal of the national interest.

Fiscal reform alone will, however, never enable Great Britain to compete more vigorously with either the United States or Germany. The diminished economic vitality of England must be partly traced to her tradition of political and social subserviency, which serves to rob both the ordinary and the exceptional Englishmen of energy and efficiency. American energy, so far as it is applied to economic tasks, is liberated not merely by the abundance of its opportunities, but by the prevailing idea that every man should make as much of himself as he can; and in obedience to this idea the average American works with all his might towards some special personal goal. The energy of the average Englishman, on the other hand, is impaired by his complacent acceptance of positions of social inferiority and by his worship of degrading social distinctions; and even successful Englishmen suffer from a similar handicap. The latter rarely push their business successes home, because they themselves immediately begin to covet a place in the social hierarchy, and to that end are content with a certain established income. The pleasure which the average Englishman seems to feel in looking up to the "upper classes" is only surpassed by the pleasure which the exceptional Englishman seems to feel in looking down on the "lower classes." Englishmen have always congratulated themselves because their nobility was not a caste; but the facts that the younger sons of the peers are commoners, and that a distinguished commoner may earn a peerage, only makes the poison of these arbitrary social discriminations the more deadly. An Englishman always has a chance of winning an irrelevant but very gratifying social and political privilege. He may by acceptable services of the ordinary kind become as good as a lord. Some such ambition is nearly always the end to which the energy of the successful Englishman is directed, and its particular nature hinders him from realizing the special purpose of his own life with an unimpeded will.

The net result of the English system is to infect English social, political, military, and industrial life with social favoritism, and the poison of the infection is only mitigated by the condition that the "favorites" must deserve their selection by the maintenance of a certain standard.

This standard was formed a good many years ago when the conditions of efficiency were not so exacting as they are to-day. At that time it was a sufficiently high standard and made, on the whole, for successful achievement. It demanded of the "favorite" that he be honest, patriotic, well-educated, gentlemanly, courageous, and a "good sort," but it wholly failed to demand high special training, intense application, unremitting energy, or any exclusive devotion to one's peculiar work. If an Englishman comes up to the regular standard, he can usually obtain his share of the good things of English life; but if he goes beyond, he falls under the social disqualification of being abnormal and peculiar. The standard, consequently, is not now an efficient standard; and it is frequently applied with some laxity to the members of the privileged classes. A tacit conspiracy naturally exists among people in such a position to make it easy for their associates, friends, and relatives. The props and chances offered to a boy born into this class make the very most of his probably moderate deserts and abilities, and in occupying a position of responsibility he inevitably displaces a more competent substitute. In our own country the enjoyment of such political favors is known as a "pull," and is a popular but disreputable method of political advancement, whereas in England the whole social, and a large part of the political, structure is constituted on the basis of a systematic and hereditary "pull." The spirit thereof is highly honored in the most sacred precincts of English life. It is supported heartily and unscrupulously by English public opinion, and its critics are few and insignificant.

When Englishmen come to understand the need of dissociating their national idea from its existing encumbrances of political privilege and social favoritism, they will be confronted by a reconstructive task of peculiar difficulty. The balance of the national life, which has been so slowly and painfully recovered, will be endangered by the weakening of any of its present supports. For centuries the existing system has been wrought with the utmost patience and patriotism; and an Englishman may well shudder at the notion of any essential modification. The good of the system is so mixed with the evil that it seems impossible to extricate and eradicate the latter without endangering English national cohesion. Their traditional faith in compromise, their traditional dread of ideas, their traditional habit of acting first and reasoning afterwards, has made the English system a hopelessly confused bundle of semi-efficiency and semi-inefficiency—just as it has made the best English social type a gentleman, but a gentleman absolutely conditioned, tempered, and supplemented by a flunky.

While the process of becoming more of a democracy may very well injure—at any rate for a while—English national consistency, England's future as a nation is compromised by her fear of democracy. She has built her national organization on the idea that the national welfare is better promoted by a popular loyalty which entails popular immobility, than by the exercise on the part of the people of a more individual and less subservient intellectual and moral energy. In so doing she has for the time being renounced one of the greatest advantages of a national political and social organization—the advantage of combining great popular energy with loyalty and fertility of association. No doubt certain nations, because of their perilous international situation, may be obliged to sacrifice the moral and economic individuality of the people to the demands of political security and efficiency. But Great Britain suffered from no such necessity. After the fall of Napoleon, she was more secure from foreign interference than ever before in her history; and she could have afforded, with far less risk than France, to identify her national principle with the work of popular liberation and amelioration. As a matter of fact, the logic of the reform movement which began in England soon after the Treaty of Vienna, required the adoption by England either of more democracy or of less. The privileged classes should either have fought to preserve their peculiar responsibility for the national welfare, or else, if they were obliged to surrender their inherited leadership, they should have also surrendered their political and social privileges. But Englishmen, terrified by the disasters which French democratic nationalism had wrought upon France, preferred domestic harmony to the perils of any radical readjustment of the balance of their national life. The aristocracy and the middle classes compromised their differences; and in the compromise each of them sacrificed the principle upon which the vitality of its action as a class depended, while both of them combined to impose subordination on the mass of the people.

Englishmen have, it is true, always remained faithful to their dominant political idea—the idea of freedom, and the English political and economic system is precisely the example of the ultimate disadvantage of basing national cohesion upon the application of such a limited principle. This principle, as we have seen in the preceding chapter, always operates for the benefit of a minority, whose whole object, after they have once won certain peculiar advantages, is to secure their perpetuation. The wealthy middle class, which at one time was the backbone of the Liberal party, has for the most part gone over to the Conservatives, because its interest has become as much opposed to political and economic egalitarianism as is that of the aristocracy: and the mass of the English people, whose liberation can never be accomplished under the existing régime of political and economic privilege, looks with complacency and awe upon the good time enjoyed by their betters. Popular bondage is the price of national consistency. A century of industrial expansion and over half a century of free trade has left the English people miserably poor and contentedly hopeless; and in the future the people cannot depend upon any increase even of the small share of the benefits of industrial expansion, which they have hitherto obtained, because the national expansion is itself proceeding at a much slower rate. The dole, which is now being accorded in the shape of old-age pensions, may fairly be compared to the free transportation to their homes with which the Bank of Monte Carlo assuages the feelings of its destitute victims. The national organization and policy is so arranged that the majority must lose. The result will be inevitably a diminution of the ability of the United Kingdom to hold its own in competition with its economic and political rivals; and in all probability this pressure from the outside will eventually force the English nation to reconsider the basis of its political and economic organization and policy.

IV Democracy and Nationality in France

The recent history and the present position of France illustrate another phase of the interdependence of the national and the democratic principles. The vitality of English national life has been impaired by its identification with an inadequate and aristocratic political principle. In France the effective vitality of the democracy has been very much lowered by certain flaws in the integrity of French national life. France is strong where England is weak and is weak where England is strong; and this divergence of development is by no means accidental. Just because they were the first countries to become effectively nationalized, their action and reaction have been constant and have served at once to develop and distinguish their national temperaments. The English invasions accelerated the growth of the French royal power and weakened domestic resistance to its ambitions. The English revolutions of the seventeenth century made the Bourbons more than ever determined to consolidate the royal despotism and to stamp out Protestantism. The excesses of the French royal despotism brought as a consequence the excesses of the Revolutionary democracy. The Reign of Terror in its turn made Englishmen more than ever suspicious of the application of rational political ideas to the fabric of English society. So the ball was tossed back and forth— the national temperament of each people being at once profoundly modified by this action and reaction and for the same cause profoundly distinguished one from the other. The association has been more beneficial to France than to England, because the French, both before and after the Revolution, really tried to learn something from English political experience, whereas the English have never been able to discover anything in the political experience of their neighbors, except an awful example of the danger of democratic ideas and political and social rationalism.

The ideas of the French democracy were in the beginning revolutionary, disorderly, and subversive of national consistency and good faith. No doubt the French democracy had a much better excuse for identifying democracy with a system of abstract rights and an indiscriminate individualism than had the American democracy. The shadow of the Old Régime hung over the country; and it seemed as if the newly won civil and political rights could be secured only by erecting them into absolute conditions of just political association and by surrounding them with every possible guarantee. Moreover, the natural course of the French democratic development was perverted by foreign interference and a constant condition of warfare; and if the French nation had been allowed to seek its own political salvation without interference, as was this English nation, the French democracy might have been saved many an error and excess. But whatever excuses may be found for the disorders of the French democracy, the temporary effect of the democratic idea upon the national fabric was, undoubtedly, a rending of the roots of their national stability and good feeling. The successive revolutionary explosions, which have constituted so much of French history since 1789, have made France the victim of what sometimes seem to be mutually exclusive conceptions of French national well-being. The democratic radicals are "intransigeant." The party of tradition and authority is "ultramontane." The majority of moderate and sensible people are usually in control; but their control is unstable. The shadow of the Terror and the Commune hangs over every serious crisis in French politics. The radicals jump to the belief that the interests and rights of the people have been betrayed and that the traitors should be exterminated. Good Frenchmen suffer during those crises from an obsession of suspicion and fear. Their mutual loyalty, their sense of fair play, and their natural kindliness are all submerged under a tyranny of desperate apprehension. The social bond is unloosed, and the prudent bourgeois thinks only of the preservation of person and property.

This aspect of the French democracy can, however, easily be over-emphasized and usually is over-emphasized by foreigners. It is undoubtedly a living element in the composition of the contemporary France; but it was less powerful at the time of the Commune than at the time of the Terror, and is less powerful today than it was in 1871. French political history in the nineteenth century is not to be regarded as a succession of meaningless revolutions, born of a spirit of reckless and factious insubordination, but as the route whereby a people, inexperienced in self-government, have been gradually traveling towards the kind of self-government best fitted to their needs. It is entirely possible that the existing Republic, modified perhaps for the purpose of obtaining a more independent and a more vigorous executive authority, may in the course of time give France the needed political and social stability. That form of government which was adopted at the time, because it divided Frenchmen the least, may become the form of government which unites Frenchmen by the strongest ties. Bismarck's misunderstanding of the French national character and political needs was well betrayed when he favored a Republic rather than a Legitimist monarchy in France, because a French Republic would, in his opinion, necessarily keep France a weak and divided neighbor. The Republic has kept France divided, but it has been less divided than it would have been under any monarchical government. It has successfully weathered a number of very grave domestic crises; and its perpetuity will probably depend primarily upon its ability to secure and advance by practical means the international standing of France. The Republic has been obliged to meet a foreign peril more prolonged and more dangerous than that which has befallen any French government since 1600. From the time of Richelieu until 1870, France was stronger than any of her continental neighbors. Unless they were united against her she had little to fear from them; and her comparative strength tempted her to be aggressive, careless, and experimental in her foreign policy. That policy was vacillating, purposeless, and frequently wasteful of the national resources. Eventually, it compromised the international position of France. After 1871, for the first time in almost three hundred years, the very safety of France in a time of peace became actively and gravely imperiled.

The third Republic reaped the fruit of all the former trifling with the national interest of France and that of its neighbors; and the resulting danger was and is so ominous and so irretrievable that it has made and will make for internal stability. If the Republic can provide for French national defense and can keep for France the position in Europe to which she is entitled, the Republic will probably endure. And in that case it will certainly deserve to endure, because it will have faced and overcome the most exacting possible national peril.

Even the most loyal friend of France can, however, hardly claim that the French democracy is even yet thoroughly nationalized. It has done something to obtain national cohesion at home, and to advance the national interest abroad; but evidences of the traditional dissociation between French democracy and French national efficiency and consistency are still plainly visible. Both the domestic and the foreign policies of the Republic have of late years been weakened by the persistence of a factious and anti-national spirit among radical French democrats.

The most dangerous symptom of this anti-national democracy is that an apparently increasing number of educated Frenchmen are rebelling against the burdens imposed upon the Republic by its perilous international position. They are tending to seek security and relief, not by strengthening the national bond and by loyalty to the fabric of their national life, but by personal disloyalty and national dissolution. The most extreme of democratic socialists do not hesitate to advocate armed rebellion against military service in the interest of international peace. They would fight their fellow-countrymen in order to promote a union with foreigners. How far views of this kind have come to prevail, an outsider cannot very well judge; but they are said to be popular among the school teachers, and to have impaired the discipline of the army itself. Authoritative French journals claim that France cannot afford to run the risk of incurring the ill-will of Germany, even in a good cause, because the country is no longer sure of its military efficiency. There is no present danger of this anti-nationalist democracy capturing control of the French government, as did the revolutionary democracy at an earlier date; but its existence is a source of weakness to a nation whose perilous international situation requires the most absolute patriotic devotion on the part of her sons.

Unfortunately, it is also true that the official domestic policy of the Republic is not informed by a genuinely national spirit. Just as the English national interest demands the temporary loosening of traditional bonds for the sake of securing national cohesion at a smaller sacrifice of popular vitality, so, on the contrary, the French national interest demands more of the English spirit of compromise for the sake of national consistency. The wounds dealt to the integrity of French national life by the domestic conflicts of four generations require binding and healing. The Third Republic has on the whole been more national in its domestic policy than were any of the preceding French governments for over two hundred years; but it has still fallen far short of its duty in that respect. The healing of one wound has always been followed by the opening of another. Irreconcilable differences of opinion still subsist; and they are rarely bridged or dissolved by any fundamental loyalty of patriotic feeling. The French have as yet been unable to find in their democracy any conscious ideal of mutual loyalty which provides a sufficient substitute for a merely instinctive national tradition. They have not yet come to realize that the success of their whole democratic experiment depends upon their ability to reach a good understanding with their fellow-countrymen, and, that just in so far as their democracy fails to be nation-ally constructive, it is ignoring the most essential condi-tion of its own vitality and perpetuity.

The French democracy is confronted by an economic, as well as a political, problem of peculiar difficulty. The effects of the Revolution were no less important upon the distribution of wealth in France than upon the dis-tribution of political power. The people came into the ownership of the land; and in the course of time the area of this distribution has been increased rather than diminished. Furthermore, the laws under which prop-erty in France is inherited have promoted a similarly wide distribution of personal estate. France is a rich country; and its riches are much more evenly divided than is the case in Great Britain, Germany, or the United States. There are fewer large fortunes, and fewer cases of poverty. The average Frenchman is a small, but ex-tremely thrifty proprietor, who abhors speculation and is always managing to add something to his accumula-tions; and the French economic system is adapted to this peculiar distribution of wealth. The scarcity in France of iron and coal has checked the tendency to industrial organization on a huge scale. The strength of the French industrial system does not consist in the large and ef-ficient use of machinery, but in its multitude of skilled craftsmen and the excellence of their handiwork. In a system of this kind, labor naturally receives a large per-centage of the gross product, and a larger proportion of wage-earners reach an independent economic position. At first sight it looks as if France was something like a genuine economic democracy, and ought to escape the evils which threaten other countries from an economic organization, in which concentrated capital plays a more important part.

But the situation is not without another and less fa-vorable aspect. France, in becoming a country of small and extremely thrifty property owners, has also become a country of partial economic parasites with very little personal initiative and energy. Individual freedom has been sacrificed to economic and social equality; and this economic and social equality has not made for national cohesion. The bourgeois, the mechanic, and the farmer, in so far as they have accumulated property, are exhibiting an extremely calculating individualism, of which the most dangerous symptom is the decline in the birth-rate. Frenchmen are becoming more than ever disinclined to take the risks and assume the expense of having more than one or two children. The recent outbreak of anti-militarism is probably merely another illustration of the increasing desire of the French bourgeois for personal security, and the opportunity for personal enjoyment. To a foreigner it looks as if the grave political and social risks, which the French nation has taken since 1789, had gradually cultivated in individual Frenchmen an excessive personal prudence, which adds to the store of national wealth, but which no more conduces to economic, social, and political efficiency than would the incarceration of a fine army in a fortress conduce to military success. A nation or an individual who wishes to accomplish great things must be ready, in Nietzsche's phrase, "to lived angerously"—to take those risks, without which no really great achievement is possible; and if Frenchmen persist in erecting the virtue of thrift and the demand for safety into the predominant national characteristic, they are merely beginning a process of national corruption and dissolution.

That any such result is at all imminent, I do not for a moment believe. The time will come when the danger of the present drift will be understood, and will create its sufficient remedy; and all good friends of democracy and human advancement should hope and believe that France will retain indefinitely her national vitality. If she should drift into an insignificant position in relation to her neighbors, a void would be created which it would be impossible to fill and which would react deleteriously upon the whole European system. But such a result is only to be avoided by the general recognition among Frenchmen that the means which they are adopting to render their personal position more secure is rendering their national situation more precarious. The fate of the French democracy is irrevocably tied up with the fate of French national life, and the best way for a Frenchman to show himself a good democrat is to make those sacrifices and to take those risks necessary for the prestige and welfare of his country.

V   The Relation of German Nationality to Democracy

The German Empire presents still another phase of the relation between democracy and nationality, and one which helps considerably towards an understanding of the varied possibilities of that relationship. The German national organization and policy was wrought in a manner entirely different from that of either France or England. In the two latter countries political freedom was conquered only as the result of successive revolutions; and the ruling classes were obliged to recognize the source of these political reformations by renouncing all or a large part of their inherited responsibilities. In Germany, on the other hand, or rather in Prussia as the maker of modern Germany, the various changes in the national organization and policy, which have resulted in the founding of a united nation, originated either with the crown or with the royal counselors. The Prussian monarchy has, consequently, passed through the revolutionary period without abandoning its political leadership of the Prussian state. It has created a national representative body; but it has not followed the English example and allowed such a body to tie its hands; and it has remained, consequently, the most completely responsible and representative monarchy in Europe.

Up to the present time this responsibility and power have on the whole been deserved by the manner in which they have been exercised. German nationality as an efficient political and economic force has been wrought by skillful and patriotic management out of materials afforded by military and political opportunities and latent national ties and traditions. During the eighteenth century the Prussian monarchy came to understand that the road to effective political power in Germany was by way of a military efficiency, disproportionate to the resources and population of the Kingdom. In this way it was able to take advantage of almost every important crisis to increase its dominion and its prestige. Neither was Prussian national efficiency built up merely by a well-devised and practicable policy of military aggression. The Prussian monarchy had the good sense to accept the advice of domestic reformers during its period of adversity, and so contributed to the economic liberation and the educational training of its subjects. Thus the modern German nation has been at bottom the work of admirable leadership on the part of officially responsible leaders; and among those leaders the man who planned most effectively and accomplished the greatest results was Otto von Bismarck.

❧

It requires a very special study of European history after 1848 to understand how bold, how original, how comprehensive, and how adequate for their purpose Bismarck's ideas and policy gradually became; and it requires a very special study of Bismarck's own biography to understand that his personal career, with all its transformations, exhibits an equally remarkable integrity. The Bismarck of from 1848 to 1851 is usually

described as a country squire, possessed by obscurantist mediæval ideas wholly incompatible with his own
subsequent policy. But while there are many superficial
contradictions between the country squire of 1848 and
the Prussian Minister and German Chancellor, the really
peculiar quality of Bismarck's intelligence was revealed
in his ability to develop a constructive German national
policy out of the prejudices and ideas of a Prussian
"junker." Bismarck, in 1848, was primarily an ardent
Prussian patriot who believed that the monarchy was
divinely authorized to govern the Prussian people, and
that any diminution of this responsibility was false in
principle and would be baleful in its results. These ideas
led him, in 1848, to oppose the constitution, granted
by Frederick William IV and to advocate the repression
of all revolutionary upheavals. He never essentially departed from these principles; but his experience gradually taught him that they were capable of a different and
more edifying application. The point of view from which
his policy, his achievements, and his career can best be
understood is that of a patriotic Prussian who was exclusively, intelligently, and unscrupulously devoted to
the welfare (as he conceived it) of his country and his
king. As a loyal Prussian he wished to increase Prussian
influence among the other German states, because that
was the only way to improve her standing and greatness
as a European Power; and he soon realized that Austria
constituted the great obstacle to any such increase of
Prussian influence. He and he only drew the one sufficient inference from this fact. Inasmuch as Prussia's
future greatness and efficiency depended absolutely on
the increase of her influence in Germany, and inasmuch
as Austria barred her path, Prussia must be prepared to
fight Austria, and must make every possible provision,
both diplomatic and military, to bring such a war to a
successful issue. Such a purpose meant, of course, the

abandonment of the policy which Prussia had pursued for a whole generation. The one interest which Bismarck wanted the Prussian government to promote was the Prussian interest, no matter whether that interest meant opposition to the democracy or coöperation therewith; and the important point in the realization of this exclusive policy is that he soon found himself in need of the help of the German democratic movement. His resolute and candid nationalism in the end forced him to enter into an alliance with the very democracy which he had begun by detesting.

It must be admitted, also, that he had in the beginning reason to distrust the Prussian and the German democracy. The German radicals had sought to compass the unification of Germany by passing resolutions and making speeches; but such methods, which are indispensable accessories to the good government of an established national community, were utterly incompetent to remove the obstacles to German unity. These obstacles consisted in the particularism of the German princes, the opposition of Austria, and looming in the background the possible opposition of France; and Bismarck alone thoroughly understood that such obstacles could be removed by war and war only. But in order to wage war successfully, a country must be well-armed; and in the attempt to arm Prussia so that she would be equal to asserting her interests in Germany, Bismarck and the king had to face the stubborn opposition of the Prussian representative assembly. Bismarck did not flinch from fighting the Prussian assembly in the national interest any more than he flinched under different circumstances from calling the German democracy to his aid. When by this policy, at once bold and cautious, of Prussian aggrandizement, he had succeeded in bringing about war with Austria, he fearlessly announced a plan of partial unification, based upon the supremacy of Prussia and a national parliament elected by universal suffrage; and after the defeat of Austria, he successfully carried this plan into effect. It so happened that the special interest of Prussia coincided with the German national interest. It was Prussia's effective military power which defeated Austria and forced the princes to abate their particularist pretensions. It was Prussia's comparatively larger population which made Bismarck insist that the German nation should be an efficient popular union rather than a mere federation of states. And it was Bismarck's experience with the anti-nationalism "liberalism" of the Prussian assembly, elected as it was by a very restricted suffrage, which convinced him that the national interest could be as well trusted to the good sense and the patriotism of the whole people as to the special interests of the "bourgeoisie." Thus little by little the fertile seed of Bismarck's Prussian patriotism grew into a German semi-democratic nationalism, and it achieved this transformation without any essential sacrifice of its own integrity. He had been working in Prussia's interest throughout, but he saw clearly just where the Prussian interest blended with the German national interest, and just what means, whether by way of military force or popular approval, were necessary for the success of his patriotic policy.

When the Prussian Minister-President became the Imperial Chancellor, he pursued in the larger field a similar purpose by different means. The German national Empire had been founded by means of the forcible coercion of its domestic and foreign opponents. It remained now to organize and develop the new national state; and the government, under Bismark's lead, made itself responsible for the task of organization and development, just as it had made itself responsible for the task of unification. According to the theories of democratic individualistic "liberalism," such an effort could only result in failure, because from the liberal point of view the one way to develop a modern industrial nation was simply to allow the individual every possible liberty. But Bismarck's whole scheme of national industrial organization looked in a very different direction. He believed that the nation itself, as represented by its official leaders, should actively assist in preparing an adequate national domestic policy, and in organizing the machinery for its efficient execution. He saw clearly that the logic and the purpose of the national type of political organization was entirely different from that of a so-called free democracy, as explained in the philosophy of the German liberals of 1848, the Manchester school in England, or our own Jeffersonian Democrats; and he successfully transformed his theory of responsible administrative activity into a comprehensive national policy. The army was, if anything, increased in strength, so that it might remain fully adequate either for national defense or as an engine of German international purposes. A beginning was made toward the creation of a navy. A moderate but explicit protectionist policy was adopted, aimed not at the special development either of rural or manufacturing industries, but at the all-round development of Germany as an independent national economic unit. In Prussia itself the railways were bought by the government, so that they should be managed, not in the interest of the shareholders, but in that of the national economic system. The government encouraged the spread of better farming methods, which have resulted in the gradual increase in the yield per acre of every important agricultural staple. The educational system of the country was made of direct assistance to industry, because it turned out skilled scientific experts, who used their knowledge to promote industrial efficiency. In every direction German activity was organized and was placed under skilled professional leadership, while at the same time each of these special lines of work was subordinated to its particular place in a comprehensive scheme of national economy. This "paternalism" has, moreover, accomplished its purpose. German industrial expansion surpasses in some respects that of the United States, and has left every European nation far behind. Germany alone among the modern European nations is, in spite of the temporary embarrassment of Imperial finance, carrying the cost of modern military prepara- tion easily, and looks forward confidently to greater successes in the future. She is at the present time a very striking example of what can be accomplished for the popular welfare by a fearless acceptance on the part of the official leaders of economic as well as political re- sponsibility, and by the efficient and intelligent use of all available means to that end.

Inevitably, however, Germany is suffering somewhat from the excess of her excellent qualities. Her leaders were not betrayed by the success of their foreign and domestic policies to attempt the immediate accomplish- ment of purposes, incommensurate with the national power and resources; but they were tempted to become somewhat overbearing in their attitude toward their domestic and foreign opponents. No doubt a position which was conquered by aggressive leadership must be maintained by aggressive leadership; and no doubt, consequently, the German Imperial Power could not well avoid the appearance and sometimes the substance of being domineering. But the consequence of the Bis- marckian tradition of bullying and browbeating one's opponents has been that of intensifying the opposition to the national policy and of compromising its suc- cess. France has been able to escape from the isolation in which she was long kept by Bismarck after the war, and has gradually built up a series of understandings with other Powers, more or less inimical to Germany.

The latter's standing in Europe is not as high as it was ten years ago, in spite of the increased relative efficiency of her army, her navy, and her economic system. Moreover, an equally serious and dangerous opposition has been created at home. The government has not succeeded in retaining the loyal support of a large fraction of the German people. A party which is composed for the most part of workingmen, and which has been increasing steadily in the number of its adherents, is utterly opposed to the present policy and organization of the Imperial government; and those Social Democrats have for the most part been treated by the authorities with repressive laws and abusive epithets. Thus a schism is being created in the German national system which threatens to become a source of serious weakness to the national efficiency and strength.

That the existence of some such domestic opposition is to a certain extent unavoidable must be admitted. A radical incompatibility exists between the national policy of the Imperial and Prussian governments and the Social Democratic programme; and the Imperial authorities could not conciliate the Social Democrats without abandoning the peculiar organization and policy which have been largely so responsible for the extraordinary increase in the national well-being. On the other hand, it must also be remembered that the Prussian royal power has maintained its nationally representative character and its responsible leadership quite as much by its ability to meet legitimate popular grievances and needs as by its successful foreign policy. The test of German domestic statesmanship hereafter will consist in its ability to win the support of the industrial democracy, created by the industrial advance of the country, without impairing the traditional and the existing practice of expert and responsible leadership. The task is one of extreme difficulty, but it is far from being wholly impossible, because the Social Democratic party in Germany is every year becoming less revolutionary and more national in its outlook. But at present little attempt is being made at conciliation; and the attitude of the ruling classes is such that in the near future none is likely to be made. In this respect they are false to the logic of the origin of German political unity. The union was accomplished with the assistance of the democracy and on a foundation of universal suffrage. As Germany has become more of a nation, the democracy has acquired more substantial power; but its increase in numbers and weight has not been accompanied by any increase of official recognition. The political organization of Germany is consequently losing touch with those who represent one essential aspect of the national growth. It behooves the ruling classes to tread warily, or they may have to face a domestic opposition more dangerous than any probable foreign opposition.

The situation is complicated by the dubious international standing of the German Empire. She is partly surrounded by actual and possible enemies, against whom she can make headway only by means of continuous vigilance and efficient leadership; while at the same time her own national ambitions still conflict in some measure with the interests of her neighbors. Her official foreign policy since 1872 has undoubtedly been determined by the desire to maintain the peace of Europe under effective guarantees, because she needed time to consolidate her position and reap the advantages of her increasing industrial efficiency; but both German and European statesmen are none the less very conscious of the fact that the German Empire is the European Power which has most to gain in Europe from a successful war. Some Frenchmen still cherish plans of revenge for 1870; but candid French opinion is beginning to admit that the constantly increasing resources of Germany in men and money make any deliberate policy of that kind al-most suicidal. France would lose much more by a defeat than she could gain from a victory, and the fruits of vic-tory could not be permanently held. Italy, also, has no unsatisfied ambition which a war could gratify, except the addition of a few thousand Austrian-Italians to her population. Russia still looks longingly toward Con-stantinople; but until she has done something to solve her domestic problem and reorganize her finances, she needs peace rather than war. But the past successes of Germany and her new and increasing expansive power tempt her to cherish ambitions which constitute the chief menace to the international stability of Europe. She would have much to lose, but she would also have something to gain from the possible disintegration of Austria-Hungary. She has possibly still more to gain from the incorporation of Holland within the Empire. Her increasing commerce has possessed her with the idea of eventually disputing the supremacy of the sea with Great Britain. And she unquestionably expects to profit in Asia Minor from the possible break-up of the Ottoman Empire. How seriously such ambitions are entertained, it is difficult to say; and it is wholly im-probable that more than a small part of this enormous programme of national aggrandizement will ever be re-alized. But when Germany has the chance of gaining and holding such advantages as these from a successful war, it is no wonder that she remains the chief possible disturber of the European peace. In her case certainly the fruits of victory look more seductive than the penal-ties of defeat look dangerous; and the resolute opposi-tion to the partial disarmament, which she has always offered at the Hague Conference, is the best evidence of the unsatisfied nature of her ambitions.

Germany's standing in the European system is, then, very far from being as well-defined as are those of the

older nations, like France and Great Britain. The gradual growth of a better understanding between France,
Great Britain, and Russia is largely due to an instinctive
coalition of those powers who would be most injured
by an increase of the German influence and dominion;
and the sense that Europe is becoming united against
them makes German statesmen more than ever on their
guard and more than ever impatient of an embarrassing
domestic opposition. Thus Germany's aggressive foreign
policy has so far tended to increase the distance between
her responsible leaders and the popular party; and there
are only two ways in which this schism can be healed.
If German foreign policy should continue to be as bril-
liantly successful as it was in the days of Bismarck, the
authorities will have no difficulty in retaining the support of a sufficient majority of the German people—just
as the victory over Austria brought King William and
Bismarck forgiveness from their parliamentary opponents. On the other hand, any severe setback to Germany in the realization of its aggressive plans would
strengthen the domestic opposition and might lead to a
severe internal crisis. It all depends upon whether German national policy has or has not overstepped the limits of practical and permanent achievement.

VI   Militarism and Nationality

The foregoing considerations in respect to the existing
international situation of Germany bring me to another
and final aspect of the relation in Europe between nationality and democracy. One of the most difficult and
(be it admitted) one of the most dubious problems raised
by any attempt to establish a constructive relationship
between those two principles hangs on the fact that
hitherto national development has not apparently made
for international peace. The nations of Europe are to all

appearances as belligerent as were the former European dynastic states. Europe has become a vast camp, and its governments are spending probably a larger proportion of the resources of their countries for military and naval purposes than did those of the eighteenth century. How can these warlike preparations, in which all the European nations share, and the warlike spirit which they have occasionally displayed, be reconciled with the existence of any constructive relationship between the national and the democratic ideas?

The question can best be answered by briefly reviewing the claims already advanced on behalf of the national principle. I have asserted from the start that the national principle was wholly different in origin and somewhat different in meaning from the principle of democracy. What has been claimed for nationality is, not that it can be identified with democracy, but that as a political principle it remained unsatisfied without an infusion of democracy. But the extent to which this infusion can go and the forms which it takes are determined by a logic and a necessity very different from that of an absolute democratic theory. National politics have from the start aimed primarily at efficiency—that is, at the successful use of the force resident in the state to accomplish the purposes desired by the Sovereign authority. Among the group of states inhabited by Christian peoples it has gradually been discovered that the efficient use of force is contingent in a number of respects upon its responsible use; and that its responsible use means a limited policy of external aggrandizement and a partial distribution of political power and responsibilities. A national polity, however, always remains an organization based upon force. In internal affairs it depends at bottom for its success not merely upon public opinion, but, if necessary, upon the strong arm. It is a matter of government and coercion as well as a matter of influence and persuasion. So in its external relations its standing and success have depended, and still depend, upon the efficient use of force, just in so far as force is demanded by its own situation and the attitudes of its neighbors and rivals. The democrats who disparage efficient national organization are at bottom merely seeking to exorcise the power of physical force in human affairs by the use of pious incantations and heavenly words. That they will never do. The Christian warrior must accompany the evangelist; and Christians are not by any means angels. It is none the less true that the modern nations control the expenditure of more force in a more responsible manner than have any preceding political organizations; and it is none the less true that a further development of the national principle will mean in the end the attachment of still stricter responsibilities to the use of force both in the internal and external policies of modern nations.

War may be and has been a useful and justifiable engine of national policy. It is justifiable, moreover, not merely in such a case as our Civil War, in which a people fought for their own national integrity. It was, I believe, justifiable, in the case of the two wars which preceded the formation of the modern German Empire. These wars may, indeed, be considered as decisive instances. Prussia did not drift into them, as we drifted into the Civil War. They were deliberately provoked by Bismarck at a favorable moment, because they were necessary to the unification of the German people under Prussian leadership; and I do not hesitate to say that he can be justified in the assumption of this enormous responsibility. The German national organization means increased security, happiness, and opportunity of development for the whole German people; and inasmuch as the selfish interests of Austria and France blocked the path, Bismarck had his sufficient warrant for a deliberately planned attack. No doubt such an attack and its results injured France and the French people just as it has benefited Germany; but France had to suffer that injury as a penalty for the part she had as a matter of policy played in German affairs. For centuries a united France had helped to maintain for her own purposes a divided Germany; and when Germany herself became united, it was inevitable, as Bismarck foresaw in 1848, that French opposition must be forcibly removed, and some of the fruits of French aggression be reclaimed. That the restitution demanded went further than was necessary, I fully believe; but the partial abuse of victory does not diminish the legitimacy of the German aggression. A war waged for an excellent purpose contributes more to human amelioration than a merely artificial peace,— such as that established by the Holy Alliance. The unification of Germany and Italy has not only helped to liberate the energies of both the German and the Italian people, but it has made the political divisions of Europe conform much more nearly to the lines within which the people of Europe can loyally and fruitfully associate one with another. In fact, the whole national movement, if it has increased the preparations for war, has diminished in number of probable causes thereof; and it is only by diminishing the number of causes whereby a nation has more to gain from victory than it has to lose by defeat that war among the civilized powers can be gradually extinguished.

At the present time it is, as we have seen, the international situation and the national ambitions of Russia and Germany which constitute the chief threat to European peace. Germany's existing position in Europe depends upon its alliance with Austria-Hungary. The Habsburg Empire is an incoherent and unstable state which is held together only by dynastic ties and external pressure. The German, the Austrian, and the

Hungarian interests all demand the perpetuation of the Habsburg dominion; but it is doubtful whether in the long run its large Slavic population will not combine with its blood neighbors to break the bond. But whether the German, Austrian, and Hungarian interest does or does not prevail, the fundamental national interests, which are compromised by the precarious stability of Austria-Hungary, are alone sufficient to make disarmament impossible. Disarmament means the preservation of Europe in its existing condition; and such a policy, enforced by means of international guarantees, would be almost as inimical to the foundation of a permanent and satisfactory international system now as it was in 1820. The fact has to be recognized that the ultimate object of a peaceable and stable European international situation cannot in all probability be reached without many additional wars; and the essential point is that these wars, when they come, should, like the wars between Austria or France and Prussia, or like our Civil War, be fought to accomplish a desirable purpose and should be decisive in result.

Modern conflicts between efficiently organized nations tend to obtain just this character. They are fought for a defensible purpose, and they accomplish a definite result. The penalties of defeat are so disastrous that warfare is no longer wantonly incurred; and it will not be provoked at all by nations, such as Italy or France, who have less to gain from victory than they have to lose from defeat. Moreover, the cost of existing armaments is so crushing that an ever increasing motive exists in favor of their ultimate reduction. This motive will not operate as long as the leading Powers continue to have unsatisfied ambitions which look practicable; but eventually it will necessarily have its effect. Each war, as it occurs, even if it does not finally settle some conflicting claims, will most assuredly help to teach the warring nations just how far they can go, and will help, consequently, to restrict its subsequent policy within practicable and probably inoffensive limits. It is by no means an accident that England and France, the two oldest European nations, are the two whose foreign policies are best defined and, so far as Europe is concerned, least offensive. For centuries these Powers fought and fought, because one of them had aggressive designs which apparently or really affected the welfare of the other; but the result of this prolonged rivalry has been a constantly clearer understanding of their respective national interests. Clear-headed and moderate statesmen like Talleyrand recognized immediately after the Revolution that the substantial interests of a liberalized France in Europe were closely akin to those of Great Britain, and again and again in the nineteenth century this prophecy was justified. Again and again the two Powers were brought together by their interests only to be again divided by a tradition of antagonism and misunderstanding. At present, however, they are probably on better terms than ever before in the history of their relations; and this result is due to the definite and necessarily unaggressive character of their European interests. They have finally learned the limits of their possible achievement and could transgress them only by some act of folly.

In the course of another fifty years the limits of possible aggression by Germany and Russia in Europe will probably be very much better defined than they are today. These two Powers will seek at the favorable moment to accomplish certain aggressive purposes which they secretly or openly entertain, and they will succeed or fail. Each success or failure will probably be decisive in certain respects, and will remove one or more existing conflicts of interest or ambiguities of position. Whether this progressive specification of the practicable foreign policies of the several Powers will soon or will ever go so far as to make some general international understanding possible, is a question which no man can answer; but as long as the national principle retains its vitality, there is no other way of reaching a permanent and fruitful international settlement. That any one nation, or any small group of nations, can impose its dominion upon Europe is contrary to every lesson of European history. Such a purpose would be immeasurably beyond the power even of 90,000,000 Germans or 150,000,000 Russians, or even beyond the power of 90,000,000 Germans allied with 150,000,000 Russians. Europe is capable of combining more effectually than ever before to resist any possible revival of imperialism; and the time will come when Europe, threatened by the aggression of any one domineering Power, can call other continents to her assistance. The limits to the possible expansion of any one nation are established by certain fundamental and venerable political conditions. The penalties of persistent transgression would be not merely a sentence of piracy similar to that passed on Napoleon I, but a constantly diminishing national vitality on the part of the aggressor. As long as the national principle endures, political power cannot be exercised irresponsibly without becoming inefficient and sterile.

Inimical as the national principle is to the carrying out either of a visionary or a predatory foreign policy in Europe, it does not imply any similar hostility to a certain measure of colonial expansion. In this, as in many other important respects, the constructive national democrat must necessarily differ from the old school of democratic "liberals." A nationalized democracy is not based on abstract individual rights, no matter whether the individual lives in Colorado, Paris, or Calcutta. Its consistency is chiefly a matter of actual historical association in the midst of a general Christian community of nations. A people that lack the power of basing their

political association on an accumulated national tradition and purpose is not capable either of nationality or
democracy; and that is the condition of the majority of
Asiatic and African peoples. A European nation can undertake the responsibility of governing these politically
disorganized societies without any necessary danger to
its own national life. Such a task need not be beyond
its physical power, because disorganized peoples have
a comparatively small power of resistance, and a few
thousand resolute Europeans can hold in submission
many million Asiatics. Neither does it conflict with the
moral basis of a national political organization, because
at least for a while the Asiatic population may well be
benefited by more orderly and progressive government.
Submission to such a government is necessary as a condition of subsequent political development. The majority of Asiatic and African communities can only got a
fair start politically by some such preliminary process
of tutelage; and the assumption by a European nation
of such a responsibility in a desirable phase of national
discipline and a frequent source of genuine national
advance.

Neither does an aggressive colonial policy make for
unnecessary or meaningless wars. It is true, of course,
that colonial expansion increases the number of possible occasions for dispute among the expanding nations;
but these disputes have the advantage of rarely turning
on questions really vital to the future prosperity of a
European nation. They are just the sort of international
differences of interest which ought to be settled by ar-
bitration or conciliation, because both of the disputants
have so much more to lose by hostilities than they have
to gain by military success. A dispute turning upon a
piece of African territory would, if it waxed into war,
involve the most awful and dangerous consequences in
Europe. The danger of European wars, except for na-

tional purposes of prime importance, carries its consequence into Africa and Asia. France, for instance, was very much irritated by the continued English occupation of Egypt in spite of certain solemn promises of evacuation; and the expedition of Marchand, which ended in the Fashoda incident, indirectly questioned the validity of the British occupation of Egypt by making that occupation strategically insecure. In spite, however, of the deliberate manner in which France raised this question and of the highly irritated condition of French public opinion, she could not, when the choice had to be made, afford the consequences of a Franco-English war. In the end she was obliged to seek compensation elsewhere in Africa and abandon her occupation of Fashoda. This incident is typical; and it points directly to the conclusion that wars will very rarely occur among European nations over disputes as to colonies, unless the political situation in Europe is one which itself makes war desirable or inevitable. A Bismarck could handle a Fashoda incident so as to provoke hostilities, but in that case Fashoda, like the Hohenzollern candidacy in Spain, would be a pretext, not a cause. The one contemporary instance in which a difference of colonial interests has caused a great war is the recent conflict between Russia and Japan; and in this instance the issues raised by the dispute were essentially different from the issues raised by a dispute over a colonial question between two European nations. The conflict of interests turned upon matter essential to the future prosperity of Japan, while at the same time the war did not necessarily involve dangerous European complications.

The truth is that colonial expansion by modern national states is to be regarded, not as a cause of war, but as a safety-valve against war. It affords an arena in which the restless and adventurous members of a national body can have their fling without dangerous consequences, while at the same time it satisfies the desire of a people for some evidence of and opportunity for national expansion. The nations which, one after another, have recognized the limits of their expansion in Europe have been those which have adopted a more or less explicit policy of colonial acquisition. Spain was, indeed, a great colonial power at a time when her policy in Europe continued to be aggressive; but her European aggressions soon undermined her national vitality, and her decadence in Europe brought her colonial expansion to a standstill. Portugal and Holland were too small to cherish visions of European aggrandizement, and they naturally sought an outlet in Asia and Africa for their energies. After Great Britain had passed through her revolutionary period, she made rapid advances as a colonial power, because she realized that her insular situation rendered a merely defensive European policy obligatory. France made a failure of her American and Asiatic colonies as long as she cherished schemes of European aggrandizement. Her period of colonial expansion, Algeria apart, did not come until after the Franco-Prussian War and the death of her ambition for a Rhine frontier. Bismarck was opposed to colonial development because he believed that Germany should husband her strength for the preservation and the improvement of her standing in Europe; but Germany's power of expansion demanded some outlet during a period of European rest. Throughout the reign of the present Emperor she has been picking up colonies wherever she could in Asia and Africa; and she cherishes certain plans for the extension of German influence in Asia Minor. It is characteristic of the ambiguous international position of Germany that she alone among the European Powers (except the peculiar case of Russia) is expectant of an increase of power both in Europe and other continents.

In the long run Germany will, like France, discover that under existing conditions an aggressive colonial and aggressive European policy are incompatible. The more important her colonies become and the larger her oceanic commerce, the more Germany lays herself open to injury from a strong maritime power, and the more hostages she is giving for good behavior in Europe. Unless a nation controls the sea, colonies are from a military point of view a source of weakness. The colonizing nation is in the position of a merchant who increases his business by means of a considerable increase of his debts. His use of the borrowed capital may be profitable, but none the less he makes his standing at the time of an emergency much more precarious. In the same way colonies add to the responsibilities of a nation and scatter its military resources; and a nation placed in such a situation is much less likely to break the peace.

The economic and political development of Asia and Africa by the European Powers is in its infancy; and no certain predictions can be made as to its final effects upon the political relations among civilized nations. Many important questions in respect thereto remain ambiguous. What, for instance, are the limits of a practicable policy of colonial expansion? In view of her peculiar economic condition and her threatened decrease in population have those limits been transgressed by France? Have they been transgressed by Great Britain? Considering the enormous increase in British responsibilities imposed by the maritime expansion of Germany, will not Great Britain be obliged to adopt a policy of concentration rather than expansion? Is not her partial retirement from American waters the first step in such a policy? Is not the Japanese alliance a dubious device for the partial shifting of burdens too heavy to bear? How long can Great Britain afford to maintain her existing control of the sea? Is there any way of ending such a control save either by the absolute exhaustion of Great Britain or by the establishment of a stable international system under adequate guarantees? Will the economic development of Asia lead to the awakening of other Asiatic states like Japan, and the re-arrangement of international relations for the purpose of giving them their appropriate places? A multitude of such questions are raised by the transformation which is taking place from a European international system into a political system composed chiefly of European nations, but embracing the whole world; and these questions will prove to be sufficiently difficult of solution. But in spite of the certainty that colonial expansion will in the end merely transfer to a larger area the conflicts of idea and interest whose effects have hitherto chiefly been confined to Europe—in spite of this certainty the process of colonial expansion is a wholly legitimate aspect of national development, and is not necessarily inimical to the advance of democracy. It will not make immediately for a permanent international settlement; but it is accomplishing a work without which a permanent international settlement is impossible; and it indubitably places every colonizing nation in a situation which makes the risk of hostilities dangerous compared to the possible advantages of military success.

The chief object of this long digression, has, I hope, now been achieved. My purpose has been to exhibit the European nations as a group of historic individuals with purposes, opportunities, and limitations analogous to those of actual individuals. An individual has no meaning apart from the society in which his individuality has been formed. A national state is capable of development only in relation to the society of more or less nationalized states in the midst of which its history has been unfolded. The growing and maturing individual is he who comes to take a more definite and serviceable position in his surrounding society,—he who performs excellently a special work adapted to his abilities. The maturing nation is in the same way the nation which is capable of limiting itself to the performance of a practicable and useful national work,—a work which in some specific respect accelerates the march of Christian civilization. There is no way in which a higher type of national life can be obtained without a corresponding individual improvement on the part of its constituent members. There is similarly no way in which a permanently satisfactory system of international relations can be secured, save by the increasing historical experience and effective self-control of related nations. Any country which declares that it is too good (or too democratic) to associate with other nations and share the responsibilities and opportunities resulting from such association is comparable to the individual who declares himself to be too saintly for association with his fellow-countrymen. Whatever a man or a nation gains by isolation, he or it necessarily loses in the discipline of experience with its possible fruits of wisdom and self-control. Association is a condition of individuality. International relations are a condition of nationality. A universal nation is as much a contradiction in terms as a universal individual. A nation seeking to destroy other nations is analogous to a man who seeks to destroy the society in which he was born. Little by little European history has been teaching this lesson; and in the course of time the correlation of national development with the improvement and definition of international relations will probably be embodied in some set of international institutions.

In the meantime the existing rivalries and enmities among European states must not be under-estimated either in their significance or their strength. In a way those rivalries have become more intense than ever before; and it is only too apparent that the many-headed rulers of modern nations are as capable of cherishing personal and national dislikes as were the sovereign kings of other centuries. These rivalries and enmities will not be dissolved by kind words and noble sentiments. The federation of Europe, like the unification of Germany, will never be brought about by congresses and amicable resolutions. It can be effected only by the same old means of blood and iron. The nations will never agree upon a permanent settlement until they have more to gain from peace than from military victory. But such a time will be postponed all the longer unless the nations, like France, Italy, England and the United States, which are at present sincerely desirous of peace, keep as well armed as their more belligerent neighbors. When the tug comes, the issue will depend upon the effective force which such nations, when loyally combined, can exert. It would be fatal, consequently, for the pacific Powers to seek to establish peace by a partial diminution of their military efficiency. Such an action would merely encourage the belligerent Powers to push their aggressive plans to the limit. The former must, on the contrary, keep as well armed as their resources and policy demand. Nationality is impaired and the national principle is violated just as soon as a nation neglects any sort of efficiency which is required either by its international position or by its national purposes.

9.

The American Democracy and
Its National Principles

I

The foregoing review of the relation which has come to
subsist in Europe between nationality and democracy
should help us to understand the peculiar bond which
unites the American democratic and national principles.
The net result of that review was encouraging but not
decisive. As a consequence of their development as nations, the European peoples have been unable to get
along without a certain infusion of democracy; but it
was for the most part essential to their national interest
that such an infusion should be strictly limited. In Europe the two ideals have never been allowed a frank and
unconstrained relation one to the other other. They have
been unable to live apart; but their marriage has usually been one of convenience, which was very far from
implying complete mutual dependence and confidence.
No doubt the collective interests of the German or British people suffer because such a lack of dependence and
confidence exists; but their collective interests would
suffer more from a sudden or violent attempt to destroy
the barriers. The nature and the history of the different democratic and national movements in the several
European countries at once tie them together and keep
them apart.

The peoples of Europe can only escape gradually
from the large infusion of arbitrary and irrational ma-

terial in their national composition. Monarchical and aristocratic traditions and a certain measure of political and social privilege have remained an essential part of their national lives; and no less essential was an element of defiance in their attitude toward their European neighbors. Hence, when the principle of national Sovereignty was proclaimed as a substitute for the principal of royal Sovereignty, that principle really did not mean the sudden bestowal upon the people of unlimited Sovereign power. "The true people," said Bismarck, in 1847, then a country squire, "is an invisible multitude of spirits. It is the living nation—the nation organized for its historical mission—the nation of yesterday and of to-morrow." A nation, that is, is a people in so far as they are united by traditions and purposes; and national Sovereignty implies an attachment to national history and traditions which permits only the very gradual alteration of these traditions in the direction of increasing democracy. The mistake which France made at the time of the French Revolution was precisely that of interpreting the phrase "souvreneté nationale" as equivalent to immediate, complete, and (in respect to the past) irresponsible popular sovereignty.

The European nations are, consequently, not in a position to make their national ideals frankly and loyally democratic. Their national integrity depends upon fidelity to traditional ideas and forms quite as much as it does upon the gradual modification of those ideas and forms in a democratic direction. The orderly unfolding of their national lives calls for a series of compromises which carry the fundamental democratic implication of the national principle as far as it can under the circumstances be safely carried; and in no other way does a people exhibit its political common sense so clearly as in its ability to be contemporary and progressive without breaking away from its historical anchorage. A comparatively definite national mission and purpose clearly emerge at some particular phase of the indefinite process of internal and external readjustment; but such a mission and such purposes necessarily possess a limited significance and a special character. Restricted as they are by the facts of national history, they lack the ultimate moral significance of the democratic ideal, which permits the transformation of patriotic fidelity into devotion to the highest and most comprehensive interests of humanity and civilization.

That an analogous condition exists in our own country, it would be vain to deny. The American people possessed a collective character even before they possessed a national organization; and both before and after the foundation of a national government, these common traditions were by no means wholly democratic. Furthermore, as we have frequently had occasion to observe, the American democracy in its traditional form has more often than not been anti-national in instinct and idea. Our own country has, consequently, a problem to solve, similar in certain respects to that of the European nations. Its national cohesion is a matter of historical association, and the facts of its historical association have resulted in a partial division and a misunderstanding between its two fundamental principles— the principles of nationality and democracy.

In the case of the United States there is, however, to be observed an essential difference. A nation, and particularly a European nation, cannot afford to become too complete a democracy all at once, because it would thereby be uprooting traditions upon which its national cohesion depends. But there is no reason why a democracy cannot trust its interests absolutely to the care of the national interest, and there is in particular every reason why the American democracy should become in sentiment and conviction frankly, unscrupulously, and loyally nationalist. This, of course, is a heresy from the point of view of the American democratic tradition; but it is much less of a heresy from the point of view of American political practice, and, whether heretical or not, it indicates the road whereby alone the American people can obtain political salvation.

The American democracy can trust its interest to the national interest, because American national cohesion is dependent, not only upon certain forms of historical association, but upon fidelity to a democratic principle. A nation is a very complex political, social, and economic product—so complex that political thinkers in emphasizing one aspect of it are apt to forget other and equally essential aspects. Its habits and traditions of historical association constitute an indispensable bond; but they do not constitute the only bond. A specific national character is more than a group of traditions and institutions. It tends to be a formative idea, which defines the situation of a country in reference to its neighbors, and which is constantly seeking a better articulation and understanding among the various parts of its domestic life. The English national idea is chiefly a matter of freedom, but the principle of freedom is associated with a certain measure of responsibility. The German national idea is more difficult of precise description, but it turns upon the principle of efficient and expert official leadership toward what is as yet a hazy goal of national greatness. The French national idea is democratic, but its democracy is rendered difficult by French national insecurity, and its value is limited by its equalitarian bias. The French, like the American, democracy needs above all to be thoroughly nationalized; and a condition of such a result is the loyal adoption of democracy as the national idea. Both French and American national cohesion depend upon the fidelity of the national organization to the democratic idea, and the gradual but intentional transformation of the substance of the national life in obedience to a democratic interest.

Let us seek for this complicated formula a specific application. How can it be translated into terms of contemporary American conditions? Well, in the first place, Americans are tied together by certain political, social, and economic habits, institutions, and traditions. From the political point of view these forms of association are at once constitutional, Federal, and democratic. They are accustomed to some measure of political centralization, to a larger measure of local governmental responsibility, to a still larger measure of individual economic freedom. This group of political institutions and habits has been gradually pieced together under the influence of varying political ideas and conditions. It contains many contradictory ingredients, and not a few that are positively dangerous to the public health. Such as it is, however, the American people are attached to this national tradition; and no part of it could be suddenly or violently transformed or mutilated without wounding large and important classes among the American people, both in their interests and feelings. They have been accustomed to associate under certain conditions and on certain terms; and to alter in any important way those conditions and terms of association without fair notice, full discussion, a demonstrable need and a sufficient consent of public opinion, would be to drive a wedge into the substance of American national cohesion. The American nation, no matter how much (or how little) it may be devoted to democratic political and social ideas, cannot uproot any essential element in its national tradition without severe penalties—as the American people discovered when they decided to cut negro slavery out of their national composition.

On the other hand, their national health and consistency were in the long run very much benefited by the surgical operation of the Civil War; and it was benefited because the War eradicated the most flagrant existing contradiction among the various parts of the American national tradition. This instance sufficiently showed, consequently, that although nationality has its traditional basis, it is far from being merely a conservative principle. At any one time the current of national public opinion embodies a temporary accommodation among the different traditional ideas, interests, conditions, and institutions. This balance of varying and perhaps conflicting elements is constantly being destroyed by new conditions,—such, for instance, as the gradual increase before the Civil War of the North as compared to the South in wealth, population, and industrial efficiency. The effect of this destruction of the traditional balance was to bring out the contradiction between the institution of negro slavery and the American democratic purpose—thereby necessitating an active conflict, and the triumph of one of these principles over the other. The unionist democracy conquered, and as the result of that conquest a new balance was reached between the various ingredients of American national life. During the past generation, the increased efficiency of organization in business and politics, the enormous growth of an irresponsible individual money-power, the much more definite division of the American people into possibly antagonistic classes, and the pressing practical need for expert, responsible, and authoritative leadership,—these new conditions and demands have been by way of upsetting once more the traditional national balance and of driving new wedges into American national cohesion. New contradictions have been developed between various aspects of the American national composition; and if the American people wish to escape the necessity of regaining their health by means of another surgical operation, they must consider carefully how much of a reorganization of traditional institutions, policy, and ideas are necessary for the achievement of a new and more stable national balance.

In the case of our own country, however, a balance is not to be struck merely by the process of compromise in the interest of harmony. Our forbears tried that method in dealing with the slavery problem from 1820 to 1850, and we all know with what results. American national cohesion is a matter of national integrity; and national integrity is a matter of loyalty to the requirements of a democratic ideal. For better or worse the American people have proclaimed themselves to be a democracy, and they have proclaimed that democracy means popular economic, social, and moral emancipation. The only way to regain their national balance is to remove those obstacles which the economic development of the country has placed in the path of a better democratic fulfillment. The economic and social changes of the past generation have brought out a serious and a glaring contradiction between the demands of a constructive democratic ideal and the machinery of methods and institutions, which have been considered sufficient for its realization. This is the fundamental discrepancy which must be at least partially eradicated before American national integrity can be triumphantly re-affirmed. The cohesion, which is a condition of effective nationality, is endangered by such a contradiction, and as long as it exists the different elements composing American society will be pulling apart rather than together. The national principle becomes a principle of reform and reconstruction, precisely because national consistency is constantly demanding the solution of contradictory economic and political tendencies, brought out by alterations in the conditions of economic and political efficiency. Its function is not only to preserve a balance among these diverse tendencies, but to make that bal-

ance more than ever expressive of a consistent and constructive democratic ideal. Any disloyalty to democracy
on the part of American national policy would in the
end prove fatal to American national unity.

The American democracy can, consequently, safely
trust its genuine interests to the keeping of those who
represent the national interest. It both can do so, and
it must do so. Only by faith in an efficient national organization and by an exclusive and aggressive devotion
to the national welfare, can the American democratic
ideal be made good. If the American local commonwealths had not been wrought by the Federalists into
the form of a nation, they would never have continued
to be democracies; and the people collectively have become more of a democracy in proportion as they have
become more of a nation. Their democracy is to be realized by means of an intensification of their national life,
just as the ultimate moral purpose of an individual is
to be realized by the affirmation and intensification of
its own better individuality. Consequently the organization of the American democracy into a nation is not to
be regarded in the way that so many Americans have
regarded it,—as a necessary but hazardous surrender of
certain liberties in order that other liberties might be
better preserved,—as a mere compromise between the
democratic ideal and the necessary conditions of political cohesion and efficiency. Its nationalized political organization constitutes the proper structure and veritable
life of the American democracy. No doubt the existing
organization is far from being a wholly adequate expression of the demands of the democratic ideal, but it
falls equally short of being an adequate expression of
the demands of the national ideal. The less confidence
the American people have in a national organization,
the less they are willing to surrender themselves to the
national spirit, the worse democrats they will be. The

most stubborn impediments which block the American national advance issue from the imperfections in our democracy. The American people are not prepared for a higher form of democracy, because they are not prepared for a more coherent and intense national life. When they are prepared to be consistent, constructive, and aspiring democrats, their preparation will necessarily take the form of becoming consistent, constructive, and aspiring nationalists.

The difficulty raised by European political and economic development hangs chiefly on a necessary loyalty to a national tradition and organization which blocks the advance of democracy. Americans cannot entirely escape this difficulty; but in our country by far the greater obstacle to social amelioration is constituted by a democratic theory and tradition, which blocks the process of national development. We Americans are confronted by two divergent theories of democracy. According to one of these theories, the interest of American democracy can be advanced only by an increasing nationalization of the American people in ideas, in institutions, and in spirit. According to the other of these theories, the most effective way of injuring the interest of democracy is by an increase in national authority and a spread of the national leaven. Thus Americans, unlike Englishmen, have to choose, not between a specific and efficient national tradition and a vague and perilous democratic ideal—they have to choose between two democratic ideals, and they have to make this choice chiefly on logical and moral grounds. An Englishman or a German, no matter how clear his intelligence or fervid his patriotism, cannot find any immediately and entirely satisfactory method of reconciling the national traditions and forms of organization with the demands of an uncompromising democracy. An American, on the other hand, has it quite within his power to accept a conception of democracy which provides for the substantial integrity of his country, not only as a nation with an exclusively democratic mission, but as a democracy with an essentially national career.

II Nationality and Centralization

The Federal political organization has always tended to confuse to the American mind the relation between democracy and nationality. The nation as a legal body was, of course, created by the Constitution, which granted to the central government certain specific powers and responsibilities, and which almost to the same extent diminished the powers and the responsibilities of the separate states. Consequently, to the great majority of Americans, the process of increasing nationalization has a tendency to mean merely an increase in the functions of the central government. For the same reason the affirmation of a constructive relation between the national and the democratic principles is likely to be interpreted merely as an attempt on the grounds of an abstract theory to limit state government and to disparage states rights. Such an interpretation, however, would be essentially erroneous. It would be based upon the very idea against which I have been continually protesting— the idea that the American nation, instead of embodying a living formative political principle, is merely the political system created by the Federal Constitution; and it would end in the absurd conclusion that the only way in which the Promise of American democracy can be fulfilled would be by the abolition of American local political institutions.

The nationalizing of American political, economic, and social life means something more than Federal centralization and something very different therefrom. To nationalize a people has never meant merely to centralize their government. Little by little a thoroughly national political organization has come to mean in Europe an organization which combined effective authority with certain responsibilities to the people; but the national interest has been just as likely to demand de-centralization as it has to demand centralization. The Prussia of Frederick the Great, for instance, was over-centralized; and the restoration of the national vitality, at which the Prussian government aimed after the disasters of 1806, necessarily took the form of reinvigorating the local members of the national body. In this and many similar instances the national interest and welfare was the end, and a greater or smaller amount of centralized government merely the necessary machinery. The process of centralization is not, like the process of nationalization, an essentially formative and enlightening political transformation. When a people are being nationalized, their political, economic, and social organization or policy is being coördinated with their actual needs and their moral and political ideals. Governmental centralization is to be regarded as one of the many means which may or may not be taken in order to effect this purpose. Like every other special aspect of the national organization, it must be justified by its fruits. There is no presumption in its favor. Neither is there any general presumption against it. Whether a given function should or should not be exercised by the central government in a Federal system is from the point of view of political logic a matter of expediency—with the burden of proof resting on those who propose to alter any existing Constitutional arrangement.

It may be affirmed, consequently, without paradox, that among those branches of the American national organization which are greatly in need of nationalizing is the central government. Almost every member of the American political body has been at one time or another or in one way or another perverted to the service of special interests. The state governments and the municipal administrations have sinned more in this respect than the central government; but the central government itself has been a grave sinner. The Federal authorities are responsible for the prevailing policy in respect to military pensions, which is one of the most flagrant crimes ever perpetrated against the national interest. The Federal authorities, again, are responsible for the existing tariff schedules, which benefit a group of special interests at the expense of the national welfare. The Federal authorities, finally, are responsible for the Sherman Anti-Trust Law, whose existence on the statute books is a fatal bar to the treatment of the problem of corporate aggrandizement from the standpoint of genuinely national policy. Those instances might be multiplied, but they suffice to show that the ideal of a constructive relation between the American national and democratic principles does not imply that any particular piece of legislation or policy is national because it is Federal. The Federal no less than the state governments has been the victim of special interests; and when a group of state or city officials effectively assert the public interest against the private interests, either of the machine or of the local corporations, they are noting just as palpably, if not just as comprehensively, for the national welfare, as if their work benefited the whole American people. The process of nationalization in its application to American political organization means that political power shall be distributed among the central, state, and municipal officials in such a manner that it can be efficiently and responsibly exerted in the interest of those affected by its action.

Be it added, however, in the same breath, that under existing conditions and simply as a matter of expediency, the national advance of the American democracy does demand an increasing amount of centralized action and responsibility. In what respect and for what purposes an increased Federal power and responsibility is desirable will be considered in a subsequent chapter. In this connection it is sufficient to insist that a more scrupulous attention to existing Federal responsibilities, and the increase of their number and scope, is the natural consequence of the increasing concentration of American industrial, political, and social life. American government demands more rather than less centralization merely and precisely because of the growing centralization of American activity. The state governments, either individually or by any practicable methods of coöperation, are not competent to deal effectively in the national interest and spirit with the grave problems created by the aggrandizement of corporate and individual wealth and the increasing classification of the American people. They have, no doubt, an essential part to play in the attempted solution of these problems; and there are certain aspects of the whole situation which the American nation, because of its Federal organization, can deal with much more effectually than can a rigidly centralized democracy like France. But the amount of responsibility in respect to fundamental national problems, which, in law almost as much as in practice, is left to the states, exceeds the responsibility which the state governments are capable of efficiently redeeming. They are attempting (or neglecting) a task which they cannot be expected to perform with any efficiency.

The fact that the states fail properly to perform certain essential functions such as maintaining order or administering justice, is no sufficient reason for depriving them thereof. Functions which should be bestowed upon the central government are not those which the states happen to perform badly. They are those which the states, even with the best will in the world, cannot be expected to perform satisfactorily; and among these functions the regulation of commerce, the organization of labor, and the increasing control over property in the public interest are assuredly to be included. The best friends of local government in this country are those who seek to have its activity confined with the limits of possible efficiency, because only in case its activity is so confined can the states continue to remain an essential part of a really efficient and well-coördinated national organization.

Proposals to increase the powers of the central government are, however, rarely treated on their merits. They are opposed by the majority of American politicians and newspapers as an unqualified evil. Any attempt to prove that the existing distribution of responsibility is necessarily fruitful of economic and political abuses, and that an increase of centralized power offers the only chance of eradicating these abuses is treated as irrelevant. It is not a question of the expediency of a specific proposal, because from the traditional point of view any change in the direction of increased centralization would be a violation of American democracy. Centralization is merely a necessary evil which has been carried as far as it should, and which cannot be carried any further without undermining the foundations of the American system. Thus the familiar theory of many excellent American democrats is rather that of a contradictory than a constructive relation between the democratic and the national ideals. The process of nationalization is perverted by them into a matter merely of centralization, but the question of the fundamental relation between nationality and democracy is raised by their attitude, because the reasons they advance against increasingly centralized authority would, if they should continue to prevail, definitely and absolutely forbid a gradually improving coördination between American political organization and American national economic needs or moral and intellectual ideals. The conception of democracy out of which the supposed contradiction between the democratic and national ideals issues is the great enemy of the American national advance, and is for that reason the great enemy of the real interests of democracy.

To be sure, any increase in centralized power and responsibility, expedient or inexpedient, is injurious to certain aspects of traditional American democracy. But the fault in that case lies with the democratic tradition; and the erroneous and misleading tradition must yield before the march of a constructive national democracy. The national advance will always be impeded by these misleading and erroneous ideas, and, what is more, it always should be impeded by them, because at bottom ideas of this kind are merely an expression of the fact that the average American individual is morally and intellectually inadequate to a serious and consistent conception of his responsibilities as a democrat. An American national democracy must always prove its right to a further advance, not only by the development of a policy and method adequate for the particular occasion, but by its ability to overcome the inevitable opposition of selfish interests and erroneous ideas. The logic of its position makes it the aggressor, just as the logic of its opponents' position ties them to a negative and protesting or merely insubordinate part. If the latter should prevail, their victory would become tantamount to national dissolution, either by putrefaction, by revolution, or by both.

Under the influence of certain practical demands, an increase has already taken place in the activity of the Federal government. The increase has not gone as far as governmental efficiency demands, but it has gone far enough to provoke outbursts of protest and anguish

from the "old-fashioned Democrats." They profess to
see the approaching extinction of the American democracy in what they call the drift towards centralization.
Such calamitous predictions are natural, but they are
none the less absurd. The drift of American politics—its
instinctive and unguided movement—is almost wholly
along the habitual road; and any effective increase of
Federal centralization can be imposed only by most
strenuous efforts, by one of the biggest sticks which has
ever been flourished in American politics. The advance
made in this direction is small compared to the actual
needs of an efficient national organization, and considering the mass of interest and prejudice which it must
continue to overcome, it can hardly continue to progress at more than a snail's pace. The great obstacle to
American national fulfillment must always be the danger that the American people will merely succumb to
the demands of their local and private interests and will
permit their political craft to drift into a compromising
situation—from which the penalties of rescue may be
almost as distressing as the penalties of submission.

The tradition of an individualist and provincial democracy, which is the mainstay of an anti-national policy, does not include ideals which have to be realized by
aggressive action. Their ideals are the ones embodied
in our existing system, and their continued vitality demands merely a policy of inaction enveloped in a cloud
of sacred phrases. The advocates and the beneficiaries
of the prevailing ideas and conditions are little by little
being forced into the inevitable attitude of the traditional Bourbon—the attitude of maintaining customary or legal rights merely because they are customary
or legal, and predicting the most awful consequences
from any attempt to impair them. Men, or associations
of men, who possess legal or customary rights inimical
to the public welfare, always defend those rights as the

essential part of a political system, which, if it is overthrown, will prove destructive to public prosperity and security. On no other ground can they find a plausible public excuse for their opposition. The French royal authority and aristocratic privileges were defended on these grounds in 1780, and as the event proved, with some show of reason. In the same way the partial legislative control of nationalized corporations now exercised by the state government, is defended, not on the ground that it has been well exercised, not even plausibly on the ground that it can be well exercised. It is defended almost exclusively on the ground that any increase in the authority of the Federal government is dangerous to the American people. But the Federal government belongs to the American people even more completely than do the state governments, because a general current of public opinion can act much more effectively on the single Federal authority than it can upon the many separate state authorities. Popular interests have nothing to fear from a measure of Federal centralization, which bestows on the Federal government powers necessary to the fulfillment of its legitimate responsibilities; and the American people cannot in the long run be deceived by pleas which bear the evidence of such a selfish origin and have such dubious historical associations. The rights and the powers both of states and individuals must be competent to serve their purposes efficiently in an economical and coherent national organization, or else they must be superseded. A prejudice against centralization is as pernicious, provided centralization is necessary, as a prejudice in its favor. All rights under the law are functions in a democratic political organism and must be justified by their actual or presumable functional adequacy.

The ideal of a constructive relation between American nationality and American democracy is in truth equivalent to a new Declaration of Independence. It affirms that the American people are free to organize their political, economic, and social life in the service of a comprehensive, a lofty, and far-reaching democratic purpose. At the present time there is a strong, almost a dominant tendency to regard the existing Constitution with superstitious awe, and to shrink with horror from modifying it even in the smallest detail; and it is this superstitious fear of changing the most trivial parts of the fundamental legal fabric which brings to pass the great bondage of the American spirit. If such an abject worship of legal precedent for its own sake should continue, the American idea will have to be fitted to the rigid and narrow lines of a few legal formulas; and the ruler of the American spirit, like the ruler of the Jewish spirit of old, will become the lawyer. But it will not continue, in case Americans can be brought to understand and believe that the American national political organization should be constructively related to their democratic purpose. Such an ideal reveals at once the real opportunity and the real responsibility of the American democracy. It declares that the democracy has a machinery in a nationalized organization, and a practical guide in the national interest, which are adequate to the realization of the democratic ideal; and it declares also that in the long run just in so far as Americans timidly or superstitiously refuse to accept their national opportunity and responsibility, they will not deserve the names either of freemen or of loyal democrats. There comes a time in the history of every nation, when its independence of spirit vanishes, unless it emancipates itself in some measure from its traditional illusions; and that time is fast approaching for the American people. They must either seize the chance of a better future, or else become a nation which is satisfied in spirit merely to repeat indefinitely the monotonous measures of its own past.

III The People and the Nation

At the beginning of this discussion popular Sovereignty was declared to be the essential condition of democracy; and a general account of the nature of a constructive democratic ideal can best be brought to a close by a definition of the meaning of the phrase, popular Sovereignty, consistent with a nationalist interpretation of democracy. The people are Sovereign; but who and what are the people? and how can a many-headed Sovereignty be made to work? Are we to answer, like Bismarck, that the "true people is an invisible multitude of spirits—the nation of yesterday and of to-morrow"? Such an answer seems scarcely fair to living people of to-day. On the other hand, can we reply that the Sovereign people is constituted by any chance majority which happens to obtain control of the government, and that the decisions and actions of the majority are inevitably and unexceptionally democratic? Such an assertion of the doctrine of popular Sovereignty would bestow absolute Sovereign authority on merely a part of the people. Majority rule, under certain prescribed conditions, is a necessary constituent of any practicable democratic organization; but the actions or decisions of a majority need not have any binding moral and national authority. Majority rule is merely one means to an extremely difficult, remote and complicated end; and it is a piece of machinery which is peculiarly liable to get out of order. Its arbitrary and dangerous tendencies can, as a matter of fact, be checked in many effectual and legitimate ways, of which the most effectual is the cherishing of a tradition, partly expressed in some body of fundamental law, that the true people are, as Bismarck declared, in some measure an invisible multitude of spirits—the nation of yesterday and to-morrow, organized for its national historical mission.

The phrase popular Sovereignty is, consequently, for us Americans equivalent to the phrase "national Sovereignty." The people are not Sovereign as individuals. They are not Sovereign in reason and morals even when united into a majority. They become Sovereign only in so far as they succeed in reaching and expressing a collective purpose. But there is no royal and unimpeachable road to the attainment of such a collective will; and the best means a democratic people can take in order to assert its Sovereign authority with full moral effect is to seek fullness and consistency of national life. They are Sovereign in so far as they are united in spirit and in purpose; and they are united in so far as they are loyal one to another, to their joint past, and to the Promise of their future. The Promise of their future may sometimes demand the partial renunciation of their past and the partial sacrifice of certain present interests; but the inevitable friction of all such sacrifices can be mitigated by mutual loyalty and good faith. Sacrifices of tradition and interest can only be demanded in case they contribute to the national purpose—to the gradual creation of a higher type of individual and associated life. Hence it is that an effective increase in national coherence looks in the direction of the democratic consummation—of the morally and intellectually authoritative expression of the Sovereign popular will. Both the forging and the functioning of such a will are constructively related to the gradual achievement of the work of individual and social amelioration.

Undesirable and inadequate forms of democracy always seek to dispense in one way or another with this tedious process of achieving a morally authoritative Sovereign will. We Americans have identified democracy with certain existing political and civil rights, and we have, consequently, tended to believe that the democratic consummation was merely a matter of exercising and preserving those rights. The grossest form of this error was perpetrated when Stephen A. Douglas confused authoritative popular Sovereignty with the majority vote of a few hundred "squatters" in a frontier state, and asserted that on democratic principles such expressions of the popular will should be accepted as final. But an analogous mistake lurks in all static forms of democracy. The bestowal and the exercise of political and civil rights are merely a method of organization, which if used in proper subordination to the ultimate democratic purpose, may achieve in action something of the authority of a popular Sovereign will. But to cleave to the details of such an organization as the very essence of democracy is utterly to pervert the principle of national democratic Sovereignty. From this point of view, the Bourbon who wishes the existing system with its mal-adaptations and contradictions preserved in all its lack of integrity, commits an error analogous to that of the radical, who wishes by virtue of a majority vote immediately to destroy some essential part of the fabric. Both of them conceive that the whole moral and national authority of the democratic principle can be invoked in favor of institutions already in existence or of purposes capable of immediate achievement.

On the other hand, there are democrats who would seek a consummate democracy without the use of any political machinery. The idea that a higher type of associated life can be immediately realized by a supreme act of faith must always be tempting to men who unite social aspirations with deep religious faith. It is a more worthy and profound conception of democracy than the conventional American one of a system of legally constituted and equally exercised rights, fatally resulting in material prosperity. Before any great stride can be made towards a condition of better democracy, the constructive democratic movement must obtain more effective support both from scientific discipline and religious faith. Nevertheless, the triumph of Tolstoyan democracy at the present moment would be more pernicious in its results than the triumph of Jeffersonian Democracy. Tolstoy has merely given a fresh and exalted version of the old doctrine of non-resistance, which, as it was proclaimed by Jesus, referred in the most literal way to another world. In this world faith cannot dispense with power and organization. The sudden and immediate conversion of unregenerate men from a condition of violence, selfishness, and sin into a condition of beatitude and brotherly love can obtain even comparative permanence only by virtue of exclusiveness. The religious experience of our race has sufficiently testified to the permanence of the law. One man can be evangelized for a lifetime. A group of men can be evangelized for many years. Multitudes of men can be evangelized only for a few hours. No faith can achieve comparatively stable social conquests without being established by habit, defined by thought, and consolidated by organization. Usually the faith itself subsequently sickens of the bad air it breathes in its own house. Indeed, it is certain to lose initiative and vigor, unless it can appeal intermittently to some correlative source of enthusiasm and devotion. But with the help of efficient organization it may possibly survive, whereas in the absence of such a worldly body, it must in a worldly sense inevitably perish. Democracy as a living movement in the direction of human brotherhood has required, like other faiths, an efficient organization and a root in ordinary human nature; and it obtains such an organization by virtue of the process of national development—on condition, of course, that the nation is free to become a genuine and thorough-going democracy.

A democracy organized into a nation, and imbued with the national spirit, will seek by means of experimentation and discipline to reach the object which Tolstoy would reach by an immediate and a miraculous act of faith. The exigencies of such schooling frequently demand severe coercive measures, but what schooling does not? A nation cannot merely discharge its unregenerate citizens; and the best men in a nation or in any political society cannot evade the responsibility which the fact of human unregeneracy places upon the whole group. After men had reached a certain stage of civilization, they frequently began to fear that the rough conditions of political association excluded the highest and most fruitful forms of social life; and they sought various ways of improving the quality of the association by narrowing its basis. They tried to found small communities of saints who were connected exclusively by moral and religious bonds, and who in this way freed themselves from the hazards, the distraction, and the violence inseparable from political association. Such communities have made at different times great successes; but their success has not been permanent. The political aspect of associated life is not to be evaded. In proportion as political organization gained in prosperity, efficiency, and dignity, special religious associations lost their independence and power. Even the most powerful religious association in the world, the Catholic Church, has been fighting a losing battle with political authority, and it is likely in the course of time to occupy in relation to the political powers a position analogous to that of the Greek or the English church. The ultimate power to command must rest with that authority which, if necessary, can force people to obey; and any plan of association which seeks to ignore the part which physical force plays in life is necessarily incomplete. Just as formerly the irresponsible and meaningless use of political power created the need of special religious associations, independent of the state, so now the responsible, the purposeful, and the efficient use of physical force, characteristic of modern nations, has in its turn made such independence less necessary, and tends to attach a different function to the church. A basis of association narrower than the whole complex of human powers and interests will not serve. National organization provides such a basis. The perversity of human nature may cause its ultimate failure; but it will not fail because it omits any essential constituent in the composition of a permanent and fruitful human association. So far as it fulfills its responsibilities, it guarantees protection against predatory powers at home and abroad. It provides in appropriate measure for individual freedom, for physical, moral, and intellectual discipline, and for social consistency. It has prizes to offer as well as coercion to exercise; and with its foundations planted firmly in the past, its windows and portals look out towards a better future. The tendency of its normal action is continually, if very slowly, to diminish the distance between the ideal of human brotherhood, and the political, economic, and social conditions, under which at any one time men manage to live together.

That is the truth to which the patriotic Americans should firmly cleave. The modern nation, particularly in so far as it is constructively democratic, constitutes the best machinery as yet developed for raising the level of human association. It really teaches men how they must feel, what they must think, and what they must do, in order that they may live together amicably and profitably. The value of this school for its present purposes is increased by its very imperfections, because its imperfections issue inevitably from the imperfections of human nature. Men being as unregenerate as they are, all worthy human endeavor involves consequences of battle and risk. The heroes of the struggle must maintain their achievements and at times even promote their objects by compulsion. The policeman and the soldier will continue for an indefinite period to be guardians of the national schools, and the nations have no reason to be ashamed of this fact. It is merely symbolic of the very comprehensiveness of their responsibilities—that they have to deal with the problem of human inadequacy and unregeneracy in all its forms,—that they cannot evade this problem by allowing only the good boys to attend school—that they cannot even mitigate it by drawing too sharp a distinction between the good boys and the bad. Such indiscriminate attendance in these national schools, if it is to be edifying, involves one practical consequence of dominant importance. Everybody within the school-house—masters, teachers, pupils and janitors, old pupils and young, good pupils and bad, must feel one to another an indestructible loyalty. Such loyalty is merely the subjective aspect of their inevitable mutual association; it is merely the recognition that as a worldly body they must all live or die and conquer or fail together. The existence of an invincible loyalty is a condition of the perpetuity of the school. The man who believes himself wise is always tempted to ignore or undervalue the foolish brethren. The man who believes himself good is always tempted actively to dislike the perverse brethren. The man who insists at any cost upon having his own way is always twisting the brethren into his friends or his enemies. But the teaching of the national school constantly tends to diminish these causes of disloyalty. Its tendency is to convert traditional patriotism into a patient devotion to the national ideal, and into a patient loyalty towards one's fellow-countrymen as the visible and inevitable substance through which that ideal is to be expressed.

In the foregoing characteristic of a democratic nation, we reach the decisive difference between a nation which is seeking to be wholly democratic and a nation which is content to be semi-democratic. In the semi-democratic nation devotion to the national ideal does not to the same extent sanctify the citizen's relation in feeling and in idea to his fellow-countrymen. The loyalty demanded by the national ideal of such a country may imply a partly disloyal and suspicious attitude towards large numbers of political associates. The popular and the national interests must necessarily in some measure diverge. In a nationalized democracy or a democratic nation the corresponding dilemma is mitigated. The popular interest can only be efficiently expressed in a national policy and organization. The national interest is merely a more coherent and ameliorating expression of the popular interest. Its consistency, so far as it is consistent, is the reflection of a more humanized condition of human nature. It increases with the increasing power of its citizens to deal fairly and to feel loyally towards their fellow-countrymen; and it cannot increase except through the overthrow of the obstacles to fair dealing and loyal feeling.

The responsibility and loyalty which the citizens of a democratic nation must feel one towards another is comprehensive and unmitigable; but the actual behavior which at any one time the national welfare demands must, of course, be specially and carefully discriminated. National policies and acts will be welcome to some citizens and obnoxious to others, according to their special interests and opinions; and the citizens whose interests and ideas are prejudiced thereby have every right and should be permitted every opportunity to protest in the most vigorous and persistent manner. The nation may, however, on its part demand that these protests, in order to be heeded and respected, must conform to certain conditions. They must not be carried to the point of refusing obedience to the law. When private interests are injured by the national policy, the protestants must be able to show either that such injuries are unnecessary, or else they involve harm to an essential public interest. All such protest must find an ultimate sanction in a group of constructive democratic ideas. Finally, the protest must never be made the excuse for personal injustice or national disloyalty. Even if the national policy should betray indifference to the fundamental interests of a democratic nation, as did that of the United States from 1820 to 1860, the obligation of patient good faith on the part of the protestants is not diminished. Their protests may be as vivacious and as persistent as the error demands. The supporters of the erroneous policy may be made the object of most drastic criticism and the uncompromising exposure. No effort should be spared to secure the adoption of a more genuinely national policy. But beyond all this there remains a still deeper responsibility—that of dealing towards one's fellow-countrymen in good faith, so that differences of interest, of conviction, and of moral purpose can be made the agency of a better understanding and a firmer loyalty.

If a national policy offends the integrity of the national idea, as for a while that of the American nation did, its mistake is sure to involve certain disastrous consequences; and those consequences constitute, usually, the vehicle of necessary national discipline. The national school is, of course, the national life. So far as the school is properly conducted, the methods of instruction are, if you please, pedagogic; but if the masters are blind or negligent, or if the scholars are unruly, there remains as a resource the more painful and costly methods of nature's instruction. A serious error will be followed by its inevitable penalty, proportioned to the blindness and the perversity in which it originated; and thereafter the prosperity of the country's future will hang partly on the ability of the national intelligence to trace the penalty to its cause and to fix the responsibility. No matter how loyal the different members of a national body may be one to another, their mutual good faith will bleed to death, unless some among them have the intelligence to trace their national ills to their appropriate causes, and the candid courage to advocate the necessary remedial measures. At some point in the process, disinterested patriotism and good faith must be reënforced by intellectual insight. A people are saved many costly perversions, in case the official school-masters are wise, and the pupils neither truant nor insubordinate; but if the lessons are foolishly phrased, or the pupils refuse to learn, the school will never regain its proper disciplinary value until new teachers have arisen, who understand both the error and its consequences, and who can exercise an effective authority over their pupils.

The mutual loyalty and responsibility, consequently, embodied and inculcated in a national school, depends for its efficient expression upon the amount of insight and intelligence which it involves. The process of national education means, not only a discipline of the popular will, but training in ability to draw inferences from the national experience, so that the national consciousness will gradually acquire an edifying state of mind towards its present and its future problems. Those problems are always closely allied to the problems which have been more or less completely solved during the national history; and the body of practical lessons which can be inferred from that history is the best possible preparation for present and future emergencies. Such history requires close and exact reading. The national experience is always strangely mixed. Even the successes of our own past, such as the Federal organization, contain much dubious matter, demanding the most scrupulous disentanglement. Even the worst enemies of our national integrity, such as the Southern planters, offer in some respects an edifying political example to a disinterested democracy. Nations do not have to make serious mistakes in order to learn valuable lessons. Every national action, no matter how trivial, which is scrutinized with candor, may contribute to the stock of national intellectual discipline—the result of which should be to form a constantly more coherent whole out of the several elements in the national composition—out of the social and economic conditions, the stock of national opinions, and the essential national ideal. And it is this essential national ideal which makes it undesirable for the national consciousness to dwell too much on the past or to depend too much upon the lessons of experience alone. The great experience given to a democratic nation must be just an incorrigible but patient attempt to realize its democratic ideal—an attempt which must mold history as well as hang upon its lessons. The function of the patriotic political intelligence in relation to the fulfillment of the national Promise must be to devise means for its redemption—means which have their relations to the past, their suitability to the occasion, and their contribution towards a step in advance. The work is both critical, experienced, and purposeful. Mistakes will be made, and their effects either corrected or turned to good account. Successes will be achieved, and their effects must be coolly appraised and carefully discriminated. The task will never be entirely achieved, but the tedious and laborious advance will for every generation be a triumphant affirmation of the nationalized democratic ideal as the one really adequate political and social principle.

10.

A National Foreign Policy

I

The logic of a national democratic ideal and the responsibilities of a national career in the world involve a number of very definite consequences in respect to American
foreign policy. They involve, in fact, a conception of the
place of a democratic nation in relation to the other
civilized nations, different from that which has hitherto
prevailed in this country. Because of their geographical
situation and their democratic institutions, Americans
have claimed and still claim a large degree of national
aloofness and independence; but such a claim could have
been better defended several generations ago than it can
to-day. Unquestionably the geographical situation of the
United States must always have a decisive effect upon
the nature of its policy in foreign affairs; and undoubtedly no course of action in respect to other nations can
be national without serving the interests of democracy.
But precisely because an American foreign policy must
be candidly and vigorously national, it will gradually
bring with it an increasingly complicated group of international ties and duties. The American nation, just in so
far as it believes in its nationality and is ready to become
more of a nation, must assume a more definite and a
more responsible place in the international system. It
will have an increasingly important and an increasingly
specific part to play in the political affairs of the world;
and, in spite of "old-fashioned democratic" scruples and

prejudices, the will to play that part for all it is worth will constitute a beneficial and a necessary stimulus to the better realization of the Promise of our domestic life.

A genuinely national policy must, of course, be based upon a correct understanding of the national interest in relation to those of its neighbors and associates. That American policy did obtain such a foundation during the early years of American history is to be traced to the sound political judgment of Washington and Hamilton. Jefferson and the Republicans did their best for a while to persuade the American democracy to follow the dangerous course of the French democracy, and to base its international policy not upon the firm ground of national interest, but on the treacherous sands of international democratic propagandism. After a period of hesitation, the American people, with their usual good sense in the face of a practical emergency, rallied to the principles subsequently contained in Washington's Farewell Address; and the Jeffersonian Republicans, when they came into control of the Federal government, took over this conception of American national policy together with the rest of the Federalist outfit. But like the rest of the Federalist organization and ideas, the national foreign policy was emasculated by the expression it received at the hands of the Republicans. The conduct of American foreign affairs during the first fifteen years of the century are an illustration of the ills which may befall a democracy during a critical international period, when its foreign policy is managed by a party of anti-national patriots.

After 1815 the foreign policy of the United States was determined by a strict adherence to the principles enunciated in Washington's Farewell Address. The adherence was more in the letter than in the spirit, and the ordinary popular interpretation, which prevails until the present day, cannot be granted undivided approval; but so far as

its immediate problems were concerned, American foreign policy did not, on the whole, go astray. The United
States kept resolutely clear of European entanglements,
and did not participate in international councils, except
when the rights of neutrals were under discussion; and
this persistent neutrality was precisely the course which
was needed in order to confirm the international position of the country as well as to leave the road clear
for its own national development. But certain consequences were at an early date deduced from a neutral
policy which require more careful examination. During
the presidency of Monroe the systematic isolation of the
United States in respect to Europe was developed, so
far as the two Americas were concerned, into a more
positive doctrine. It was proclaimed that abstention
on the part of the United States from European affairs
should be accompanied by a corresponding abstention
by the European Powers from aggressive action in the
two Americas. What our government proposed to do
was to divide sharply the democratic political system
of the Americas from the monarchical and aristocratic
political system of Europe. The European system, based
as it was upon royalist legitimacy and privileges, and
denying as it did popular political rights, was declared
to be inimical in spirit and in effect to the American
democratic state.

The Monroe Doctrine has been accepted in this form
ever since as an indisputable corollary of the Farewell Address. The American people and politicians cherish it as
a priceless political heirloom. It is considered to be the
equivalent of the Declaration of Independence in the field
of foreign affairs; and it arouses an analogous volume
and fury of conviction. Neither is this conviction merely
the property of Fourth-of-July Americans. Our gravest
publicists usually contribute to the Doctrine a no less
emphatic adherence; and not very many years ago one of

the most enlightened of American statesmen asserted that American foreign policy as a whole could be sufficiently summed up in the phrase, "The Monroe Doctrine and the Golden Rule." Does the Monroe Doctrine, as stated above, deserve such uncompromising adherence? Is it an adequate expression of the national interest of the American democracy in the field of foreign affairs?

At the time the Monroe Doctrine was originally proclaimed, it did unquestionably express a valid national interest of the American democracy. It was the American retort to the policy of the Holy Alliance which sought to erect the counter-revolutionary principles into an international system, and which suppressed, so far as possible, all nationalist or democratic agitation. The Spanish-American colonies had been winning their independence from Spain; and there was a fear, not entirely ill-founded, that the Alliance would apply its anti-democratic international policy to the case of Spain's revolted colonies. Obviously the United States, both as a democracy and as a democracy which had won its independence by means of a revolutionary war, could not admit the right of any combination of European states to suppress national and democratic uprisings on the American continents. Our government would have been wholly justified in resisting such interference with all its available military force. But in what sense and upon what grounds was the United States justified in going farther than this, and in asserting that under no circumstances should there be any increase of European political influence upon the American continents? What is the propriety and justice of such a declaration of continental isolation? What are its implications? And what, if any, are its dangers?

In seeking an answer to these questions we must return to the source of American foreign policy in the Farewell Address. That address contains the germ of a prudent and wise American national policy; but Hamilton, in preparing its phrasing, was guided chiefly by a consideration of the immediate needs and dangers of his country. The Jeffersonian Republicans in their enthusiasm for the French Revolution proposed for a while to bring about a permanent alliance between France and the United States, the object whereof should be the propagation of the democratic political faith. Both Washington and Hamilton saw clearly that such behavior would entangle the United States in all the vicissitudes and turmoil which might attend the development of European democracy; and their favorite policy of neutrality and isolation implied both that the national interest of the United States was not concerned in merely European complications, and that the American people, unlike those of France, did not propose to make their political principles an excuse for international aggression. The Monroe Doctrine, as proclaimed in 1825, rounded out this negative policy with a more positive assertion of principles. It declared that the neutrality of the American democracy, so far as Europe was concerned, must be balanced by the non-intervention of European legitimacy and aristocracy in the affairs of the American continents. Now this extension of American foreign policy was, as we have seen, justified, in so far as it was a protest against any possible interference on the part of the Holy Alliance in American politics. It was, moreover, justified in so far as it sought to identify the attainment of a desirable democratic purpose with American international policy. Of course Hamilton, when he tried to found the international policy of his country upon the national interest, wholly failed to identify that interest with any positive democratic purpose; but in this, as in other respects, Hamilton was not a thorough-going democrat. While he was right in seeking to prevent the American people from allying themselves with the aggressive French democracy, he was wrong in failing to foresee that the national interest of the United States was identified with the general security and prosperity of liberal political institutions—that the United States must by every practical means encourage the spread of democratic methods and ideas. As much in foreign as in domestic affairs must the American people seek to unite national efficiency with democratic idealism. The Monroe Doctrine, consequently, is not to be condemned, as it has been condemned, merely because it went far beyond the limited foreign policy of Hamilton. The real question in regard to the Doctrine is whether it seeks in a practicable way—in a way consistent with the national interest and inevitable international responsibilities—the realization of the democratic idea. Do the rigid advocates of that Doctrine fall into an error analogous to the error against which Washington and Hamilton were protesting? Do they not tend, indirectly, and within a limited compass, to convert the American democratic idea into a dangerously aggressive principle?

The foregoing question must, I believe, be answered partly in the affirmative. The Monroe Doctrine, as usually stated, does give a dangerously militant tendency to the foreign policy of the United States; and unless its expression is modified, it may prevent the United States from occupying a position towards the nations of Europe and America in conformity with its national interest and its national principle. It should be added, however, that this unwholesomely aggressive quality is only a tendency, which will not become active except under certain possible conditions, and which can gradually be rendered less dangerous by the systematic development of the Doctrine as a positive principle of political action in the Western hemisphere.

The Monroe Doctrine has, of course, no status in the accepted system of International Law. Its interna-

tional standing is due almost entirely to its express proclamation as an essential part of the foreign policy of
the United States, and it depends for its weight upon
the ability of this country to compel its recognition by
the use of latent or actual military force. Great Britain
has, perhaps, tacitly accepted it, but no other European
country has done so, and a number of them have expressly stated that it entails consequences against which
they might sometime be obliged strenuously and forcibly to protest. No forcible protest has as yet been made,
because no European country has had anything to gain
from such a protest, comparable to the inevitable cost of
a war with the United States.

The dangerously aggressive tendency of the Monroe
Doctrine is not due to the fact that it derives its standing
from the effective military power of the United States.
The recognition which any proclamation of a specific
principle of foreign policy receives will depend, in case
it conflicts with the actual or possible interests of other
nations, upon the military and naval power with which
it can be maintained. The question as to whether a particular doctrine is unwholesomely aggressive depends,
consequently, not upon the mere fact that it may provoke a war, but upon the doubt that, if it provokes a
war, such a war can be righteously fought. Does the
Doctrine as usually stated, possibly or probably commit the United States to an unrighteous war—a war in
which the United States would be opposing a legitimate
interest on the part of one or a group of European nations? Does an American foreign policy of the "Monroe
Doctrine and the Golden Rule" proclaim two parallel
springs of national action in foreign affairs which may
prove to be incompatible?

There is a danger that such may be the case. The
Monroe Doctrine in its most popular form proclaims a
rigid policy of continental isolation—of America for the

Americans and of Europe for the Europeans. European nations may retain existing possessions in the Americas, but such possessions must not be increased. So far, so good. A European nation, which sought defiantly to increase its American possessions, in spite of the express declaration of the United States that such action would mean war, would deserve the war thereby incurred. But there are many ways of increasing the political influence of European Powers in the Americas without actual territorial appropriation. The emigration from several European states and from Japan to South America is already considerable, and is likely to increase rather than diminish. European commercial interests in South America are greater than ours, and in the future will become greater still. The South Americans have already borrowed large quantities of European capital, and will need more. The industrial and agricultural development of the South American states is constantly tying them more closely to Europe than it is to the United States. It looks, consequently, as if irresistible economic conditions were making in favor of an increase of effective European influence in South America. The growth of that influence is part of the world-movement in the direction of the better utilization of the economic resources of mankind. South America cannot develop without the benefits of European capital, additional European labor, European products, and European experience and training; and in the course of another few generations the result will be a European investment in South America, which may in a number of different ways involve political complications. We have already had a foretaste of those consequences in the steps which the European Powers took a few years ago to collect debts due to Europeans by Venezuela.

The increasing industrial, social, and financial bonds might not have any serious political consequences, provided the several South American states were possessed of stable governments, orderly political traditions, and a political standing under definite treaties similar to that of the smaller European states. But such is not the case. The alien investment in South America may involve all sorts of political complications which would give European or Asiatic Powers a justifiable right under the law of nations to interfere. Up to the present time, as we have seen, such interference has promised to be too costly; but the time may well come when the advantages of interference will more than counterbalance the dangers of a forcible protest. Moreover, in case such a protest were made, it might not come from any single European Power. A general European interest would be involved. The United States might well find her policy of America for the Americans result in an attempt on the part of a European coalition to bring about a really effectual isolation. We might find ourselves involved in a war against a substantially united Europe. Such a danger seems sufficiently remote at present; but in the long run a policy which carries isolation too far is bound to provoke justifiable attempts to break it down. If Europe and the Americas are as much divided in political interest as the Monroe Doctrine seems to assert, the time will inevitably arrive when the two divergent political systems must meet and fight; and plenty of occasions for such a conflict will arise, as soon as the policy of isolation begins to conflict with the establishment of that political relation between Europe and South America demanded by fundamental economic and social interests. Thus under certain remote but entirely possible conditions, the Doctrine as now proclaimed and practiced might justify Europe in seeking to break it down by reasons at least as valid as those of our own country in proclaiming it.

But if the Monroe Doctrine could only be maintained by a war of this kind, or a succession of wars, it would defeat the very purpose which it is supposed to accomplish. It would embroil the United States and the two American continents in continual trouble with Europe; and it would either have to be abandoned or else would carry with it incessant and enormous expenditures for military and naval purposes. The United States would have to become a predominantly military power, armed to the teeth, to resist or forestall European attack; and our country would have to accept these consequences, for the express purpose of keeping the Americas unsullied by the complications of European politics. Obviously there is a contradiction in such a situation. The United States could fight with some show of reason a single European Power, like France in 1865, which undertook a policy of American territorial aggrandizement; but if it were obliged to fight a considerable portion of Europe for the same purpose, it would mean that our country was opposing a general, and presumably a legitimate, European interest. In that event America would become a part of the European political system with a vengeance—a part which in its endeavor to escape from the vicissitudes of European politics had brought upon itself a condition of permanent military preparation and excitement. Consequently, in case the "Monroe Doctrine and the Golden Rule" are to remain the foundation of American foreign policy, mere prudence demands a systematic attempt to prevent the Doctrine from arousing just and effective European opposition.

No one can believe more firmly than myself that the foreign policy of a democratic nation should seek by all practicable and inoffensive means the affirmation of democracy; but the challenge which the Monroe Doctrine in its popular form issues to Europe is neither an inoffensive nor a practicable means of affirmation. It is based usually upon the notion of an essential incompatibility between American and European political institutions; and the assertion of such an incompatibility at the present time can only be the result of a stupid or willful American democratic Bourbonism. Such an incompatibility did exist when the Holy Alliance dominated Europe. It does not exist to-day, except in one particular. The exception is important, as we shall see presently; but it does not concern the domestic institutions of the European and the American states. The emancipated and nationalized European states of to-day, so far from being essentially antagonistic to the American democratic nation, are constantly tending towards a condition which invites closer and more fruitful association with the United States; and any national doctrine which proclaims a rooted antagonism lies almost at right angles athwart the road of American democratic national achievement. Throughout the whole of the nineteenth century the European nations have been working towards democracy by means of a completer national organization; while this country has been working towards national cohesion by the mere logic and force of its democratic ideal. Thus the distance between America and Europe is being diminished; and Americans in their individual behavior bear the most abundant and generous testimony to the benefits which American democracy can derive from association with the European nations. It is only in relation to the Monroe Doctrine that we still make much of the essential incompatibility between European and American institutions, and by so doing we distort and misinterpret the valid meaning of a national democratic foreign policy. The existing domestic institutions of the European nations are for the most part irrelevant to such a policy.

The one way in which the foreign policy of the United States can make for democracy is by strengthening and encouraging those political forces which make for international peace. The one respect in which the political system, represented by the United States, is still antagonistic to the European political system is that the European nation, whatever its ultimate tendency, is actually organized for aggressive war, that the cherished purposes of some of its states cannot be realized without war, and that the forces which hope to benefit by war are stronger than the forces which hope to benefit by peace. That is the indubitable reason why the United States must remain aloof from the European system and must avoid scrupulously any entanglements in the complicated web of European international affairs. The policy of isolation is in this respect as wise to-day as it was in the time of its enunciation by Washington and Hamilton; and nobody seriously proposes to depart from it. On the other hand, the basis for this policy is wholly independent of the domestic institutions of the European nations. It derives from the fact that at any time those nations may go to war about questions in which the United States has no vital interest. The geographical situation of the United States emancipates her from these conflicts, and enables her to stand for the ultimate democratic interest in international peace.

This justifiable policy of isolation has, moreover, certain important consequences in respect to the foreign policy of the United States in the two Americas. In this field, also, the United States must stand in every practicable way for a peaceful international system, and whatever validity the Monroe Doctrine may have in its relation to the European nations is the outcome of that obligation. If South and Central America were thrown open to European colonial ambitions, they would be involved very much more than they are at present in the consequences of European wars. In this sense the increase of European political influence in the two Americas would be an undesirable thing which the United States would have good reason to oppose. In this sense the extension of the European system to the American hemisphere would involve consequences inimical to democracy. In 1801 the North was fighting, not merely to preserve American national integrity, but to prevent the formation of a state on its southern frontier which could persist only by virtue of a European alliance, and which would consequently have entangled the free republic of the Northern states in the network of irrelevant European complications. Such would be the result of any attempt on the part of the European states to seek alliances or to pursue an aggressive policy on this side of the Atlantic.

But it may be asked, how can European aggressions in America be opposed, even on the foregoing ground, without requiring enormous and increasing military preparations? Would not the Monroe Doctrine, even in that modified form, involve the same practical inconsistency which has already been attached to its popular expression? The answer is simple. It will involve a similar inconsistency unless effective means are taken to avoid the inevitable dangers of such a challenge to Europe— unless, that is, means are taken to prevent Europe from having any just cause for intervention in South America for the purpose of protecting its own investment of men and money. The probable necessity of such intervention is due to the treacherous and unstable political conditions prevailing on that continent; and the Monroe Doctrine, consequently, commits the United States at least to the attempt to constitute in the two Americas a stable and peaceful international system. During the next two or three generations the European states will be too much preoccupied elsewhere to undertake or even to threaten any serious or concerted interference in South America. During that interval, while the Monroe

Doctrine remains in its present situation of being un-recognized but unchallenged, American statesmen will have their opportunity. If the American system can be made to stand for peace, just as the European system stands at present for war, then the United States will have an unimpeachable reason in forbidding European intervention. European states would no longer have a legitimate ground for interference; it would be impos-sible for them to take any concerted action. The Ameri-can nation would testify to its sincere democracy both by its negative attitude towards a militant European system and by its positive promotion of a peaceful in-ternational system in the two Americas.

On the other hand, if a stable international system either is not or cannot be constituted in the two Ameri-cas, the Monroe Doctrine will probably involve this country in wars which would be not merely exhausting and demoralizing, but fruitless. We should be fighting to maintain a political system which would be in no essential respect superior to the European political sys-tem. The South and Central American states have been almost as ready to fight among themselves, and to cher-ish political plans which can be realized only by war, as the European states. In the course of time, as they grow in population and wealth, they also will entertain more or less desirable projects of expansion; and the result-ing conflicts would, the United States permitting, be sure to involve European alliances and complications. Why should the United States prepare for war in order to pre-serve the integrity of states which, if left to themselves, might well have an interest in compromising their own independence, and which, unless subjected to an edify-ing pressure, would probably make comparatively poor use of the independence they enjoyed? Surely the only valid reason for fighting in order to prevent the growth of European political influence in the two Americas is the creation of a political system on behalf of which it is worth while to fight.

II   A Stable American International System

Possibly some of my readers will have inferred by this time that the establishment of a peaceable international system in the two Americas is only a sanctimonious paraphrase for a policy on the part of this country of political aggrandizement in the Western hemisphere. Such an inference would be wholly unjust. Before such a system can be established, the use of compulsion may on some occasions be necessary; but the United States acting individually, could rarely afford to employ forcible means. An essential condition of the realization of the proposed system would be the ability of American statesmen to convince the Latin-Americans of the disinterestedness of their country's intentions; and to this end the active coöperation of one or more Latin-American countries in the realization of the plan would be indispensable. The statesmen of this country can work without coöperation as long as they are merely seeking to arouse public sentiment in favor of such a plan, or as long as they are clearing away preliminary obstacles; but no decisive step can be taken without assurance of support on the part of a certain proportion of the Latin-American states, and the best way gradually to obtain such support has already been indicated by Mr. Elihu Root during his official term as Secretary of State. He has begun the work of coming to an understanding with the best element in South American opinion by his candid and vigorous expression of the fundamental interest of the United States in its relations with its American neighbors.

Fifteen years ago the attempt to secure effective support from any of the Latin-American states in the foundation of a stable American international system would have looked hopeless. Countries with so appalling a record of domestic violence and instability could apparently be converted to a permanently peaceable behavior in respect to their neighbors only by the use of force. But recently several niches have been built into the American political structure on which a foothold may eventually be obtained. In general the political condition of the more powerful Latin-American states, such as Mexico, Brazil, Argentina, and Chile, has become more stable and more wholesome. If their condition of stability and health persists, their industrial and commercial prosperity will also continue; and little by little their political purposes will become more explicit and more significant. As soon as this stage is reached, it should be possible for American statesmen to estimate accurately the weight of the probable obstacles which any movement towards an international agreement would encounter. A series of particular steps could then be taken, tending to remove such obstacles, and, if wise, the whole question of an international agreement could be raised in some definite way.

Such obstacles may prove to be insurmountable; but provided the Latin-Americans can be convinced of the disinterestedness of this country, they do not look insurmountable. Acquiescence in a permanent American international system would, of course, imply a certain sacrifice of independence on the part of the several contracting states; but in return for this sacrifice their situation in respect to their neighbors would receive a desirable certification. They would renounce the right of going to war in return for a guarantee of their independence in other respects, and for the consequent chance of an indefinite period of orderly economic and social development. Whether they can ever be brought to such a renunciation will depend, of course, on the conception of their national interest which the more important Latin-American states will reach. As long as any one of them cherishes objects which can only be realized by war, the international situation in the Western hemisphere will remain similar to that of Europe. An actual or latent aggressiveness on the part of any one nation inevitably provokes its neighbors into a defiant and suspicious temper. It is too soon to predict whether the economic and political development of the Latin-Americans during the next generation will make for a warlike or a peaceful international organization; but considering the political geography of South America and the manifest economic interests of the several states, it does not look as if any one of them had as much to gain from a militant organization as it had from a condition of comparative international security.

The domestic condition of some of the Latin-American states presents a serious obstacle to the creation of a stable American international system. Such a system presupposes a condition of domestic peace. The several contracting states must possess permanent and genuinely national political organizations; and no such organization is possible as long as the tradition and habit of revolution persists. As we have seen, the political habits of the more important states have in this respect enormously improved of late years, but there remain a number of minor countries wherein the right of revolution is cherished as the essential principle of their democracy. Just what can be done with such states is a knotty problem. In all probability no American international system will ever be established without the forcible pacification of one or more such centers of disorder. Coercion should, of course, be used only in the case of extreme necessity; and it would not be just to deprive the people of such states of the right of revolution, unless effective measures were at the same time taken to do away with the more or less legitimate excuses for revolutionary protest. In short, any international American political system might have to undertake a task in states like Venezuela, similar to that which the United States is now performing in Cuba. That any attempt to secure domestic stability would be disinterested, if not successful, would be guaranteed by the participation or the express acquiescence therein of the several contracting states.

The United States has already made an effective beginning in this great work, both by the pacification of Cuba and by the attempt to introduce a little order into the affairs of the turbulent Central American republics. The construction of the Panama Canal has given this country an exceptional interest in the prevalence of order and good government in the territory between Panama and Mexico; and in the near future our best opportunity for improving international political conditions in the Western hemisphere will be found in this comparatively limited but, from a selfish point of view, peculiarly important field. Within this restricted area the same obstacles will be encountered as in the larger area, and success will depend upon the use of similar means and the exhibition of similar qualities. Very little can be achieved in Central America without the coöperation of Mexico, and without the ability to convince Mexican statesmen of the disinterested intentions of this country. In the same way any recrudescence of revolutionary upheavals in Mexico would enormously increase the difficulties and perils of the attempt. On the other hand, success in bringing about with Mexican coöperation a condition of political security and comparative stability in Central America would augur well for the success of the larger and more difficult attempt to perform a similar work for the whole American hemisphere.

The most difficult task, however, connected with the establishment of a peaceful American international system is presented by Canada. In case such a system were constituted, Canada should most assuredly form a part of it. Yet she could not form a part of it without a radical alteration in her relations with Great Britain. Canada is tied to the British Imperial system, and her policy and destiny depends upon the policy and destiny of the British Empire. She is content with this situation, not merely because she is loyal to the mother country, but because she believes that her association with Great Britain guarantees her independence in respect to the United States. Many Canadians cherish a profound conviction that the United States wishes nothing so much as the annexation of the Dominion; and the one thing in the world which they propose to prevent is a successful attack upon their independence. This is the natural attitude of a numerically weak people, divided by a long and indefensible frontier from a numerous and powerful neighbor; and while the people of this country have done nothing since the War of 1812 positively to provoke such suspicions, they have, on the other hand, done nothing to allay them. We have never attempted to secure the good will of the Canadians in any respect; and we have never done anything to establish better relations. Yet unless such better relations are established, the United States will lose an indispensable ally in the making of a satisfactory political system in the Western hemisphere while at the same time the American people will be in the sorry situation for a sincere democracy of having created only apprehension and enmity on the part of their nearest and most intelligent neighbors.

Under such circumstances the very first object of the foreign policy of the United States should be to place its relations with Canada on a better footing. There was a time when this object could have been accomplished by the negotiation of a liberal treaty of commercial reciprocity. If the commercial policy of the United States had been determined by its manifest national interest instead of by the interests of a group of special industries, such a treaty would have been signed many years ago. A great opportunity was lost when the negotiations failed early in the eighties, because ever since Canada has been tightening her commercial ties with Great Britain; and these ties will be still further tightened as Canada grows into a large grain-exporting country. But while it will be impossible to make an arrangement as advantageous as the one which might have been made twenty-five years ago, the national interest plainly demands the negotiation of the most satisfactory treaty possible at the present time; and if the special interests of a few industries are allowed to stand indefinitely in the way, we shall be plainly exhibiting our incompetence to carry out an enlightened and a truly national foreign policy. We shall be branding ourselves with the mark of a merely trading democracy which is unable to subordinate the selfish interests of a few of its citizens to the realization of a policy combining certain commercial advantages with an essential national object. Just as the maintenance of the present high protective tariff is the clearest possible indication of the domination of special over national interests in domestic politics, so the resolute opposition which these industries show to the use of the tariff as an instrument of a national foreign policy, suggests that the first duty of the United States as a nation is to testify to its emancipation from such bondage by revising the tariff. The matter concerns not merely Canada, but the South American Republics; and it is safe to say that the present policy of blind protection is an absolute bar to the realization of that improved American political system which is the correlative in foreign affairs of domestic individual and social amelioration.

The desirable result of the utmost possible commercial freedom between Canada and the United States would be to prepare the way for closer political association. By closer political association I do not mean the annexation of Canada to the United States. Such annexation might not be desirable even with the consent of Canada. What I do mean is some political recognition of the fact that the real interests of Canada in foreign affairs coincide with the interests of the United States rather than with the interests of Great Britain. Great Britain's interest in the independence of Holland or in the maintenance of the Turkish power in Europe might involve England in a European war, in which Canada would have none but a sentimental stake, but from which she might suffer severe losses. At bottom Canada needs for her political and commercial welfare disentanglement from European complications just as much as does the United States; and the diplomacy, official and unofficial, of the United States, should seek to convince Canada of the truth of this statement. Neither need a policy which looked in that direction necessarily incur the enmity of Great Britain. In view of the increasing cost of her responsibilities in Europe and in Asia, England has a great deal to gain by concentration and by a partial retirement from the American continent, so far as such a retirement could be effected without being recreant to her responsibilities towards Canada. The need of such retirement has already been indicated by the diminution of her fleet in American waters; and if her expenses and difficulties in Europe and Asia increase, she might be glad to reach some arrangement with Canada and the United States which would recognize a dominant Canadian interest in freedom from exclusively European political vicissitudes.

Such an arrangement is very remote; but it looks as if under certain probable future conditions, a treaty along the following lines might be acceptable to Great Britain, Canada, and the United States. The American and the English governments would jointly guarantee the independence of Canada. Canada, on her part, would enter into an alliance with the United States, looking towards the preservation of peace on the American continents and the establishment of an American international political system. Canada and the United States in their turn would agree to lend the support of their naval forces to Great Britain in the event of a general European war, but solely for the purpose of protecting the cargoes of grain and other food which might be needed by Great Britain. Surely the advantages of such an arrangement would be substantial and well-distributed. Canada would feel secure in her independence, and would be emancipated from irrelevant European complications. The United States would gain support, which is absolutely essential for the proper pacification of the American continent, and would pay for that support only by an engagement consonant with her interest as a food-exporting power. Great Britain would exchange a costly responsibility for an assurance of food in the one event, which Britons must fear—viz., a general European war with strong maritime powers on the other side. Such an arrangement would, of course, be out of the question at present; but it suggests the kind of treaty which might lead Great Britain to consent to the national emancipation of Canada, and which could be effected without endangering Canadian independence.

Any systematic development of the foreign policy of the United States, such as proposed herewith, will seem very wild to the majority of Americans. They will not concede its desirability, because the American habit is to proclaim doctrines and policies, without considering either the implications, the machinery necessary to carry them out, or the weight of the resulting responsibilities. But in estimating the practicability of the policy proposed, the essential idea must be disentangled from any possible methods of realizing it—such as the suggested treaty between the United States, Great Britain, and Canada. An agreement along those lines may never be either practicable or prudent, but the validity of the essential idea remains unaffected by the abandonment of a detail. That idea demands that effective and far-sighted arrangements be made in order to forestall the inevitable future objections on the part of European nations to an uncompromising insistence on the Monroe Doctrine; and no such arrangement is possible, except by virtue of Canadian and Mexican coöperation as well as that of some of the South American states. It remains for American statesmanship and diplomacy to discover little by little what means are practicable and how much can be accomplished under any particular set of conditions. A candid man must admit that the obstacles may prove to be insuperable. One of any number of possible contingencies may serve to postpone its realization indefinitely. Possibly neither Canada nor Great Britain will consent to any accommodation with the United States. Possibly one or more South American states will assume an aggressive attitude towards their neighbors. Possibly their passions, prejudices, and suspicions will make them prefer the hazards and the costs of military preparations and absolute technical independence, even though their interests counsel another course. Possibly the consequences of some general war in Europe or Asia will react on the two Americas and embroil the international situation to the point of hopeless misunderstanding and confusion. Indeed, the probabilities are that in America as in Europe the road to any permanent international settlement will be piled mountain high with dead bodies, and will be traveled, if at all, only after a series of abortive and costly experiments. But remote and precarious as is the establishment of any American international system, it is not for American statesmen necessarily either an impracticable, an irrelevant, or an unworthy object. Fail though we may in the will, the intelligence, or the power to carry it out, the systematic effort to establish a peaceable American system is just as plain and just as inevitable a consequence of the democratic national principle, as is the effort to make our domestic institutions contribute to the work of individual and social amelioration.

III Democracy and Peace

A genuinely national foreign policy for the American democracy is not exhausted by the Monroe Doctrine. The United States already has certain colonial interests; and these interests may hereafter be extended. I do not propose at the present stage of this discussion to raise the question as to the legitimacy in principle of a colonial policy on the part of a democratic nation. The validity of colonial expansion even for a democracy is a manifest deduction from the foregoing political principles, always assuming that the people whose independence is thereby diminished are incapable of efficient national organization. On the other hand, a democratic nation cannot righteously ignore an unusually high standard of obligation for the welfare of its colonial population. It would be distinctly recreant to its duty, in case it failed to provide for the economic prosperity of such a population, and for their educational discipline and social improvement. It by no means follows, however, that because there is no rigid objection on democratic principles to colonial expansion, there may not be the strongest practical objection on the score of national interest to the acquisition of any particular territory. A remote colony is, under existing international conditions, even more of a responsibility than it is a source of national power and efficiency; and it is always a grave question how far the assumption of any particular responsibility is worth while.

Without entering into any specific discussion, there can, I think, be little doubt that the United States was justified in assuming its existing responsibilities in respect to Cuba and its much more abundant responsibilities in respect to Porto Rico. Neither can it be fairly claimed that hitherto the United States has not dealt disinterestedly and in good faith with the people of these islands. On the other hand, our acquisition of the Philippines raises a series of much more doubtful questions. These islands have been so far merely an expensive obligation, from which little benefit has resulted to this country and a comparatively moderate benefit to the Filipinos. They have already cost an amount of money far beyond any chance of compensation, and an amount of American and Filipino blood, the shedding of which constitutes a grave responsibility. Their future defense against possible attack presents a military and naval problem of the utmost difficulty. In fact, they cannot be defended from Japan except by the maintenance of a fleet in Pacific waters at least as large as the Japanese fleet; and it does not look probable that the United States will be able to afford for another generation any such concentration of naval strength in the Pacific. But even though from the military point of view the Philippines may constitute a source of weakness and danger, their possession will have the political advantage of keeping the American people alive to their interests in the grave problems which will be raised in the Far East by the future development of China and Japan.

The future of China raises questions of American foreign policy second only in importance to the establishment of a stable American international organization; and in relation to these questions, also, the interests of the United States and Canada tend both to coincide and to diverge (possibly) from those of Great Britain. Just what form the Chinese question will assume, after the industrial and the political awakening of China has resulted in a more effective military organization and in greater powers both of production and consumption, cannot be predicted with any certainty; but at present, it looks as if the maintenance of the traditional American policy with respect to China, viz., the territorial integrity and the free commercial development of that country, might require quite as considerable a concentration of naval strength in the Pacific as is required by the defense of the Philippines. It is easy enough to enunciate such a policy, just as it is easy to proclaim a Monroe Doctrine which no European Power has any sufficient immediate interest to dispute; but it is wholly improbable that China can be protected in its territorial integrity and its political independence without a great deal of diplomacy and more or less fighting. During the life of the coming generation there will be brought home clearly to the American people how much it will cost to assert its own essential interests in China; and the peculiar value of the Philippines as an American colony will consist largely in the fact that they will help American public opinion to realize more quickly than it otherwise would the complications and responsibilities created by Chinese political development and by Japanese ambition.

The existence and the resolute and intelligent facing of such responsibilities are an inevitable and a wholesome aspect of national discipline and experience. The American people have too easily evaded them in the past, but in the future they cannot be evaded; and it is better so. The irresponsible attitude of Americans in respect to their national domestic problems may in part be traced to freedom from equally grave international responsibilities. In truth, the work of internal reconstruction and amelioration, so far from being opposed to that of the vigorous assertion of a valid foreign policy, is really correlative and supplementary thereto; and it is entirely possible that hereafter the United States will be forced into the adoption of a really national domestic policy because of the dangers and duties incurred through her relations with foreign countries.

The increasingly strenuous nature of international competition and the constantly higher standards of international economic, technical, and political efficiency prescribe a constantly improving domestic political and economic organization. The geographical isolation which affords the United States its military security against foreign attack should not blind Americans to the merely comparative nature of their isolation. The growth of modern sea power and the vast sweep of modern national political interests have at once diminished their security, and multiplied the possible sources of contact between American and European interests. No matter how peaceably the United States is inclined, and no matter how advantageously it is situated, the American nation is none the less constantly threatened by political warfare, and constantly engaged in industrial warfare. The American people can no more afford than can a European people to neglect any necessary kind or source of efficiency. Sooner than ever before in the history of the world do a nation's sins and deficiencies find it out. Under modern conditions a country which takes its responsibilities lightly, and will not submit to the discipline necessary to political efficiency, does not gradually decline, as Spain did in the seventeenth century. It usually goes down with a crash, as France did in

1870, or as Russia has just done. The effect of diminishing economic efficiency is not as suddenly and dramatically exhibited; but it is no less inevitable and no less severe. And the service which the very intensity of modern international competition renders to a living nation arises precisely from the searching character of the tests to which it subjects the several national organizations. Austria-Hungary has been forced to assume a secondary position in Europe, because the want of national cohesion and vitality deprived her political advance of all momentum. Russia has suddenly discovered that a corrupt bureaucracy is incapable of a national organization as efficient as modern military and political competition requires. It was desirable in the interest of the Austrians, the Hungarians, and the Russians, that these weaknesses should be exposed; and if the Christian states of the West ever become so organized that their weaknesses are concealed until their consequences become irremediable, Western civilization itself will be on the road to decline. The Atlantic Ocean will, in the long run, fail to offer the United States any security from the application of the same searching standards. Its democratic institutions must be justified, not merely by the prosperity which they bestow upon its own citizens, but by its ability to meet the standards of efficiency imposed by other nations. Its standing as a nation is determined precisely by its ability to conquer and to hold a dignified and important place in the society of nations.

The inference inevitably is that the isolation which has meant so much to the United States, and still means so much, cannot persist in its present form. Its geographical position will always have a profound influence on the strategic situation of the United States in respect to the European Powers. It should always emancipate the United States from merely European complications. But, while the American nation should never seek a positive place in an exclusively European system, Europe, the United States, Japan, and China must all eventually take their respective places in a world system. While such a system is still so remote that it merely shows dimly through the obscurity of the future, its manifest desirability brings with it certain definite but contingent obligations in addition to the general obligation of comprehensive and thorough-going national efficiency. It brings with it the obligation of interfering under certain possible circumstances in what may at first appear to be a purely European complication; and this specific obligation would be the result of the general obligation of a democratic nation to make its foreign policy serve the cause of international peace. Hitherto, the American preference and desire for peace has constituted the chief justification for its isolation. At some future time the same purpose, just in so far as it is sincere and rational, may demand intervention. The American responsibility in this respect is similar to that of any peace-preferring European Power. If it wants peace, it must be spiritually and physically prepared to fight for it. Peace will prevail in international relations, just as order prevails within a nation, because of the righteous use of superior force— because the power which makes for pacific organization is stronger than the power which makes for a warlike organization. It looks as if at some future time the power of the United States might well be sufficient, when thrown into the balance, to tip the scales in favor of a comparatively pacific settlement of international complications. Under such conditions a policy of neutrality would be a policy of irresponsibility and unwisdom.

The notion of American intervention in a European conflict, carrying with it either the chance or the necessity of war, would at present be received with pious horror by the great majority of Americans. Non-interference in European affairs is conceived, not as a policy dependent upon certain conditions, but as absolute law—derived from the sacred writings. If the issue should be raised in the near future, the American people would be certain to shirk it; and they would, perhaps, have some reason for a failure to understand their obligation, because the course of European political development has not as yet been such as to raise the question in a decisive form. All one can say as to the existing situation is that there are certain Powers which have very much more to lose than they have to gain by war. These Powers are no longer small states like Belgium, Switzerland, and Holland, but populous and powerful states like Great Britain, Italy, and France. It may be one or it may be many generations before the issue of a peaceful or a warlike organization is decisively raised. When, if ever, it is decisively raised, the system of public law, under which any organization would have to take place, may not be one which the United States could accept. But the point is that, whenever and however it is raised, the American national leaders should confront it with a sound, well-informed, and positive conception of the American national interest rather than a negative and ignorant conception. And there is at least a fair chance that such will be the case. The experience of the American people in foreign affairs is only beginning, and during the next few generations the growth of their traffic with Asia and Europe will afford them every reason and every opportunity to ponder seriously the great international problem of peace in its relation to the American national democratic interest.

The idea which is most likely to lead them astray is the idea which vitiates the Monroe Doctrine in its popular form,—the idea of some essential incompatibility between Europeanism and Americanism. That idea has given a sort of religious sanctity to the national tradition of isolation; and it will survive its own utility because it flatters American democratic vanity. But if such an idea should prevent the American nation from contributing its influence to the establishment of a peaceful system in Europe, America, and Asia, such a refusal would be a decisive stop toward American democratic degeneracy. It would either mean that the American nation preferred its apparently safe and easy isolation to the dangers and complications which would inevitably attend the final establishment of a just system of public law; or else it would mean that the American people believed more in Americanism than they did in democracy. A decent guarantee of international peace would be precisely the political condition which would enable the European nations to release the springs of democracy; and the Americanism which was indifferent or suspicious of the spread of democracy in Europe would incur and deserve the enmity of the European peoples. Such an attitude would constitute a species of continental provincialism and chauvinism. Hence there is no shibboleth that patriotic Americans should fight more tenaciously and more fiercely than of America for the Americans, and Europe for the Europeans. To make Pan-Americanism merely a matter of geography is to deprive it of all serious meaning. Pan-Slavism or Pan-Germanism, based upon a racial bond, would be a far more significant political idea. The only possible foundation of Pan-Americanism is an ideal democratic purpose—which, when translated into terms of international relations, demands, in the first place, the establishment of a pacific system of public law in the two Americas, and in the second place, an alliance with the pacific European Powers, just in so far as a similar system has become in that continent one of the possibilities of practical politics.

11.

Problems of Reconstruction: Part 1

I State Institutional Reform

In the foregoing chapter I have traced the larger aspects of a constructive relation between the national and democratic principles in the field of foreign politics. The task remains of depicting somewhat in detail the aspect which our more important domestic problems assume from the point of view of the same relationship. The general outlines of this picture have already been roughly sketched; but the mere sketch of a fruitful general policy is not enough. A national policy must be justified by the flexibility with which, without any loss of its integrity, it can be applied to specific problems, differing radically one from another in character and significance. That the idea of a constructive relationship between nationality and democracy is flexible without being invertebrate is one of its greatest merits. It is not a rigid abstract and partial ideal, as is that of an exclusively socialist or an exclusively individualist democracy. Neither is it merely a compromise, suited to certain practical exigencies, between individualism and socialism. Its central formative idea can lend itself to many different and novel applications, while still remaining true to its own fundamental interest.

Flexible though the national ideal may be, its demands are in one respect inflexible. It is the strenuous and irrevocable enemy of the policy of drift. It can counsel patience; but it cannot abide collective indifference or irresponsibility. A constructive national ideal must at least seek humbly to be constructive. The only question is, as to how this responsibility for the collective welfare can at any one time be most usefully redeemed. In the case of our own country at the present time an intelligent conception of the national interest will counsel patient agitation rather than any hazardous attempts at radical reconstruction. No such reform can be permanent, or even healthy, until American public opinion has been converted to a completer realization of the nature and extent of its national responsibilities. The ship of reform will gather most headway from the association of certain very moderate practical proposals with the issue of a deliberate, persistent, and far more radical challenge to popular political prejudices and errors. It will be sufficient, in case our practical proposals seek to accomplish some small measure both of political and economic reconstruction, and in case they occupy some sort of a family relation to plans of the same kind with which American public opinion is already more or less familiar.

In considering this matter of institutional reform, I shall be guided chiefly by the extent to which certain specific reforms have already become living questions. From this point of view it would be a sheer waste of time just at present to discuss seriously any radical modification, say, of the Federal Constitution. Certain transformations of the Constitution either by insidious effect of practice, by deliberate judicial construction, or by amendment are, of course, an inevitable aspect of the contemporary American political problem; but all such possible and proposed changes must be confined to specific details. They should not raise any question as to the fundamental desirability of a system of checks and balances or of the other principles upon which the Federal political organization is based. Much, consequently, as a political theorist may be interested in some ideal plan of American national organization, it will be of little benefit under existing conditions to enter into such a discussion. Let it wait until Americans have come to think seriously and consistently about fundamental political problems. The Federal Constitution is not all it should be, but it is better than any substitute upon which American public opinion could now agree. Modifications may and should somehow be made in details, but for the present not in fundamentals. On the other hand, no similar sanctity attaches to municipal charters and state constitutions. The ordinary state constitution is a sufficiently ephemeral piece of legislation. State and municipal political forms are being constantly changed, and they are being changed because they have been so extremely unsatisfactory in their actual operation. The local political machinery becomes, consequently, the natural and useful subject of reconstructive experiments. A policy of institutional reform must prove its value and gain its experience chiefly in this field; and in formulating such a policy reformers will be placing their hands upon the most palpable and best-recognized weakness in the American political system.

A popular but ill-founded American political illusion concerns the success of their state governments. Americans tend to believe that these governments have on the whole served them well, whereas in truth they have on the whole been ill served by their machinery of local administration and government. The failure has not, perhaps, been as egregious or as scandalous as has been that of their municipal institutions; but it has been sufficiently serious to provoke continual but abortive attempts to improve them; and it has had so many dangerous consequences that the cause and cure of their inefficiency constitute one of the most fundamental of American political problems. The consequences of the failure have been mitigated because the weakness of the state governments has been partly concealed and redeemed by the comparative strength and efficiency of the central government. But the failures have none the less been sufficiently distressing; and if they are permitted to continue, they will compromise the success of the American democratic experiment. The Federal government has done much to ameliorate the condition of the American people, whereas the state governments have done little or nothing. Instead of representing, as a government should, the better contemporary ideals and methods, they have reflected at best the average standard of popular behavior and at worst a standard decidedly below the average. The lawlessness which so many Americans bemoan in American life must be traced to the inefficiency of the state governments. If the central government had shared this weakness, the American political organism would have already dissolved in violence and bloodshed.

The local authorities retain under the American Federal organization many of the primary functions of government. They preserve order, administer civil and criminal justice, collect taxes for general and local purposes, and are directly or indirectly responsible for the system of public education. If it can be proved that the state governments have exercised any of these functions in an efficient manner, that proof certainly does not lie upon the surface of the facts. The provisions they have made for keeping order have been utterly inadequate, and have usually broken down when any serious reason for disorder has existed. A certain part of this violence is, moreover, the immediate result of the failure of American criminal justice. The criminal laws have been so carefully framed and so admirably expounded for the benefit of the lawyers and their clients, the malefactors, that a very large proportion of American murderers escape the proper penalty of their acts; and these dilatory and dubious judicial methods are undoubtedly one effective cause of the prevalence of lynching in the South. There is more to be said in favor of our civil than of our criminal courts. In spite of a good deal of corruption and of subserviency to special interests, the judges are usually honest men and good average lawyers; but the fact that they are elected for comparatively short terms has made them the creatures of the political machine, and has demoralized their political standards. They use court patronage largely for the benefit of the machine; and whatever influence they have in politics is usually exercised in favor of the professional politician. If they do not constitute a positive weakness in the system of local government, they are certainly far from constituting a source of strength; and considering the extent to which our government is a government of judges, they should exercise a far more beneficent influence than they do.

Neither are the administrative and legislative responsibilities of the states redeemed with any more success. The tax systems of the several states are in a chaotic condition. Their basis consists of the old property tax, which under its application to modern conditions has become both unjust and unproductive, but which the state legislatures seem to be wholly incapable of either abandoning or properly transforming. In the matter of education the states have been, except in the South, liberal; but they have not been as intelligent and well-informed as they have been well-intentioned. The educational system of the country is not only chaotic, but it is very imperfectly adapted to the needs of an industrial and agricultural democracy. Finally, if the legislatures of the several states have ever done anything to increase respect for the wisdom and conservatism of American representative government, it is certainly hard to discover indications thereof. The financial and economic legislation of the states has usually shown incompetence and frequently dishonesty. They have sometimes been ready to repudiate their debts. In their relations to the corporations they have occupied the positions alternately of blackmailers and creatures. They have been as ready to confiscate private property as they have to confer on it excessive privileges. If the word "law" means something less majestic and authoritative to Americans than it should, the mass of trivial, contradictory, unwise, ephemeral, and corrupt legislation passed by the state legislatures is largely responsible.

No doubt a certain part of this failure of the state governments is irremediable as long as existing standards of public and private morality prevail; but most assuredly a certain part is the direct result of unwise organization. American state governments have been corrupt and inefficient largely because they have been organized for the benefit of corrupt and inefficient men; and as long as they continue to be organized on such a basis, no permanent or substantial improvement can be expected. Moreover, any reorganization in order to be effective must not deal merely with details and expedients. It must be as radical as are the existing disorganization and abuses. It must be founded on a different relation between the executive and legislative branches and a wholly different conception of the function of a state legislative body.

The demand for some such reorganization has already become popular, particularly in the West. A generation or more ago the makers of new state constitutions, being confronted by palpable proofs of the inefficiency and corruption of the state governments, sought to provide a remedy chiefly by limiting the power of the legislature. All sorts of important details, which would have formerly been left to legislative action, were incorporated in the fundamental law; and in the same spirit severe restrictions were imposed on legislative procedure, designed to prevent the most flagrant existing abuses. These prudential measures have not served to improve the legislative output, and the reformers are now crying for more drastic remedies. In the West the tendency is to transfer legislative authority from a representative body directly to the people. A movement in favor of the initiative and the referendum is gaining so much headway, that in all probability it will spread throughout the country much as the Australian ballot did over a decade ago. But the adoption of the initiative and the referendum substitutes a new principle for the one which has hitherto underlain American local institutions. Representative government is either abandoned thereby or very much restricted; and direct government, so far as possible, is substituted for it. Such a fundamental principle and tradition as that of representation should not be thrown away, unless the change can be justified by a specific, comprehensive, and conclusive analysis of the causes of the failure of the state governments.

The analysis upon which the advocates of the initiative and the referendum base their reform has the merit of being obvious. American legislatures have betrayed the interests of their constituents, and have been systematically passing laws for the benefit of corrupt and special interests. The people must consequently take back the trust, which has been delegated to representative bodies. They must resume at least the power to initiate the legislation they want; and no law dealing with a really important subject should be passed without their direct consent.

Such an analysis of the causes of legislative corruption and incompetence is not as correct as it is obvious. It is based upon the old and baleful democratic tendency of always seeking the reason for the failure of a democratic enterprise in some personal betrayal of trust. It is never the people who are at fault. Neither is the betrayal attributed to some defect of organization, which neglects to give the representative individual a sufficient chance. The responsibility for the failure is fastened on the selected individual himself, and the conclusion is drawn that the people cannot trust representatives to serve them honestly and efficiently. The course of reasoning is precisely the same as that which prompted the Athenian democracy to order the execution of an unsuccessful general. In the case of our state legislatures, a most flagrant betrayal of trust has assuredly occurred, but before inferring from this betrayal that selected individuals cannot be trusted to legislate properly on behalf of their constituents, it would be just as well to inquire whether individual incompetence and turpitude are any sufficient reason for this particular failure of representative institutions.

As a matter of fact they are no sufficient reason. When a large number of individuals to whom authority is delegated exercise that authority improperly, one may safely infer that the system is at fault as much as the individual. Local American legislative organization has courted failure. Both the system of representation and functions of the representative body have been admirably calculated to debase the quality of the representatives and to nullify the value of their work. American state legislatures have really never had a fair opportunity. They have almost from the beginning been deprived of any effective responsibility. The state constitutions have gradually hedged them in with so many restrictions, have gone so much into detail in respect to state organization and policy that the legislatures really had comparatively little to do, except to deal with matters of current business. They offered no opportunity for a man of ability and public spirit. When such men drifted into a local legislature, they naturally escaped as soon as they could to some larger and less obstructed field of action. If the American people want better legislatures, they must adopt one of two courses. Either they must give their legislative bodies something more and better to do, or else they must arrange so that these bodies will have a chance to perform an inferior but definite service more capably.

The legislatures have been corrupt and incapable, chiefly because they have not been permitted any sufficient responsibility, but this irresponsibility itself has had more than one cause. It cannot be traced exclusively to the diminished confidence and power reposed in representative bodies by the state constitutions. Early in the nineteenth century, the legislatures were granted almost full legislative powers; and if they did not use those powers well, they used them much better than at a later period. Their corruption began with the domination of the political machine; and it is during the last two generations that their powers and responsibilities have been more and more restricted. They have undoubtedly been more corrupt and incompetent in proportion as they have been increasingly deprived of power; but the restrictions imposed upon them have been as much an effect as a cause of their corruption. There is a deeper reason for their deficiencies; and this reason is connected with mal-adaptation of the whole system of American state government to its place in a Federal system. The Federal organization took away from the states a number of the most important governmental functions, and in certain respects absolutely subordinated the state to the nation. In this way the actual responsibilities and the powers of the state governments were very much diminished, while at the same time no sufficient allowance for such a diminution was made in framing their organization. Their governments were organized along the same lines as that of an independent state—in spite of the fact that they had abandoned so many of the responsibilities and prerogatives of independence.

The effect of this mal-adaptation of the state political institutions to their place in a Federal system has been much more important than is usually supposed. The former were planned to fulfill a much completer responsibility than the one which they actually possessed. The public business of a wholly or technically independent state naturally arouses in its citizens a much graver sense of responsibility than does the public business of a state in the American Union. The latter retained many important duties; but it surrendered, if not the most essential of its functions, at least the most critical and momentous, while in the exercise of the remainder it was to a certain extent protected against the worst consequences of mistakes or perversities. It surrendered the power of making peace or declaring war. Its relation to the other states in the Union was strictly defined, so that it had no foreign policy and responsibilities corresponding to its purely domestic ones. Its citizens were aware that the protection of such fundamental institutions as that of private property was lodged in the Federal government, and that in the end that government had the power to guarantee them even against the worst consequences of domestic disorder. Thus the state governments were placed in the easy situation of rich annuitants, who had surrendered the control of some political capital in order to enjoy with less care the opportunities of a plethoric income.

The foregoing comment is not intended as any disparagement of a Federal as contrasted with a centralized political system. Its purpose is to justify the statement that, in a Federal system, local political institutions should be adapted to their necessarily restricted functions. The state governments were organized as smaller copies of the central government, and the only alterations in the type permitted by the Democrats looked in the direction of a further distribution of responsibility. But a system which was adapted to the comprehensive task of securing the welfare of a whole people might well fail as an engine of merely local government,—even though the local government retained certain major political functions. As a matter of fact, such has been the case. The system of a triple division of specific powers, each one of which was vigorous in its own sphere while at the same time checked and balanced by the other branches of the government, has certain advantages and certain disadvantages. Its great advantage is its comparative safety, because under it no one function of government can attain to any dangerous excess of power. Its great disadvantage consists in the division of responsibility among three independent departments, and the possibility that the public interest would suffer either from lack of coöperation or from actual conflicts. In the case of the general government, the comparative safety of the system of checks and balances was of paramount importance, because the despotic exercise of its vast powers would have wrecked the whole American political system. On the other hand, the disadvantages of such a system—its division of responsibility and the possible lack of coöperation among the several departments—were mitigated to a considerable, if not to a sufficient, extent. National parties came into existence with the function of assuming a responsibility which no single group of Federal officials possessed; and in their management of national affairs, the partisan leaders were prompted by a certain amount of patriotism and interest in the public welfare. Even at Washington the system works badly enough in certain respects; but in general the dominant party can be held to a measure of responsibility; and effective coöperation is frequently obtained in matters of foreign policy and the like through the action of patriotic and disinterested motives.

In the state governments the advantages of a system of checks and balances were of small importance, while its disadvantages were magnified. The state governments had no reason to sacrifice concentrated efficiency to safety, because in a Federal organization the temporary exercise of arbitrary executive or legislative power in one locality would not have entailed any irretrievable consequences, and could not impair the fundamental integrity of the American system. But if a state had less to lose from a betrayal by a legislature or an executive of a substantially complete responsibility for the public welfare, it was not protected to the same extent as the central government against the abuses of a diffused responsibility. In the state capitals, as at Washington, the national parties did, indeed, make themselves responsible for the management of public affairs and for the harmonious coöperation of the executive and the legislature; but in their conduct of local business the national parties retained scarcely a vestige of national patriotism. Their behavior was dictated by the most selfish factional and personal motives. They did, indeed, secure the coöperation of the different branches of the government, but largely for corrupt or undesirable purposes; and after the work was done the real authors of it could hide behind the official division of responsibility.

If the foregoing analysis is correct, the partial failure of American state governments is to be imputed chiefly to their lack of a centralized responsible organization. In their case a very simple and very efficient legislative and administrative system is the more necessary, because only through such a machinery can the local public spirit receive any effective expression. It can hardly be expected that American citizens will bring as much public spirit to their local public business as to the more stirring affairs of the whole nation; and what local patriotism there is should be confronted by no unnecessary obstacles. If a mistake or an abuse occurs, the responsibility for it should be unmistakable and absolute, while if a reform candidate or party is victorious, they should control a machinery of government wholly sufficient for their purposes.

As soon as any attempt is made to devise a system which does concentrate responsibility and power, serious difficulties are encountered. Concentration of responsibility can be brought about in one of two ways—either by subordinating the legislature to the executive or the executive to the legislature. There are precedents both here and abroad in favor of each of these methods, and their comparative advantages must be briefly sketched.

The subordination of the executive to the legislature would conform to the early American political tradition. We have usually associated executive authority with arbitrary and despotic political methods, and we have tended to assume that a legislative body was much more representative of popular opinion. During or immediately succeeding the Revolutionary War, the legislatures of the several states were endowed with almost complete control—a control which was subject only to the constitutional bills of rights; and it has been seriously and frequently proposed to revive this complete legislative responsibility. Under such a system, the legislature would elect the chief executive, if not the judicial officials; and it would become like the British Parliament exclusively and comprehensively responsible for the work of government—both in its legislative and administrative branches.

The foregoing type of organization has so many theoretical advantages that one would like to see it tried in some American states. But for the present it is not likely to be tried. The responsibility of the legislature could not be exercised without the creation of some institution corresponding to the British Cabinet: and the whole tendency of American political development has been away from any approach to the English Parliamentary system. Whatever the theoretical advantages of legislative omnipotence, it would constitute in this country a dangerous and dubious method of concentrating local governmental responsibility and power. It might succeed, in case it were accompanied by the adoption of some effective measures for improving the quality of the representation—such, for instance, as the abandonment of all existing traditions necessitating the residence of the representative in the district he represents. This American political practice always has and always will tend to give mediocrity to the American popular representation, but it corresponds to one of the most fundamental of American political prejudices, and for the present its abandonment is out of the question. The work of improving the quality of the average American representative from a small district appears to be hopeless, because as a matter of fact such small districts and the work imposed on their representatives can hardly prove tempting to able men; and unless the American legislator is really capable of becoming exceptionally representative, the fastening of exclusive responsibility upon the state legislatures could hardly result in immediate success. Its intrinsic merits might carry it to ultimate success, but not until it had transformed many American political practices and traditions.

The truth is, that certain very deep and permanent causes underlie American legislative degeneracy. When the American legislative system was framed, a representative assembly possessed a much better chance than it does now of becoming a really representative body. It constituted at the time an effective vehicle for the formation and expression of public opinion. Public questions had not received the complete ventilation on the platform and in the press that they obtain at the present time; and in the debate of a representative assembly the chance existed of a really illuminating and formative conflict of opinion. Representatives were often selected, who were capable of adding something to the candid and serious consideration of a question of public policy. The need helped to develop men capable of meeting it. Now, however, American legislatures, with the partial exception of the Federal Senate, have ceased to be deliberative bodies. Public questions receive their effective discussion in the press and on the platform. Public opinion is definitely formed before the meeting of the legislature; and the latter has become simply a vehicle for realizing or betraying the mandates of popular opinion. Its function is or should be to devise or to help in the devising of means, necessary to accomplish a predetermined policy. Its members have little or no initiative and little or no independence. Legislative projects are imposed upon them either by party leaders, by special interests, or at times by the executive and public opinion. Their work is at best that of committee-men and at worst that of mercenaries, paid to betray their original employers. A successful attempt to bestow upon legislative bodies, composed of such doubtful material and subject to such equivocal traditions anything resembling complete governmental responsibility, would be a dangerous business. Legislatures have degenerated into the condition of being merely agents, rather than principals in the work of government; and the strength and the propriety of the contemporary movement in favor of the initiative and the referendum is to be attributed to this condition.

The increasing introduction of the referendum into the local political organization is partly a recognition of the fact that the legislatures have ceased to play an independent part in the work of government. There is every reason to believe that hereafter the voters will obtain and keep a much more complete and direct control over the making of their laws than that which they have exerted hitherto; and the possible desirability of the direct exercise of this function cannot be disputed by any loyal democrat. The principle upon which the referendum is based is unimpeachable; but a question remains as to the manner in which the principle of direct legislation can be best embodied in a piece of practical political machinery; and the attempt to solve this question involves a consideration of the general changes in our system of local government, which may be required, as a result of the application of the new principle.

The necessary limits of this discussion forbid any exhaustive consideration of the foregoing questions; and I must content myself with a brief summary of the method in which the principle of direct legislation can be made the part of an efficient local political system. The difficulty is to find some means of distinguishing that part of the legislative responsibility which should be retained by the people and that part which, in order to be effectively redeemed, must be delegated. Obviously the part to be retained is the function of accepting or rejecting certain general proposals respecting state organization or policy. An American electorate is or should be entirely competent to decide whether in general it wishes gambling or the sale of intoxicating liquors to be suppressed, whether it is willing or unwilling to delegate large judicial and legislative authority to commissions, or whether it wishes to exempt buildings from local taxation. In retaining the power of deciding for itself these broad questions of public legislative policy, it is exercising a function, adapted to the popular intelligence and both disciplinary and formative in its effect on those who take the responsibility seriously. Under any system of popular government—even under a parliamentary system—such general questions are eventually submitted to popular decision; and the more decisively they can be submitted, the better. On the other hand, there is a large part of the work of government, which must be delegated by the people to select individuals, because it can be efficiently exercised only by peculiarly experienced or competent men. The people are capable of passing upon the general principle embodied in a proposed law; but they cannot be expected to decide with any certainty of judgment about amendments or details, which involve for their intelligent consideration technical and special knowledge. Efficient law-making is as much a matter of well-prepared and well-tempered detail as it is of an excellent general principle, and this branch of legislation must necessarily be left to experts selected in one way or another to represent the popular interest. How can they best be selected and what should be their functions?

An answer to these questions involves a consideration of the changes which the referendum should bring with it in the whole system of local government—an aspect of the matter which according to the usual American habit has hitherto been neglected. In states like Oregon the power of initiating and consummating legislation is bestowed on the electorate without being taken away from the legislature; and a certain share of necessary political business is left to a body which has been expressly declared unworthy to exercise a more important share of the same task. A legislative body, whose responsibilities and power are still further reduced, will probably exercise their remaining functions with even greater incompetence, and will, if possible, be composed of a still more inferior class of legislative agents. If the legislature is to perform the inferior but still necessary functions that will necessarily remain in its hands, an at-

tempt should certainly be made to obtain a better quality of representation. No direct system of state government can constitute any really substantial improvement
on the existing system, unless either the legislature is
deprived of all really essential functions, or the quality
of its membership improved.

The legislature, or some representative body corresponding to it, cannot, however, be deprived of certain
really essential functions. The task of preparing legislation for reference to the people, so that a question of
public policy will be submitted in a decisive and acceptable form, belongs naturally to a representative body;
and the same statement is true respecting the legislative
work essential to the administration of a state's business
affairs. The supply bills demand an amount of inspection in detail, which can obtain only by expert supervision; and so it is in respect to various minor legislative
matters which do not raise question of general policy
but which amount to little more than problems of local
administrative detail. A representative body must be
provided which shall perform work of this kind; and
again, it must be said that existing legislatures would
perform these more restricted functions even worse than
they have performed a completer legislative duty. Their
members are experts in nothing but petty local politics.
They are usually wholly incapable of drawing a bill, or
of passing intelligently on matters either of technical or
financial detail. If they represent anything, it is the interest of their district rather than that of the state. The
principle of direct legislation, in order to become really
constructive, must bring with it a more effective auxil-
iary machinery than any which existing legislatures can
supply.

The kind of machinery needed can be deduced from
the character of the work. The function of the representative body, needed under a system of direct legislation,

is substantially that of a legislative and administrative council or commission. It should be an experienced body of legal, administrative, and financial experts, comparatively limited in numbers, and selected in a manner to make them solicitous of the interests of the whole state. They should be elected, consequently, from comparatively large districts, or, if possible, by the electorate of the whole state under some system of cumulative voting. The work of such a council would not be in any real sense legislative; and its creation would simply constitute a candid recognition of the plain fact that our existing legislatures, either with or without the referendum, no longer perform a responsible legislative function. It would be tantamount to a scientific organization of the legislative committees, which at the present time exercise an efficient control over the so-called legislative output. This council would mediate between the governor, who administered the laws, and the people, who enacted them. It would constitute a check upon the governor, and would in turn be checked by him; while it would act in relation to the people as a sort of technical advisory commission, with the duty of preparing legislation for popular enactment or rejection.

But how would such specific legislative proposals originate? Before answering this question let us consider how important bills actually originate under the existing system. They are in almost every case imposed upon the legislature by some outside influence. Sometimes they are prepared by corporation lawyers and are introduced by the special corporation representatives. Sometimes they originate with the party "bosses," and are intended to promote some more or less important partisan purpose. Sometimes they are drawn by associations of reformers, and go to the legislature with whatever support from public opinion the association can collect. Finally, they are frequently introduced at the suggestion of the governor; and of late years during the growth of the reform movement, the executive has in point of fact become more and more responsible for imposing on the legislature laws desired or supposed to be desired by the electorate. Of these different sources of existing legislation, the last suggests a manner of initiating legislation, which is most likely to make for the efficient concentration of governmental responsibility. The governor should be empowered not merely to suggest legislation to the council, but to introduce it into the council. His right to introduce legislation need not be exclusive, but bills introduced by him should have a certain precedence and their consideration should claim a definite amount of the council's time. The council would possess, of course, full right of rejection or amendment. In the case of rejection or an amendment not acceptable to the governor the question at issue would be submitted to popular vote.

The method of originating legislation suggested above is, of course, entirely different from that ordinarily associated with the referendum. According to the usual methods of direct legislation, any body of electors of a certain size can effect the introduction of a bill and its submission to popular vote; but a method of this kind is really no method at all. It allows the electorate to be bombarded with a succession of legislative proposals, turning perhaps on radical questions of public policy like the single tax, which may be well or ill drawn, which may or may not be living questions of the day, which may or may not have received sufficient preparatory discussion, and which would keep public opinion in a wholly unnecessary condition of ferment. Some organized control over the legislative proposals submitted to popular approval is absolutely necessary; and the sort of control suggested above merely conforms to the existing unofficial practice of those states wherein

public opinion has been aroused. The best reform legislation now enacted usually originates in executive
mansions. Why should not the practice be made official? If it were so, every candidate for governor would
have to announce either a definite legislative policy or
the lack of one; and the various items composing this
policy would be fully discussed during the campaign.
In proposing such a policy the governor would be held
to a high sense of responsibility. He could not escape
from the penalties of an unwise, an ill-drawn, or a fool-
hardy legislative proposal. At the same time he would
be obliged constantly to meet severe criticism both as
to the principle and details of his measures on the part
of the legislative council. Such criticism would fasten
upon any weakness and would sufficiently protect the
public against the submission of unnecessary, foolish, or
dangerous legislative proposals.

I am aware, of course, that the plan of legislative
organization, vaguely sketched above, will seem to be
most dubious to the great majority of Americans, intelligently interested in political matters; but before absolutely condemning these suggestions as wild or dangerous, the reader should consider the spirit in which
and the purpose for which they are made. My intention
has not been to prepare a detailed plan of local governmental organization and to stamp it as the only one,
which is correct in principle and coherent in detail. In a
sense I care nothing about the precise suggestions submitted in the preceding paragraphs. They are offered,
not as a definite plan of local political organization, but
as the illustration of a principle. The principle is that
both power and responsibility in affairs of local government should be peculiarly concentrated. It cannot be
concentrated without some simplification of machinery
and without giving either the legislature or the executive
a dominant authority. In the foregoing plan the execu-

tive has been made dominant, because as a matter of fact recent political experience has conclusively proved that the executives, elected by the whole constituency, are much more representative of public opinion than are the delegates of petty districts. One hundred district agents represent only one hundred districts and not the whole state, or the state in so far as it is whole. In the light of current American political realities the executive deserves the greater share of responsibility and power; and that is why the proposal is made to bestow it on him. The other details of the foregoing plan have been proposed in a similar spirit. They are innovations; but they are innovations which may naturally (and perhaps should) result from certain living practices and movements in American local politics. They merely constitute an attempt to give those ideas and practices candid recognition. No such reorganization may ever be reached in American local government; and I may have made essential mistakes in estimating the real force of certain current practices and the real value of certain remedial expedients. But on two points the argument admits of no concession. Any practical scheme of local institutional reform must be based on the principle of more concentrated responsibility and power, and it must be reached by successive experimental attempts to give a more consistent and efficient form to actual American political practices.

The bestowal upon an executive of increased official responsibility and power will be stigmatized by "old-fashioned Democrats" as dangerously despotic; and it may be admitted that in the case of the central government, any official increase of executive power might bring with it the risk of usurpation. The Constitution of the United States has made the President a much more responsible and vigorous executive in his own sphere of action than are the governors of the several states in theirs; and he can with his present power exercise a tolerably effective control over legislation. But the states, for reasons already given, are protected against the worst possible consequences of illegal usurpation; and in any event the people, in case their interests were threatened, could make use of a simple and absolutely effective remedy. The action of the governor or of any member of the legislative council could be challenged by the application of the recall. He could be made to prove his loyalty to the Constitution and to the public interest by the holding of a special election at the instance of a sufficient number of voters; and if he could not justify any possibly dubious practices, he could be displaced and replaced. The recall is for this purpose a useful and legitimate political device. It has the appearance at the first glance of depriving an elected official of the sense of independence and security which he may derive from his term of office; and unquestionably if applied to officials who served for very short terms and exercised no effective responsibility during service it would deprive them of what little power of public service they possessed. On the other hand, it is right that really responsible and vigorous officials serving for comparatively long terms should be subjected to the check of a possible recall of the popular trust.

No plan of political organization can in the nature of things offer an absolute guarantee that a government will not misuse its powers; but a government of the kind suggested, should it prove to be either corrupt or incompetent, could remain in control only by the express acquiescence of the electorate. Its corruption and incompetence could not be concealed, and would inevitably entail serious consequences. On the other hand, the results of any peculiar efficiency and political wisdom would be equally conspicuous. Men of integrity, force, and ability would be tempted to run for office by the

stimulating opportunity offered for effective achievement. Such a government would, consequently, press
into its service whatever public-spirited and energetic
men the community possessed; and it would represent
not an inferior or even an average standard public opinion and ideas, but the highest standard which the people
could be made to accept. Provided only the voters themselves were on the whole patriotic, well-intentioned, and
loyal, it would be bound to make not for a stagnant
routine, but for a gradually higher level of local political
action.

II State Administrative Reform

The foregoing discussion of the means which may be
taken to make American local governments more alive
to their responsibilities has been confined to the department of legislation. The department of administration
is, however, almost equally important; and some attempt must be made to associate with a reform of the
local legislature a reform of the local administration.
The questions of administrative efficiency and the best
method of obtaining it demand special and detailed
consideration. In this case the conclusions reached will
apply as much to the central and municipal as they do
to the state administrations; but the whole matter of
administrative efficiency can be most conveniently discussed in relation to the proper organization of a state
government. The false ideas and practices which have
caused so much American administrative inefficiency
originated in the states and thence infected the central
government. On the other hand, the reform of these
practices made its first conquests at Washington and
thereafter was languidly and indifferently taken over
by many of the states. The state politicians have never
adopted it in good faith, because real administrative ef-

ficiency would, by virtue of the means necessarily taken to accomplish it, undermine the stability of the political machine. The power of the machine can never be broken without a complete reform of our local administrative systems; and the discussion of that reform is more helpful in relation to the state than in relation to the central government.

Civil service reform was the very first movement of the kind to make any headway in American politics. Within a few years after the close of the War it had waxed into an issue which the politicians could not ignore; and while its first substantial triumph was postponed until late in the seventies, it has, on the whole, been more completely accepted than any important reforming idea. It has secured the energetic support of every President during the last twenty-five years; it has received at all events the verbal homage of the two national parties; and it can point to affirmative legislation in the great majority of the states. It meets at the present time with practically no open and influential opposition. Nevertheless, the "merit system" has not met the expectations of its most enthusiastic supporters. Abuses have been abolished wherever the reform has been introduced, but the abolition of abuses has not made for any marked increase of efficiency. The civil service is still very far from being in a satisfactory condition either in the central, state, or municipal offices. Moreover, the passage of reform laws has not had any appreciable effect upon the vitality or the power of the professional politician. The machine has, on the whole, increased rather than diminished in power, during the past twenty-five years. Civil service reform is no longer as vigorously opposed as it used to be, because it is no longer feared. The politicians have found that in its ordinary shape it really does not do them any essential harm. The consequence is that the

agitation has drifted to the rear of the American political battle, and fails to excite either the enthusiasm, the
enmity, or the interest that it did fifteen years ago.

Its partial failure has been due to the fact that the
reformers merely attacked one of the symptoms of a
disease which was more deeply rooted and more virulent than they supposed. They were outraged by the appointment of administrative officials solely as a reward
for partisan service and without reference to their qualifications for their official duties; and two means were
devised to strike at this abuse. Lower administrative
officials were protected in their positions by depriving
their superiors of the power of removing them except
for cause; and it was provided that new appointments
should be made from lists of candidates whose eligibil-
ity was guaranteed by their ability to pass examina-
tions in subjects connected with the work of the office.
These were undoubtedly steps in a better direction; but
they have failed to be effective, because the attempt to
secure a more meritorious selection of public servants
was not applied to higher grades of the service. At the
head of every public office was a man who had been
appointed or elected chiefly for partisan reasons; who
served only for a short time; who could become familiar
with the work of his office, if at all, only slowly; and
who, because of his desire to be surrounded by his own
henchmen, was the possible enemy of the permanent
staff. The civil service laws have been designed, consequently, to a very considerable extent for the purpose
of protecting the subordinates against their chiefs; and
that is scarcely to be conceived as a method of organizing administrative employees helpful to administrative
efficiency. The chiefs were allowed comparatively little
effective authority over their subordinates, and subordinates could not be held to any effective responsibility. A

premium was placed upon ordinary routine work which observed carefully all the official forms, but which was calculated with equal care not to task its perpetrators.

The American civil service will never be really reformed by the sort of civil service laws which have hitherto been passed—no matter how faithfully those laws may be executed. The only way in which administrative efficiency can be secured is by means of an organization which makes a departmental chief absolutely responsible for energetic work and economical administration in his office; and no such responsibility can exist as long as his subordinates are independent of him. He need not necessarily have the power to discharge his subordinates, except with the consent of a Board of Inspectors; but he should have the power to promote them to positions of greater responsibility and income, or to degrade them to comparatively insignificant positions. Efficiency cannot be secured in any other way, because no executive official can be held accountable for good work unless his control over his subordinates is effective. So far as the existing civil service laws in city, state, and the United States fail to bestow full responsibility, coupled with sufficient authority, upon departmental chiefs, they should be altered; and their alteration should be made part of any plan of constructive reform in the civil service.

The responsibility of departmental chiefs and their effective authority over their subordinates necessarily imply changes in the current methods of selecting these officials. The prevailing methods are unwise and chaotic. In some cases they are appointed by the chief executive. In other cases they are elected. But whether appointed or elected, they are selected chiefly for partisan service. They hold office only for a few years. They rarely have any particular qualification for their work. They cannot be expected either to take very much interest in their official duties or use their powers in an efficient manner. To give such temporary officeholders a large measure of authority over their subordinates would mean in the long run that such authority would be used chiefly for political purposes. Administrative efficiency, consequently, can only be secured by the adoption of a method of selecting departmental chiefs which will tend to make them expert public servants rather than politicians. They must be divorced from political associations. They must be emancipated from political vicissitudes. The success of their career must depend exclusively upon the excellence of their departmental work.

As long as these public servants are elected, no such result can be expected. The practice of electing the incumbents of subordinate executive positions inevitably invites the evasion of responsibility and the selection of the candidate chiefly for partisan service. When such a man stands for renomination or reëlection, his administrative efficiency or inefficiency (unless the latter should chance to be particularly flagrant) does not affect his chances. He is renominated in case he has served his party well, or in case no one else who wants the job has in the meantime served it better. He is reëlected in case his party happens to have kept public confidence. Departmental chiefs can be made responsible for their work only by being subordinated to a chief executive whose duty it is to keep his eye on his subordinates and who is accountable to the people for the efficient conduct of all the administrative offices. The former, consequently, must be selected by appointment, they must be installed in office for an indefinite period, and they must be subject to removal by the chief executive. Those are terms upon which all private employees serve; and on no other terms will equally efficient results be obtained from public officials.

Under a democratic political system there is, of course, no way of absolutely guaranteeing that any method of administrative organization, however excellent in itself, will accomplish the desired and the desirable result. Administrative authority must at some point always originate in an election. The election can delegate power only for a limited period. At the end of the limited period another executive will be chosen—possibly a man representing a wholly different political policy. Such a man will want his immediate advisers to share his political point of view; and it is always possible that in electing him the voters will make a mistake and choose an incompetent and irresponsible person. An incompetent or disloyal executive could undoubtedly under such a system do much to disorganize the public service; but what will you have? There can be no efficiency without responsibility. There can be no responsibility without authority. The authority and responsibility residing ultimately in the people must be delegated; and it must not be emasculated in the process of delegation. If it is abused, the people should at all events be able to fix the offense and to punish the offender. At present our administration is organized chiefly upon the principle that the executive shall not be permitted to do much good for fear that he will do harm. It ought to be organized on the principle that he shall have full power to do either well or ill, but that if he does do ill, he will have no defense against punishment. The principle is the same as it is in the case of legislative responsibility. If under those conditions the voters should persist in electing incompetent or corrupt executives, they would deserve the sort of government they would get and would probably in the end be deprived of their vote.

A system of local government, designed for concentrating power and responsibility, might, consequently, be shaped along the following general lines. Its core would be a chief executive, elected for a comparatively long term, and subject to recall under certain defined conditions. He would be surrounded by an executive council, similar to the President's Cabinet, appointed by himself and consisting of a Controller, Attorney General, Secretary of State, Commissioner of Public Works, and the like. So far his position would not differ radically from that of the President of the United States, except that he would be subject to recall. But he would have the additional power of introducing legislation into a legislative council and, in case his proposed legislation were rejected or amended in an inacceptable manner, of appealing to the electorate. The legislative council would be elected from large districts and, if possible, by some cumulative system of voting. They, also, might be subject to recall. They would have the power, dependent on the governor's veto, of authorizing the appropriation of public money and, also, of passing on certain minor classes of legislation—closely associated with administrative functions. But in relation to all legislation of substantial importance express popular approval would be necessary. The chief executive should possess the power of removing any administrative official in the employ of the state and of appointing a successor. He would be expected to choose an executive council who agreed with him in all essential matters of public policy, just as the President is expected to appoint his Cabinet. His several councilors would be executive officials, responsible for particular departments of the public service; but they would exercise their authority through permanent departmental chiefs—just as the Secretary of War delegates much of his authority to a chief of staff, or an English minister to a permanent under-secretary. The system could offer no guarantee that the subordinate departmental chiefs would be absolutely permanent; but at all events they would not be changed at fixed periods or for irrelevant reasons. They would be just as permanent or as transient as the good of the service demanded. In so far, that is, as the system was carried out in good faith they would be experts, absolutely the masters of the technical business of the offices and of the abilities and services of their subordinates. The weak point in such administrative organization is undoubtedly the relation between the members of the governor's council and their chiefs of staff; but there must be a weak link in any organization which seeks to convert the changing views of public policy, dependent upon an election, into responsible, efficient, and detailed administrative acts. If the system were not accepted in good faith, if in the long run it were not carried out by officials, who were disinterestedly and intelligently working in the public interest, it would be bound to fail; but so would any method of political organization. This particular plan simply embodies the principle that the way to get good public service out of men is to give them a sufficient chance.

Under the proposed system the only powers possessed by the state executive, not now bestowed upon the President of the United States, would consist in an express and an effective control over legislation. It would be his duty to introduce legislation whenever it was in his opinion desirable; and in case his bills were amended to death or rejected, it would be his right to appeal to the people. He would, in addition, appoint all state officials except the legislative council, and perhaps the judges of the highest court. On the other hand, he would be limited by the recall and he could not get any important legislative measure on the statute books except after severe technical criticism, and express popular consent. He could accomplish nothing without the support of public opinion; yet he could be held absolutely responsible for the good government of the state.

A demagogue elected to a position of such power and responsibility might do a great deal of harm; but if a democratic political body cannot distinguish between the leadership of able and disinterested men and self-seeking charlatans, the loss and perhaps the suffering, resulting from their indiscriminate blindness, would constitute a desirable means of political education,— particularly when the demagogue, as in the case under consideration, could not really damage the foundations of the state. And the charlatan or the incompetent could be sent into retreat just as soon as exposed. The danger not only has a salutary aspect, but it seems a small price to pay for the chance, thereby afforded, for really efficient and responsible government. The chief executive, when supported by public opinion, would become a veritable "Boss"; and he would inevitably be the sworn enemy of unofficial "Bosses" who now dominate local politics. He would have the power to purify American local politics, and this power he would be obliged to use. The logic of his whole position would convert him into an enemy of the machine, in so far as the machine was using any governmental function for private, special, or partisan purposes. The real "Boss" would destroy the sham "Bosses"; and no other means, as yet suggested, will, I believe, be sufficient to accomplish such a result.

After the creation of such a system of local government the power of the professional politician would not last a year longer than the people wanted it to last. The governor would control the distribution of all those fruits of the administrative and legislative system upon which the machine has lived. There could be no trafficking in offices, in public contracts, or in legislation; and the man who wished to serve the state unofficially would have to do so from disinterested motives. Moreover, the professional politician could not only be destroyed, but he would not be needed. At present he is needed, because of the prodigious amount of business entailed by the multiplicity of elective officials. Somebody must take charge of this political detail; and it has, as we have already remarked, drifted into the hands of specialists. These specialists cannot be expected to serve for nothing. Their effort to convert their work into a means of support is the source of the greater part of the petty American political corruption; and such corruption will persist as long as any real need exists for the men who live upon it. The simplest way to dispense with the professional politician is to dispense with the service he performs. Reduce the number of elective officials. Under the proposed method of organization the number of elections and the number of men to be elected would be comparatively few. The voter would cast his ballot only for his local selectmen or commissioners, a governor, one or more legislative councilmen, the justices of the state court of appeals, and his Federal congressman and executive. The professional politician would be left without a profession. He would have to pass on his power to men who would be officially designated to rule the people for a limited period, and who could not escape full responsibility for their public performances.

I have said that no less drastic plan of institutional reorganization will be sufficient to accomplish the proposed result; and a brief justification must be afforded for this statement. It was expected, for instance, that the secret Australian ballot would do much to undermine the power of the professional politician. He would be prevented thereby from controlling his followers and, in case of electoral trades, from, "delivering the goods." Well! the Australian ballot has been adopted more or less completely in the majority of the states; and it has undoubtedly made open electoral corruption more difficult and less common than it once was. But it has not diminished the personal and partisan allegiance on which the power of the local "Boss" is based; and it has done the professional politician as little serious harm as have the civil service laws. Neither can it be considered an ideal method of balloting for the citizens of a free democracy. Independent voting and the splitting of tickets is essential to a wholesome expression of public opinion; but in so far as such independence has to be purchased by secrecy its ultimate value may be doubted. American politics will never be "purified" or its general standards improved by an independence which is afraid to come out into the open; and it is curious that with all the current talk about the wholesome effects of "publicity" the reformed ballot sends a voter sneaking into a closet in order to perform his primary political duty. If American voters are more independent than they used to be, it is not because they have been protected by the state against the penalties of independence, but because they have been aroused to more independent thought and action by the intrusion and the discussion of momentous issues. In the long run that vote which is really useful and significant is the vote cast in the open with a full sense of conviction and responsibility.

Another popular reforming device which belongs to the same class and which will fail to accomplish the expected result is the system of direct primaries. It may well be that this device will in the long run merely emphasize the evil which it is intended to abate. It will tend to perpetuate the power of the professional politician by making his services still more necessary. Under it the number of elections will be very much increased, and the amount of political business to be transacted will grow in the same proportion. In one way or another the professional politician will transact this business; and in one way or another he will make it pay. Under a system of direct primaries the machine could not prevent the nomination of the popular candidate whenever public opinion was aroused; so it is with the existing system. But whenever public interest flags,—and it is bound to flag under such an absurd multiplication of elections and under such a complication of electoral machinery,—the politicians can easily nominate their own candidates. Up to date no method has been devised which would prevent them from using their personal followers in the primary elections of both parties; and no such method can be devised without enforcing some comparatively fixed distinction between a Republican and a Democrat, and thus increasing the difficulties of independent voting. In case the number of elective officials were decreased, as has been proposed above, there would be fewer objections to the direct primary. Under the suggested method of organization each election would become of such importance that public opinion would be awakened and would be likely to obtain effective expression; and the balloting for the party candidates would arouse as much interest, particularly in the case of the dominant party, as the final election itself. In fact, the danger would be under such circumstances that the primaries would arouse too much interest, and that the parties would become divided into embittered and unscrupulous factions. Genuinely patriotic and national parties may exist; but a genuinely patriotic faction within a party would be a plant of much rarer growth. From every point of view, consequently, the direct primary has its doubtful aspects. The device is becoming so popular that it will probably prevail; and as it prevails, it may have the indirect beneficial result of diminishing the number of regular elections; but at bottom it is a clumsy and mechanical device for the selection of party candidates. It is merely one of the many means generated by American political practice for cheapening the ballot. The way to make votes important and effective is not to increase but to diminish their number.

A democracy has no interest in making good government complicated, difficult, and costly. It has, on the
contrary, every interest in so simplifying its machinery
that only decisive decisions and choices are submitted
to the voter. Every attempt should be made to arouse
his interest and to turn his public spirit to account; and
for that reason it should not be fatigued by excessive
demands and confused by complicated decisions. The
cost of government in time, ability, training, and energy
should fall not upon the followers but upon the leaders;
and the latter should have every opportunity to make
the expenditure pay. Such is the object of the foregoing suggestions towards reconstruction which, radical
as they may seem, have been suggested chiefly by an examination of the practical conditions of contemporary
reform. Only by the adoption of some such plan can
the reformers become something better than perpetual
moral protestants who are fighting a battle in which a
victory may be less fruitful than defeat. As it is, they are
usually flourishing in the eyes of the American people
a flask of virtue which, when it is uncorked, proves to
be filled with oaths of office. The reformers must put
strong wine into their bottle. They must make office-
holding worth while by giving to the officeholders the
power of effecting substantial public benefits.

III Possibilities of Effective State Action

The questions relating to the kind of reforms which
these reorganized state governments might and should
attempt to bring about need not be considered in any
detail. In the case of the states institutional reconstruction is necessarily prior to social reconstruction; and the
objects for which their improved powers can be best
used need at present only be indicated. These objects include, in fact, practically all the primary benefits which

a state ought to confer upon its citizens; and it is because the states have so largely failed to confer these primary benefits that the reconstruction necessarily assumes a radical complexion. It is absurd to discuss American local governments as agents of individual and social amelioration until they begin to meet their most essential and ordinary responsibilities in a more satisfactory manner.

Take, for instance, the most essential function of all— that of maintaining order. A state government which could not escape and had the courage to meet its responsibilities would necessarily demand from the people a police force which was really capable of keeping the peace. It could not afford to rely upon local "posses" and the militia. It would need a state constabulary, subject to its control and numerous enough for all ordinary emergencies. Such bodies of state police, efficiently used, could not only prevent the lawlessness which frequently accompanies strikes, but it could gradually stamp out lynch law. Lynching, which is the product of excited local feeling, will never be stopped by the sheriffs, because they are afraid of local public opinion. It will never be stopped by the militia, because the militia is slow to arrive and is frequently undisciplined. But it can be stopped by a well-trained and well-disciplined state constabulary, which can be quickly concentrated, and which would be independent of merely local public opinion. When other states besides Pennsylvania establish constabularies, it will be an indication that they really want to keep order; and when the Southern states in particular organize forces of this kind, there will be reason to believe that they really desire to do justice to the negro criminal and remove one of the ugliest aspects of the race question.

A well-informed state government would also necessarily recognize the intimate connection between the prevention of lynching and the speedy and certain administration of criminal justice. It would seek not merely to stamp out disorder, but to anticipate it by doing away with the substantial injustice wrought by the procedure of the great majority of American criminal courts. It is unnecessary to dwell at any length upon the work of reorganization which would confront a responsible state government in relation to the punishment and the prevention of crime, because public opinion is becoming aroused to the dangers which threaten American society from the escape of criminals and the lax and sluggish administration of the criminal laws. But the remark must be made that our existing methods of framing, executing, and expounding criminal laws are merely an illustration of the extent to which the state governments, under the influence of traditional legal and political preconceptions, have subordinated the collective social interest to that of the possible individual criminal; and no thorough-going reform will be possible until these traditional preconceptions have themselves been abandoned, and a system substituted which makes the state the efficient friend of the collective public interest and the selected individual.

Assuming, then, that they use their increased powers more effectually for the primary duty of keeping order, and administering civil and criminal justice, reforming state governments could proceed to many additional tasks. They could redeem very much better than they do their responsibility to their wards—the insane and the convicted criminals. At the present time some states have fairly satisfactory penitentiaries, reformatories, and insane asylums, while other states have utterly unsatisfactory ones; but in all the states both the machinery and the management are capable of considerable improvement. The steady increase both of crime and insanity is demanding the most serious consideration of the whole problem presented by social dereliction—particularly for the purpose of separating out those criminals and feeble-minded people who are capable of being restored to the class of useful citizens. In fact a really regenerated state government might even consider the possible means of preventing crime and insanity. It might have the hardihood to inquire whether the institution of marriage, which would remain under exclusive state protection, does not in its existing form have something to do with the prevalence and increase of insanity and crime; and it might conceivably reach the conclusion that the enforced celibacy of hereditary criminals and incipient lunatics would make for individual and social improvement even more than would a maximum passenger fare on the railroads of two cents a mile. Moreover, while their eyes were turned to our American success in increasing the social as well as the economic output, they might pause a moment to consider the marvelous increase of divorces. They might reflect whether this increase, like that of the criminals and the insane, did not afford a possible subject of legislation, but I doubt whether even a regenerate state government would reach any very quick or satisfactory conclusions in respect to this matter. Public opinion does not appear to have decided whether the social fact of divorce abounding is to be considered as an abuse or as a fulfillment of the existing institution of marriage.

Neither need the pernicious activity of such a government cease, after it has succeeded in radically improving its treatment of the criminal and its lunatics, and in possibly doing something to make the American home less precarious, if less cheerful. It might then turn its attention to the organization of labor, in relation to which, as we shall see presently, the states may have the opportunity for effective work. Or an inquiry might be made as to whether the educational system of the country, which should remain under exclusive state jurisdiction, is well adapted to the extremely complicated purpose of endowing its various pupils with the general and special training most helpful to the creation of genuine individuals, useful public servants, and loyal and contented citizens of their own states. In this matter of education the state governments, particularly in the North, have shown abundant and encouraging good will; but it is characteristic of their general inefficiency that a good will has found its expression in a comparatively bad way.

It would serve no good purpose to push any farther the list of excellent objects to which the state governments might devote their liberated and liberalized energies. We need only add that they would then be capable, not merely of more efficient separate action, but also of far more profitable coöperation. In case the states were emancipated from their existing powerless subjection to individual, special, and parochial interests, the advantages of a system of federated states would be immediately raised to the limit. The various questions of social and educational reform can only be advanced towards a better understanding and perhaps a partial solution by a continual process of experimentation—undertaken with the full appreciation that they were tentative and would be pushed further or withdrawn according to the nature of their results. Obviously a state government is a much better political agency for the making of such experiments than is a government whose errors would affect the population of the whole country. No better machinery for the accomplishment of a progressive programme of social reform could be advised than a collection of governments endowed with the powers of an American state, and really desirous of advancing particular social questions towards their solution. Such a system would be flexible; it would provoke emulation; it would encourage initiative; and it would take advantage of local ebullitions of courage and insight and any peculiarly happy local collection of circumstances. Finally, if in addition to the merits of a system of generous competition, it could add those of occasional consultation and coöperation, such as is implied by the proposed "House of Governors," the organization for social reform would leave little to be desired. The governors who would meet in consultation would be the real political leaders of their several states; and they should meet, not so much for the purpose of agreeing upon any single group of reforming measures, as for the purpose of comparing notes obtained under widely different conditions and as the result of different legislative experiments. Just in so far as this mixture of generous competition and candid coöperation was seeking to accomplish constructive social purposes, for which the powers of the states, each within its geographical limits, were fully adequate, just to that extent it could hardly fail to make headway in the direction of social reform.

If the state governments are to reach their maximum usefulness in the American political system, they must not only be self-denying in respect to the central government, but generous in respect to their creatures—the municipal corporations. There are certain business and social questions of exclusively or chiefly local importance which should be left to the municipal governments; and it is as characteristic of the unregenerate state governments of the past and the present that they have interfered where they ought not to interfere as that they have not interfered where they had an excellent opportunity for effective action. A politically regenerated state would guarantee in its constitution a much larger measure of home rule to the cities than they now enjoy, while at the same time the reformed legislative authority would endeavor to secure the edifying exercise of these larger powers, not by an embarrassing system of super-vision, but by the concentration of the administrative power and responsibility of the municipal authorities. I shall not attempt to define in detail how far the measure of home rule should go; but it may be said in general that the functions delegated or preserved should so far as possible be completely delegated or preserved. This rule cannot be rigidly applied to such essential functions of the state governments as the preservation of order and the system of education. The delegation of certain police powers and a certain control over local schools is considered at present both convenient and necessary, al-though in the course of time such may no longer be the case; but if these essential functions are delegated, the state should retain a certain supervision over the man-ner of their exercise. On the other hand, the municipal-ity as an economic and business organism should be left pretty much to its own devices; and it is not too much to say that the state should not interfere in these mat-ters at all, except under the rarest and most exceptional conditions.

The reasons for municipal home rule in all economic and business questions are sufficiently obvious. A state is a political and legal body; and as a political and legal body it cannot escape its appropriate political and so-cial responsibilities. But a state has in the great majority of cases no meaning at all as a center of economic orga-nization and direction. The business carried on within state limits is either essentially related by competition to the national economic system,—or else it is essentially municipal in its scope and meaning. Of course, such a statement is not strictly true. The states have certain es-sential economic duties in respect to the conservation and development of agricultural resources and methods and to the construction and maintenance of a compre-hensive system of highways. But these legitimate economic responsibilities are not very numerous or very onerous compared to those which should be left to the central government on the one hand or to the municipal governments on the other. A municipality is a living center of economic activity—a genuine case of essentially local economic interests. To be sure, the greater part of the manufacturing or commercial business transacted in a city belongs undubitably to the national economic system; but there is a minor part which is exclusively local. Public service corporations which control franchises in cities do not enter into inter-state commerce at all—except in those unusual cases (as in New York) where certain parts of the economic municipal body are situated in another state. They should be subject, consequently, to municipal jurisdiction and only that. The city alone has anything really important to gain or to lose from their proper or improper treatment; and its legal responsibility should be as complete as its economic localization is real.

There is no need of discussing in any detail the way in which a municipal government which does enjoy the advantage of home rule and an efficient organization can contribute to the work of national economic and social reconstruction. Public opinion is tending to accept much more advanced ideas in this field of municipal reform than it is in any other part of the political battle-field. Experiments are already being tried, looking in the direction of an increasingly responsible municipal organization, and an increasing assumption by the city of economic and social functions. Numerous books are being written on various aspects of the movement, which is showing the utmost vitality and is constantly making progress in the right direction. In all probability, the American city will become in the near future the most fruitful field for economically and socially constructive experimentation; and the effect of the example set therein will have a beneficially reactive effect upon both state and Federal politics. The benefits which the city governments can slowly accomplish within their own jurisdiction are considerable. They do not, indeed, constitute the exclusive "Hope of Democracy," because the ultimate democratic hope depends on the fulfillment of national responsibilities; and they cannot deal effectively with certain of the fundamental social questions. But by taking advantage of its economic opportunities, the American city can gradually diminish the economic stress within its own jurisdiction. It has unique chance of appropriating for the local community those sources of economic value which are created by the community, and it has an equally unique opportunity of spending the money so obtained for the amelioration of the sanitary, if not of the fundamental economic and social, condition of the poorer people.

There is, finally, one fundamental national problem with which the state governments, no matter to what extent they may be liberated and invigorated, are wholly incompetent to deal. The regulation of commerce, the control of corporations, and the still more radical questions connected with the distribution of wealth and the prevention of poverty—questions of this kind should be left exclusively to the central government; or in case they are to any extent allowed to remain under the jurisdiction of the states, they should exercise such jurisdiction as the agents of the central government. The state governments lack and must always lack the power and the independence necessary to deal with this whole group of problems; and as long as they remain preoccupied therewith, their effective energy and good intentions will be diverted from the consideration of those aspects of political and social reform with which they are peculiarly competent to deal. The whole future prosperity and persistence of the American Federal system is bound up in the progressive solution of this group of problems; and if it is left to the conflicting jurisdictions of the central and local governments, the American democracy will have to abandon in this respect the idea of seeking the realization of a really national policy. Justification for these statements will be offered in the following chapter.

12.

Problems of Reconstruction: Part 2

Any proposal to alter the responsibilities and powers now enjoyed by the central and the state governments in respect to the control of corporations and the distribution of wealth involves, of course, the Federal rather than the state constitutions; and the amendment of the former is both a more difficult and a more dangerous task than is the amendment of the latter. A nation cannot afford to experiment with its fundamental law as it may and must experiment with its local institutions. As a matter of fact the Federal Constitution is very much less in need of amendment than are those of the several states. It is on the whole an admirable system of law and an efficient organ of government; and in most respects it should be left to the ordinary process of gradual amendment by legal construction until the American people have advanced much farther towards the realization of a national democratic policy. Eventually certain radical amendments will be indispensable to the fulfillment of the American national purpose; but except in one respect nothing of any essential importance is to be gained at present by a modification of the Federal Constitution. This exception is, however, of the utmost importance. For another generation or two any solution of the problem of corporation control, and of all the other critical problems connected therewith, will be complicated, confused, and delayed by the inter-state commerce clause, and by the impossibility, under that clause, of the exercise of any really effective responsibility and power by the central government. The distinction between domestic and inter-state commerce which is implied by the Constitutional distribution of powers is a distinction of insignificant economic or industrial importance; and its necessary legal enforcement makes the carrying out of an efficient national industrial policy almost impossible.

Under the inter-state commerce clause, a corporation conducting, as all large companies do, both a state and an inter-state business, is subject to several supplementary jurisdictions. It is subject, of course, primarily to the laws of the state under which it is organized, and to the laws of the same state regulating its own particular form of industrial operation. It is subject, also, to any conditions which the legislatures of other states may wish to impose upon its business,—in so far as that business is transacted within their jurisdictions. Finally, it is subject to any regulation which the central government may impose upon its inter-state transactions. From the standpoint of legal supervision, consequently, the affairs of such a corporation are divided into a series of compartments, each compartment being determined by certain arbitrary geographical lines—lines which do not, like the boundaries of a municipality, correspond to any significant economic division. As long as such a method of supervision endures, no effective regulation of commerce or industry is possible. A corporation is not a commercial Pooh-Bah, divided into unrelated sections. It is an industrial and commercial individual. The business which it transacts in one state is vitally related to the business which it transacts in other states; and even in those rare cases of the restriction of a business to the limits of a single state, the purchasing and selling made in its interest necessarily compete with inter-state transactions in the same products. Thus the Constitutional distinction between state and inter-state commerce is irrelevant to the real facts of American industry and trade.

In the past the large corporations have, on the whole, rather preferred state to centralized regulation, because of the necessary inefficiency of the former. Inter-state railroad companies usually exercised a dominant influence in those states under the laws of which they had incorporated; and this influence was so beneficial to them that they were quite willing for the sake of preserving it to subsidize the political machine and pay a certain amount of blackmail. In this way the Pennsylvania Railroad Company exercised a dominant influence in the politics of Pennsylvania and New Jersey; the New York Central was not afraid of anything that could happen at Albany; the Boston and Maine pretty well controlled the legislation of the state of New Hampshire; and the Southern Pacific had its own will in California. Probably in these and other instances the railroads acquired their political influence primarily for purposes of protection. It was the cheapest form of blackmail they could pay to the professional politicians; and in this respect they differed from the public service corporations, which have frequently been active agents of corruption in order to obtain public franchises for less than their value. But once the railroads had acquired their political influence, they naturally used it for their own purposes. They arranged that the state railroad commissioners should be their clerks, and that taxation should not press too heavily upon them. They were big enough to control the public officials whose duty it was to supervise them; and they were content with a situation which left them free from embarrassing interference without being over-expensive.

The situation thereby created, however, was not only extremely undesirable in the public interest, but it was at bottom extremely dangerous to the railroads. These companies were constantly extending their mileage, increasing their equipment, improving their terminals, and enlarging their capital stock. Their operations covered many different states, and their total investments ran far into the hundreds of millions of dollars. In the meantime they remained subject to one or several different political authorities whose jurisdiction extended over only a portion of their line and a fraction of their business, but who could none the less by unwise interference throw the whole system out of gear, and compromise the earning power of many millions of dollars invested in other states. Moreover, they could, if they chose, make all this trouble with a comparative lack of responsibility, because only a fraction of the ill effects of this foolish regulation would be felt within the guilty state. As a matter of fact many railroads had experiences of this kind with the Western states, and were obliged to defend themselves against legislative and administrative dictation, which if it did not amount to confiscation, always applied narrow and rigid restrictive methods to a delicate and complicated economic situation. Most of the large Eastern and some of the large Western companies purchased immunity from such "supervision," and were well content; but it was mere blindness on their part not to understand that such a condition, with the ugly corruption it involved, could not continue. The time was bound to come when an aroused public opinion would undermine their "influence," and would retaliate by imposing upon them restrictions of a most embarrassing and expensive character. In so doing the leaders of a reformed and aroused public opinion might be honestly seeking only legitimate regulation; but the more the state authorities sought conscientiously to regulate the railroads the worse the confusion they would create. The railroads could not escape some restrictive supervision; neither were they obliged wholly to submit to it on the part of any one state. The situation of a railroad running through half a dozen states, and subject to the contradictory and irresponsible orders of half a dozen legislatures or commissions might well become intolerable.

Just this sort of thing has been recently happening. The state authorities began to realize that their lax methods of railway supervision were being used as an argument for increased Federal interference. So the state governments arose in their might and began furiously to "regulate" the railroads. Commissions were constituted or re-constituted, and extremely drastic powers were granted to these officials in respect to the operation of the railroads, the rates and the fares charged, and their financial policies. Bills were passed severely restricting the rights which companies had enjoyed of owning the stock of connecting railroads. Many of the states sought to forbid the companies from charging more than two cents a mile for passenger fares. The issuing of passes except under severe restrictions was made illegal. The railroad companies were suddenly confronted by a mass of hostile and conflicting legislation which represented for the most part an honest attempt to fulfill a neglected responsibility, but whose effort on the whole merely embarrassed the operations of the roads, and which in many instances failed to protect the real public interests involved. Even when this legislation was not ignorantly and unwisely conceived, and even when it was prepared by well-informed and well-intentioned men, it was informed by contradictory ideas and a false conception of the genuine abuses and their necessary remedies. Consequently, a certain fraction of intelligent and disinterested public opinion began soon to realize that the results of a vigorous attempt on the part of the state governments to use their powers and to fulfill their responsibilities in respect to the railroads were actually worse and more dangerous to the public interest than was the previous neglect. The neglect of the responsibility implied corruption, because it provoked blackmail. The vigorous fulfillment of the responsibility implied confusion, cross-purposes, and excessive severity, because the powers of a single state were too great within its specific jurisdiction and absolutely negligible beyond.

The railroad companies suffer more from this piecemeal and conflicting regulation than do corporations engaged in manufacturing operations, not only because they discharge a peculiarly public function, but because their business, particularly in its rate-making aspect, suffers severely from any division by arbitrary geographical lines. But all large inter-state corporations are more or less in the same situation. Corporations such as the Standard Oil Company and some of the large New York life insurance companies are confronted by the alternative either of going out of business in certain states, or of submitting to restrictions which would compromise the efficiency of their whole business policy. Doubtless they have not exhausted the evasive and dilatory methods which have served them so well in the past; but little by little the managers of these corporations are coming to realize that they are losing more than they gain from subjection to so many conflicting and supplementary jurisdictions. Little by little they are coming to realize that the only way in which their businesses can obtain a firm legal standing is by means of Federal recognition and exclusive Federal regulation. They would like doubtless to continue to escape any effective regulation at all; but without it they cannot obtain effective recognition, and in the existing ferment of public opinion recognition has become more important to them than regulation is dangerous.

Many important financiers and corporation lawyers are still bitterly opposed to any effective centralized regulation, even if accompanied by recognition; but such opposition is not merely inaccessible to the les-

sons of experience, but is blinded by theoretical prejudice. Doubtless the position of being, on the one hand,
inefficiently regulated by the state governments, and,
on the other hand, of being efficiently protected in all
their essential rights by the Federal courts—doubtless
such a situation seems very attractive to men who need
a very free hand for the accomplishment of their business purposes; but they should be able to understand
that it would necessarily produce endless friction. The
states may well submit to the constant extension of a
protecting arm to corporations by the Federal courts,
provided the central government is accomplishing more
efficiently than can any combination of state governments the amount of supervision demanded by the public interest. But if the Federal courts are to be constantly
invoked, in order to thwart the will of state legislatures
and commissions, and if at the same time the authority
which protects either neglects or is unable effectively to
supervise, there is bound to be a revival of anti-Federal
feeling in its most dangerous form. Whatever the corporations may suffer from the efficient exercise of Federal
regulative powers, they have far more to fear from the
action of the state governments—provided such action
proceeds from an irresponsible local radicalism embittered by being thwarted. The public opinion on which
the corporations must depend for fair treatment is national rather than local; and just in as far as they can be
made subject to exclusive centralized jurisdiction, just
to that extent is there a good chance of their gradual
incorporation into a nationalized economic and legal
system.

The control of the central government over commerce and the corporations should consequently be
substituted for the control of the states rather than
added thereto; and this action should be taken not in
order to enfeeble American local governments, but to

invigorate them. The enjoyment by any public authority of a function which it cannot efficiently perform is always a source of weakness rather than of strength; and in this particular case it is a necessary source, not merely of weakness, but of corruption. The less the state governments have to do with private corporations whose income is greater than their own, the better it will be for their morals, and the more effectively are they likely to perform their own proper and legitimate functions. Several generations may well elapse before the American public opinion will learn this lesson; and even after it is well learned there will be enormous and peculiar obstacles to be removed before they can turn their instruction to good account. But in the end the American Federal Constitution, like all the Federal Constitutions framed during the past century, will have to dispense with the distinction between state and inter-state commerce; and the national authority will prevail, not because there is any peculiar virtue in the action of the central government, but because there is a peculiar vice in asking the state governments to regulate matters beyond their effective jurisdiction.

II The Recognition of Industrial Organization

The central government in its policy toward the large corporations must adopt one of two courses. Either it must discriminate in their favor or it must discriminate against them. The third alternative—that of being what is called "impartial"—has no real existence; and it is essential that the illusory nature of a policy of impartiality should in the beginning be clearly understood.

A policy of impartiality is supposed to consist in recognizing the existence of the huge industrial and railroad organizations, while at the same time forbidding them the enjoyment of any of those little devices whereby they have obtained an unfair advantage over competitors. It would consist, that is, of a policy of recognition tempered by regulation; and a policy of this kind is the one favored by the majority of conservative and fair-minded reformers. Such a policy has unquestionably a great deal to recommend it as a transitional means of dealing with the problem of corporate aggrandizement, but let there be no mistake: it is not really a policy of strict neutrality between the small and the large industrial agent. Any recognition of the large corporations, any successful attempt to give them a legal standing as authentic as their economic efficiency, amounts substantially to a discrimination in their favor.

The whole official programme of regulation does not in any effective way protect their competitors. Unquestionably these large corporations have in the past thrived partly on illegal favors, such as rebates, which would be prevented by the official programme of regulation; but at the present time the advantage which they enjoy over their competitors is independent of such practices. It depends upon their capture and occupation of certain essential strategic positions in the economic battle-field. It depends upon abundant capital, which enables it to take advantage of every opportunity, and to buy and sell to the best advantage. It depends upon the permanent appropriation of essential supplies of raw materials, such as iron ore and coal, or of terminals in large cities, which cannot now be duplicated. It depends upon possibilities of economic industrial management and of the systematic development of individual industrial ability and experience which exist to a peculiar degree in large industrial enterprises. None of these sources of economic efficiency will be in any way diminished by the official programme of regulation. The corporations will still possess substantially all of their existing advantages over their competitors, while to these will be added the additional one of an unimpeachable legal standing. Like the life insurance companies after the process of purgation, they will be able largely to reduce expenses by abolishing their departments of doubtful law.

Thus the recognition of the large corporation is equivalent to the perpetuation of its existing advantages. It is not an explicit discrimination against their smaller competitors, but it amounts to such discrimination. If the small competitor is to be allowed a chance of regaining his former economic importance, he must receive the active assistance of the government. Its policy must become, not one of recognition, but one of recognition under conditions which would impair the efficiency of the large industrial organizations. Mr. William J. Bryan's policy of a Federal license granted only under certain rigid conditions as to size, is aimed precisely at the impairment of the efficiency of the "trusts," and the consequent active discrimination in favor of the small competitor; but the Roosevelt-Taft programme allows the small competitor only such advantages as he is capable of earning for himself; and it must be admitted that these advantages are, particularly in certain dominant industries, not of a very encouraging nature.

Nevertheless, at the last general election the American people cast a decisively preponderant vote in favor of the Roosevelt-Taft programme; and in so doing they showed their customary common sense. The huge corporations have contributed to American economic efficiency. They constitute an important step in the direction of the better organization of industry and commerce. They have not, except in certain exceptional cases, suppressed competition; but they have regulated it; and it should be the effort of all civilized societies to substitute coöperative for competitive methods, wherever coöperation can prove its efficiency. Deliberately to undo this work of industrial and commercial organization would constitute a logical application of the principle of equal rights, but it would also constitute a step backward in the process of economic and social advance. The process of industrial organization should be allowed to work itself out. Whenever the smaller competitor of the large corporation is unable to keep his head above water with his own exertions, he should be allowed to drown. That the smaller business man will entirely be displaced by the large corporation is wholly improbable. There are certain industries and lines of trade in which he will be able to hold his own; but where he is not able to hold his own, there is no public interest promoted by any expensive attempt to save his life.

The Sherman Anti-Trust Law constitutes precisely such an attempt to save the life of the small competitor; and in case the Roosevelt-Taft policy of recognition tempered by regulation is to prevail, the first step to be taken is the repeal or the revision of that law. As long as it remains on the statute books in its existing form, it constitutes an announcement that the national interest of the American people demands active discrimination in favor of the small industrial and commercial agent. It denies the desirability of recognizing what has already been accomplished in the way of industrial and commercial organization; and according to prevalent interpretations, it makes the legal standing of all large industrial combinations insecure—no matter how conducive to economic efficiency their business policy may be.

Assuming, however, that the Sherman Anti-Trust Law can be repealed, and that the Roosevelt-Taft policy of recognition tempered by regulation be adopted, the question remains as to the manner in which such a policy can best be carried out. Certain essential aspects of this question will not be discussed in the present connection. The thorough carrying out of a policy of recognition would demand a Federal incorporation act, under

which all corporations engaged in anything but an exclusively local business would be obliged to organize;
but, as we have already seen, such an act would be unconstitutional as applied to many technically domestic
corporations, and it would probably be altogether unconstitutional, except, perhaps, under limitations which
would make it valueless. It may be that some means
will be found to evade these Constitutional difficulties,
or it may not be. These are matters on which none but
the best of Constitutional lawyers have any right to an
opinion. But in any event, I shall assume that the Federal
government can eventually find the legal means to make
its policy of recognition effective and to give the "trust"
a definite legal standing. What sort of regulation should
supplement such emphatic recognition?

The purpose of such supervision is, of course, to prevent those abuses which have in the past given the larger
corporation an illegal or an "unfair" advantage over its
competitors; and the engine which American legislatures, both Federal and state, are using for the purpose is
the commission. The attempt to define in a comprehensive statute just what corporations may do, or must in
the public interest be forbidden from doing, is not being
tried, because of the apparent impossibility of providing
in advance against every possible perversion of the public interest in the interest of the private corporation. The
responsibility of the legislature for the protection of the
public interest is consequently delegated to a commission whose duties are partly administrative and partly
either legislative or judicial. The most complete existing
type of such a delegated power is not the Federal Inter-
state Commerce Commission, but the Public Service
Commissions of New York State; and in considering the
meaning and probable effects of this kind of supervision I shall consider only the completed type. A Federal Inter-state Commerce Commission which was fully

competent to supervise all inter-state commerce and all commerce competing therewith would necessarily possess powers analogous to those bestowed upon the New York Public Service Commissions.

The powers bestowed upon those commissions are based upon the assumption that the corporations under their jurisdiction cannot be trusted to take any important decision in respect to their business without official approval. All such acts must be known to the commission, and be either expressly or tacitly approved, and the official body has the power of ordering their wards to make any changes in their service or rates which in the opinion of the commission are desirable in the public interest. Thus the commission is required not only to approve all agreements among corporations, all mergers, all issues of securities, but they are in general responsible for the manner in which the corporations are operated. The grant of such huge powers can be explained only on the ground that the private interest of these corporations is radically opposed to the interest of their patrons. Public opinion must have decided that if left to themselves, the corporations will behave, on the whole, in a manner inimical to the public welfare; and their business must consequently be actually or tacitly "regulated" in every important detail.

One may well hesitate wholly to condemn this government by commission, because it is the first emphatic recognition in American political and economic organization of a manifest public responsibility. In the past the public interests involved in the growth of an extensive and highly organized industrial system have been neither recognized nor promoted. They have not been promoted by the states, partly because the states neither wanted to do so, nor when they had the will, did they have the power. They have not been promoted by the central government because irresponsibility in relation to national economic interest was, the tariff apart, supposed to be an attribute of the central authority. Any legislation which seeks to promote this neglected public interest is consequently to be welcomed; but the welcome accorded to these commissions should not be very enthusiastic. It should not be any more enthusiastic than the welcome accorded by the citizens of a kingdom to the birth of a first child to the reigning monarchs,—a child who turns out to be a girl, incapable under the law of inheriting the crown. A female heir is under such circumstances merely the promise of better things; and so these commissions are merely an evidence of good will and the promise of something better. As initial experiments in the attempt to redeem a neglected responsibility, they may be tolerated; but if they are tolerated for too long, they may well work more harm than good.

The constructive idea behind a policy of the recognition of semi-monopolistic corporations, is, of course, the idea that they can be converted into economic agents which will make unequivocally for the national economic interest; and it is natural that in the beginning legislators should propose to accomplish this result by rigid and comprehensive official supervision. But such supervision, while it would eradicate many actual and possible abuses, would be just as likely to damage the efficiency which has been no less characteristic of these corporate operations. The only reason for recognizing the large corporations as desirable economic institutions is just their supposed economic efficiency; and if the means taken to regulate them impair that efficiency, the government is merely adopting in a roundabout way a policy of destruction. Now, hitherto, their efficiency has been partly the product of the unusual freedom they have enjoyed. Unquestionably they cannot continue to enjoy any similar freedom hereafter; but in restricting it care should be taken not to destroy with the freedom the essential condition of the efficiency. The essential condition of efficiency is always concentration of responsibility; and the decisive objection to government by commission as any sufficient solution of the corporation problem is the implied substitution of a system of divided for a system of concentrated responsibility.

This objection will seem fanciful and far-fetched to the enthusiastic advocates of reform by commission. They like to believe that under a system of administrative regulation abuses can be extirpated without any diminution of the advantages hitherto enjoyed under private management; but if such proves to be the case, American regulative commissions will establish a wholly new record of official good management. Such commissions, responsible as they are to an insistent and uninformed public opinion, and possessed as they inevitably become of the peculiar official point of view, inevitably drift or are driven to incessant, vexatious, and finally harmful interference. The efficient conduct of any complicated business, be it manufacturing, transportation, or political, always involves the constant sacrifice of an occasional or a local interest for the benefit of the economic operation of the whole organization. But it is just such sacrifices of local and occasional to a comprehensive interest which official commissions are not allowed by public opinion to approve. Under their control rates will be made chiefly for the benefit of clamorous local interests; and little by little the economic organization of the country, so far as affected by the action of commission government, would become the increasing rigid victim of routine management. The flexibility and enterprise, characteristic of our existing national economic organization, would slowly disappear; and American industrial leaders would lose the initiative and energy which has contributed so much to the efficiency of the national economic system. Such a result would, of course, only take place gradually; but it would none the less be the eventual result of any complete adoption of such a method of supervision. The friends of commission government who expect to discipline the big corporations severely without injuring their efficiency are merely the victims of an error as old as the human will. They "want it both ways." They want to eat their cake and to have it. They want to obtain from a system of minute official regulation and divided responsibility the same economic results as have been obtained from a system of almost complete freedom and absolutely concentrated responsibility.

The reader must not, however, misinterpret the real meaning of the objection just made to corporation reform by means of commissions. I can see no ground for necessarily opposing the granting of increased power and responsibility to an official or a commission of officials, merely because such officials are paid by the government rather than by a private employer. But when such a grant is considered necessary, the attempt should be to make the opportunity for good work comprehensive and commensurate with the responsibility. The sort of officialism of which the excavations at Panama or the reclamation service is a sample has as much chance of being efficient under suitable conditions as has the work of a private corporation. The government assumes complete charge of a job, and pushes it to a successful or unsuccessful conclusion, according to the extent with which its tradition or organization enables it to perform efficient work. Moreover, there is a certain kind of official supervision of a private business which does not bring with it any divided responsibility. Perhaps the best illustration thereof is the regulation to which the national banks are obliged to submit. In this case the bank examiners and the Controller do not interfere in the management of the bank, except when the manage-

ment is violating certain conditions of safe banking—
which have been carefully defined in the statute. So long
as the banks obey the law, they need have no fear of the
Treasury Department. But in commission government
the official authority, in a sense, both makes and ad-
ministers the law. The commission is empowered to use
its own discretion about many matters, such as rates,
service, equipment, and the like, in relation to which the
law places the corporation absolutely in its hands. Such
official interference is of a kind which can hardly fail in
the long run to go wrong. It is based on a false principle,
and interferes with individual liberty, not necessarily in
an unjustifiable way, but in a way that can hardly be
liberating in spirit or constructive in result.

The need for regulation should not be made the excuse for bestowing upon officials a responsibility which
they cannot in the long run properly redeem. In so far
as the functions of such commissions are really regulative, like the functions of the bank examiners, they may
for the present perform a useful public service. These
commissions should be constituted partly as bureaus of
information and publicity, and partly as an administrative agency to secure the effective enforcement of the
law. In case the Sherman Anti-Trust Law were repealed,
the law substituted therefor should define the kind of
combination among corporations and the kind of agreements among railroads which were permissible, and the
commission should be empowered to apply the law to
any particular consolidation or contract. Similar provision should be made in respect to railroad mergers, and
the purchases by one railroad of the stock of another.
The purposes for which new securities might be legiti-
mately issued should also be defined in the statute, and
the commission allowed merely to enforce the definitions. Common carriers should be obliged, as at present,
to place on record their schedules of rates, and when

a special or a new rate was made, notification should be required to the commission, together with a statement of reasons. Finally the commission should have the completest possible power of investigating any aspect of railway and corporation management or finance the knowledge of which might be useful to Congress. The unflinching use of powers, vaguely sketched above, would be sufficient to prevent mere abuses, and they could be granted without making any body of officials personally responsible for any of the essential details of corporation management.

If the commission is granted the power to promulgate rates, to control the service granted to the public, or to order the purchase of new equipment, it has become more than a regulative official body. It has become responsible for the business management of the corporation committed to its charge; and again it must be asserted that mixed control of this kind is bound to take the energy and initiative out of such business organizations. Neither has any necessity for reducing public service corporations to the level of industrial minors been sufficiently demonstrated. In the matter of service and rates the interest of a common carrier is not at bottom and in the long run antagonistic to the interest of its patrons. The fundamental interest of a common carrier is to develop traffic, and this interest coincides with the interest in general of the communities it serves. This interest can best be satisfied by allowing the carrier freedom in the making of its schedules—subject only to review in particular cases. Special instances may always exist of unnecessarily high or excessively discriminatory rates; and provisions should be made for the consideration of such cases, perhaps, by some court specially organized for the purpose; but the assumption should be, on the whole, that the matter of rates and service can be left to the interest of the corporation itself. In no other way can the American economic system retain that flexibility with which its past efficiency has been associated. In no other way can the policy of these corporations continue to be, as it has so often been in the past, in an economic sense genuinely constructive. This flexibility frequently requires readjustments in the conditions of local industry which cause grave losses to individuals or even communities; but it is just such readjustments which are necessary to continued economic efficiency; and it is just such readjustments which would tend to be prevented by an official rate-making authority. An official rate-making power would necessarily prefer certain rigid rules, favorable to the existing distribution of population and business. Every tendency to a new and more efficient distribution of trade would be checked, because of its unfairness to those who suffer from it. Thus the American industrial system would gradually become petrified, and the national organization of American industry would be sacrificed for the benefit of an indiscriminate collection of local interests.

If the interest of a corporation is so essentially hostile to the public interest as to require the sort of official supervision provided by the New York Public Service Commission Law, the logical inference therefrom is not a system of semi-official and semi-private management, but a system of exclusively public management. The logical inference therefrom is public ownership, if not actual public operation. Public ownership is not open to the same theoretical objections as is government by commission. It is not a system of divided responsibility. Political conditions and the organization of the American civil service being what they are, the attempt of the authorities to assume such a responsibility might not be very successful; but the fault would in that case reside in the general political and administrative organization. The community could not redeem the particular responsibility of owning and operating a railroad, because it was not organized for the really efficient conduct of any practical business. The rejection of a system of divided personal responsibility between public and private officials does not consequently bring with it necessarily the rejection of a system of public ownership, if not public operation; and if it can be demonstrated in the case of any particular class of corporations that its interest has become in any essential respect hostile to the public interest, a constructive industrial policy demands, not a partial, but a much more complete, shifting of the responsibility.

That cases exist in which public ownership can be justified on the foregoing grounds, I do not doubt; but before coming to the consideration of such cases it must be remarked that this new phase of the discussion postulates the existence of hitherto neglected conditions and objects of a constructive industrial policy. Such a policy started with the decision, which may be called the official decision, of the American electorate, to recognize the existing corporate economic organization; and we have been inquiring into the implications of this decision. Those implications include, according to the results of the foregoing discussion, not only a repeal of the Sherman Anti-Trust Law, but the tempering of the recognition with certain statutory regulations. It by no means follows that such regulation satisfies all the objects of a constructive national economic policy. In fact it does not satisfy the needs of a national economic policy at all, just in so far as such a policy is concerned not merely with the organization of industry, but with the distribution of wealth. But inasmuch as the decision has already been reached in preceding chapters that the national interest of a democratic state is essentially concerned with the distribution of wealth, the corporation problem must be considered quite as much in its

relation to the social problem as to the problem of economic efficiency.

The American corporation problem will never be understood in its proper relations and full consequences
until it is conceived as a sort of an advanced attack on
the breastworks of our national economic system by
this essential problem of the distribution of wealth. The
current experiments in the direction of corporate "regulation" are prompted by a curious mixture of divergent
motives. They endeavor to evade a fundamental responsibility by meeting a superficial one. They endeavor to
solve the corporation problem merely by eradicating
abuses, the implication being that as soon as the abuses
are supervised out of existence, the old harmony between public and private interest in the American economic system will be restored, and no more "socialistic"
legislation will be required. But the extent to which this
very regulation is being carried betrays the futility of the
expectation. And as we have seen, the intention of the
industrial reformers is to introduce public management
into the heart of the American industrial system; that is,
into the operation of railroads and public service corporations, and in this way to bring about by incessant
official interference that harmony between public and
private interest which must be the object of a national
economic system. But this proposed remedy is simply
one more way of shirking the ultimate problem; and
it is the logical consequence of the persistent misinterpretation of our unwholesome economic inequalities as
the result merely of the abuse, instead of the legal use,
of the opportunities provided by the existing economic
system.

An economic organization framed in the national
interest would conform to the same principles as a political organization framed in the national interest. It
would stimulate the peculiarly efficient individual by

offering him opportunities for work commensurate with his abilities and training. It would grant him these opportunities under conditions which would tend to bring about their responsible use. And it would seek to make the results promote the general economic welfare. The peculiar advantage of the organization of American industry which has gradually been wrought during the past fifty years is precisely the opportunity which it has offered to men of exceptional ability to perform really constructive economic work. The public interest has nothing to gain from the mutilation or the destruction of these nationalized economic institutions. It should seek, on the contrary, to preserve them, just in so far as they continue to remain efficient; but it should at the same time seek the better distribution of the fruits of this efficiency. The great objection to the type of regulation constituted by the New York Public Service Commission Law is that it tends to deprive the peculiarly capable industrial manager of any sufficient opportunity to turn his abilities and experience to good account. It places him under the tutelage of public officials, responsible to a public opinion which has not yet been sufficiently nationalized in spirit or in purpose, and in case this tutelage fails of its object (as it assuredly will) the responsibility for the failure will be divided. The corporation manager will blame the commissions for vexatious, blundering, and disheartening interference. The commissions will blame the corporation manager for lack of cordial coöperation. The result will be either the abandonment of the experiment or the substitution of some degree of public ownership. But in either event the constructive economic work of the past two generations will be in some measure undone; and the American economic advance will be to that extent retarded. Such obnoxious regulation has been not unjustly compared to the attempt to discipline a somewhat too vivacious bull by the simple process of castration. For it must be substituted an economic policy which will secure to the nation and the individual the opportunities and the benefits of the existing organization, while at the same time seeking the diffusion of those benefits over a larger social area.

III The Fruits of Industrial Organization

The only sound point of departure for a national economic policy is, as we have seen, the acceptance by the state of certain of the results of corporate industrial organization. Such state recognition is equivalent to discrimination in their favor, because it leaves them in possession of those fundamental economic advantages, dependent on terminals, large capital, and natural resources, which place them beyond effective competition; and the state has good reason to suffer this discrimination, because a wise government can always make more social capital out of a coöperative industrial organization than it can out of an extremely competitive one.

It is extremely improbable that, even when officially recognized in this way, the process of corporate combination would go beyond a certain point. It might result in a condition similar to that which now prevails in the steel industry or that of sugar refining; but it should be added that in industries organized to that extent there is not very much competition in prices. Prices are usually regulated by agreement among the leading producers; and competition among the several producers turns upon quickness of delivery and the quality of the service or product. Whether or not this restriction of competition works badly depends usually upon the enlightened shrewdness with which the schedule of rates and prices is fixed. A corporation management which was thoroughly alive to its own interest would endeavor to arrange a scale of prices, which, while affording a sufficient profit, would encourage the increased use of the product, and that is precisely the policy which has been adopted by the best managed American railroad and industrial corporations. But it must always be kept in mind that, in the absence of a certain amount of competition, such a policy cannot be taken wholly for granted. A short-sighted management may prefer to reap large profits for a short time and at the expense of the increased use of its product or service. Moreover, the margin between the cost of production and the particular price at which the product or service can be sold consistent with its largely increasing use may enable the producer to gather enormous profits; and such profits may not stimulate competition to any effective extent, precisely because they depend upon advantages in production which cannot be duplicated. No state desirous of promoting the economic welfare of its citizens can remain indifferent to the chance thus afforded of earnings disproportionately large to the economic service actually rendered.

In dealing with this question of possibly excessive profits under such a method of economic organization, the state has many resources at its disposal besides the most obvious one of incessant official interference with the essentials of corporation management. Of these the most useful consists unquestionably in its power of taxation. It can constitute a system of taxation, in respect to the semi-monopolistic corporations, which would deprive them of the fruits of an excessively large margin between the cost of production and the price at which the product or service could be increasingly sold. Net profits could be taxed at a rate which was graduated to the percentage paid; and beyond a certain point the tax should amount to much the larger fraction of the profits. In this way a semi-monopolistic corporation would not have any interest in seeking profits beyond a certain percentage. A condition would be established which, while it would not deprive the managers of a corporation of full responsibility for the conduct of its business, would give them an additional inducement always to work for the permanent improvement of the economic relation of the corporation to the community. They would have no interest in preferring large but insecure net earnings to smaller ones, founded on a thoroughly satisfactory service, a low schedule of prices, and the constantly increasing efficiency of the plant and organization of the company.

The objection will, no doubt, be immediately urged that a system of this kind would prevent any improvement of service from going beyond a certain point, just because it would cease to be profitable beyond a certain point. But such an objection would not be valid, provided the scale of taxation were properly graduated. I shall not attempt to define any precise scale which would serve the purpose because the possible adoption of such a plan is still too remote; but the state should, in return for the protection it extends to these semimonopolistic corporations, take a certain percentage of all profits, and, while this percentage should increase until it might at a certain level reach as much as one half or three quarters, it should not become larger than three quarters—except in the case of a corporation earning, say, more than 20 per cent on its capital. To be sure the establishment even of such a level would conceivably destroy the interested motive for increased efficiency at a certain point, but such a point could hardly be reached except in the case of companies whose monopoly was almost complete.

The foregoing plan, however, is not suggested as a final and entirely satisfactory method of incorporating semimonopolistic business organizations into the economic system of a nationalizing democracy. I do not believe that any formula can be framed which will by the magic of some chemical process convert a purely selfish economic motive into an unqualified public economic benefit. But some such plan as that proposed above may enable an industrial democracy to get over the period of transition between the partial and the complete adaptation of these companies to their place in a system of national economy. They can never be completely incorporated so long as the interest of their owners is different from that of the community as a whole, but in the meantime they can be encouraged to grow and perhaps to become more efficient, while at the same time they can be prevented from becoming a source of undesirable or dangerous individual economic inequalities; and I do not believe that such a transitional system of automatically regulated recognition would be open to the same objections as would a system of incessant official interference. In so far, indeed, as the constructive industrial leader is actuated merely by the motive of amassing more millions than can be of any possible use to himself or his children—in so far as such is the case, the inducement to American industrial organization on a national scale would be impaired. But if an economic democracy can purchase efficient industrial organization on a huge scale only at the price of this class of fortunes, then it must be content with a lower order of efficiency, and American economic statesmanship has every reason to reject such an alternative until there is no help for it. The best type of American millionaire seems always to have had as much interest in the work and in the game as in its prodigious rewards; and much of his work has always been done for him by employees who, while they were paid liberally, did not need the inducement of more money than they could wholesomely spend in return, for service of the highest efficiency.

In any event the plan of an automatically regulated recognition of semi-monopolistic corporations would be intended only as a transitional measure. Its object would be to give these somewhat novel industrial agents a more prolonged and thorough test than any they have yet received. If they survived for some generations and increased in efficiency and strength, it could only be because the advantages they enjoyed in the way of natural resources, abundant capital, organization, terminals, and responsible management were decisive and permanent; and in that case the responsibility of the state could not be limited to their automatic regulation and partial assimilation. A policy must be adopted of converting them into express economic agents of the whole community, and of gradually appropriating for the benefit of the community the substantial economic advantages which these corporations had succeeded in acquiring. Just in so far, that is, as a monopoly or a semi-monopoly succeeded in surviving and growing, it would partake of the character of a natural monopoly, and would be in a position to profit beyond its deserts from the growth of the community. In that event a community which had any idea of making economic responsibility commensurate with power would be obliged to adopt a policy of gradual appropriation.

The public service corporations in the large cities have already reached the stage of being recognized natural monopolies. In the case of these corporations public opinion is pretty well agreed that a monopoly controlling the whole service is more likely to be an efficient servant of the city than a number of separate corporations, among whom competition in order to be effective must be destructive and wasteful. American municipal policy is consequently being adapted to the idea of monopolized control of these public services. The best manner of dealing with these monopolies, after they have been created and recognized, is not settled by any means to the same extent; but the principle of restricting the franchises under which they operate to a limited term of years is well established, and the tendency is towards a constant reduction of the length of such leases and towards the retention of a right of purchase, exercisable at all or at certain stated times. The American city has come to realize that such privileges possess a value which increases automatically with the growth of the city and with the guarantee against competition; and this source of value should never be alienated except for a short period and on the most stringent terms. Wherever, consequently, a city has retained any control over such franchises, it is converting the public service corporations merely into temporary tenants of what are essentially exclusive economic privileges. During the period of its tenancy the management of a corporation has full opportunity to display any ability and energy whereof it may be possessed; and such peculiarly efficient management should be capable of earning sufficient if not excessive rewards. In the meantime, any increase in value which would result inevitably from the possession of a monopoly in a growing community would accrue, as it should, to the community itself.

The only alternative to such a general scheme of municipal policy in relation to public service corporations would be one of municipal operation as well as municipal ownership; and municipal operation unquestionably has certain theoretical advantages. When a corporation enjoys a tenancy for a stated term only, there is always a danger that it will seek temporarily larger profits by economizing on the quality of its service. It has not the same interest in building up a permanently profitable business that it would in case it were owner as well as operator. This divergence of interest may lead to a good deal of friction; but for the present at least the mixed

system of public ownership and private operation offers the better chance of satisfactory results. As long as
the municipal civil service remains in its existing disorganized and inefficient condition, the public administration should not be granted any direct responsibility
which can be withheld without endangering an essential
public interest. A system of public operation would be
preferable to one of divided personal responsibility between public and private officials; but when a mixed
system can be created which sharply distinguishes the
two responsibilities one from another without in any
way confusing them, it combines for the time being a
maximum of merit with a minimum of friction.

Such a system carries with it, however, two results,
not always appreciated. A municipality which embarks
upon a policy of guaranteeing monopolies and leasing
the enjoyment thereof should make all permanent improvements to the system at its own expense, and its
financial organization and methods must be adapted to
the necessity of raising a liberal supply of funds for such
essential purposes. Its borrowing capacity must not be
arbitrarily restricted as in the case of so many American
cities at the present time; and, of course, any particular
lease must be arranged so as to provide not only the
interest on the money raised for all work of construction, but for the extinction of the debt thereby incurred.
Furthermore a city adopting such a policy should push
it to the limit. Wherever, as is so often the case, private
companies now enjoy a complete or a substantial monopoly of any service, and do so by virtue of permanent
franchises, every legal means should be taken to nullify such an intolerable appropriation of the resources
of the community. Persistent and ruthless war should be
declared upon these unnatural monopolies, because as
long as they exist they are an absolute bar to any thoroughly democratic and constructive system of municipal

economy. Measures should be taken which under other circumstances would be both unfair and unwise for the deliberate purpose of bringing them to terms, and getting them to exchange their permanent possession of these franchises for a limited tenancy. Permanent commissions should be placed over them with the right and duty of interfering officiously in their business. Taxation should be made to bear heavily upon them. Competitive services should be established wherever this could be done without any excessive loss. They should be annoyed and worried in every legal way; and all those burdens should be imposed upon them with the explicit understanding that they were measures of war. In adopting such a policy a community would be fighting for an essential condition of future economic integrity and well-being, and it need not be any more scrupulous about the means employed (always "under the law") than would an animal in his endeavor to kill some blood-sucking parasite. The corporation should plainly be told that the fight would be abandoned wherever it was ready to surrender its unlimited franchises for a limited but exclusive monopoly, which in these cases should in all fairness run for a longer term than would be ordinarily permissible.

I have lingered over the case of corporations enjoying municipal franchises, because they offer the only existing illustration of a specific economic situation—a situation in which a monopolized service is based upon exclusive and permanent economic advantages. Precisely the same situation does not exist in any other part of the economic area; but the idea is that under a policy of properly regulated recognition such a situation may come to exist in respect to those corporations which should be subject to the jurisdiction of the central government; and just in so far as it does come to exist, the policy of the central government should

resemble the one suggested for the municipal governments and already occasionally adopted by them. That
any corporations properly subject to the jurisdiction of
the Federal government will attain to the condition of
being a "natural" monopoly may be disputed; but according to the present outlook, if such is not the case,
the only reason will be that the government by means
of official and officious interference "regulates" them
into inefficiency, and consequent inability to hold their
own against smaller and less "regulated" competitors. If
these corporations are left in the enjoyment of the natural advantages which wisely or unwisely they have been
allowed to appropriate, some of them at any rate will
gradually attain to the economic standing of "natural"
monopolies.

The railroad system of the country is gradually ap-
proximating to such a condition. The process of combination which has been characteristic of American
railroad development from the start has been checked
recently both by government action and by anti-railroad
agitation; but if the railroads were exempted from the
provisions of the Anti-Trust Law and were permitted, subject to official approval, either to make agreements or to merge, according as they were competing
or non-competing lines, there can be no doubt that the
whole country would be gradually divided up among
certain large and essentially non-competitive systems.
A measure of competition would always remain, even
if one corporation controlled the entire railway system,
because the varying and conflicting demands of different localities and businesses for changes in rates would
act as a competitive force; and in the probable system
of a division of territory, this competitive force would
have still more influence. But at the same time by far
the larger part of the freight and passenger traffic of
the country would under such a system be shared by

arrangement among the several corporations. The ultimate share of each of the big corporations would not
be determined until the period of building new through
routes had passed. But this period is not likely to endure for more than another generation. Thereafter additional railroad construction will be almost exclusively
a matter of branch extensions and connections, or of
duplicating tracks already in existence; and when such a
situation is reached, the gross traffic will be just as much
divided among the coöperative companies as if it were
distributed among different lines by a central management. Certain lines would be managed more efficiently
than others and might make more money, just as certain
departments of a big business might, because of peculiarly able management, earn an unusually large contribution to the total profits; but such variations could not
be of any essential importance. From the point of view
of the community as a whole the railroad system of the
country would be a monopoly.

The monopoly, like that of a municipal street railroad, would depend upon the possession of exclusive
advantages. It would depend upon the ownership of
terminals in large and small cities which could no longer be duplicated save at an excessive expense. It would
depend upon the possession of a right of way in relation to which the business arrangements of a particular territory had been adjusted. It would have become
essentially a special franchise, even if it had not been
granted as a special franchise by any competent legal
authority; and, like every similar franchise, it would
increase automatically in value with the growth of the
community in population and business. This automatic
increase in value, like that of a municipal franchise,
should be secured to the community which creates it;
and it can be secured only by some such means as those
suggested in the case of municipal franchises. The Fed-

eral government must, that is, take possession of that share of railroad property represented by the terminals, the permanent right of way, the tracks, and the stations. It is property of this kind which enables the railroads to become a monopoly, and which, if left in private hands, would absolutely prevent the gradual construction of a national economic system.

In the existing condition of economic development and of public opinion, the man who believes in the ultimate necessity of government ownership of railroad road-beds and terminals must be content to wait and to watch. The most that he can do for the present is to use any opening, which the course of railroad development affords, for the assertion of his ideas; and if he is right, he will gradually be able to work out, in relation to the economic situation of the railroads, some practical method of realizing the ultimate purpose. Even if public opinion eventually decided that the appropriation of the railroads was necessary in the national economic interest, the end could in all probability be very slowly realized. In return, for instance, for the benefit of government credit, granted under properly regulated conditions, the railroads might submit to the operation of some gradual system of appropriation, which would operate only in the course of several generations, and the money for which would be obtained by the taxation of railroad earnings. It might, however, be possible to arrange a scheme of immediate purchase and the conversion of all railway securities, except those representing equipment and working capital, into one special class of government security. In that case the whole railroad system of the country could be organized into a certain limited number of special systems, which could be leased for a definite term of years to private corporations. These independent systems would in their mutual relations stimulate that economic rivalry among localities which is the wholesome aspect of railroad competition. Each of these companies should, of course, be free to fix such rates as were considered necessary for the proper development and distribution of traffic within its own district.

Any such specific suggestions cannot at the present time be other than fanciful; and they are offered, not because of their immediate or proximate practical value, but because of the indication they afford of the purposes which must be kept in mind in drawing up a radical plan of railroad reorganization in the ultimate national interest. All such plans of reorganization should carefully respect existing railroad property values, unless the management of those railroads obstinately and uncompromisingly opposed all concessions necessary to the realization of the national interest. In that event the nation would be as much justified in fighting for its essential interests as would under analogous circumstances a municipality. Furthermore, any such reorganization should aim at keeping the benefits of the then existing private organization—whatever they might be. It should remain true to the principle that, so far as economic authority and power is delegated in the form of terminable leases to private corporations, such power should be complete within certain defined limits. If agents of the national economic interest cannot be trusted to fulfill their responsibilities without some system of detailed censure and supervision they should be entirely dispensed with. It may be added that if the proposed or any kindred method of reorganization becomes politically and economically possible, the circumstances which account for its possibility will in all probability carry with them some practicable method of realizing the proposed object.

Wherever the conditions, obtaining in the case of railroad and public service corporations, are duplicated in that of an industrial corporation, a genuinely national economic system would demand the adoption of similar measures. How far or how often these measures would be necessarily applied to industrial corporations could be learned only after a long period of experimentation, and during this period the policy of recognition, tempered by regulation under definite conditions and graduated taxation of net profits would have to be applied. But when such a policy had been applied for a period sufficiently prolonged to test their value as national economic agents, further action might become desirable in their case as in that of the railroads. The industrial, unlike the service corporations, cannot, however, be considered as belonging to a class which must be all treated in the same way. Conditions would vary radically in different industries; and the case of each industry should be considered in relation to its special conditions. Wherever the tendency in any particular industry continued to run in the direction of combination, and wherever the increasingly centralized control of that industry was associated with a practical monopoly of some mineral, land, or water rights, the government might be confronted by another instance of a natural monopoly, which it would be impolitic and dangerous to leave in private hands. In all such cases some system of public ownership and private operation should, if possible, be introduced. On the other hand, in case the tendency to combination was strengthened in an industry, such, for instance, as that of the manufacture of tobacco, which does not depend upon the actual ownership of any American natural resources, the manner of dealing with it would be a matter of expediency, which would vary in different cases. In the case of a luxury like tobacco, either a government monopoly might be created, as has been already done so frequently abroad, or the state might be satisfied with a sufficient share of the resulting profits. No general rule can be laid down for such cases; and they will not come up for serious consideration until the more fundamental question of the railroads has been agitated to the point of compelling some kind of a definite settlement.

This sketch of a constructive national policy in relation to corporations need not be carried any further. Its purpose has been to convert to the service of a national democratic economic system the industrial organization which has gradually been built up in this country; and to make this conversion, if possible, without impairing the efficiency of the system, and without injuring individuals in any unnecessary way. The attempt will be criticised, of course, as absolutely destructive of American economic efficiency and as wickedly unjust to individuals; and there will be, from the point of view of the critics, some truth in the criticism. No such reorganization of our industrial methods could be effected without a prolonged period of agitation, which would undoubtedly injure the prosperity and unsettle the standing of the victims of the agitation; and no matter what the results of the agitation, there must be individual loss and suffering. But there is a distinction to be made between industrial efficiency and business prosperity. Americans have hitherto identified prosperity with a furious economic activity, and an ever-increasing economic product—regardless of genuine economy of production and any proper distribution of the fruits. Unquestionably, the proposed reorganization of American industrial methods would for a while make many individual Americans less prosperous. But it does not follow that the efficiency of the national economic organization need be compromised, because its fruits are differently distributed and are temporarily less abundant. It is impossible to judge at present how far that efficiency depends upon the chance, which Americans have enjoyed, of appropriating far more money than they have earned, and far more than they can spend except either by squandering it or giving it away. But in any event the dangerous lack of national economic balance involved by the existing distribution of wealth must be redressed. This object is so essential that its attainment is worth the inevitable attendant risks. In seeking to bring it about, no clear-sighted democratic economist would expect to "have it both ways." Even a very gradual displacement of the existing method of distributing economic fruits will bring with it regrettable wounds and losses. But provided they are incurred for the benefit of the American people as an economic whole, they are worth the penalty. The national economic interest demands, on the one hand, the combination of abundant individual opportunity with efficient organization, and on the other, a wholesome distribution, of the fruits; and these joint essentials will be more certainly attained under some such system as the one suggested than they are under the present system.

The genuine economic interest of the individual, like the genuine political interest, demands a distribution of economic power and responsibility, which will enable men of exceptional ability an exceptional opportunity of exercising it. Industrial leaders, like political leaders, should be content with the opportunity of doing efficient work, and with a scale of reward which permits them to live a complete human life. At present the opportunity of doing efficient industrial work is in the case of the millionaires (not in that of their equally or more efficient employees) accompanied by an excessive measure of reward, which is, in the moral interest of the individual, either meaningless or corrupting. The point at which these rewards cease to be earned is a difficult one to define; but there certainly can be no injustice in appropriating for the community those increases in value

which are due merely to a general increase in population and business; and this increase in value should be
taken over by the community, no matter whether it is
divided among one hundred or one hundred thousand
stockholders in a corporation. The essential purpose
is to secure for the whole community those elements
in value which are made by the community. The semi-
monopolistic organization of certain American industries is little by little enabling the government to separate from the total economic product a part at least of
that fraction which is created by social rather than individual activity; and a democracy which failed to take
advantage of the opportunity would be blind to its fundamental interest. To be sure, the opportunity cannot be
turned to the utmost public benefit until industrial leaders, like political leaders, are willing to do efficient work
partly from disinterested motives; but that statement is
merely a translation into economic terms of the fundamental truth that democracy, as a political and social
ideal, is founded essentially upon disinterested human
action. A democracy can disregard or defy that truth at
its peril.

IV   Taxation and Inequalities in Wealth

Before dismissing this subject of a national industrial organization and a better distribution of the fruits thereof
brief references must be made to certain other aspects
of the matter. The measures which the central and local
governments could take for the purpose of adapting our
economic and social institutions to the national economic and social interest would not be exhausted by
the adoption of the proposed policy of reconstruction;
and several of these supplementary means, which have
been proposed to accomplish the same object, deserve
consideration. Some of these proposals look towards a

further use of the power of taxation, possessed by both the state and the Federal governments; but it must not be supposed that in their entirety they constitute a complete system of taxation. They are merely examples, like the protective tariff, of the use of the power of taxation to combine a desirable national object with the raising of money for the expenses of government.

It may be assumed that the adoption of the policy outlined in the last section would gradually do away with certain undesirable inequalities in the distribution of wealth: but this process, it is scarcely necessary to add, would do nothing to mitigate existing inequalities. Existing inequalities ought to be mitigated; and they can be mitigated without doing the slightest injustice to their owners. The means to such mitigation are, of course, to be found in a graduated inheritance tax—a tax which has already been accepted in principle by several American states and by the English government, which certainly cannot be considered indifferent to the rights of individual property owners.

At the present stage of the argument, no very elaborate justification can be necessary, either for the object proposed by a graduated inheritance tax, or for the use of precisely these means to attain it. The preservation intact of a fortune over a certain amount is not desirable either in the public or individual interest. No doubt there are certain people who have the gift of spending money well, and whose personal value as well as the general social interest is heightened by the opportunity of being liberal. But to whatever extent such considerations afford a moral justification for private property, they have no relevancy to the case of existing American fortunes. The multi-millionaire cannot possibly spend his income save by a recourse to wild and demoralizing extravagance, and in some instances not even extravagance is sufficient for the purpose. Fortunes of a certain size either remorselessly accumulate or else are given away. There is a general disposition to justify the possession of many millions by the frequent instances among their owners of intelligent public benefaction, but such an argument is a confession that a justification is needed without constituting in itself a sufficient excuse. If wealth, particularly when accumulated in large amounts, has a public function, and if its possession imposes a public duty, a society is foolish to leave such a duty to the accidental good intentions of individuals. It should be assumed and should be efficiently performed by the state; and the necessity of that assumption is all the plainer when it is remembered that the greatest public gifts usually come from the first generation of millionaires. Men who inherit great wealth and are brought up in extravagant habits nearly always spend their money on themselves. That is one reason why the rich Englishman is so much less generous in his public gifts than the rich American. In the long run men inevitably become the victims of their wealth. They adapt their lives and habits to their money, not their money to their lives. It pre-occupies their thoughts, creates artificial needs, and draws a curtain between them and the world. If the American people believe that large wealth really requires to be justified by proportionately large public benefactions, they should assuredly adopt measures which will guarantee public service for a larger proportion of such wealth.

Whether or not the state shall permit the inheritance of large fortunes is a question which stands on a totally different footing from the question of their permissible accumulation. Many millions may, at least in part, be earned by the men who accumulate them; but they cannot in the least be earned by the people who inherit them. They could not be inherited at all save by the intervention of the state; and the state has every right to impose conditions in its own interest upon the whole business of inheritance. The public interests involved go very much beyond the matter of mitigating flagrant inequalities of wealth. They concern at bottom the effect of the present system of inheritance upon the inheritors and upon society; and in so far as the system brings with it the creation of a class of economic parasites, it can scarcely be defended. But such is precisely its general tendency. The improbability that the children will inherit with the wealth of the parent his possibly able and responsible use of it is usually apparent to the father himself; and not infrequently he ties up his millions in trust, so that they are sure to have the worst possible moral effect upon his heirs. Children so circumstanced are deprived of any economic responsibility save that of spending an excessive income; and, of course, they are bound to become more or less respectable parasites. The manifest dissociation thereby implied between the enjoyment of wealth and the personal responsibility attending its ownership, has resulted in the proposal that fathers should be forbidden by the state to arrange so carefully for the demoralization of their children and grandchildren. Even if we are not prepared to acquiesce in so radical an impairment of the rights of testators, there can be no doubt that, under a properly framed system of inheritance taxation, all property placed in trust for the benefit of male heirs above a certain amount should be subject to an exceptionally severe deduction. Whatever justification such methods of guaranteeing personal financial irresponsibility may have in aristocratic countries, in which an upper class may need a peculiar economic freedom, they are hostile both to the individual and public interest of a democratic community.

Public opinion is not, however, even remotely prepared for any radical treatment of the whole matter of inheritance; and it will not be prepared, until it has

learned from experience that the existing freedom enjoyed by rich testators means the sacrifice of the quick
to the dead—the mutilation of living individuals in the
name of individual freedom and in order that a dead
will may have its way. Until this lesson is learned the
most that can be done is to work for some kind of a
graduated inheritance tax, the severity of which should
be dictated chiefly by conditions of practical efficiency.
Considerations of practical efficiency make it necessary that the tax should be imposed exclusively by the
Federal government. State inheritance taxes, sufficiently
large to accomplish the desirable result, will be evaded
by change of residence to another state. A Federal tax
could be raised to a much higher level without prompt-
ing the two possible methods of evasion—one of which
would be the legal transfer of the property during lifetime, and the other a complete change of residence to
some foreign country. This second method of evasion
would not constitute a serious danger, because of the
equally severe inheritance laws of foreign countries. The
tax at its highest level could be placed without danger
of evasion at as much as twenty per cent. The United
Kingdom now raises almost $100,000,000 of revenue
from the source; and a slightly increased scale of taxation might yield double that amount to the American
Treasury, a part of which could be turned into the state
Treasuries.

There has been associated with the graduated inheritance tax the plan of a graduated income tax; but the
graduated income tax would serve the proposed object
both less efficiently and less equitably. It taxes the man
who earns the money as well as him who inherits it.
It taxes earned income as well as income derived from
investments; and in taxing the income derived from
investments, it cannot make any edifying discrimination as to its source. Finally, it would interfere with a

much more serviceable plan of taxing the net profits of corporations subject to the jurisdiction of the Federal government—a plan which is an indispensable part of any constructive treatment of the corporation problem in the near future.

The suggestion that the inheritance tax should constitute a pillar of central rather than local taxation implicitly raises a whole series of difficult Constitutional and fiscal questions concerning the relation between central and local taxation. The discussion of these questions would carry me very much further than my present limits permit; and there is room in this connection for only one additional remark. The real estate tax and saloon licenses should, I believe, constitute the foundation of the state revenues; but inasmuch as certain states have derived a considerable part of their income from corporation and inheritance taxes, allowance would have to be made for this fact in revising the methods of Federal taxation. It is essential to any effective control over corporations and over the "money power" that corporation and inheritance taxes should be uniform throughout the country, and should be laid by the central government; but no equally good reason can be urged on behalf of the exclusive appropriation by the Federal Treasury of the proceeds of these taxes. If the states need revenues derived from these sources, a certain proportion of the net receipts could be distributed among the states. The proportion should be the same in the case of all the states; but it should be estimated in the case of any particular state upon the net yield which the Federal Treasury had derived from its residents.

V   The Organization of Labor

Only one essential phase of a constructive national policy remains to be considered—and that is the organization of labor. The necessity for the formulation of some constructive policy in respect to labor is as patent as is that for the formulation of a similar policy in respect to corporate wealth. Any progress in the solution of the problem of the better distribution of wealth will, of course, have a profound indirect effect on the amelioration of the condition of labor; but such progress will be at best extremely slow, and in the meantime the labor problem presses for some immediate and direct action. As we have seen, American labor has not been content with the traditional politico-economic optimism. Like all aggressive men alive to their own interest, the laborer soon decided that what he really needed was not equal rights, but special opportunities. He also soon learned that in order to get these special opportunities he must conquer them by main force—which he proceeded to do with, on the whole, about as much respect for the law as was exhibited by the big capitalists. In spite of many setbacks the unionizing of industrial labor has been attended with almost as much success as the consolidating of industrial power and wealth; and now that the labor unions have earned the allegiance of their members by certain considerable and indispensable services, they find themselves placed, in the eyes of the law, in precisely the same situation as combinations of corporate wealth. Both of these attempts at industrial organization are condemned by the Sherman Anti-Trust Law and by certain similar state legislation as conspiracies against the freedom of trade and industry.

The labor unions, consequently, like the big corporations, need legal recognition; and this legal recognition means in their case, also, substantial discrimination by the state in their favor. Of course, the unionist leaders appeal to public opinion with the usual American cant. According to their manifestoes they demand nothing but "fair play"; but the demand for fair play is as usual merely the hypocritical exterior of a demand for substantial favoritism. Just as there can be no effective competition between the huge corporation controlling machinery of production which cannot be duplicated and the small manufacturer in the same line, so there can be no effective competition between the individual laborer and the really efficient labor union. To recognize the labor union, and to incorporate it into the American legal system, is equivalent to the desertion by the state of the non-union laborer. It means that in the American political and economic system the organization of labor into unions should be preferred to its disorganized separation into competing individuals. Complete freedom of competition among laborers, which is often supposed to be for the interest of the individual laborer, can only be preserved as an effective public policy by active discrimination against the unions.

An admission that the recognition of labor unions amounts to a substantial discrimination in their favor would do much to clear up the whole labor question. So far as we declare that the labor unions ought to be recognized, we declare that they ought to be favored; and so far as we declare that the labor union ought to be favored, we have made a great advance towards the organization of labor in the national interest. The labor unions deserve to be favored, because they are the most effective machinery which has as yet been forged for the economic and social amelioration of the laboring class. They have helped to raise the standard of living, to mitigate the rigors of competition among individual laborers, and in this way to secure for labor a larger share of the total industrial product. A democratic government has little or less reason to interfere on behalf of the non-union laborer than it has to interfere in favor of the small producer. As a type the non-union laborer is a species of industrial derelict. He is the laborer who has gone astray and who either from apathy, unintelligence, incompetence, or some immediately pressing need prefers his own individual interest to the joint interests of himself and his fellow-laborers. From the point of view of a constructive national policy he does not deserve any special protection. In fact, I am willing to go farther and assert that the non-union industrial laborer should, in the interest of a genuinely democratic organization of labor, be rejected; and he should be rejected as emphatically, if not as ruthlessly, as the gardener rejects the weeds in his garden for the benefit of fruit- and flower-bearing plants.

The statement just made unquestionably has the appearance of proposing a harsh and unjust policy in respect to non-union laborers; but before the policy is stigmatized as really harsh or unjust, the reader should wait until he has pursued the argument to its end. Our attitude towards the non-union laborer must be determined by our opinion of the results of his economic action. In the majority of discussions of the labor question the non-union laborer is figured as the independent working man who is asserting his right to labor when and how he prefers against the tyranny of the labor union. One of the most intelligent political and social thinkers in our country has gone so far as to describe them as industrial heroes, who are fighting the battle of individual independence against the army of class oppression. Neither is this estimate of the non-union laborer wholly without foundation. The organization and policy of the contemporary labor union being what they are, cases will occasionally and even frequently occur in which the non-union laborer will represent the protest of an individual against injurious restrictions imposed by the union upon his opportunities and his work. But such cases are rare compared to the much larger number of instances in which the non-union laborer is to be

considered as essentially the individual industrial derelict. In the competition among laboring men for work
there will always be a certain considerable proportion
who, in order to get some kind of work for a while,
will accept almost any conditions of labor or scale of
reward offered to them. Men of this kind, either because
of irresponsibility, unintelligence, or a total lack of social standards and training, are continually converting
the competition of the labor market into a force which
degrades the standard of living and prevents masses of
their fellow-workmen from obtaining any real industrial
independence. They it is who bring about the result that
the most disagreeable and dangerous classes of labor remain the poorest paid; and as long as they are permitted
to have their full effects upon the labor situation, progress to a higher standard of living is miserably slow and
always suffers a severe setback during a period of hard
times. From any comprehensive point of view union
and not non-union labor represents the independence
of the laborer, because under existing conditions such
independence must be bought by association. Worthy
individuals will sometimes be sacrificed by this process
of association; but every process of industrial organization or change, even one in a constructive direction,
necessarily involves individual cases of injustice.

Hence it is that the policy of so-called impartiality is
both impracticable and inexpedient. The politician who
solemnly declares that he believes in the right of the laboring man to organize, and that labor unions are de-
serving of approval, but that he also believes in the right
of the individual laborer to eschew unionism whenever
it suits his individual purpose or lack of purpose,—
such familiar declarations constitute merely one more
illustration of our traditional habit of "having it both
ways." It is always possible to have it both ways, in case
the two ways do not come into conflict; but where they

do conflict in fact and in theory, the sensible man must make his choice. The labor question will never be advanced towards solution by proclaiming it to be a matter of antagonistic individual rights. It involves a fundamental public interest—the interest which a democracy must necessarily take in the economic welfare of its own citizens; and this interest demands that a decisive preference be shown for labor organization. The labor unions are perfectly right in believing that all who are not for them are against them, and that a state which was really "impartial" would be adopting a hypocritical method of retarding the laborer from improving his condition. The unions deserve frank and loyal support; and until they obtain it, they will remain, as they are at present, merely a class organization for the purpose of extorting from the political and economic authorities the maximum of their special interests.

The labor unions should be granted their justifiable demand for recognition, partly because only by means of recognition can an effective fight be made against their unjustifiable demands. The large American employer of labor, and the whole official politico-economic system, is placed upon the defensive by a refusal frankly to prefer unionism. Union labor is allowed to conquer at the sword's point a preferential treatment which should never have been refused; and the consequence is that its victory, so far as it is victorious, is that of an industrial faction. The large employer and the state are disqualified from insisting on their essential and justifiable interests in respect to the organization of labor, because they have rejected a demand essential to the interest of the laborer. They have remained consistently on the defensive; and a merely defensive policy in warfare is a losing policy. Every battle the unions win is a clear gain. Every fight which they lose means merely a temporary suspension of their aggressive tactics. They lose nothing by it but a part of their equipment and prestige, which can be restored by a short period of inaction and accumulation. A few generations more of this sort of warfare will leave the unions in substantial possession of the whole area of conflict; and their victory may well turn their heads so completely that its effects will be intolerable and disastrous.

The alternative policy would consist in a combination of conciliation and aggressive warfare. The spokesman of a constructive national policy in respect to the organization of labor would address the unions in some such words as these: "Yes! You are perfectly right in demanding recognition, and in demanding that none but union labor be employed in industrial work. That demand will be granted, but only on definite terms. You should not expect an employer to recognize a union which establishes conditions and rules of labor inimical to a desirable measure of individual economic distinction and independence. Your recognition, that is, must depend upon conformity to another set of conditions, imposed in the interest of efficiency and individual economic independence. In this respect you will be treated precisely as large corporations are treated. The state will recognize the kind of union which in contributing to the interest of its members contributes also to the general economic interest. On the other hand, it will not only refuse to recognize a union whose rules and methods are inimical to the public economic interest, but it will aggressively and relentlessly fight such unions. Employment will be denied to laborers who belong to unions of that character. In trades where such unions are dominant, counter-unions will be organized, and the members of these counter-unions alone will have any chance of obtaining work. In this way the organization of labor like the organization of capital may gradually be fitted into a nationalized economic system."

The conditions to which a "good" labor union ought to conform are more easily definable than the conditions to which a "good" trust ought to conform. In the first place the union should have the right to demand a minimum wage and a minimum working day. This minimum would vary, of course, in different trades, in different branches of the same trade, and in different parts of the country; and it might vary, also, at different industrial seasons. It would be reached by collective bargaining between the organizations of the employer and those of the employee. The unions would be expected to make the best terms that they could; and under the circumstances they ought to be able to make terms as good as trade conditions would allow. These agreements would be absolute within the limits contained in the bond. The employer should not have to keep on his pay-roll any man who in his opinion was not worth the money; but if any man was employed, he could not be obliged to work for less than for a certain sum. On the other hand, in return for such a privileged position the unions would have to abandon a number of rules upon which they now insist. Collective bargaining should establish the minimum amount of work and pay; but the maximum of work and pay should be left to individual arrangement. An employer should be able to give a peculiarly able or energetic laborer as much more than the minimum wage as in his opinion the man was worth; and men might be permitted to work overtime, provided they were paid for the over-time one and one half or two times as much as they were paid for an ordinary working hour. The agreement between the employers and the union should also provide for the terms upon which men would be admitted into the union. The employer, if he employed only union men, should have a right to demand that the supply of labor should not be artificially restricted, and that he could depend upon procuring as much labor as the growth of his business might require. Finally in all skilled trades there should obviously be some connection between the unions and the trade schools; and it might be in this respect that the union would enter into closest relations with the state. The state would have a manifest interest in making the instruction in these schools of the very best, and in furnishing it free to as many apprentices as the trade agreement permitted.

In all probability the general policy roughly sketched above will please one side to the labor controversy as little as it does another. Union leaders might compare the recognition received by the unions under the proposed conditions to the recognition which the bear accords to the man whom he hugs to death. They would probably prefer for the time being their existing situation—that of being on the high road to the conquest of almost unconditional submission. On the other hand, the large employers believe with such fine heroism of conviction in the principle of competition among their employees that they dislike to surrender the advantages of industrial freedom to the oppressive exigencies of collective bargaining. In assuming such an attitude both sides would be right from their own class points of view. The plan is not intended to further the selfish interest of either the employer or the union. Whatever merits it has consist in its possible ability to promote the national economic interest in a progressively improving general standard of living, in a higher standard of individual work, and in a general efficiency of labor. The existing system has succeeded hitherto in effecting a progressive improvement in the standard of living, but the less said the better about its effects upon labor-quality and labor-efficiency. In the long run it looks as if the improvement in the standard of living would be brought to an end by the accompanying inefficiency of labor. At any rate the employers are now fighting for an illusory benefit; and because they are fighting for an illusory benefit they are enabling the unions to associate all sorts of dangerous conditions with their probable victory. The proposed plan does not do away with the necessity of a fight. The relations between labor and capital are such that only by fighting can they reach a better understanding. But it asks the employers to consider carefully what they are fighting for, and whether they will not lose far more from a defeat than they will gain from a successful defense. And it asks the unions to consider whether a victory, gained at the expense of labor-efficiency, will not deprive them of its fruits. Let the unions fight for something they can keep; and let the employers fight for something they will not be sure to lose.

The writer is fully aware of the many difficulties attending the practical application of any such policy. Indeed it could not be worked at all, unless the spirit and methods of collective bargaining between the employers and the labor organizations were very much improved. The consequences of a strike would be extremely serious for both of the disputants and for the consumers. If disagreements terminating in strikes and lock-outs remained as numerous as they are at present, there would result both for the producer and consumer a condition of perilous and perhaps intolerable uncertitude. But this objection, although serious, is not unanswerable. The surest way in which a condition of possible warfare, founded on a genuine conflict of interest, can be permanently alleviated is to make its consequences increasingly dangerous. When the risks become very dangerous, reasonable men do not fight except on grave provocation or for some essential purpose. Such would be the result in any industry, both the employers and laborers of which were completely organized. Collective bargaining would, under such circumstances, assume a serious character; and no open fight would ensue except under exceptional conditions and in the event of grave and essential differences of opinion. Moreover, the state could make them still less likely to happen by a policy of discreet supervision. Through the passage of a law similar to the one recently enacted in the Dominion of Canada, it could assure the employers and the public that no strike would take place until every effort had been made to reach a fair understanding or a compromise; and in case a strike did result, public opinion could form a just estimate of the merits of the controversy. In an atmosphere of discussion and publicity really prudent employers and labor organizations would fight very rarely, if at all; and this result would be the more certain, provided a consensus of public opinion existed as the extent to which the clashing interests of the two combatants could be fitted into the public interest. It should be clearly understood that the public interest demanded, on the one hand, a standard of living for the laborer as high as the industrial conditions would permit, and on the other a standard of labor-efficiency equivalent to the cost of labor and an opportunity for the exceptional individual laborer to improve on that standard in his own interest. The whole purpose of such an organization would be the attempt to develop efficient labor and prosperous laboring men, whereas the tendency of the existing organization is to associate the prosperity of the laboring man with the inefficiency of labor. The employers are usually fighting not for the purpose of developing good labor, but for the purpose of taking advantage of poor, weak, and dependent laborers.

How far the central, state, and municipal governments could go in aiding such a method of organization, is a question that can only be indefinitely answered. The legislatures of many American states and municipalities

have already shown a disposition to aid the labor unions
in certain indirect ways. They seek by the passage of
eight-hour and prevailing rate-of-wages laws to give an
official sanction to the claims of the unions, and they do
so without making any attempt to promote the parallel
public interest in an increasing efficiency of labor. But
these eight-hour and other similar laws are frequently
being declared unconstitutional by the state courts, and
for the supposed benefit of individual liberty. Without
venturing on the disputed ground as to whether such
decisions are legitimate or illegitimate interpretations of
constitutional provisions, it need only be said in this,
as in other instances, that the courts are as much influenced in such decisions by a political theory as they
are by any fidelity to the fundamental law, and that if
they continue indefinitely in the same course, they are
likely to get into trouble. I shall, however, as usual,
merely evade constitutional obstacles, the full seriousness of which none but an expert lawyer is competent
to appraise. Both the state and the municipal governments ought, just in so far as they have the power, to
give preference to union labor, but wherever possible
they should also not hesitate to discriminate between
"good" and "bad" unions. Such a discrimination would
be beyond the courage of existing governments, but a
mild hope may be entertained that it would not be beyond the courage of the regenerated governments. The
adoption of some such attitude by the municipal and
state authorities might encourage employers to make
the fight along the same lines; and wherever an employer did make the fight along those lines, he should,
in his turn, receive all possible support. In the long run
the state could hardly impose by law such a method
of labor organization upon the industrial fabric. Unless
the employers themselves came to realize just what they
could fight for with some chance of success, and with

the best general results if successful, the state could not force him into a better understanding of the relation between their own and the public interest. But in so far as any tendency existed among employers to recognize the unions, but to insist on efficiency and individual opportunity; and in so far as any tendency existed among the unions to recognize the necessary relation between an improving standard of living and the efficiency of labor—then the state and municipal governments could interfere effectively on behalf of those employers and those unions who stand for a constructive labor policy. And in case the tendency towards an organization of labor in the national interest became dominant, it might be possible to embody it in a set of definite legal institutions. But any such set of legal institutions would be impossible without an alteration in the Federal and many state constitutions; and consequently they could not in any event become a matter for precisely pressing consideration. In general, however, the labor, even more than the corporation, problem will involve grave and dubious questions of constitutional interpretation; and not much advance can be made towards its solution until, in one way or another, the hands of the legislative authority have been untied.

Before ending this very inadequate discussion of the line of advance towards a constructive organization of labor, one more aspect thereof must be briefly considered. Under the proposed plan the fate of the non-union laborer, of the industrial dependent, would hang chiefly on the extent to which the thorough-going organization of labor was carried. In so far as he was the independent industrial individual which the opponents of labor unions suppose him to be, he could have no objection to joining the union, because his individual power of efficient labor would have full opportunity of securing its reward. On the other hand, in so far as he was unable to maintain a standard of work commensurate with the prevailing rate of wages in any trade, he would, of course, be excluded from its ranks. But it should be added that in an enormous and complicated industrial body, such as that of the United States, a man who could not maintain the standard of work in one trade should be able to maintain it in another and less exacting trade. The man who could not become an efficient carpenter might do for a hod-carrier; and a man who found hod-carrying too hard on his shoulders might be able to dig in the ground. There would be a sufficient variety of work for all kinds of industrial workers; while at the same time there would be a systematic attempt to prevent the poorer and less competent laborers from competing with those of a higher grade and hindering the latter's economic amelioration. Such a result would be successful only in so far as the unions were in full possession of the field; but if the unions secure full possession even of part of the field, the tendency will be towards an ever completer monopoly. The fewer trades into which the non-union laborers were crowded would drift into an intolerable condition, which would make unionizing almost compulsory.

If all, or almost all, the industrial labor of the country came to be organized in the manner proposed, the only important kind of non-union laborer left in the country would be agricultural; and such a result could be regarded with equanimity by an economic statesman. The existing system works very badly in respect to supplying the farmer with necessary labor. In every period of prosperity the tendency is for agricultural laborers to rush off to the towns and cities for the sake of the larger wages and the less monotonous life; and when a period of depression follows, their competition lowers the standard of living in all organized trades. If the supply of labor were regulated, and its efficiency increased as

it would be under the proposed system, agricultural laborers would not have the opportunity of finding industrial work, except of the most inferior class, until their
competence had been proved; and it would become less
fluid and unstable than it is at present. Moreover, farm
labor is, on the whole, much more wholesome for economically dependent and mechanically untrained men
than labor in towns or cities. They are more likely under
such conditions to maintain a higher moral standard.
If they can be kept upon the farm until or unless they
are prepared for a higher class of work, it will be the
greatest possible boon to American farming. Agricul-
ture suffers in this country peculiarly from the scarcity,
the instability, and the high cost of labor; and unless it
becomes more abundant, less fluid, and more efficient
compared to its cost, intensive farming, as practiced in
Europe, will scarcely be possible in the United States.
Neither should it be forgotten that the least intelligent
and trained grade of labor would be more prosperous
on the farms than in the cities, because of the lower cost
of living in an agricultural region. Their scale of wages
would be determined in general by that of the lowest
grade of industrial labor, but their expenses would be
materially smaller.

That the organization of labor herewith suggested
would prove to be any ultimate solution of the labor
problem, is wholly improbable. It would constitute, like
the proposed system of corporate regulation, at best
a transitional method of reaching some very different
method of labor-training, distribution, and compensation; and what that method might be, is at present
merely a matter of speculation. The proposed reorganization of labor, like the proposed system of institutional
reform, and like the proposed constructive regulation
of large industrial corporations, simply takes advantage
of those tendencies in our current methods which look

in a formative direction; and in so far as these several tendencies prevail, they will severally supplement and strengthen one another. The more independent, responsible, and vigorous political authority will be the readier to seek some formative solution of the problem of the distribution of wealth and that of the organization of labor. Just in so far as the combination of capital continues to be economically necessary, it is bound to be accompanied by the completer unionizing of labor. Just in so far as capital continues to combine, the state is bound to appropriate the fruits of its monopoly for public purposes. Just in so far as the corporations become the lessees of special franchises from the state, pressure can be brought to bear in favor of the more systematic and more stimulating organization of labor; and finally, just in so far as labor was systematically organized, public opinion would demand a vigorous and responsible concentration of political and economic power, in order to maintain a proper balance. An organic unity binds the three aspects of the system together; and in so far as a constructive tendency becomes powerful in any one region, it will tend by its own force to introduce constructive methods of organization into the other divisions of the economic, political, and social body.

Such are the outlines of a national policy which seeks to do away with existing political and economic abuses, not by "purification" or purging, but by substituting for them a more positive mode of action and a more edifying habit of thought. The policy seeks to make headway towards the most far-reaching and thorough-going democratic ideals by the taking advantage of real conditions and using realistic methods. The result may wear to advanced social reformers the appearance of a weak compromise. The extreme socialist democrat will find a discrepancy between the magnificent end and the paltry means. "Why seek to justify," he will ask, "a series of proposals for economic and institutional reform most of which have already been tried in Europe for purely practical reasons, why seek to justify such a humble scheme of reconstruction by such a remote and lofty purpose?" It might remind him of a New Yorker who started for the North Pole, but proposed to get there by the Subway. The justification for the association of such a realistic practical programme with an end which is nothing short of moral and social improvement of mankind, is to be found, however, by the manner in which even the foregoing proposals will be regarded by the average American democrat. He will regard them as in meaning and effect subversive of the established political and economic system of the country; and he would be right. The American people could never adopt the accompanying programme, moderate as it is from the point of view of its ultimate object, without unsettling some of their most settled habits and transforming many of their most cherished ideas. It would mean for the American people the gradual assumption of a new responsibility, the adoption of a new outlook, the beginning of a new life. It would, consequently, be radical and revolutionary in implication, even though it were modest in its expectation of immediate achievement; and the fact that it is revolutionary in implication, but moderate in its practical proposals, is precisely the justification for my description of it as a constructive national programme. It is national just because it seeks to realize the purpose of American national association without undermining or overthrowing the living conditions of American national integrity.

13.

Conclusions: The Individual and the National Purposes

I   Individual vs. Collective Education

Hitherto we have been discussing the ways in which existing American economic and political methods and institutions should be modified in order to make towards the realization of the national democratic ideal. In course of this discussion, it has been taken for granted that the American people under competent and responsible leadership could deliberately plan a policy of individual and social improvement, and that with the means at their collective disposal they could make headway towards its realization. These means consisted, of course, precisely in their whole outfit of political, economic, and social institutions; and the implication has been, consequently, that human nature can be raised to a higher level by an improvement in institutions and laws. The majority of my readers will probably have thought many times that such an assumption, whatever its truth, has been overworked. Admitting that some institutions may be better than others, it must also be admitted that human nature is composed of most rebellious material, and that the extent to which it can be modified by social and political institutions of any kind is, at best, extremely small. Such critics may, consequently, have reached the conclusion that the proposed system of reconstruction, even if desirable, would not accomplish anything really effectual or decisive towards the fulfillment of the American national Promise.

It is no doubt true that out of the preceding chapters many sentences could be selected which apparently imply a credulous faith in the possibility of improving human nature by law. It is also true that I have not ventured more than to touch upon a possible institutional reformation, which, in so far as it was successful in its purpose, would improve human nature by the most effectual of all means—that is, by improving the methods whereby men and women are bred. But if I have erred in attaching or appearing to attach too much efficacy to legal and institutional reforms, the error or its appearance was scarcely separable from an analytic reconstruction of a sufficient democratic ideal. Democracy must stand or fall on a platform of possible human perfectibility. If human nature cannot be improved by institutions, democracy is at best a more than usually safe form of political organization; and the only interesting inquiry about its future would be: How long will it continue to work? But if it is to work better as well as merely longer, it must have some leavening effect on human nature; and the sincere democrat is obliged to assume the power of the leaven. For him the practical questions are: How can the improvement best be brought about? and, How much may it amount to?

As a matter of fact, Americans have always had the liveliest and completest faith in the process of individual and social improvement and in accepting the assumption, I am merely adhering to the deepest and most influential of American traditions. The better American has continually been seeking to "uplift" himself, his neighbors, and his compatriots. But he has usually favored means of improvement very different from those suggested hereinbefore. The real vehicle of improvement is education. It is by education that the American is trained for such democracy as he possesses; and it is by better education that he proposes to better his democracy. Men are uplifted by education much more surely than they are by any tinkering with laws and institutions, because the work of education leavens the actual social substance. It helps to give the individual himself those qualities without which no institutions, however excellent, are of any use, and with which even bad institutions and laws can be made vehicles of grace.

The American faith in education has been characterized as a superstition; and superstitious in some respects it unquestionably is. But its superstitious tendency is not exhibited so much in respect to the ordinary process of primary, secondary, and higher education. Not even an American can over-emphasize the importance of proper teaching during youth; and the only wonder is that the money so freely lavished on it does not produce better results. Americans are superstitious in respect to education, rather because of the social "uplift" which they expect to achieve by so-called educational means. The credulity of the socialist in expecting to alter human nature by merely institutional and legal changes is at least equaled by the credulity of the good American in proposing to evangelize the individual by the reading of books and by the expenditure of money and words. Back of it all is the underlying assumption that the American nation by taking thought can add a cubit to its stature,—an absolute confidence in the power of the idea to create its own object and in the efficacy of good intentions.

Do we lack culture? We will "make it hum" by founding a new university in Chicago. Is American art neglected and impoverished? We will enrich it by organizing art departments in our colleges, and popularize it by lectures with lantern slides and associations for the study of its history. Is New York City ugly? Perhaps, but if we could only get the authorities to appropriate a few hundred millions for its beautification, we could make it look like a combination of Athens, Florence, and Paris. Is it desirable for the American citizen to be something of a hero? I will encourage heroes by establishing a fund whereby they shall be rewarded in cash. War is hell, is it? I will work for the abolition of hell by calling a convention and passing a resolution denouncing its iniquities. I will build at the Hague a Palace of Peace which shall be a standing rebuke to the War Lords of Europe. Here, in America, some of us have more money than we need and more good will. We will spend the money in order to establish the reign of the good, the beautiful, and the true.

This faith in a combination of good intentions, organization, words, and money is not confined to women's clubs or to societies of amiable enthusiasts. In the state of mind which it expresses can be detected the powerful influence which American women exert over American men; but its guiding faith and illusion are shared by the most hard-headed and practical of Americans. The very men who have made their personal successes by a rigorous application of the rule that business is business—the very men who in their own careers have exhibited a shrewd and vivid sense of the realities of politics and trade; it is these men who have most faith in the practical, moral, and social power of the Subsidized Word. The most real thing which they carry over from the region of business into the region of moral and intellectual ideals is apparently their bank accounts. The fruits of their hard work and their business ability are to be applied to the purpose of "uplifting" their fellow-countrymen. A certain number of figures written on a check and signed by a familiar name, what may it not accomplish? Some years ago at the opening exercises of the Carnegie Institute in Pittsburg, Mr. Andrew Carnegie burst into an impassioned and mystical vision of the miraculously constitutive power of first mortgage steel bonds. From his point of view and from that of the average American there is scarcely anything which the combination of abundant resources and good intentions may not accomplish.

The tradition of seeking to cross the gulf between American practice and the American ideal by means of education or the Subsidized Word is not be dismissed with a sneer. The gulf cannot be crossed without the assistance of some sort of educational discipline; and that discipline depends partly on a new exercise of the "money power" now safely reposing in the strong boxes of professional millionaires. There need be no fundamental objection taken to the national faith in the power of good intentions and re-distributed wealth. That faith is the immediate and necessary issue of the logic of our national moral situation. It should be, as it is, innocent and absolute; and if it does not remain innocent and absolute, the Promise of American Life can scarcely be fulfilled.

A faith may, however, be innocent and absolute without being inexperienced and credulous. The American faith in education is by way of being credulous and superstitious, not because it seeks individual and social amelioration by what may be called an educational process, but because the proposed means of education are too conscious, too direct, and too superficial. Let it be admitted that in any one decade the amount which can be accomplished towards individual and social amelioration by means of economic and political reorganization is comparatively small; but it is certainly as large as that which can be accomplished by subsidizing individual good intentions. Heroism is not to be encouraged by cash prizes any more than is genius; and a man's friends should not be obliged to prove that he is a hero in order that he may reap every appropriate reward. A hero officially conscious of his heroism is a mutilated hero. In the same way art cannot become a power in a community unless many of its members are possessed of a native and innocent love of beautiful things; and the extent to which such a possession can be acquired by any one or two generations of traditionally inartistic people is extremely small. Its acquisition depends not so much upon direct conscious effort, as upon the growing ability to discriminate between what is good and what is bad in their own native art. It is a matter of the training and appreciation of American artists, rather than the cultivation of art. Illustrations to the same effect might be multiplied. The popular interest in the Higher Education has not served to make Americans attach much importance to the advice of the highly educated man. He is less of a practical power in the United States than he is in any European country; and this fact is in itself a sufficient commentary on the reality of the American faith in education. The fact is, of course, that the American tendency to disbelieve in the fulfillment of their national Promise by means of politically, economically, and socially reconstructive work has forced them into the alternative of attaching excessive importance to subsidized good intentions. They want to be "uplifted," and they want to "uplift" other people; but they will not use their social and political institutions for the purpose, because those institutions are assumed to be essentially satisfactory. The "uplifting" must be a matter of individual, or of unofficial associated effort; and the only available means are words and subsidies.

There is, however, a sense in which it is really true that the American national Promise can be fulfilled only by education; and this aspect of our desirable national education can, perhaps, best be understood by seeking its analogue in the training of the individual. An individual's education consists primarily in the discipline which he undergoes to fit him both for fruitful association with his fellows and for his own special work. Important as both the liberal and the technical aspect of this preliminary training is, it constitutes merely the beginning of a man's education. Its object is or should be to prepare him both in his will and in his intelligence to make a thoroughly illuminating use of his experience in life. His experience,—as a man of business, a husband, a father, a citizen, a friend,—has been made real to him, not merely by the zest with which he has sought it and the sincerity with which he has accepted it, but by the disinterested intelligence which he has brought to its understanding. An educational discipline which has contributed in that way to the reality of a man's experience has done as much for him as education can do; and an educational discipline which has failed to make any such contribution has failed of its essential purpose. The experience of other people acquired at second hand has little value,—except, perhaps, as a means of livelihood,—unless it really illuminates a man's personal experience.

Usually a man's ability to profit by his own personal experience depends upon the sincerity and the intelligence which he brings to his own particular occupation. The rule is not universal, because some men are, of course, born with much higher intellectual gifts than others; and to such men may be given an insight which has little foundation in any genuine personal experience. It remains true, none the less, for the great majority of men, that they gather an edifying understanding of men and things just in so far as they patiently and resolutely stick to the performance of some special and (for the most part) congenial task. Their education in life must be grounded in the persistent attempt to realize in action some kind of a purpose—a purpose usually connected with the occupation whereby they live. In the pursuit of that purpose they will be continually making experiments—opening up new lines of work, establishing new relations with other men, and taking more or less serious risks. Each of these experiments offers them an opportunity both for personal discipline and for increasing personal insight. If a man is capable of becoming wise, he will gradually be able to infer from this increasing mass of personal experience, the extent to which or the conditions under which he is capable of realizing his purpose; and his insight into the particular realities of his own life will bring with it some kind of a general philosophy—some sort of a disposition and method of appraisal of men, their actions, and their surroundings. Wherever a man reaches such a level of intelligence, he will be an educated man, even though his particular job has been that of a mechanic. On the other hand, a man who fails to make his particular task in life the substantial support of a genuine experience remains essentially an unenlightened man.

National education in its deeper aspect does not differ from individual education. Its efficiency ultimately depends upon the ability of the national consciousness to draw illuminating inferences from the course of the national experience; and its power to draw such inferences must depend upon the persistent and disinterested sincerity with which the attempt is made to realize the national purpose—the democratic ideal of individual and social improvement. So far as Americans are true to that purpose, all the different aspects of their national experience will assume meaning and momentum; while in so far as they are false thereto, no amount of "education" will ever be really edifying. The fundamental process of American education consists and must continue to consist precisely in the risks and experiments which the American nation will make in the service of its national ideal. If the American people balk at the sacrifices demanded by their experiments, or if they attach finality to any particular experiment in the distribution of political, economic, and social power, they will remain morally and intellectually at the bottom of a well, out of which they will never be "uplifted" by the most extravagant subsidizing of good intentions and noble words.

The sort of institutional and economic reorganization suggested in the preceding chapters is not, consequently, to be conceived merely as a more or less dubious proposal to improve human nature by laws. It is to be conceived as (possibly) the next step in the realization of a necessary collective purpose. Its deeper significance does not consist in the results which it may accomplish by way of immediate improvement. Such results may be worth having; but at best they will create almost as many difficulties as they remove. Far more important than any practical benefits would be the indication it afforded of national good faith. It would mean that the American nation was beginning to educate itself up to its own necessary standards. It would imply a popular realization that our first experiment in democratic political and economic organization was founded partly on temporary conditions and partly on erroneous theories. A new experiment must consequently be made; and the great value of this new experiment would derive from the implied intellectual and moral emancipation. Its trial would demand both the sacrifice of many cherished interests, habits, and traditions for the sake of remaining true to a more fundamental responsibility and a much larger infusion of disinterested motives into the economic and political system. Thus the sincere definite decision that the experiment was necessary, would probably do more for American moral and social amelioration than would the specific measures actually adopted and tried. Public opinion can never be brought to approve any effectual measures, until it is converted to a constructive and consequently to a really educational theory of democracy.

Back of the problem of educating the individual lies the problem of collective education. On the one hand, if the nation is rendered incapable of understanding its own experience by the habit of dealing insincerely with its national purpose, the individual, just in so far as he himself has become highly educated, tends to be divided from his country and his fellow-countrymen. On the other hand, just in so far as a people is sincerely seeking the fulfillment of its national Promise, individuals of all kinds will find their most edifying individual opportunities in serving their country. In aiding the accomplishment of the collective purpose by means of increasingly constructive experiments, they will be increasing the scope and power of their own individual action. The opportunities, which during the past few years the reformers have enjoyed to make their personal lives more interesting, would be nothing compared to the opportunities for all sorts of stirring and responsible work, which would be demanded of individuals under the proposed plan of political and economic reorganization. The American nation would be more disinterestedly and sincerely fulfilling its collective purpose, partly because its more distinguished individuals had been called upon to place at the service of their country a higher degree of energy, ability, and unselfish devotion. If a nation, that is, is recreant to its deeper purpose, individuals, so far as they are well educated, are educated away from the prevailing national habits and traditions; whereas when a nation is sincerely attempting to meet its collective responsibility, the better individuals are inevitably educated into active participation in the collective task.

The reader may now be prepared to understand why the American faith in education has the appearance of being credulous and superstitious. The good average American usually wishes to accomplish exclusively by individual education a result which must be partly accomplished by national education. The nation, like the individual, must go to school; and the national school is not a lecture hall or a library. Its schooling consists chiefly in experimental collective action aimed at the realization of the collective purpose. If the action is not aimed at the collective purpose, a nation will learn little even from its successes. If its action is aimed at the collective purpose, it may learn much even from its mistakes. No process of merely individual education can accomplish the work of collective education, because the nation is so much more than a group of individuals. Individuals can be "uplifted" without "uplifting" the nation, because the nation has an individuality of its own, which cannot be increased without the consciousness of collective responsibilities and the collective official attempt to redeem them. The processes of national and individual education should, of course, parallel and supplement each other. The individual can do much to aid national education by the single-minded and intelligent realization of his own specific purposes; but all individual successes will have little more than an individual interest unless they frequently contribute to the work of national construction. The nation can do much to aid individual education; but the best aid within its power is to offer to the individual a really formative and inspiring opportunity for public service. The whole round of superficial educational machinery—books, subsidies, resolutions, lectures, congresses—may be of the highest value, provided they are used to digest and popularize the results of a genuine individual and national educational experience, but when they are used, as so often at present, merely as a substitute for well-purposed individual and national action, they are precisely equivalent to an attempt to fly in a vacuum.

That the direct practical value of a reform movement may be equaled or surpassed by its indirect educational value is a sufficiently familiar idea—an idea admirably expressed ten years ago by Mr. John Jay Chapman in the chapter on "Education" in his "Causes and Consequences." But the idea in its familiar form is vitiated, because the educational effect of reform is usually conceived as exclusively individual. Its effect *must*, indeed, be considered wholly as an individual matter, just so long as reform is interpreted merely as a process of purification. From that point of view the collective purpose has already been fulfilled as far as it can be fulfilled by collective organization, and the *only* remaining method of social amelioration is that of the self-improvement of its constituent members. As President Nicholas Murray Butler of Columbia says, in his "True and False Democracy": "We must not lose sight of the fact that the corporate or collective responsibility which it (socialism) would substitute for individual initiative is only such corporate or collective responsibility as a group of these very same individuals could exercise. Therefore, socialism is primarily an attempt to overcome man's individual imperfections by adding them together, in the hope that they will cancel each other." But what is all organization but an attempt, not to overcome man's individual imperfections by adding them together, so much as to make use of many men's varying individual abilities by giving each a sufficient sphere of exercise? While all men are imperfect, they are not all imperfect to the same extent. Some have more courage, more ability, more insight, and more training than others; and an efficient organization can accomplish more than can a mere collection of individuals, precisely because it may represent a standard of performance far above that of the average individual. Its merit is simply that of putting the collective power of the group at the service of its ablest members; and the ablest members of the group will never attain to an individual responsibility commensurate with their powers, until they are enabled to work efficiently towards the redemption of the collective responsibility. The nation gives individuality an increased scope and meaning by offering individuals a chance for effective service, such as they could never attain under a system of collective irresponsibility. Thus under a system of collective responsibility the process of social improvement is absolutely identified with that of individual improvement. The antithesis is not between nationalism and individualism, but between an individualism which is indiscriminate, and an individualism which is selective.

II Conditions of Individual Emancipation

It is, then, essential to recognize that the individual American will never obtain a sufficiently complete chance of self-expression, until the American nation has earnestly undertaken and measurably achieved the realization of its collective purpose. As we shall see presently, the cure for this individual sterility lies partly with the individual himself or rather with the man who proposes to become an individual; and under any plan of economic or social organization, the man who proposes to become an individual is a condition of national as well as individual improvement. It is none the less true that any success in the achievement of the national purpose will contribute positively to the liberation of the individual, both by diminishing his temptations, improving his opportunities, and by enveloping him in an invigorating rather than an enervating moral and intellectual atmosphere.

It is the economic individualism of our existing national system which inflicts the most serious damage
on American individuality; and American individual
achievement in politics and science and the arts will
remain partially impoverished as long as our fellow-
countrymen neglect or refuse systematically to regulate
the distribution of wealth in the national interest. I am
aware, of course, that the prevailing American conviction is absolutely contradictory of the foregoing assertion. Americans have always associated individual
freedom with the unlimited popular enjoyment of all
available economic opportunities. Yet it would be far
more true to say that the popular enjoyment of practically unrestricted economic opportunities is precisely
the condition which makes for individual bondage.
Neither does the bondage which such a system fastens
upon the individual exist only in the case of those individuals who are victimized by the pressure of unlimited
economic competition. Such victims exist, of course,
in large numbers, and they will come to exist in still
larger number hereafter; but hitherto, at least, the characteristic vice of the American system has not been the
bondage imposed upon its victims. Much more insidious has been the bondage imposed upon the conquerors and their camp-followers. A man's individuality is
as much compromised by success under the conditions
imposed by such a system as it is by failure. His actual
occupation may tend to make his individuality real and
fruitful; but the quality of the work is determined by a
merely acquisitive motive, and the man himself thereby
usually debarred from obtaining any edifying personal
independence or any peculiar personal distinction. Different as American business men are one from another
in temperament, circumstances, and habits, they have a
way of becoming fundamentally very much alike. Their
individualities are forced into a common mold, because

the ultimate measure of the value of their work is the same, and is nothing but its results in cash.

Consider for a moment what individuality and individual independence really mean. A genuine individual must at least possess some special quality which distinguishes him from other people, which unifies the successive phases and the various aspects of his own life and which results in personal moral freedom. In what way and to what extent does the existing economic system contribute to the creation of such genuine individuals? At its best it asks of every man who engages in a business occupation that he make as much money as he can, and the only conditions it imposes on this pursuit of money are those contained in the law of the land and a certain conventional moral code. The pursuit of money is to arouse a man to individual activity, and law and custom determine the conditions to which the activity must conform. The man does not become an individual merely by obeying the written and unwritten laws. He becomes an individual because the desire to make money releases his energy and intensifies his personal initiative. The kind of individuals created by such an economic system are not distinguished one from another by any special purpose. They are distinguished by the energy and success whereby the common purpose of making money is accompanied and followed. Some men show more enterprise and ingenuity in devising ways of making money than others, or they show more vigor and zeal in taking advantage of the ordinary methods. These men are the kind of individuals which the existing economic system tends to encourage; and critics of the existing system are denounced, because of the disastrous effect upon individual initiative which would result from restricting individual economic freedom.

But why should a man become an individual because he does what everybody else does, only with more energy and success? The individuality so acquired is merely that of one particle in a mass of similar particles. Some particles are bigger than others and livelier; but from a sufficient distance they all look alike; and in substance and meaning they all are alike. Their individual activity and history do not make them less alike. It merely makes them bigger or smaller, livelier or more inert. Their distinction from their fellows is quantitative; the unity of their various phases a matter of repetition; their independence wholly comparative. Such men are associated with their fellows in the pursuit of a common purpose, and they are divided from their fellows by the energy and success with which that purpose is pursued. On the other hand, a condition favorable to genuine individuality would be one in which men were divided from one another by special purposes, and reunited in so far as these individual purposes were excellently and successfully achieved.

The truth is that individuality cannot be dissociated from the pursuit of a disinterested object. It is a moral and intellectual quality, and it must be realized by moral and intellectual means. A man achieves individual distinction, not by the enterprise and vigor with which he accumulates money, but by the zeal and the skill with which he pursues an exclusive interest—an interest usually, but not necessarily, connected with his means of livelihood. The purpose to which he is devoted—such, for instance, as that of painting or of running a railroad—is not exclusive in the sense of being unique. But it becomes exclusive for the individual who adopts it, because of the single-minded and disinterested manner in which it is pursued. A man makes the purpose exclusive for himself by the spirit and method in which the work is done; and just in proportion as the work is thoroughly well done, a man's individuality begins to take substance and form. His individual quality does not depend merely on the display of superior enterprise and energy, although, of course, he may and should be as enterprising and as energetic as he can. It depends upon the actual excellence of the work in every respect,—an excellence which can best be achieved by the absorbing and exclusive pursuit of that alone. A man's individuality is projected into his work. He does not stop when he has earned enough money, and he does not cease his improvements when they cease to bring in an immediate return. He is identified with his job, and by means of that identification his individuality becomes constructive. His achievement, just because of its excellence, has an inevitable and an unequivocal social value. The quality of a man's work reunites him with his fellows. He may have been in appearance just as selfish as a man who spends most of his time in making money, but if his work has been thoroughly well done, he will, in making himself an individual, have made an essential contribution to national fulfillment.

Of course, a great deal of very excellent work is accomplished under the existing economic system; and by means of such work many a man becomes more or less of an individual. But in so far as such is the case, it is the work which individualizes and not the unrestricted competitive pursuit of money. In so far as the economic motive prevails, individuality is not developed; it is stifled. The man whose motive is that of money-making will not make the work any more excellent than is demanded by the largest possible returns; and frequently the largest possible returns are to be obtained by indifferent work or by work which has absolutely no social value. The ordinary mercenary purpose always compels a man to stop at a certain point, and consider something else than the excellence of his achievement. It does not make the individual independent, except in so far as independence is merely a matter of cash in the bank;

and for every individual on whom it bestows excessive pecuniary independence, there are many more who are by that very circumstance denied any sort of liberation. Even pecuniary independence is usually purchased at the price of moral and intellectual bondage. Such genuine individuality as can be detected in the existing social system is achieved not because of the prevailing money-making motive, but in spite thereof.

The ordinary answer to such criticisms is that while the existing system may have many faults, it certainly has proved an efficient means of releasing individual energy; whereas the exercise of a positive national responsibility for the wholesome distribution of wealth would tend to deprive the individual of any sufficient initiative. The claim is that the money-making motive is the only one which will really arouse the great majority of men, and to weaken it would be to rob the whole economic system of its momentum. Just what validity this claim may have cannot, with our present experience, be definitely settled. That to deprive individuals suddenly of the opportunities they have so long enjoyed would be disastrous may be fully admitted. It may also be admitted that any immediate and drastic attempt to substitute for the present system a national regulation of the distribution of wealth or a national responsibility for the management even of monopolies or semi-monopolies would break down and would do little to promote either individual or social welfare. But to conclude from any such admissions that a systematic policy of promoting individual and national amelioration should be abandoned is wholly unnecessary. That the existing system has certain practical advantages, and is a fair expression of the average moral standards of to-day is not only its chief merit, but also its chief and inexcusable defect. What a democratic nation must do is not to accept human nature as it is, but to move in the direction of its improvement. The question it must answer is: How can it contribute to the increase of American individuality? The defender of the existing system must be able to show either (1) that it does contribute to the increase of American individuality; or that (2) whatever its limitations, the substitution of some better system is impossible.

Of course, a great many defenders of the existing system will unequivocally declare that it does contribute effectually to the increase of individuality, and it is this defense which is most dangerous, because it is due, not to any candid consideration of the facts, but to unreasoning popular prejudice and personal self-justification. The existing system contributes to the increase of individuality only in case individuality is deprived of all serious moral and intellectual meaning. In order to sustain their assertion they must define individuality, not as a living ideal, but as the psychological condition produced by any individual action. In the light of such a definition every action performed by an individual would contribute to individuality; and, conversely, every action performed by the state, which conceivably could be left to individuals, would diminish individuality. Such a conception derives from the early nineteenth century principles of an essential opposition between the state and the individual; and it is a deduction from the common conception of democracy as nothing but a finished political organization in which the popular will prevails. As applied in the traditional American system this conception of individuality has resulted in the differentiation of an abundance of raw individual material, but the raw material has been systematically encouraged to persist only on condition that it remained undeveloped. Properly speaking, it has not encouraged individualism at all. Individuality is necessarily based on genuine discrimination. It has encouraged particularism. While the particles have been roused into activity, they all remain dominated by substantially the same forces of attraction and repulsion. But in order that one of the particles may fulfill the promise of a really separate existence, he must pursue some special interest of his own. In that way he begins to realize his individuality, and in realizing his individuality he is coming to occupy a special niche in the national structure. A national structure which encourages individuality as opposed to mere particularity is one which creates innumerable special niches, adapted to all degrees and kinds of individual development. The individual becomes a nation in miniature, but devoted to the loyal realization of a purpose peculiar to himself. The nation becomes an enlarged individual whose special purpose is that of human amelioration, and in whose life every individual should find some particular but essential function.

It surely cannot be seriously claimed that the improvement of the existing economic organization for the sake of contributing to the increase of such genuine individuals is impossible. If genuine individuality depends upon the pursuit of an exclusive interest, promoted most certainly and completely by a disinterested motive, it must be encouraged by enabling men so far as possible to work from disinterested motives. Doubtless this is a difficult, but it is not an impossible task. It cannot be completely achieved until the whole basis of economic competition is changed. At present men compete chiefly for the purpose of securing the most money to spend or to accumulate. They must in the end compete chiefly for the purpose of excelling in the quality of their work that of other men engaged in a similar occupation. And there are assuredly certain ways in which the state can diminish the undesirable competition and encourage the desirable competition.

The several economic reforms suggested in the preceding chapter would, so far as they could be successfully introduced, promote more disinterested economic work. These reforms would not, of course, entirely do away with the influence of selfish acquisitive motives in the economic field, because such motives must remain powerful as long as private property continues to have a public economic function. But they would at least diminish the number of cases in which the influence of the mercenary motive made against rather than for excellence of work. The system which most encourages mere cupidity is one which affords too many opportunities for making "easy money," and our American system has, of course, been peculiarly prolific of such opportunities. As long as individuals are allowed to accumulate money from mines, urban real estate, municipal franchises, or semi-monopolies of any kind, just to that extent will the economic system of the country be poisoned, and its general efficiency impaired. Men will inevitably seek to make money in the easiest possible way, and as long as such easy ways exist fewer individuals will accept cordially the necessity of earning their living by the sheer excellence of achievement. On the other hand, in case such opportunities of making money without earning it can be eliminated, there will be a much closer correspondence than there is at present between the excellence of the work and the reward it would bring. Such a correspondence would, of course, be far from exact. In all petty kinds of business innumerable opportunities would still exist of earning more money either by disregarding the quality of the work or sometimes by actually lowering it. But at any rate it would be work which would earn money, and not speculation or assiduous repose in an easy chair.

In the same way, just in so far as industry became organized under national control for the public benefit, there would be a much closer correspondence between the quality of the work and the amount of the reward.

In a well-managed corporation a man is promoted because he does good work, and has shown himself capable of assuming larger responsibilities and exercising
more power. His promotion brings with it a larger salary, and the chance of obtaining a larger salary doubtless has much to do with the excellence of the work; but
at all events a man is not rewarded for doing bad work
or for doing no work at all. The successful employee of
a corporation has not become disinterested in his motives. Presumably he will not do any more work than
will contribute to his personal advancement; and if the
standard of achievement in his office is at all relaxed,
he will not be kept up to the mark by an exclusive and
disinterested devotion to the work itself. Still, under
such conditions a man might well become better than
his own motives. Whenever the work itself was really
interesting, he might become absorbed in it by the very
momentum of his habitual occupation, and this would
be particularly the case provided his work assumed a
technical character. In that case he would have to live up
to the standard, not merely of an office, but of a trade,
a profession, a craft, an art, or a science; and if those
technical standards were properly exacting, he would
be kept up to the level of his best work by a motive
which had almost become disinterested. He could not
fall below the standard, even though he derived no personal profit from striving to live up to it, because the
traditions and the honor of his craft would not let him.

The proposed economic policy of reform, in so far
as it were successful, would also tend to stimulate labor
to more efficiency, and to diminish its grievances. The
state would be lending assistance to the effort of the
workingman to raise his standard of living, and to restrict the demoralizing effect of competition among laborers who cannot afford to make a stand on behalf of
their own interest. It should, consequently, increase the

amount of economic independence enjoyed by the average laborer, diminish his "class consciousness" by doing away with his class grievances, and intensify his importance to himself as an individual. It would in every way help to make the individual workingman more of an individual. His class interest would be promoted by the nation in so far as such promotion was possible, and could be adjusted to a general policy of national economic construction. His individual interest would be left in his own charge; but he would have much more favorable opportunities of redeeming the charge by the excellence of his individual work than he has under the existing system. His condition would doubtless still remain in certain respects unsatisfactory, for the purpose of a democratic nation must remain unfulfilled just in so far as the national organization of labor does not enable all men to compete on approximately equal terms for all careers. But a substantial step would be made towards its improvement, and the road marked, perhaps, for still further advance.

Again, however, must the reader be warned that the important thing is the constructive purpose, and not the means proposed for its realization. Whenever the attempt at its realization is made, it is probable that other and unforeseen measures will be found necessary; and even if a specific policy proposed were successfully tried, this would constitute merely an advance towards the ultimate end. The ultimate end is the complete emancipation of the individual, and that result depends upon his complete disinterestedness. He must become interested exclusively in the excellence of his work; and he can never become disinterestedly interested in his work as long as heavy responsibilities and high achievements are supposed to be rewarded by increased pay. The effort equitably to adjust compensation to earnings is ultimately not only impossible, but undesirable, because it necessarily would foul the whole economic organization—so far as its efficiency depended on a generous rivalry among individuals. The only way in which work can be made entirely disinterested is to adjust its compensation to the needs of a normal and wholesome human life.

Any substantial progress towards the attainment of complete individual disinterestedness is far beyond the reach of contemporary collective effort, but such disinterestedness should be clearly recognized as the economic condition both of the highest fulfillment which democracy can bestow upon the individual and of a thoroughly wholesome democratic organization. Says Mr. John Jay Chapman in the chapter on "Democracy," in his "Causes and Consequences": "It is thought that the peculiar merit of democracy lies in this: that it gives every man a chance to pursue his own ends. The reverse is true. The merit lies in the assumption imposed upon every man that he shall serve his fellow-men. . . . The concentration of every man on his own interests has been the danger and not the safety of democracy, for democracy contemplates that every man shall think first of the state and next of himself. . . . Democracy assumes perfection in human nature." But men will always continue chiefly to pursue their own private ends as long as those ends are recognized by the official national ideal as worthy of perpetuation and encouragement. If it be true that democracy is based upon the assumption that every man shall serve his fellow-men, the organization of democracy should be gradually adapted to that assumption. The majority of men cannot be made disinterested for life by exhortation, by religious services, by any expenditure of subsidized words, or even by a grave and manifest public need. They can be made permanently unselfish only by being helped to become disinterested in their individual purposes, and how can they be disinterested except in a few little spots as long as their daily occupation consists of money seeking and spending in conformity with a few written and unwritten rules? In the complete democracy a man must in some way be made to serve the nation in the very act of contributing to his own individual fulfillment. Not until his personal action is dictated by disinterested motives can there be any such harmony between private and public interests. To ask an individual citizen continually to sacrifice his recognized private interest to the welfare of his countrymen is to make an impossible demand, and yet just such a continual sacrifice is apparently required of an individual in a democratic state. The only entirely satisfactory solution of the difficulty is offered by the systematic authoritative transformation of the private interest of the individual into a disinterested devotion to a special object.

American public opinion has not as yet begun to understand the relation between the process of national education by means of a patient attempt to realize the national purpose and the corresponding process of individual emancipation and growth. It still believes that democracy is a happy device for evading collective responsibilities by passing them on to the individual; and as long as this belief continues to prevail, the first necessity of American educational advance is the arousing of the American intellectual conscience. Behind the tradition of national irresponsibility is the still deeper tradition of intellectual insincerity in political matters. Americans are almost as much afraid of consistent and radical political thinking as are the English, and with nothing like as much justification. Jefferson offered them a seductive example of triumphant intellectual dishonesty, and of the sacrifice of theory to practice, whenever such a sacrifice was convenient. Jefferson's example has been warmly approved by many subsequent intellectual leaders. Before Emerson and after, mere consistency has been stigmatized as the preoccupation of petty minds; and our American superiority to the necessity of making ideas square with practice, or one idea with another, has been considered as an exhibition of remarkable political common sense. The light-headed Frenchmen really believed in their ideas, and fell thereby into a shocking abyss of anarchy and fratricidal bloodshed, whereas we have avoided any similar fate by preaching a "noble national theory" and then practicing it just as far as it suited our interests or was not too costly in time and money. No doubt, we also have had our domestic difficulties, and were obliged to shed a good deal of American blood, because we resolutely refused to believe that human servitude was not entirely compatible with the loftiest type of democracy; but then, the Civil War might have been avoided if the Abolitionists had not erroneously insisted on being consistent. The way to escape similar trouble in the future is to go on preaching ideality, and to leave its realization wholly to the individual. We can then be "uplifted" by the words, while the resulting deeds cannot do us, as individuals, any harm. We can continue to celebrate our "noble national theory" and preserve our perfect democratic system until the end of time without making any of the individual sacrifices or taking any of the collective risks, inseparable from a systematic attempt to make our words good.

The foregoing state of mind is the great obstacle to the American national advance; and its exposure and uprooting is the primary need of American education. In agitating against the traditional disregard of our full national responsibility, a critic will do well to dispense with the caution proper to the consideration of specific practical problems. A radical theory does not demand in the interest of consistency an equally radical action. It only demands a sincere attempt to push the application of the theory as far as conditions will permit, and the employment of means sufficient probably to accomplish the immediate purpose. But in the endeavor to establish and popularize his theory, a radical critic cannot afford any similar concessions. His own opinions can become established only by the displacement of the traditional opinions; and the way to displace a traditional error is not to be compromising and conciliatory, but to be as uncompromising and as irritating as one's abilities and one's vision of the truth will permit. The critic in his capacity as agitator is living in a state of war with his opponents; and the ethics of warfare are not the ethics of statesmanship. Public opinion can be reconciled to a constructive national programme only by the agitation of what is from the traditional standpoint a body of revolutionary ideas.

In vigorously agitating such a body of revolutionary ideas, the critic would be doing more than performing a desirable public service. He would be vindicating his own individual intellectual interest. The integrity and energy of American intellectual life has been impaired for generations by the tradition of national irresponsibility. Such irresponsibility necessarily implies a sacrifice of individual intellectual and moral interests to individual and popular economic interests. It could not persist except by virtue of intellectual and moral conformity. The American intellectual habit has on the whole been just about as vigorous and independent as that of the domestic animals. The freedom of opinion of which we boast has consisted for the most part in uttering acceptable commonplaces with as much defiant conviction as if we were uttering the most daring and sublimest heresies. In making this parade of the uniform of intellectual independence, the American is not consciously insincere. He is prepared to do battle for his convictions, but his really fundamental convictions he shares with everybody else. His differences with his fellow-countrymen are those of interest and detail. When he breaks into a vehement proclamation of his faith, he is much like a bull, who has broken out of his stall, and goes snorting around the barnyard, tossing everybody within reach of his horns. A bull so employed might well consider that he was offering the world a fine display of aggressive individuality, whereas he had in truth been behaving after the manner of all bulls from the dawn of domestication. No doubt he is quite capable of being a dangerous customer, in case he can reach anybody with his horns; but on the other hand how meekly can he be led back into the stall by the simple device of attaching a ring to his nose. His individuality always has a tender spot, situated in much the same neighborhood as his personal economic interests. If this tender spot is merely irritated, it will make him rage; but when seized with a firm grip he loses all his defiance and becomes as aggressive an individual as a good milch cow.

The American intellectual interest demands, consequently, a different sort of assertion from the American economic or political interest. Economically and politically the need is for constructive regulation, implying the imposition of certain fruitful limitations upon traditional individual freedom. But the national intellectual development demands above all individual emancipation. American intelligence has still to issue its Declaration of Independence. It has still to proclaim that in a democratic system the intelligence has a discipline, an interest, and a will of its own, and that this special discipline and interest call for a new conception both of individual and of national development. For the time being the freedom which Americans need is the freedom of thought. The energy they need is the energy of thought. The moral unity they need cannot be obtained without intensity and integrity of thought.

III   Attempts at Individual Emancipation

Americans believe, of course, that they enjoy perfect freedom of opinion, and so they do in form. There is no legal encouragement of any one set of opinions. There is no legal discouragement of another set of opinions. They have denied intellectual freedom to themselves by methods very much more insidious than those employed by a despotic government. A national tradition has been established which prevents individuals from desiring freedom; and if they should desire and obtain it, they are prevented from using it. The freedom of American speech and thought has not been essentially different from the freedom of speech which a group of prisoners might enjoy during the term of their imprisonment. The prisoners could, of course, think and talk much as they pleased, but there was nobody but themselves to hear; and in the absence both of an adequate material, discipline, and audience, both the words and thoughts were without avail. The truth is, of course, that intellectual individuality and independence were sacrificed for the benefit of social homogeneity and the quickest possible development of American economic opportunities; and in this way a vital relation has been established for Americans between the assertion of intellectual independence or moral individuality and the adoption of a nationalized economic and political system.

During the Middle Period American individual intelligence did, indeed, struggle gallantly to attain freedom. The intellectual ferment at that time was more active and more general than it is to-day. During the three decades before the war, a remarkable outbreak of heresy occurred all over the East and middle West. Every convention of American life was questioned, except those unconscious conventions of feeling and thought which pervaded the intellectual and moral atmosphere. The

Abolitionist agitation was the one practical political result of this ferment, but many of these free-thinkers wished to emancipate the whites as well as the blacks. They fearlessly challenged substantially all the established institutions of society. The institutions of marriage and the state fared frequently as ill as did property and the church. Radical, however, as they were in thought, they were by no means revolutionary in action. The several brands of heresy differed too completely one from another to be melted into a single political agitation and programme. The need for action spent itself in the formation of socialistic communities of the most varied kind, the great majority of which were soon either disbanded or transformed. But whatever its limitations the ferment was symptomatic of a genuine revolt of the American spirit against the oppressive servitude of the individual intelligence to the social will, demanded by the popular democratic system and tradition.

The revolt, however, with all the sincere enthusiasm it inspired, was condemned to sterility. It accomplished nothing and could accomplish nothing for society, because it sought by individual or unofficial associated action results which demanded official collective action; and it accomplished little even for the individual, because it was not the outcome of any fruitful individual discipline. The emancipated idea was usually defined by seeking the opposite of the conventional idea. Individuality was considered to be a matter of being somehow and anyhow different from other people. There was no authentic intellectual discipline behind the agitation. The pioneer democrat with all his limitations embodied the only living national body of opinion, and he remained untainted by this outburst of heresy. He deprived it of all vitality by depriving its separate explosions, Abolitionism excepted, of all serious attention. He crushed it far more effectually by indifference than he would have by persecution. When the shock of the Civil War aroused Americans to a realization of the unpleasant political realities sometimes associated with the neglect of a "noble national theory," the ferment subsided without leaving behind so much as a loaf of good white bread.

For practical political purposes it exhausted itself, as I have said, in Abolitionism, and in that movement both its strength and weakness are writ plain. Its revolt on behalf of emancipation was courageous and sincere. The patriotism which inspired it recognized the need of justifying its protestantism by a better conception of democracy. But the heresy was as incoherent and as credulous as the antithetic orthodoxy. It sought to accomplish an intellectual revolution without organizing either an army or an armament—just as the pioneer democrat expected to convert untutored enthusiasm into acceptable technical work, and a popular political and economic atomism into a substantially socialized community. In its meaning and effect, consequently, the revolt was merely negative and anti-national. It served a constructive democratic purpose only by the expensive and dubious means of instigating a Civil War. If any of the other heresies of the period, as well as Abolitionism, had developed into an effective popular agitation, they could have obtained a similar success only by means of incurring a similar danger. The intellectual ideals of the movement were not educational, and its declaration of intellectual independence issued in as sterile a programme for the Republic of American thought as did the Declaration of Political Independence for the American national democracy.

In truth all these mid-century American heretics were not heretics at all in relation to really stupefying and perverting American tradition. They were sturdily rebellious against all manner of respectable methods, ideas, and institutions, but none of them dreamed of protest-

ing against the real enemy of American intellectual independence. They never dreamed of associating the moral
and intellectual emancipation of the individual with the
conscious fulfillment of the American national purpose
and with the patient and open-eyed individual and social
discipline thereby demanded. They all shared the illusion of the pioneers that somehow a special Providential
design was effective on behalf of the American people,
which permitted them as individuals and as a society
to achieve their purposes by virtue of good intentions,
exuberant enthusiasm, and enlightened selfishness. The
New World and the new American idea had released
them from the bonds in which less fortunate Europeans
were entangled. Those bonds were not to be considered
as the terms under which excellent individual and social purposes were necessarily to be achieved. They were
bad habits, which the dead past had imposed upon the
inhabitants of the Old World, and from which Americans could be emancipated by virtue of their abundant
faith in human nature and the boundless natural opportunities of the new continent.

Thus the American national ideal of the Middle Period was essentially geographical. The popular thinkers
of that day were hypnotized by the reiterated suggestion of a new American world. Their fellow-countrymen
had obtained and were apparently making good use of
a wholly unprecedented amount of political and economic freedom; and they jumped to the conclusion that
the different disciplinary methods which limited both
individual and social action in Europe were unnecessary. Just as the Jacksonian Democracy had finally vin-
dicated American political independence by doing away
with the remnants of our earlier political colonialism,
so American moral and intellectual independence demanded a similar vindication. This geographical protestantism was in a measure provoked, if not justified, by

the habit of colonial dependence upon Europe in matters of opinion, which so many well-educated Americans of that period continued to cherish. But it was based upon the illusion that the economic and social conditions of the Middle Period, which favored temporarily a mixture of faith and irresponsibility, freedom and formlessness, would persist and could be translated into terms of individual intellectual and moral discipline. In truth, it was, of course, a great mistake to conceive Americanism as intellectually and morally a species of Newer-Worldliness. A national intellectual ideal did not divide us from Europe any more than did a national political ideal. In both cases national independence had no meaning except in a system of international, intellectual, moral, and political relations. American national independence was to be won, not by means of a perverse opposition to European intellectual and moral influence, but by a positive and a thorough-going devotion to our own national democratic ideal.

The national intellectual ideal could afford to be as indifferent to the sources of American intellectual life as the American political ideal was to the sources of American citizenship. The important thing was and is, not where our citizens or our special disciplinary ideals come from, but what use we make of them. Just as economic and political Americanism has been broad enough and vital enough to make a place in the American social economy for the hordes of European immigrants with their many diverse national characteristics, so the intellectual basis of Americanism must be broad enough to include and vigorous enough to assimilate the special ideals and means of discipline necessary to every kind of intellectual or moral excellence. The technical ideals and standards which the typical American of the Middle Period instinctively under-valued are neither American nor European. They are merely the special forms whereby the several kinds of intellectual eminence are to be obtained. They belong to the nature of the craft. Those forms and standards were never sufficiently naturalized in America during the Colonial Period, because the economic and social conditions of the time did not justify such naturalization. The appropriate occasion for the transfer was postponed until after American political independence had been secured; and when occasion did not arise, the naturalness of the transfer was perverted and obscured by political preconceptions.

The foregoing considerations throw a new light upon the mistake made by the American heretics of the Middle Period. In so far as their assertion of American intellectual independence was negative, it should not have been a protest against "feudalism," social classification, social and individual discipline, approved technical methods, or any of those social forms and intellectual standards which so many Americans vaguely believed to be exclusively European. It should have been a protest against a sterile and demoralizing Americanism—the Americanism of national irresponsibility and indiscriminate individualism. The bondage from which Americans needed, and still need, emancipation is not from Europe, but from the evasions, the incoherence, the impatience, and the easy-going conformity of their own intellectual and moral traditions. We do not have to cross the Atlantic in order to hunt for the enemies of American national independence and fulfillment. They sit at our political fireside and toast their feet on its coals. They poison American patriotic feeling until it becomes, not a leaven, but a kind of national gelatine. They enshrine this American democratic ideal in a temple of canting words which serves merely as a cover for a religion of personal profit. American moral and intellectual emancipation can be achieved only by a victory over the ideas, the conditions, and the standards which

make Americanism tantamount to collective irresponsibility and to the moral and intellectual subordination of
the individual to a commonplace popular average.

The heretics of the Middle Period were not cowardly,
but they were intellectually irresponsible, undisciplined,
and inexperienced. Sharing, as they did, most of the
deeper illusions of their time, they did not vindicate
their own individual intellectual independence, and they
contributed little or nothing to American national intellectual independence. With the exception of a few of
the men of letters who had inherited a formative local
tradition, their own personal careers were examples not
of gradual individual fulfillment, but at best of repetition and at worst of degeneracy. Like the most brilliant
contemporary Whig politicians, such as Henry Clay
and Daniel Webster, their intellectual individuality was
gradually cheapened by the manner in which it was expressed; and it is this fact which makes the case of Lincoln, both as a politician and a thinker, so unique and so
extraordinary. The one public man of this period who
did impose upon himself a patient and a severe intellectual and moral discipline, who really did seek the excellent use of his own proper tools, is the man who preëmi-
nently attained national intellectual and moral stature.
The difference in social value between Lincoln and, say,
William Lloyd Garrison can be measured by the difference in moral and intellectual discipline to which each
of these men submitted. Lincoln sedulously turned to
account every intellectual and moral opportunity which
his life afforded. Garrison's impatient temper and unbalanced mind made him the enthusiastic advocate of
a few distorted and limited ideas. The consequence was
that Garrison, although apparently an arch-heretic, was
in reality the victim of the sterile American convention
which makes willful enthusiasm, energy, and good intentions a sufficient substitute for necessary individual

and collective training. Lincoln, on the other hand, was in his whole moral and intellectual make-up a living protest against the aggressive, irresponsible, and merely practical Americanism of his day; while at the same time in the greatness of his love and understanding he never allowed his distinction to divide him from his fellow-countrymen. His was the unconscious and constructive heresy which looked in the direction of national intellectual independence and national moral union and good faith.

IV   Means of Individual Emancipation

We are now in a position to define more clearly just how the American individual can assert his independence, and how in asserting his independence he can contribute to American national fulfillment. He cannot make any effective advance towards national fulfillment merely by educating himself and his fellow-countrymen as individuals to a higher intellectual and moral level, because an essential condition of really edifying individual education is the gradual process of collective education by means of collective action and formative collective discipline. On the other hand, this task of collective education is far from being complete in itself. It necessarily makes far greater demands upon the individual than does a system of comparative collective irresponsibility. It implies the selection of peculiarly competent, energetic, and responsible individuals to perform the peculiarly difficult and exacting parts in a socially constructive drama; and it implies, as a necessary condition of such leadership, a progressively higher standard of individual training and achievement, unofficial as well as official, throughout the whole community. The process of educating men of moral and intellectual stature sufficient for the performance of important constructive work cannot be disentangled from the process of national fulfillment by means of intelligent collective action. American nationality will never be fulfilled except under the leadership of such men; and the American nation will never obtain the necessary leadership unless it seeks seriously the redemption of its national responsibility.

Such being the situation in general, how can the duty and the opportunity of the individual at the present time best be defined? Is he obliged to sit down and wait until the edifying, economic, political, and social transformation has taken place? Or can he by his own immediate behavior do something effectual both to obtain individual emancipation and to accelerate the desirable process of social reconstruction? This question has already been partially answered by the better American individual; and it is, I believe, being answered in the right way. The means which he is taking to reach a more desirable condition of individual independence, and inferentially to add a little something to the process of national fulfillment, consist primarily and chiefly in a thoroughly zealous and competent performance of his own particular job; and in taking this means of emancipation and fulfillment he is both building better and destroying better than he knows.

The last generation of Americans has taken a better method of asserting their individual independence than that practiced by the heretics of the Middle Period. Those who were able to gain leadership in business and politics sought to justify their success by building up elaborate industrial and political organizations which gave themselves and their successors peculiar individual opportunities. On the other hand, the men of more specifically intellectual interests tacitly abandoned the Newer-Worldliness of their predecessors and began unconsciously but intelligently to seek the attainment of some excellence in the performance of their own special work. In almost every case they discovered that the first step in the acquisition of the better standards of achievement was to go abroad. If their interests were scholarly or scientific, they were likely to matriculate at one of the German universities for the sake of studying under some eminent specialist. If they were painters, sculptors, or architects, they flocked to Paris, as the best available source of technical instruction in the arts. Wherever the better schools were supposed to be, there the American pupils gathered; and the consequence was during the last quarter of the nineteenth century a steady and considerable improvement in the standard of special work and the American schools of special discipline. In this way there was domesticated a necessary condition and vehicle of the liberation and assertion of American individuality.

A similar transformation has been taking place in the technical aspects of American industry. In this field the individual has not been obliged to make his own opportunities to the same extent as in business, politics, and the arts. The opportunities were made for him by the industrial development of the country. Efficient special work soon became absolutely necessary in the various branches of manufacture, in mining, and in the business of transportation; and in the beginning it was frequently necessary to import from abroad expert specialists. The technical schools of the country were wholly inadequate to supply the demand either for the quantity or the quality of special work needed. When, for instance, the construction of railroads first began, the only good engineering school in the country was West Point, and the consequence was that many army officers became railroad engineers. But little by little the amount and the standard of technical instruction improved; while at the same time the greater industrial organizations themselves trained their younger employees with ever increasing efficiency. Of late years even farming has become an occupation in which special knowledge is supposed to have certain advantages. In every kind of practical work specialization, founded on a more or less arduous course of preparation, is coming to prevail; and in this way individuals, possessing the advantages of the necessary gifts and discipline, are obtaining definite and stimulating opportunities for personal efficiency and independence.

It would be a grave mistake to conclude, however, that the battle is already won—that the individual has already obtained in any department of practical or intellectual work sufficient personal independence or sufficiently edifying opportunities. The comparatively zealous and competent individual performer does not, of course, feel so much of an alien in his social surroundings as he did a generation or two ago. He can usually obtain a certain independence of position, a certain amount of intelligent and formative appreciation, and a sufficiently substantial measure of reward. But he has still much to contend against in his social, economic, and intellectual environment. His independence is precarious. In some cases it is won with too little effort. In other cases it can be maintained only at too great a cost. His rewards, if substantial, can be obtained as readily by sacrificing the integrity of his work as by remaining faithful thereto. The society in which he lives, and which gives him his encouragement and support, has the limitations of a clique. Its encouragement is too conscious; its support too willful. Beyond a certain point its encouragement becomes indeed relaxing rather than stimulating, and the aspiring individual is placed in the situation of having most to fear from the inhabitants of his own household. His intellectual and moral environment is lukewarm. He is encouraged to be an individual, but not too much of an individual. He is encouraged to do good work, but not to do always and uncompromisingly his best work. He is trusted, but he is not trusted enough. He believes in himself, but he does not believe as much in himself and in his mission as his own highest achievement demands. He is not sufficiently empowered by the idea that just in so far as he does his best work, and only his best work, he is contributing most to national as well as personal fulfillment.

What the better American individual particularly needs, then, is a completer faith in his own individual purpose and power—a clearer understanding of his own individual opportunities. He needs to do what he has been doing, only more so, and with the conviction that thereby he is becoming not less but more of an American. His patriotism, instead of being something apart from his special work, should be absolutely identified therewith, because no matter how much the eminence of his personal achievement may temporarily divide him from his fellow-countrymen, he is, by attaining to such an eminence, helping in the most effectual possible way to build the only fitting habitation for a sincere democracy. He is to make his contribution to individual improvement primarily by making himself more of an individual. The individual as well as the nation must be educated and "uplifted" chiefly by what the individual can do for himself. Education, like charity, should begin at home.

An individual can, then, best serve the cause of American individuality by effectually accomplishing his own individual emancipation—that is, by doing his own special work with ability, energy, disinterestedness, and excellence. The scope of the individual's opportunities at any one time will depend largely upon society, but whatever they amount to, the individual has no excuse for not making the most of them. Before he can be of any service to his fellows, he must mold himself into the condition and habit of being a good instrument. On this point there can be no compromise. Every American who has the opportunity of doing faithful and fearless work, and who proves faithless to it, belongs to the perfect type of the individual anti-democrat. By cheapening his own personality he has cheapened the one constituent of the national life over which he can exercise most effectual control; and thereafter, no matter how superficially patriotic and well-intentioned he may be, his words and his actions are tainted and are in some measure corrupting in their social effect.

A question will, however, immediately arise as to the nature of this desirable individual excellence. It is all very well to say that a man should do his work competently, faithfully, and fearlessly, but how are we to define the standard of excellence? When a man is seeking to do his best, how shall he go about it? Success in any one of these individual pursuits demands that the individual make some sort of a personal impression. He must seek according to the nature of the occupation a more or less numerous popular following. The excellence of a painter's work does not count unless he can find at least a small group of patrons who will admire and buy it. The most competent architect can do nothing for himself or for other people unless he attracts clients who will build his paper houses. The playwright needs even a larger following. If his plays are to be produced, he must manage to amuse and to interest thousands of people. And the politician most of all depends upon a numerous and faithful body of admirers. Of what avail would his independence and competence be in case there were nobody to accept his leadership? It is not enough, consequently, to assert that the individual must emancipate himself by means of excellent and disinterested work. His emancipation has no meaning, his career as an individual no power, except with the support of a larger or smaller following. Admitting the desirability of excellent work, what kind of workmanlike excellence will make the individual not merely independent and incorruptible, but powerful? In what way and to what end shall he use the instrument, which he is to forge and temper, for his own individual benefit and hence for that of society?

These questions involve a real difficulty, and before we are through they must assuredly be answered; but they are raised at the present stage of the discussion for the purpose of explicitly putting them aside rather than for the purpose of answering them. The individual instruments must assuredly be forged and tempered to some good use, but before we discuss their employment let us be certain of the instruments themselves. Whatever that employment may be and however much of a following its attainment may demand, the instrument must at any rate be thoroughly well made, and in the beginning it is necessary to insist upon merely instrumental excellence, because the American habit and tradition is to estimate excellence almost entirely by results. If the individual will only obtain his following, there need be no close scrutiny as to his methods. The admirable architect is he who designs an admirably large number of buildings. The admirable playwright is he who by whatever means makes the hearts of his numerous audiences palpitate. The admirable politician is he who succeeds somehow or anyhow in gaining the largest area of popular confidence. This tradition is the most insidious enemy of American individual independence and fulfillment. Instead of declaring, as most Americans do, that a man may, if he can, do good work, but that he *must* create a following, we should declare that a man may, if he can, obtain a following, but that he *must* do good work. When he has done good work, he may not have done all that is required of him; but if he fails to do good work, nothing else counts. The individual democrat who has had the chance and who has failed in that essential respect is an individual sham, no matter how much of a shadow his figure casts upon the social landscape.

The good work which for his own benefit the individual is required to do, means primarily technically competent work. The man who has thoroughly mastered the knowledge and the craft essential to his own special occupation is by way of being the well-forged and well-tempered instrument. Little by little there have been developed in relation to all the liberal arts and occupations certain tested and approved technical methods. The individual who proposes to occupy himself with any one of these arts must first master the foundation of knowledge, of formal traditions, and of manual practice upon which the superstructure is based. The danger that a part of this fund of technical knowledge and practice may at any particular time be superannuated must be admitted; but the validity of the general rule is not affected thereby. The most useful and effective dissenters are those who were in the beginning children of the Faith. The individual who is too weak to assert himself with the help of an established technical tradition is assuredly too weak to assert himself without it. The authoritative technical tradition associated with any one of the arts of civilization is merely the net result of the accumulated experience of mankind in a given region. That experience may or may not have been exhaustive or adequately defined; but in any event its mastery by the individual is merely a matter of personal and social economy. It helps to prevent the individual from identifying his whole personal career with unnecessary mistakes. It provides him with the most natural and serviceable vehicle for self-expression. It supplies him with a language which reduces to the lowest possible terms the inevitable chances of misunderstanding. It is society's nearest approach to an authentic standard in relation to the liberal arts and occupations; and just so far as it is authentic society is justified in imposing it on the individual.

The perfect type of authoritative technical methods are those which prevail among scientific men in respect to scientific work. No scientist as such has anything to gain by the use of inferior methods or by the production of inferior work. There is only one standard for all scientific investigators—the highest standard; and so far as a man falls below that standard his inferiority is immediately reflected in his reputation. Some scientists make, of course, small contributions to the increase of knowledge, and some make comparatively large contributions; but just in so far as a man makes any contribution at all, it is a real contribution, and nothing makes it real but the fact that it is recognized. In the Hall of Science exhibitors do not get their work hung upon the line because it tickles the public taste, or because it is "uplifting," or because the jury is kindly and wishes to give the exhibitor a chance to earn a little second-rate reputation. The same standard is applied to everybody, and the jury is incorruptible. The exhibit is nothing if not true, or by way of becoming or being recognized as true.

A technical standard in any one of the liberal or practical arts cannot be applied as rigorously as can the standard of scientific truth, because the standard itself is not so authentic. In all these arts many differences of opinion exist among masters as to the methods and forms which should be authoritative; and in so far as such is the case, the individual must be allowed to make many apparently arbitrary personal choices. The fact that a man has such choices to make is the circumstance which most clearly distinguishes the practice of an art from that of a science, but this circumstance, instead of being

an excuse for technical irresponsibility or mere eclecti-
cism, should, on the contrary, stimulate the individual
more completely to justify his choice. In his work he is
fighting the battle not merely of his own personal career,
but of a method, of a style, of an idea, or of an ideal.
The practice of the several arts need not suffer from diversity of standard, provided the several separate standards are themselves incorruptible. In all the arts—and
by the arts I mean all disinterested and liberal practical
occupations—the difficulty is not that sufficiently authoritative standards do not exist, but that they are not
applied. The standard which is applied is merely that
of the good-enough. The juries are either too kindly or
too lax or too much corrupted by the nature of their
own work. They are prevented from being incorruptible about the work of other people by a sub-conscious
apprehension of the fate of their own performances—in
case similar standards were applied to themselves. Just
in so far as the second-rate performer is allowed to
acquire any standing, he inevitably enters into a conspiracy with his fellows to discourage exhibitions of
genuine and considerable excellence, and, of course, to
a certain extent he succeeds. By the waste which he encourages of good human appreciation, by the confusion
which he introduces into the popular critical standards,
he helps to effect a popular discrimination against any
genuine superiority of achievement.

Individual independence and fulfillment is conditioned on the technical excellence of the individual's
work, because the most authentic standard is for the
time being constituted by excellence of this kind. An
authentic standard must be based either upon acquired
knowledge or an accepted ideal. Americans have no
popularly accepted ideals which are anything but an embarrassment to the aspiring individual. In the course of
time some such ideals may be domesticated—in which

case the conditions of individual excellence would be changed; but we are dealing with the present and not with the future. Under current conditions the only authentic standard must be based, not upon the social influence of the work, but upon its quality; and a standard of this kind, while it falls short of being complete, must always persist as one indispensable condition of final excellence. The whole body of acquired technical experience and practice has precisely the same authority as any other body of knowledge. The respect it demands is similar to the respect demanded by science in all its forms. In this particular case the science is neither complete nor entirely trustworthy, but it is sufficiently complete and trustworthy for the individual's purpose, and can be ignored only at the price of waste, misunderstanding, and partial inefficiency and sterility.

A standard of uncompromising technical excellence contains, however, for the purpose of this argument, a larger meaning than that which is usually attached to the phrase. A technically competent performance is ordinarily supposed to mean one which displays a high degree of manual dexterity; and a man who has acquired such a degree of dexterity is also supposed to be the victim of his own mastery. No doubt such is frequently the case; but in the present meaning the thoroughly competent individual workman becomes necessarily very much more of an individual than any man can be who is merely the creature of his own technical facility and preoccupation. I have used the word art not in the sense merely of fine art, but in the sense of all liberal and disinterested practical work; and the excellent performance of that work demands certain qualifications which are common to all the arts as well as peculiar to the methods and materials of certain particular arts and crafts. These qualifications are both moral and intellectual. They require that no one shall be admitted to the ranks of thoroughly competent performers until he is morally and intellectually, as well as scientifically and manually, equipped for excellent work, and these appropriate moral and intellectual standards should be applied as incorruptibly as those born of specific technical practices.

A craftsman whose merits do not go beyond technical facility is probably deficient in both the intellectual and moral qualities essential to good work. The rule cannot be rigorously applied, because the boundaries between high technical proficiency and some very special examples of genuine mastery are often very indistinct. Still, the majority of craftsmen who are nothing more than manually dexterous are rarely either sincere or disinterested in their personal attitude towards their occupation. They have not made themselves the sort of moral instrument which is capable of eminent achievement, and whenever unmistakable examples of such a lack of sincerity and conviction are distinguished, they should in the interest of a complete standard of special excellence meet with the same reprobation as would manual incompetence. It must not be inferred, however, that the standard of moral judgment applied to the individual in the performance of his particular work is identical with a comprehensive standard of moral practice. A man may be an acceptable individual instrument in the service of certain of the arts, even though he be in some other respects a tolerably objectionable person. A single-minded and disinterested attempt to obtain mastery of any particular occupation may in specific instances force a man to neglect certain admirable and in other relations essential qualities. He may be a faithless husband, a treacherous friend, a sturdy liar, or a professional bankrupt, without necessarily interfering with the excellent performance of his special job. A man who breaks a road to individual distinction by such questionable means may always be tainted; but he is a better public servant than would be some comparatively impeccable nonentity. It all depends on the nature and the requirements of the particular task, and the extent to which a man has really made sacrifices in order to accomplish it. There are many special jobs which absolutely demand scrupulous veracity, loyalty in a man's personal relations, or financial integrity. The politician who ruins his career in climbing down a waterspout, or the engineer who prevents his employers from trusting his judgment and conscience in money matters, cannot plead in extenuation any other sort of instrumental excellence. They have deserved to fail, because they have trifled with their job; and it may be added that serious moral delinquencies are usually grave hindrances to a man's individual efficiency.

From the intellectual point of view also technical competence means something more than manual proficiency. Just as the master must possess those moral qualities essential to the integrity of his work, so he must possess the corresponding intellectual qualities. All the liberal arts require, as a condition of mastery, a certain specific and considerable power of intelligence; and this power of intelligence is to be sharply distinguished from all-round intellectual ability. From our present point of view its only necessary application concerns the problems of a man's special occupation. Every special performer needs the power of criticising the quality and the subject-matter of his own work. Unless he has great gifts or happens to be brought up and trained under peculiarly propitious conditions, his first attempts to practice his art will necessarily be experimental. He will be sure to commit many mistakes, not merely in the choice of alternative methods and the selection of his subject-matter, but in the extent to which he personally can approve or disapprove of his own achievements. The thoroughly competent performer must at least possess the intellectual power of profiting from this experience. A candid consideration of his own experiments must guide him in the selection of the better methods, in the discrimination of the more appropriate subject-matter, in the avoidance of his own peculiar failings, and in the cultivation of his own peculiar strength. The technical career of the master is up to a certain point always a matter of growth. The technical career of the second-rate man is always a matter of degeneration or at best of repetition. The former brings with it its own salient and special form of enlightenment based upon the intellectual power to criticise his own experience and the moral power to act on his own acquired insight. To this extent he becomes more of a man by the very process of becoming more of a master.

The intellectual power required to criticise one's own experience with a formative result will of course vary considerably in different occupations. Technical mastery of the occupation of playwriting, criticism, or statesmanship, will require more specifically intellectual qualities than will be demanded by the competent musician or painter. But no matter how much intelligence may be needed, the way in which it should be used remains the same. Mere industry, aspiration, or a fluid run of ideas make as meager an equipment for a politician, a philanthropist, or a critic as they would for an architect; and absolutely the most dangerous mistake which an individual can make is that of confusing admirable intentions expressed in some inferior manner with genuine excellence of achievement. If such men succeed, they are corrupting in their influence. If they fail, they learn nothing from their failure, because they are always charging up to the public, instead of to themselves, the responsibility for their inferiority.

The conclusion is that at the present time an individual American's intentions and opinions are of less importance than his power of giving them excellent and efficient expression. What the individual can do is to make himself a better instrument for the practice of some serviceable art; and by so doing he can scarcely avoid becoming also a better instrument for the fulfillment of the American national Promise. To be sure, the American national Promise demands for its fulfillment something more than efficient and excellent individual instruments. It demands, or will eventually demand, that these individuals shall love and wish to serve their fellow-countrymen, and it will demand specifically that in the service of their fellow-countrymen, they shall reorganize their country's economic, political, and social institutions and ideas. Just how the making of competent individual instruments will of its own force assist the process of national reconstruction, we shall consider presently; but the first truth to drive home is that all political and social reorganization is a delusion, unless certain individuals, capable of edifying practical leadership, have been disciplined and trained; and such individuals must always and in some measure be a product of self-discipline. While not only admitting but proclaiming that the processes of individual and social improvement are mutually dependent, it is equally true that the initiative cannot be left to collective action. The individual must begin and carry as far as he can the work of his own emancipation; and for the present he has an excuse for being tolerably unscrupulous in so doing. By the successful assertion of his own claim to individual distinction and eminence, he is doing more to revolutionize and reconstruct the American democracy than can a regiment of professional revolutionists and reformers.

Professional socialists may cherish the notion that their battle is won as soon as they can secure a permanent popular majority in favor of a socialistic policy;

but the constructive national democrat cannot logically accept such a comfortable illusion. The action of a majority composed of the ordinary type of convinced socialists could and would in a few years do more to make socialism impossible than could be accomplished by the best and most prolonged efforts of a majority of malignant anti-socialists. The first French republicans made by their behavior another republic out of the question in France for almost sixty years; and the second republican majority did not do so very much better. When the republic came in France it was founded by men who were not theoretical democrats, but who understood that a republic was for the time being the kind of government best adapted to the national French interest. These theoretical monarchists, but practical republicans, were for the most part more able, more patriotic, and higher-minded men than the convinced republicans; and in all probability a third republic, started without their coöperation, would also have ended in a dictatorship. Any substantial advance toward social reorganization will in the same way be forced by considerations of public welfare on a majority of theoretical anti-socialists, because it is among this class that the most competent and best disciplined individuals are usually to be found. The intellectual and moral ability required, not merely to conceive, but to realize a policy of social reorganization, is far higher than the ability to carry on an ordinary democratic government. When such a standard of individual competence has been attained by a sufficient number of individuals and is applied to economic and social questions, some attempt at social reorganization is bound to be the result,—assuming, of course, the constructive relation already admitted between democracy and the social problem.

The strength and the weakness of the existing economic and social system consist, as we have observed, in the fact that it is based upon the realities of contemporary human nature. It is the issue of a time-honored tradition, an intense personal interest, and a method of life so habitual that it has become almost instinctive. It cannot be successfully attacked by any body of hostile opinion, unless such a body of opinion is based upon a more salient individual and social interest and a more intense and vital method of life. The only alternative interest capable of putting up a sufficiently vigorous attack and pushing home an occasional victory is the interest of the individual in his own personal independence and fulfillment—an interest which, as we have seen, can only issue from integrity and excellence of individual achievement. An interest of this kind is bound in its social influence to make for social reorganization, because such reorganization is in some measure a condition and accompaniment of its own self-expression; and the strength of its position and the superiority of its weapons are so decisive that they should gradually force the existing system to give way. The defenses of that system have vulnerable points; and its defenders are disunited except in one respect. They would be able to repel any attack delivered along their whole line; but their binding interest is selfish and tends under certain conditions to divide them one from another without bestowing on the divided individuals the energy of independence and self-possession. Their position can be attacked at its weaker points, not only without meeting with combined resistance, but even with the assistance of some of their theoretical allies. Many convinced supporters of the existing order are men of superior merit, who are really fighting against their own better individual interests; and they need only to taste the exhilaration of freedom in order better to understand its necessary social and economical conditions. Others, although men of inferior achievement, are patriotic and well-intentioned in feeling; and they may little by little be brought to believe that patriotism in a democracy demands the sacrifice of selfish interests and the regeneration of individual rights. Men of this stamp can be made willing prisoners by able and aggressive leaders whose achievements have given them personal authority and whose practical programme is based upon a sound knowledge of the necessary limits of immediate national action. The disinterested and competent individual is formed for constructive leadership, just as the less competent and independent, but well-intentioned, individual is formed more or less faithfully to follow on behind. Such leadership, in a country whose traditions and ideals are sincerely democratic, can scarcely go astray.

V   Constructive Individualism

The preceding section was concluded with a statement, which the majority of its readers will find extremely questionable and which assuredly demands some further explanation. Suppose it to be admitted that individual Americans do seek the increase of their individuality by competent and disinterested special work. In what way will such work and the sort of individuality thereby developed exercise a decisive influence on behalf of social amelioration? We have already expressly denied that a desire to succor their fellow-countrymen or an ideal of social reorganization is at the present time a necessary ingredient in the make-up of these formative individuals. Their individual excellence has been defined exclusively in terms of high but special technical competence; and the manner in which these varied and frequently antagonistic individual performers are to coöperate towards socially constructive results must still remain a little hazy. How are these eminent specialists, each of whom is admittedly pursuing unscrupulously his own special purpose, to be made serviceable in a coherent national democratic organization? How, indeed, are these specialists to get at the public whom they are supposed to lead? Many very competent contemporary Americans might claim that the real difficulty in relation to the social influence of the expert specialist has been sedulously evaded. The admirably competent individual cannot exercise any constructive social influence, unless he becomes popular; and the current American standards being what they are, how can an individual become popular without more or less insidious and baleful compromises? The gulf between individual excellence and effective popular influence still remains to be bridged; and until it is bridged, an essential stage is lacking in the transition from an individually formative result to one that is also socially formative.

Undoubtedly, a gulf does exist in the country between individual excellence and effective popular influence. Many excellent specialists exercise a very small amount of influence, and many individuals who exercise apparently a great deal of influence are conspicuously lacking in any kind of excellence. The responsibility for this condition is usually fastened upon the Philistine American public, which refuses to recognize genuine eminence and which showers rewards upon any second-rate performer who tickles its tastes and prejudices. But it is at least worth inquiring whether the responsibility should not be fastened, not upon the followers, but upon the supposed leaders. The American people are what the circumstances, the traditional leadership, and the interests of American life have made them. They cannot be expected to be any better than they are, until they have been sufficiently shown the way; and they cannot be blamed for being as bad as they are, until it is proved that they have deliberately rejected better leadership. No such proof has ever been offered.

Some disgruntled Americans talk as if in a democracy the path of the aspiring individual should be made peculiarly safe and easy. As soon as any young man appears whose ideals are perched a little higher than those of his neighbors, and who has acquired some knack of performance, he should apparently be immediately taken at his own valuation and loaded with rewards and opportunities. The public should take off its hat and ask him humbly to step into the limelight and show himself off for the popular edification. He should not be obliged to make himself interesting to the public. They should immediately make themselves interested in him, and bolt whatever he chooses to offer them as the very meat and wine of the mind. But surely one does not need to urge very emphatically that popularity won upon such easy terms would be demoralizing to any but very highly gifted and very cool-headed men. The American people are absolutely right in insisting that an aspirant for popular eminence shall be compelled to make himself interesting to them, and shall not be welcomed as a fountain of excellence and enlightenment until he has found some means of forcing his meat and his wine down their reluctant throats. And if the aspiring individual accepts this condition as tantamount to an order that he must haul down the flag of his own individual purpose in order to obtain popular appreciation and reward, it is he who is unworthy to lead, not they who are unworthy of being led. The problem and business of his life is precisely that of keeping his flag flying at any personal cost or sacrifice; and if his own particular purpose demands that his flying flag shall be loyally saluted, it is his own business also to see that his flag is well worthy of a popular salutation. In occasional instances these two aspects of a special performer's business may prove to be incompatible. Every real adventure must be attended by risks. Every real battle involves a certain number of casualties. But better the risk and the wounded and the dead than sham battles and unearned victories.

There is only one way in which popular standards and preferences can be improved. The men whose standards are higher must learn to express their better message in a popularly interesting manner. The people will never be converted to the appreciation of excellent special performances by argumentation, reproaches, lectures, associations, or persuasion. They will rally to the good thing, only because the good thing has been made to look good to them; and so far as individual Americans are not capable of making their good things look good to a sufficient number of their fellow-countrymen, they will on the whole deserve any neglect from which they may suffer. They themselves constitute the only efficient source of really formative education. In so far as a public is lacking, a public must be created. They must mold their followers after their own likeness—as all aspirants after the higher individual eminence have always been obliged to do.

The manner in which the result is to be brought about may be traced by considering the case of the contemporary American architect—a case which is typical because, while popular architectural preferences are inferior, the very existence of the architect depends upon his ability to please a considerable number of clients. The average well-trained architect in good standing meets this situation by designing as well as he can, consistent with the building-up an abundant and lucrative practice. There are doubtless certain things which he would not do even to get or keep a job; but on the whole it is not unfair to say that his first object is to get and to keep the job, and his second to do good work. The consequence is that, in compromising the integrity of his work, he necessarily builds his own practice upon a shifting foundation. His work belongs to the well-populated class of the good-enough. It can have little distinctive excellence; and it cannot, by its peculiar force and quality, attract a clientele. Presumably, it has the merit of satisfying prevailing tastes; but the architect, who is designing only as well as popular tastes will permit, suffers under one serious disadvantage. There are hundreds of his associates who can do it just as well; and he is necessarily obliged to face demoralizing competition. Inasmuch as it is not his work itself that counts, he is obliged to build up his clientele by other means. He is obliged to make himself personally popular, to seek social influence and private "pulls"; and his whole life becomes that of a man who is selling his personality instead of fulfilling it. His relations with his clients suffer from the same general condition. They have come to him, not because they are particularly attracted by his work and believe in it, but, as a rule, because of some accidental and arbitrary reason. His position, consequently, is lacking in independence and authority. He has not enough personal prestige as a designer to insist upon having his own way in all essential matters. He tends to become too much of an agent, employed for the purpose of carrying out another man's wishes, instead of a professional expert, whose employer trusts his judgment and leans loyally on his advice.

Take, on the other hand, the case of the exceptional architect who insists upon doing his very best. Assuming sufficient ability and training, the work of the man who does his very best is much more likely to possess some quality of individual merit, which more or less sharply distinguishes it from that of other architects. He has a monopoly of his own peculiar qualities. Such merit may not be noticed by many people; but it will probably be noticed by a few. The few who are attracted will receive a more than usually vivid impression. They will talk, and begin to create a little current of public opinion favorable to the designer. The new clients who come to him will be influenced either by their appreciation of the actual merit of the work or by this approving body of opinion. They will come, that is, because they want *him* and believe in his work. His own personal position, consequently, becomes much more independent and authoritative than is usually the case. He is much less likely to be embarrassed by ignorant and irrelevant interference. He can continue to turn out designs genuinely expressive of his own individual purpose. If he be an intelligent as well as a sincere and gifted designer, his work will, up to a certain point, grow in distinction and individuality; and as good or better examples of it become more numerous, it will attract and hold an increasing body of approving opinion. The designer will in this way have gradually created his own special public. He will be molding and informing the architectural taste and preference of his admirers. Without in any way compromising his own standards, he will have brought himself into a constructive relation with a part at least of the public, and the effect of his work will soon extend beyond the sphere of his own personal clientele. In so far as he has succeeded in popularizing a better quality of architectural work, he would be by way of strengthening the hands of all of his associates who were standing for similar ideals and methods.

It would be absurd to claim that every excellent and competent special performer who sticks incorruptibly to his individual purpose and standard can succeed in creating a special public, molded somewhat by his personal influence. The ability to succeed is not given to everybody. It cannot always be obtained by sincere industry and able and single-minded work. The qualities needed in addition to those mentioned will vary in different occupations and according to the accidental circumstances of different cases; but they are not always the qualities which a man can acquire. Men will fail who have deserved to succeed and who might have succeeded with a little more tenacity or under slightly more favorable conditions. Men who have deserved to fail will succeed because of certain collateral but partly irrelevant merits—just as an architect may succeed who is ingenious about making his clients' houses comfortable and building them cheap. In a thousand different ways an individual enterprise, conceived and conducted with faith and ability, may prove to be abortive. Moreover, the sacrifices necessary to success are usually genuine sacrifices. The architect who wishes to build up a really loyal following by really good work must deliberately reject many possible jobs; and he must frequently spend upon the accepted jobs more money than is profitable. But the foregoing is merely tantamount to saying, as we have said, that the adventure involves a real risk. A resolute, intelligent man undertakes a doubtful and difficult enterprise, not because it is sure to succeed, but because if it succeeds, it is worth the risk and the cost, and such is the case with the contemporary American adventurer. The individual independence, appreciation, and fulfillment which he secures in the event of success are assuredly worth a harder and a more dangerous fight than the one by which frequently he is confronted. In any particular case a man, as we have admitted, may put up a good fight without securing the fruits of victory, and his adventure may end, not merely in defeat, but in self-humiliation. But if any general tendency exists to shirk, or to back down, or to place the responsibility for personal ineptitude on the public, it means, not that the fight was hopeless, but that the warriors were lacking in the necessary will and ability.

The case of the statesman, the man of letters, the phi-lanthropist, or the reformer does not differ essentially from that of the architect. They may need for their particular purposes a larger or a smaller popular following, a larger or smaller amount of moral courage, and a more or less peculiar kind of intellectual efficiency; but wherever there is any bridge to be built between their own purposes and standards and those of the public, they must depend chiefly upon their own resources for its construction. The best that society can do to assist them at present is to establish good schools of preliminary instruction. For the rest it is the particular business of the exceptional individual to impose himself on the public; and the necessity he is under of creating his own following may prove to be helpful to him as his own exceptional achievements are to his followers. The fact that he is obliged to make a public instead of finding one ready-made, or instead of being able by the subsidy of a prince to dispense with one—this necessity will in the long run tend to keep his work vital and human. The danger which every peculiarly able individual specialist runs is that of overestimating the value of his own purpose and achievements, and so of establishing a false and delusive relation between his own world and the larger world of human affairs and interests. Such a danger cannot be properly checked by the conscious moral and intellectual education of the individual, because when he is filled too full of amiable intentions and ideas, he is by way of attenuating his individual impulse and power. But the individual who is forced to create his own public is forced also to make his own special work attractive to a public; and when he succeeds in accomplishing this result without hauling down his personal flag, his work tends to take on a more normal and human character.

It tends, that is, to be socially as well as individually formative. The peculiarly competent individual is obliged to accept the responsibilities of leadership with its privileges and fruits. There is no escape from the circle by which he finds himself surrounded. He cannot obtain the opportunities, the authority, and the independence which he needs for his own individual fulfillment, unless he builds up a following; and he cannot build up a secure personal following without making his peculiar performances appeal to some general human interest. The larger and more general the interest he can arouse, the more secure and the more remunerative his personal independence becomes. It by no means necessarily follows that he will increase his following by increasing the excellence of his work, or that he will not frequently find it difficult to keep his following without allowing his work to deteriorate. No formula, reconciling the individual and the popular interest, can be devised which will work automatically. The reconciliation must always remain a matter of victorious individual or national contrivance. But it is none the less true that the chance of fruitful reconciliation always exists, and in a democracy it should exist under peculiarly wholesome conditions. The essential nature of a democracy compels it to insist that individual power of all kinds, political, economic, or intellectual, shall not be perversely and irresponsibly exercised. The individual democrat is obliged no less to insist in his own interest that the responsible exercise of power shall not be considered equivalent to individual mediocrity and dependence. These two demands will often conflict; but the vitality of a democracy hangs upon its ability to keep both of them vigorous and assertive. Just in so far as individual democrats find ways of asserting their independence in the very act of redeeming their responsibility, the social body of which they form a part is marching toward the goal of human betterment.

It cannot be claimed, however, that the foregoing account of the relation between the individual and a nationalized democracy is even yet entirely satisfactory. No relation can be satisfactory which implies such a vast amount of individual suffering and defeat and such a huge waste of social and individual effort. The relation is only as satisfactory as it can be made under the circumstances. The individual cannot be immediately transformed by individual purpose and action into a consummate social type, any more than society can be immediately transformed by purposive national action into a consummate residence for the individual. In both cases amelioration is a matter of intelligent experimental contrivance based upon the nature of immediate conditions and equipped with every available resource and weapon. In both cases these experiments must be indefinitely continued, their lessons candidly learned, and the succeeding experiments based upon past failures and achievements. Throughout the whole task of experimental educational advance the different processes of individual and social amelioration will be partly opposed, partly supplementary, and partly parallel; but in so far as any genuine advance is made, the opposition should be less costly, and coöperation, if not easier, at least more remunerative.

The peculiar kind of individual self-assertion which has been outlined in the foregoing sections of this chapter has been adapted, not to perfect, but to actual moral, social, and intellectual conditions. For the present Americans must cultivate competent individual independence somewhat unscrupulously, because their peculiar democratic tradition has hitherto discouraged and under-valued a genuinely individualistic practice and ideal. In order to restore the balance, the individual must emancipate himself at a considerable sacrifice and by somewhat forcible means; and to a certain extent he must continue those sacrifices throughout the whole of his career. He must proclaim and, if able, he must assert his own leadership, but he must be always somewhat on his guard against his followers. He must always keep in mind that the very leadership which is the fruit of his mastery and the condition of his independence is also, considering the nature and disposition of his average follower, a dangerous temptation; and while he must not for that reason scorn popular success, he must always conscientiously reckon its actual cost. And just because a leader cannot wholly trust himself to his following, so the followers must always keep a sharp lookout lest their leaders be leading them astray. For the kind of leadership which we have postulated above is by its very definition and nature liable to become perverse and distracting.

But just in so far as the work of social and individual amelioration advances, the condition will be gradually created necessary to completer mutual confidence between the few exceptional leaders and the many "plain people." At present the burden of establishing any genuine means of communication rests very heavily upon the exceptionally able individual. But after a number of exceptionally able individuals have imposed their own purposes and standards and created a following, they will have made the task of their successors easier. Higher technical standards and more adequate forms of expression will have become better established. The "public" will have learned to expect and to appreciate more simple and appropriate architectural forms, more sincere and better-formed translations of life in books and on the stage, and more independent and better equipped political leadership. The "public," that is, instead of being as much satisfied as it is at present with cheap forms and standards, will be prepared to assume part of the expense of establishing better forms and methods of social intercourse. In this way a future generation of leaders may be enabled to conquer a following with a smaller individual expenditure of painful sacrifices and wasted effort. They can take for granted a generally higher technical and formal tradition, and they themselves will be freed from an over-conscious preoccupation with the methods and the mechanism of their work. Their attention will naturally be more than ever concentrated on the proper discrimination of their subject-matter; and just in so far as they are competent to create an impression or a following, that impression should be more profound and the following more loyal and more worthy of loyalty.

Above all, a substantial improvement in the purposes and standards of individual self-expression should create a more bracing intellectual atmosphere. Better standards will serve not only as guides but as weapons. In so far as they are embodied in competent performances, they are bound also to be applied in the critical condemnation of inferior work; and the critic himself will assume a much more important practical job than he now has. Criticism is a comparatively neglected art among Americans, because a sufficient number of people do not care whether and when the current practices are really good or bad. The practice of better standards and their appreciation will give the critic both a more substantial material for his work and a larger public. It will be his duty to make the American public conscious of the extent of the individual successes or failures and the reasons therefor; and in case his practice improves with that of the other arts, he should become a more important performer, not only because of his better opportunities and public, but because of his increase of individual prowess. He should not only be better equipped for the performance of his work and the creation of a public following, but he should have a more definite and resolute conviction of the importance of his own job. It is the business of the competent individual as a type to force society to recognize the meaning and the power of his own special purposes. It is the special business of the critic to make an ever larger portion of the public conscious of these expressions of individual purpose, of their relations one to another, of their limitations, and of their promises. He not only popularizes and explains for the benefit of a larger public the substance and significance of admirable special performance, but he should in a sense become the standard bearer of the whole movement.

The function of the critic hereafter will consist in part of carrying on an incessant and relentless warfare on the prevailing American intellectual insincerity. He can make little headway unless he is sustained by a large volume of less expressly controversial individual intellectual self-expression; but on the other hand, there are many serious obstructions to any advancing intellectual movement, which he should and must overthrow. In so doing he has every reason to be more unscrupulous and aggressive even than his brethren-in-arms. He must stab away at the gelatinous mass of popular indifference, sentimentality, and complacency, even though he seems quite unable to penetrate to the quick and draw blood. For the time the possibility of immediate constructive achievement in his own special field is comparatively small, and he is the less responsible for the production of any substantial effect, or the building up of any following except a handful of free lances like himself. He need only assure himself of his own competence with his own peculiar tools, his own good-humored sincerity, and his disinterestedness in the pursuit of his legitimate purposes, in order to feel fully justified in pushing his strokes home. In all serious warfare, people have to be really wounded for some good purpose; and in this particular fight there may be some chance that not only a good cause, but the very victim of the blow, may possibly be benefited by its delivery. The stabbing of a mass of public opinion into some consciousness of its active torpor, particularly when many particles of the mass are actively torpid because of admirable patriotic intentions,—that is a job which needs sharp weapons, intense personal devotion, and a positive indifference to consequences.

Yet if the American national Promise is ever to be fulfilled, a more congenial and a more interesting task will also await the critic—meaning by the word "critic" the voice of the specific intellectual interest, the lover of wisdom, the seeker of the truth. Every important human enterprise has its meaning, even though the conduct of the affair demands more than anything else a hard and inextinguishable faith. Such a faith will imply a creed; and its realizations will go astray unless the faithful are made conscious of the meaning of their performances or failures. The most essential and edifying business of the critic will always consist in building up "a pile of better thoughts," based for the most part upon the truth resident in the lives of their predecessors and contemporaries, but not without its outlook toward an immediate and even remote future. There can be nothing final about the creed unless there be something final about the action and purposes of which it is the expression. It must be constantly modified in order to define new experiences and renewed in order to meet unforeseen emergencies. But it should grow, just in so far as the enterprise itself makes new conquests and unfolds new aspects of truth. Democracy is an enterprise of this kind. It may prove to be the most important moral and social enterprise as yet undertaken by mankind; but it is still a very young enterprise, whose meaning and promise is

by no means clearly understood. It is continually meeting unforeseen emergencies and gathering an increasing experience. The fundamental duty of a critic in a
democracy is to see that the results of these experiences
are not misinterpreted and that the best interpretation
is embodied in popular doctrinal form. The critic consequently is not so much the guide as the lantern which
illuminates the path. He may not pretend to know the
only way or all the ways; but he should know as much
as can be known about the traveled road.

Men endowed with high moral gifts and capable of
exceptional moral achievements have also their special
part to play in the building of an enduring democratic
structure. In the account which has been given of the
means and conditions of democratic fulfillment, the importance of this part has been under-estimated; but the
under-estimate has been deliberate. It is very easy and in
a sense perfectly true to declare that democracy needs
for its fulfillment a peculiarly high standard of moral
behavior; and it is even more true to declare that a
democratic scheme of moral values reaches its consummate expression in the religion of human brotherhood.
Such a religion can be realized only through the loving-
kindness which individuals feel toward their fellow-men
and particularly toward their fellow-countrymen; and
it is through such feelings that the network of mutual
loyalties and responsibilities woven in a democratic nation become radiant and expansive. Whenever an individual democrat, like Abraham Lincoln, emerges, who
succeeds in offering an example of specific efficiency
united with supreme kindliness of feeling, he qualifies
as a national hero of consummate value. But—at present—a profound sense of human brotherhood is no substitute for specific efficiency. The men most possessed by
intense brotherly feelings usually fall into an error, as
Tolstoy has done, as to the way in which those feelings

can be realized. Consummate faith itself is no substitute for good work. Back of any work of moral conversion must come a long and slow process of social reorganization and individual emancipation; and not until the reorganization has been partly accomplished, and the individual released, disciplined and purified, will the soil be prepared for the crowning work of some democratic Saint Francis.

Hence, in the foregoing account of a possible democratic fulfillment, attention has been concentrated on that indispensable phase of the work which can be attained by conscious means. Until this work is measurably accomplished no evangelist can do more than convert a few men for a few years. But it has been admitted throughout that the task of individual and social regeneration must remain incomplete and impoverished, until the conviction and the feeling of human brotherhood enters into possession of the human spirit. The laborious work of individual and social fulfillment may eventually be transfigured by an outburst of enthusiasm— one which is not the expression of a mood, but which is substantially the finer flower of an achieved experience and a living tradition. If such a moment ever arrives, it will be partly the creation of some democratic evangelist—some imitator of Jesus who will reveal to men the path whereby they may enter into spiritual possession of their individual and social achievements, and immeasurably increase them by virtue of personal regeneration.

Be it understood, however, that no prophecy of any such consummate moment has been made. Something of the kind may happen, in case the American or any other democracy seeks patiently and intelligently to make good a complete and a coherent democratic ideal. For better or worse, democracy cannot be disentangled from an aspiration toward human perfectibility, and hence from the adoption of measures looking in the direction of realizing such an aspiration. It may be that the attempt will not be seriously made, or that, if it is, nothing will come of it. Mr. George Santayana concludes a chapter on "Democracy" in his "Reason in Society" with the following words: "For such excellence to grow general mankind must be notably transformed. If a noble and civilized democracy is to subsist, the common citizen must be something of a saint and something of a hero. We see, therefore, how justly flattering and profound, and at the same time how ominous, was Montesquieu's saying that the principle of democracy is virtue." The principle of democracy *is* virtue, and when we consider the condition of contemporary democracies, the saying may seem to be more ominous than flattering. But if a few hundred years from now it seems less ominous, the threat will be removed in only one way. The common citizen can become something of a saint and something of a hero, not by growing to heroic proportions in his own person, but by the sincere and enthusiastic imitation of heroes and saints, and whether or not he will ever come to such imitation will depend upon the ability of his exceptional fellow-countrymen to offer him acceptable examples of heroism and saintliness.

Index

Austria-Hungary (cont.)
unstable condition of, renders
disarmament impossible, 316;
secondary position of, in Europe, and reasons, 382

Balance of Power, development of
doctrine of, 270
Bank, National: Hamilton's
policy in creating, 48; reasons
for hostility of Jacksonian
Democrats to, 70–71; view
of, held by Republicans, 71–
72; campaign of Jackson and
his followers against, 72–73;
Whigs' failure in attempt to re-
charter, 83–84
Bank examiners, difference between Federal commissions
and, 446–447
Birth-rate, lowering of, in France,
301
Bismarck, Otto von, 9, 297,
314–315; personal career of,
303–304; unification of Germany by, 303–306; course of,
as Imperial Chancellor, 306
ff.; inheritance left to German
Empire by, in the way of overbearing attitude to domestic
and foreign opponents, 308;
provoking of Germany's two
wars by, was justifiable, 314–
315; quoted on what constitutes the real nation, 327
"Boss": the coming of the, 145–
149; character and position of
the, 150–151; dealings of, with
big corporations, 151–153;
his specialized leadership fills
a real and permanent need,
153–154; is the unofficial ruler
of his community, 153–154; is

the logical outcome of a certain conception of the democratic state, 182–183; method
proposed for destroying the,
414–418; Australian ballot
and system of direct primaries
have no injurious effect on,
418–419
Bourbon monarchy, the, 270;
cause of downfall of, 270–271
Bryan, William J., 167, 176, 185;
particular consideration of,
as a reformer, 190 ff.; special
reforms advocated by, 192–
194; incoherence in political
thinking shown by, 194–195;
policy of, toward large corporations, 440
Business man: origins of the
typical American, 131–134;
business regarded as warfare
by, 132–134; relation between
railroads and the, 134–137;
rise of, in Great Britain, and
relations with aristocracy,
288–289
Butler, Nicholas Murray, quoted,
501

Cabinet, or executive council,
suggested for governors,
415–416
Calhoun, John, a leader of the
Whigs, 82, 97–98, 102
Canada: question of coöperation
of, in establishment of a peaceful international system, 373;
desirability of greater commercial freedom between United
States and, 375; preparing the
way for closer political association, 375; lines along which
treaty between United States,

Great Britain, and, might be made, 376

Carnegie, Andrew, 249, 494

Catholic Church, as a bond between Western European states, 266; losing battle of, with political authority, 348

Central America, opportunity for improving international political conditions in, 372

Centralization: nationality and, 335–343; demand for more rather than less, because of growing centralization of American activity, 337–338; increase in, injurious to certain aspects of traditional American democracy, 340; perniciousness of prejudice against, 342–343

Chapman, John Jay, work by: cited, 501; quoted, 513

Checks and balances, system of, 40, 387; proves especially unsuitable for state governments, 397

China, questions raised concerning American foreign policy by, 380

Christianity a common bond between early European states, 266 ff.

Church, change in function of the, resulting from change in modern nations, 349

Cities: relations of state governments to, 426–427; home rule in, 427–429; as fields for economically and socially constructive experimentation, 428–429; policy of, toward public service corporations, 457–458; measures to be taken against monopolies in, 459–460

City states, Greek and mediæval, 264

Civil service reform, 175; disappointing results of, 410–411; causes of partial failure of, 411–413

Civil War: a case of a justifiable war, 314–315; as a surgical operation, 330–331

Class discrimination, 158–159, 235

Clay, Henry: Whig doctrine of, 64, 82; reason for failure of ideas of, 85–86; as a believer in compromises, 94; an example of cheapening of intellectual individuality of leaders during Middle Period, 524

Cleveland, Grover, 206–207

Colonial expansion: the principle of nationality not hostile to, 318–319; not a cause of wars, but the contrary, 319–320; incompatibility of, for European powers, with aggrandizement at home, 319–322; question of what are limits of a practicable, 322–323; is accomplishing a work without which a permanent international settlement would be impossible, 323; validity of, even for a democracy, 378–379; of the United States, 378–380

Commerce, question of control of, by state or Federal government, 431–438

Commissions: supervision of corporations by, 442–443; the objection to government by, 444–445; false principle

Executives of states, proposed administrative system for, 414–418

Factory legislation, justifiable class discrimination in, 235
Faguet, Emile, quoted, 237–238, 255
Farmers: necessity of organization not felt by, 155; present position of British, 288
Farming: improvement of, in Prussia, 307; value of specialization in, 528
Farm laborers, 486–487
Fashoda incident, 320
Federalism: at close of Revolutionary War, represented by Hamilton, 35–36; class which supported, 37; views held by supporters of, of anti-Federalists, 39–40; supporters of, founded national government on distrust of democracy, 41; error and misfortune of so doing, 41–42; the Hamiltonian brand of, shown in constructive legislation following framing of Constitution, 47–48; reconciliation of Republicanism and, 57–58; doubtful results of combination of Republicanism and, 61–63; Whig doctrine of Clay contrasted with Hamilton's Federalism, 64
Federalist, Hamilton's, quotation from, 45–46
Federalists: the Whigs an improvement on, 82–83. *See also* Federalism
Financial policy of Hamilton, 48

Foreign policy: of Great Britain, 9; of European states, 312–325; natural method of arriving at a definite, as shown by England and France, 317; bearing of colonial expansion on, 319–322; relation between national domestic policy and, 380–381
Foreign policy, American, 355 ff.; the Monroe Doctrine in, 357–365; of Jeffersonian Republicans, 359; wisdom of continued policy of isolation, 366, 381; correct policy would be to make American system stand for peace, 368; international system advocated for South and Central America, and Mexico, 369–372; the question of relations with Canada, 373–376; suggested treaty bearing on relations between United States, Canada, and Great Britain, 376; systematic development of, an absolute necessity, 376–378; colonial expansion, 378–379; questions of, raised by future of China, 380; isolation of United States is only comparative, under modern conditions, 381
Fortunes, the inheritors of great, 250, 469–472
France: faith of Frenchmen in, 2; origins of national state in, 267–268, 269–270; effect of Revolution on national principle in, 274–275; lack of representative institutions a defect in its government to-day, 281; democracy and nationality in, 294 ff.; a Republic proved to

be best form of government
for, 297–298; democracy not
thoroughly nationalized in,
298–299; lack of national
spirit in official domestic
policy, 299–300; economic
problem in, 300–301; failure
of, as a colonial power as long
as striving for European aggrandizement, 321; national
idea of, is democratic but is
rendered difficult and its value
limited, 329

Franchises, American municipal
policy toward public service
corporations', 457–460

Freedom: American tradition
of, 518; the failure to attain,
518 ff.

Free trade in Great Britain, 288

French Revolution, the, 273 ff.

Garrison, William Lloyd, mental
attitude and policy of, contrasted with Lincoln's, 117,
524–525

George, Henry, Jr., cited, 186

Germany: effect of religious
wars and lack of national
policy in, during early development, 269; nationality in,
increased after Napoleon,
277; outstripping of England
by, industrially, 285, 286;
relation between democracy
and nationality in, 302 ff.;
system of protection, state
ownership of railways, improvement in farming, etc.,
307; result of "paternalism"
has been industrial expansion
surpassing other European
states, 307–308; position of,

not so high as ten years ago,
309; the Social Democrats,
309–310; dubious interna-
tional standing of, 310–311;
is the power which has most
to gain from a successful war,
310–311; effect of success or
failure of foreign policy on
domestic policy, 312; is the
cause of a better understanding between England, France,
and Russia, 312; further
consideration of international
position of, and bearing on
disarmament question, 315–
318; colonial expansion of,
despite her expectation of European aggrandizement, 321;
danger of this policy, 322;
national idea of, turns upon
the principle of official leadership toward a goal of national
greatness, 329

Governors of states, 146–147;
suggested reforms relative to
administration of, 414 ff.;
"House of," proposed, 426

Great Britain: effect of position
of, on domestic and foreign
policy, 9, 321; question
whether colonial expansion of,
has been carried too far, 322–
323; relations between Canada
and, 375–376; suggested arrangement between United,
States and, relative to Canada,
376. *See also* England

Hamilton, Alexander: doctrines
of, versus those of Jefferson,
35–36, 54–55, 188;
insight and energy of, saved
states from disunion, 45;

Jefferson, Thomas (cont.)

Jeffersonian Democrats',
54–55; bearing of worship of
so-called, on behavior of factions at time of slavery crisis,
97–98; responsibility of a democracy for personal, 237 ff.;
economic, of the individual,
246–254; subordinated and
made helpful to the principle
of human brotherhood, 255

Liberty and union: Hamilton's
idea of, 54; prevailing view
of, during "era of good feeling," 63

Life insurance companies, attempted regulation of, by various state governments, 436

Lincoln, Abraham: first appearance of, in debates with Douglas, 106; service of, in seeing
straighter and thinking harder
than did his contemporaries,
107–108; makes the Western
Democracy understand for
the first time that American
nationality is a living principle,
108–109; peculiar service
rendered by and wherein
his greatness lay, 109–110;
the personal worth of, 110;
early career and surroundings of, 110–111; wherein
he differed from the average
Western Democrat, 111–112;
training and development
of his intellect, 112–113;
further consideration of his
character, 115 ff.; contrasted
with Jefferson, 117; with Garrison, 117, 524–525; with
Jackson, 119; necessity for
emphasis of the difference between, and his contemporary

fellow-countrymen, 121–122;
national intellectual and moral
stature of, 525

Low, Seth, as a reformer, 176

Lynching: cause of, 390; method
of stopping, 422

McClellan, George B., as a reformer, 176

Machinery, place of, in American economic development,
133–134

Machines, political, 144 ff.; created to satisfy a real need,
153–154; power of, felt in the
courts, 390; corruption and
incompetence of state legislative organizations traceable to,
394; complete reform of local
administrative systems necessary for breaking power of,
409–410; civil service reform
has not retarded progress of,
410–411

Madison, James, conduct of
second war with England by,
66–67

Manufacturing, Hamilton's
policy in encouraging, 48

Merit system in offices, 175; disappointing results of establishment of, 410–413

Mexico, coöperation, of, in establishment of stable international
system, 372

Middle Ages: city states of the,
264; origins of the national
state found in, 267 ff.

Middle class, rise of, in Great
Britain, 288–289, 293

Militarism and nationality, 312 ff.

Millionaire, the "tainted," a result
of extreme individualism, 182

Railroads (cont.)
constructive organization
of, in United States, 431 ff.;
domination of, in politics of
states, 433; undesirability
of state supervision of, and
danger to roads themselves,
433–435; ignorant and un-
wise legislation by states
concerning, 435–436; sub-
stitution of control of central
government for state control,
437–438; policy to be followed by central government
toward, 438 ff.; regulation
of, by Federal commissions a
doubtful step, 442–446, 452–
453; law should be passed
providing for agreements
between roads, and mergers,
447–448; freedom should
be left to, to make rates and
schedules, and develop their
traffic, 448–449; public ownership of, 449–450; process
of combination among, and
results, 461–462; value of
monopoly possessed by, could
be secured to the community
by Federal government taking possession of terminals,
right of way, tracks, and
stations, 462–463; the alternative plan, of government
appropriation of roads, and
its working out, 463–464. See
also Corporations
Real estate tax, 473
Rebates, 134, 136–137, 439
Recall: principle of the, 408; employment of the, in suggested
administrative system, 415

Referendum: movement in favor
of, in state governments, 392;
pros and cons of the, 400–402
Reform: course of the movement,
173–175; variety in kinds of,
175–176; variety found in ex-
ponents of, 176–177; function
of, according to the reformers,
177–178; disappointment of
hopes for, and reasons, 179–
181; a better understanding of
meaning of, and of the function of reformers, necessary
to successful correction of
abuses, 181; causes of need for,
181–184; wrong conceptions
of, and intellectual awakening essential for, 185; true
methods for accomplishing,
187–189; state institutional,
386 ff.; policy of drift should
not be allowed in, 386–387;
state administrative, 409 ff.;
impossibility of accomplishing,
by Australian ballot, direct primary system, and similar devices, 418–420; direct practical
value of a movement for, may
be surpassed by its indirect
educational value, 501
Reich, Emil, quoted, 1
Religious wars, bearing of, on
national development of European states, 268–270
Republicanism: represented by
Jefferson, 35–36, 37, 38–39;
identified with political disorder and social instability by
Federalists, 40; opposition of,
to Federalism as represented
by Hamilton, 52–56; alliance
of Federalists and party of,

57–58; effects of combination, 61–63; Jefferson's Republicanism contrasted with Jackson's Democracy, 64; views held by supporters of, on slavery question, 97

Republican party: causes leading to organization of the modern, 103; its claims to being the first genuinely national party, 103–104; rescue of, by Roosevelt, 210–211

Revolutions, question of, 258

Rockefeller, John D., 137–138, 141

Roman Empire, the, 266

Roosevelt, Theodore, 107, 167, 190, 191; as a reformer, 174, 205 ff.; nationalization of reform by, 207–208; policy of, compared with Hamiltonian creed, 208; theory and practice of, contrasted with Jefferson's, 209–210; the rescue of the Republican party by, 210–211; vulnerability of, on the point of equal rights, 211–212; has really been building better than he knew or will admit, 212–213; criticism of, as a national reformer, 213–215

Roosevelt-Taft programme, of recognition of corporations: tempered by regulation, 440–441; how best to carry out, 441–442

Root, Elihu, 166; international system indicated by, 369

Russia: faith of Russians in, 2; international situation of, at present, 311, 315, 317; weakness of, exposed, 382

Saloon licenses, 473

Santayana, George, quoted, 558

Scientists, methods of, a perfect type of authoritative technical methods, 533

Sherman Anti-Trust Law: a bar to proper treatment of corporate aggrandizement, 337; as an expensive attempt to save the life of the small competitor who cannot hold his own, should be repealed, 441

Slaveholders, an impartial estimate of, 100–101

Slavery: effect of introduction of factor of, on Democrats and Whigs, 89; sanctioned by the Constitution, and results, 89–90; attitude of the two political parties toward, 90–91; shirking of the question, and compromises, 91; brings out inconsistency of alliance between Jeffersonian democracy and American nationality as embodied in Constitutional Union, 92–93; Webster's attitude on the question, 93–96; American people separated into five parties by, 96; attitude of Constitutional Unionists toward, 96–97; beliefs of Abolitionists, Southern Democrats, Northern Democrats, and Republicans, 97–98; body of public opinion looking to denationalizing slavery, which was organized into the Republican party, 103–104

Smythe, William, 186

Social Democrats, party of, in Germany, 309

reform in, 409 ff.; maintenance of order by, 422; reorganization of criminal laws
by, 422–423; improvement of
prisons and insane asylums by,
423–424; possible activities
of, in relation to labor, educational questions, etc., 424–
425; method of attaining their
maximum usefulness, 426;
relation of, to cities, 426–427;
questions such as regulation of
commerce, control of corporations, distribution of wealth,
and prevention of poverty
outside of field of activities of,
429–430; domination of railroads in, 433; interference of,
with railroad, insurance, and
other corporations, 433–436
Steffens, Lincoln, 201
Sterilization of criminals, 424
Strikes, 157, 482
Suffrage, advantages and disadvantages of a limited, 243–244
Supreme Court: power of the,
163; success of, in the American political system, 165;
question of life tenure of office
of judges of, 246

Taft, William Howard, 166
Tammany Hall, 154, 185
Tariff: an example of class legislation, 235; Federal authorities
responsible for, 337; first duty
of United States to revise, 374
Tariff reform, 175
Taxation: remedying excessive
profits of corporations by,
454–455; as a weapon of municipalities against monopolies, 460; use of power of, to

equalize distribution of wealth
and raise money for governmental expenses, 468–473;
of inheritances, 469–473; of
incomes, 472–473; real estate
and saloon, 473
Tax systems, state, chaotic condition of, 390
Technical schools, growth of,
527–528
Tobacco manufacture, regulation
of, by government, 465–466
Tolstoy, Leo: pernicious results of
triumph of democracy of, 347;
led into error by brotherly
feelings, 556–557
Trade schools, 481
Tradition: force of accumulated
national, in forming a people
into a state, 279–280, 318–
319; the national, of England, Germany, France, and
America, 328–333; necessity
of emancipation of nations
from, 343
Trust funds, evils of, 471
Trusts. See Corporations

Un-Americanism, the reforming
spirit wrongly called, 61
Unification: of Germany by Bismarck, 303–306; wars which
helped toward, were justifiable, 314–315
United States Steel Corporation,
lease of ore lands by, 140–141

Vienna, Treaty of, 277
Virtue, the principle of democracy, 558
Voting: for state representatives,
404; American systems of,
418–420

Wage-earners: increasing standard of living for, 253; weakness of socialistic programme for, 258–259. *See also* Labor unions

War of 1812 and its lessons, 66–68

Wars: justifiability of, 314–315; likelihood of more, before establishment of a stable European situation, 316

Washington, George, foreign policy contained in Farewell Address of, 356

Wealth: necessity of opportunity for acquiring, 249–250; improvement in the distribution of, 257–258; distribution of, in France, 300–301; equalization of distribution of, by graduated inheritance tax, 468–473

Webster, Daniel, 64, 524; reason for failure of ideas of, 85–86; representative of behavior of public opinion as regarded slavery question during the Middle Period, 93–96

Wells, H. G., quoted, 5

Whigs: standards represented by, against Jacksonian or Western Democracy, 81–82; policy of internal improvements, 82; wherein they improved on the Federalists, 82–83; failure regarding re-chartering of National Bank, 83–84; its failure, 83–84; and regarding policy of protection, 84; complete failure in fight against Federal executive, 84–85; reason for failures, 85–86; attitude of, toward slavery, 90–91

Workingmen, party composed of, in Germany, 309